CLOCKWORK PLANET

IV

STORY BY YUU KAMIYA & TSUBAKI HIMANA
MANGA BY KURO
CHARACTER DESIGN BY SINO

ClockWork Planet
CONTENTS

IV

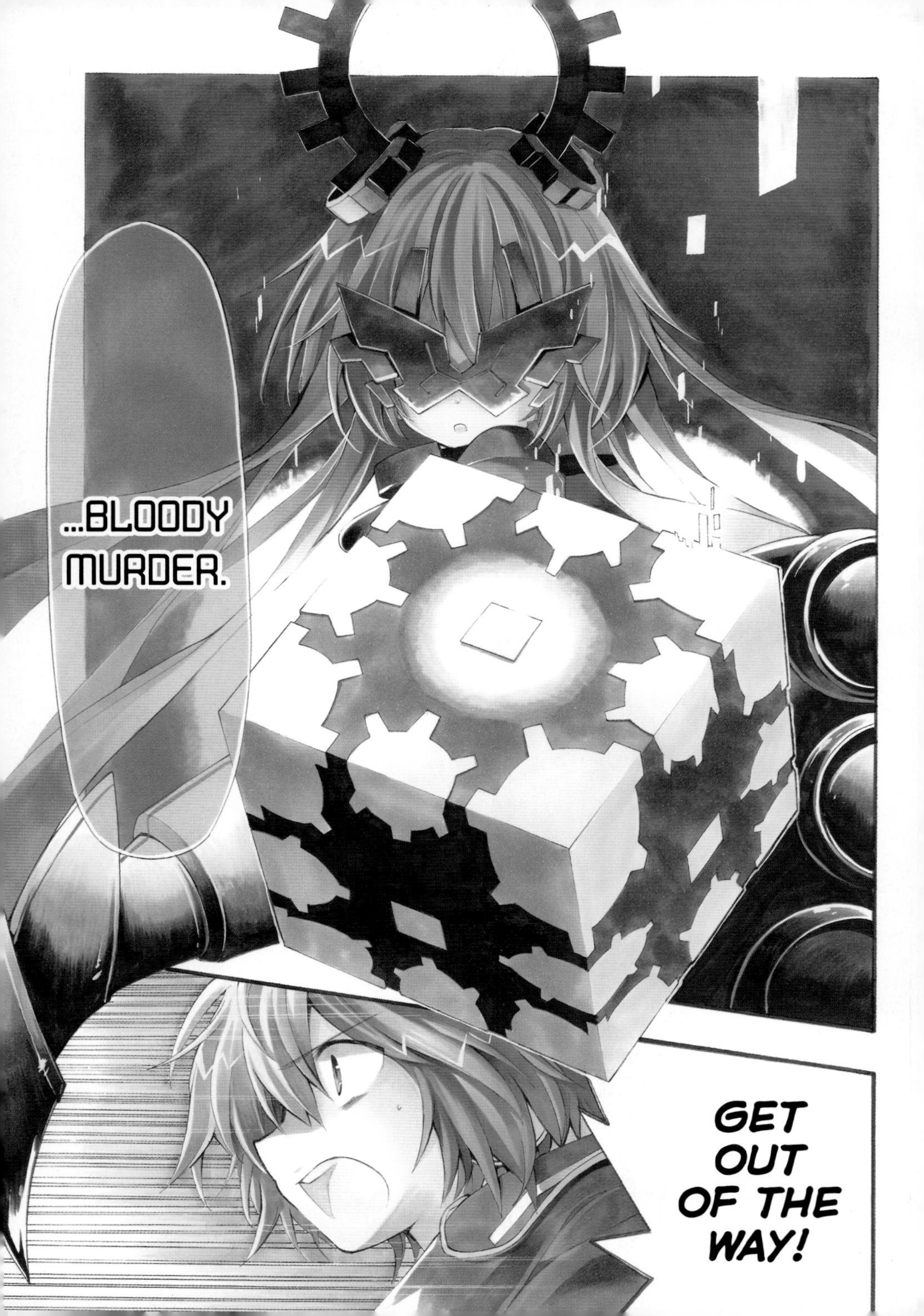
...BLOODY MURDER.
GET OUT OF THE WAY!

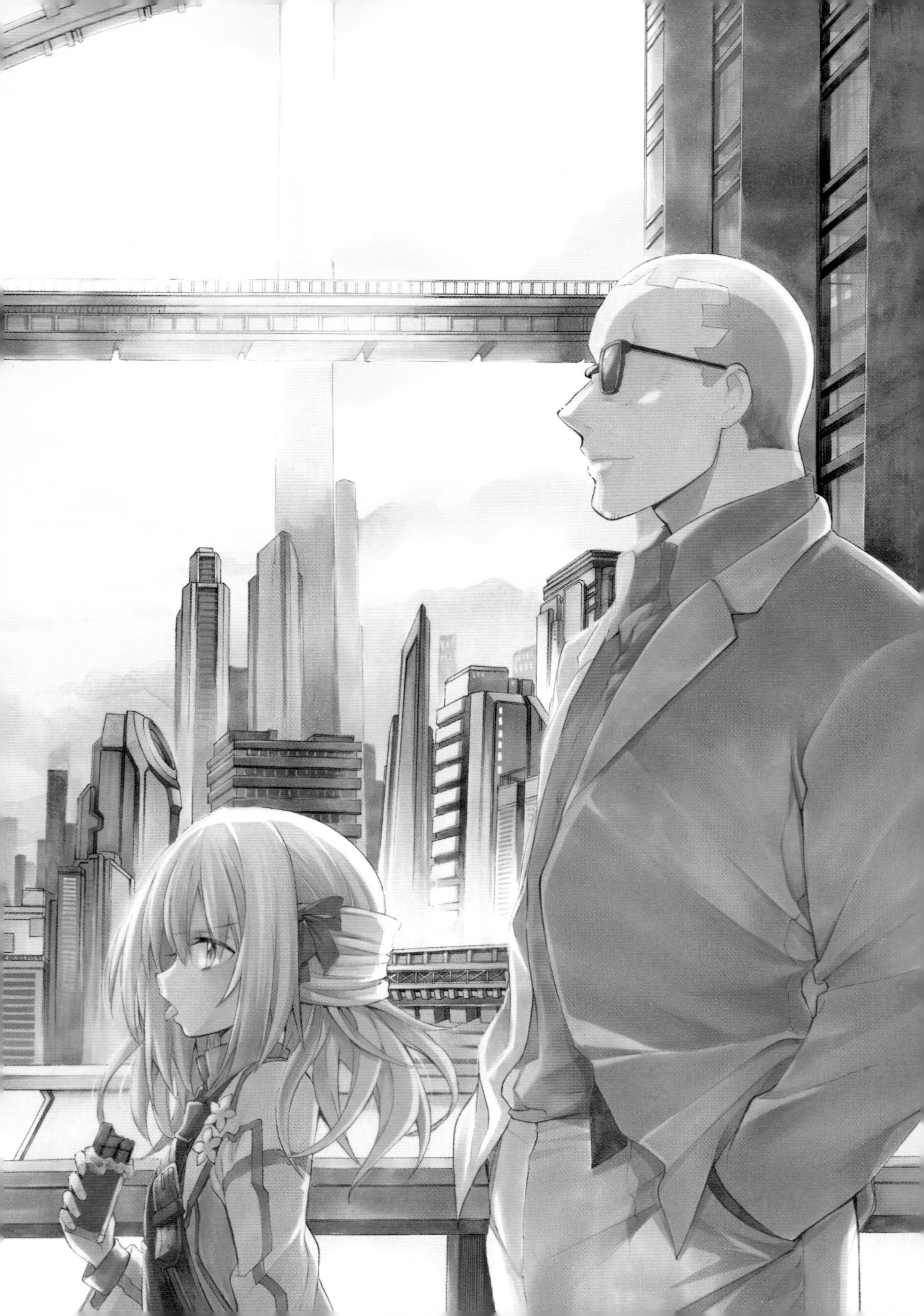

Clock 16: Fury

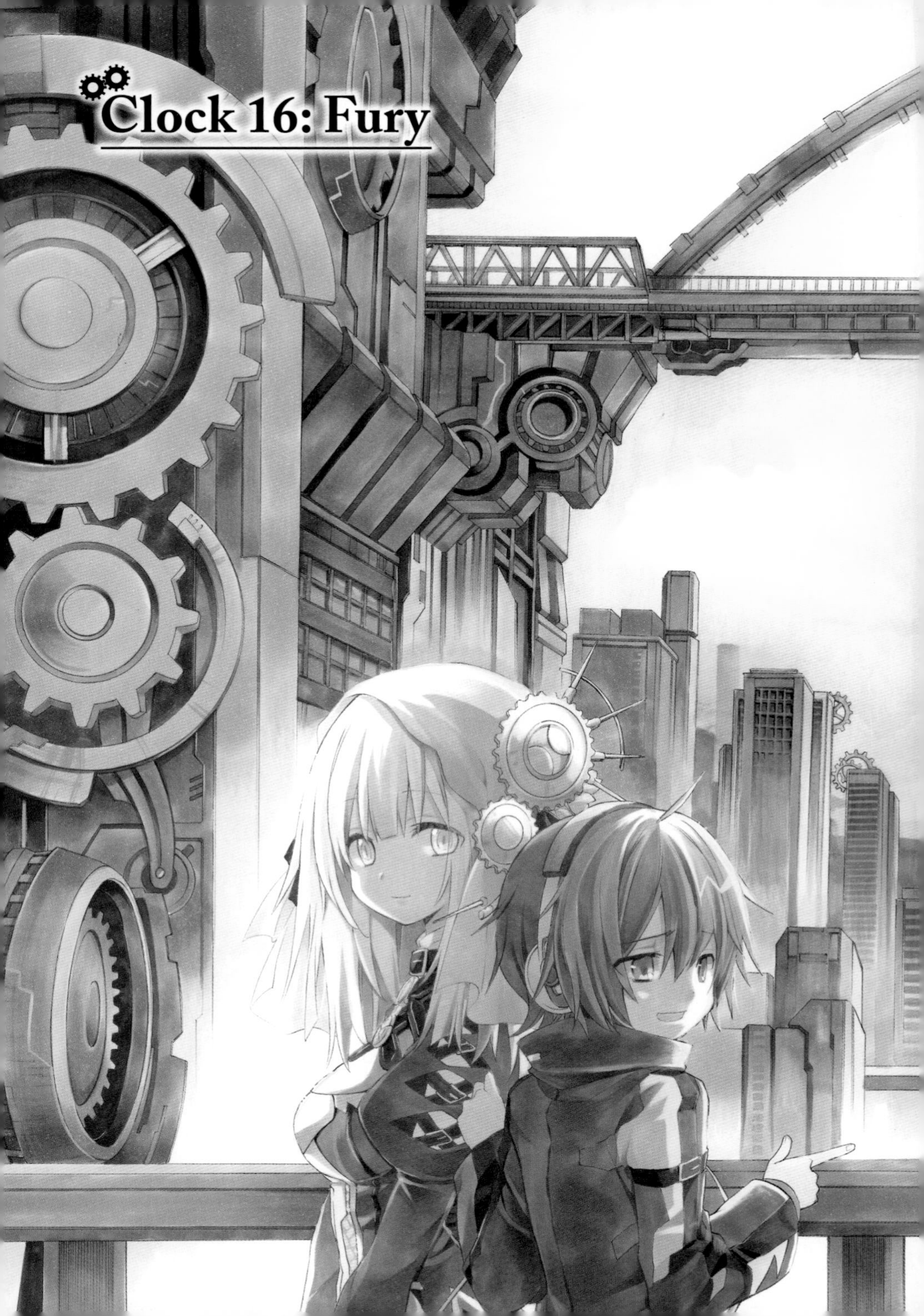

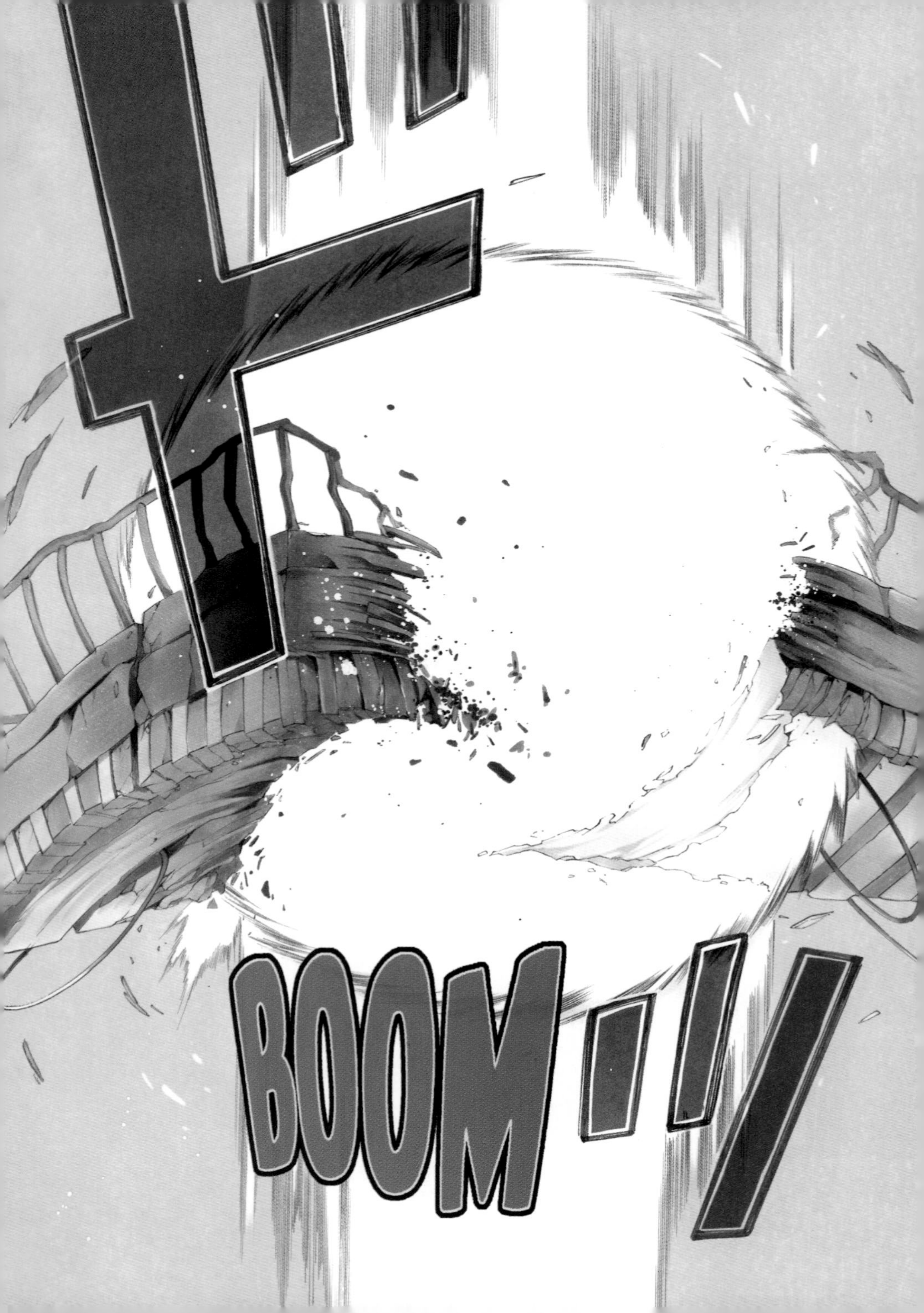
BOOM!!

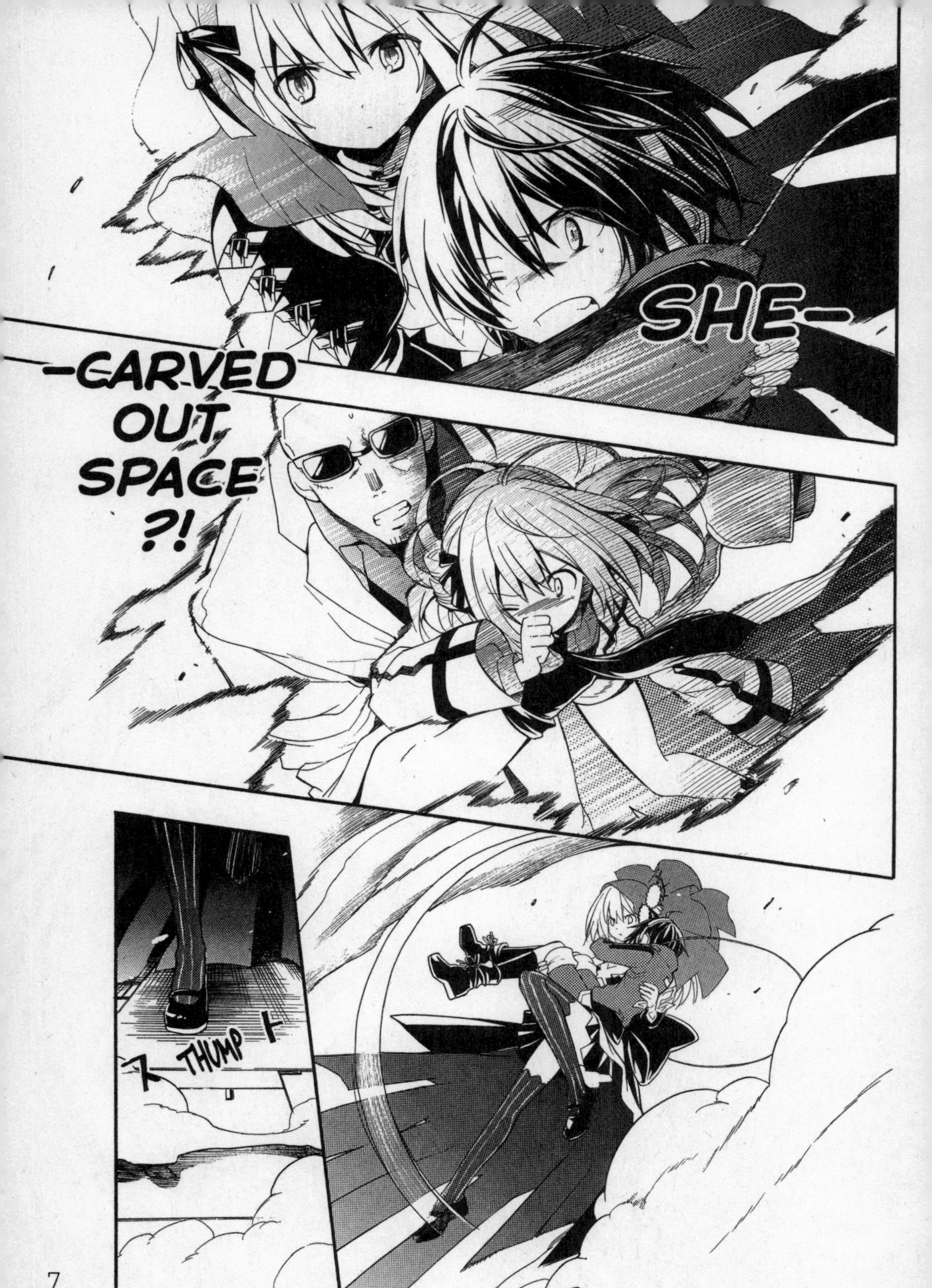
SHE—
—CARVED OUT SPACE ?!
THUMP

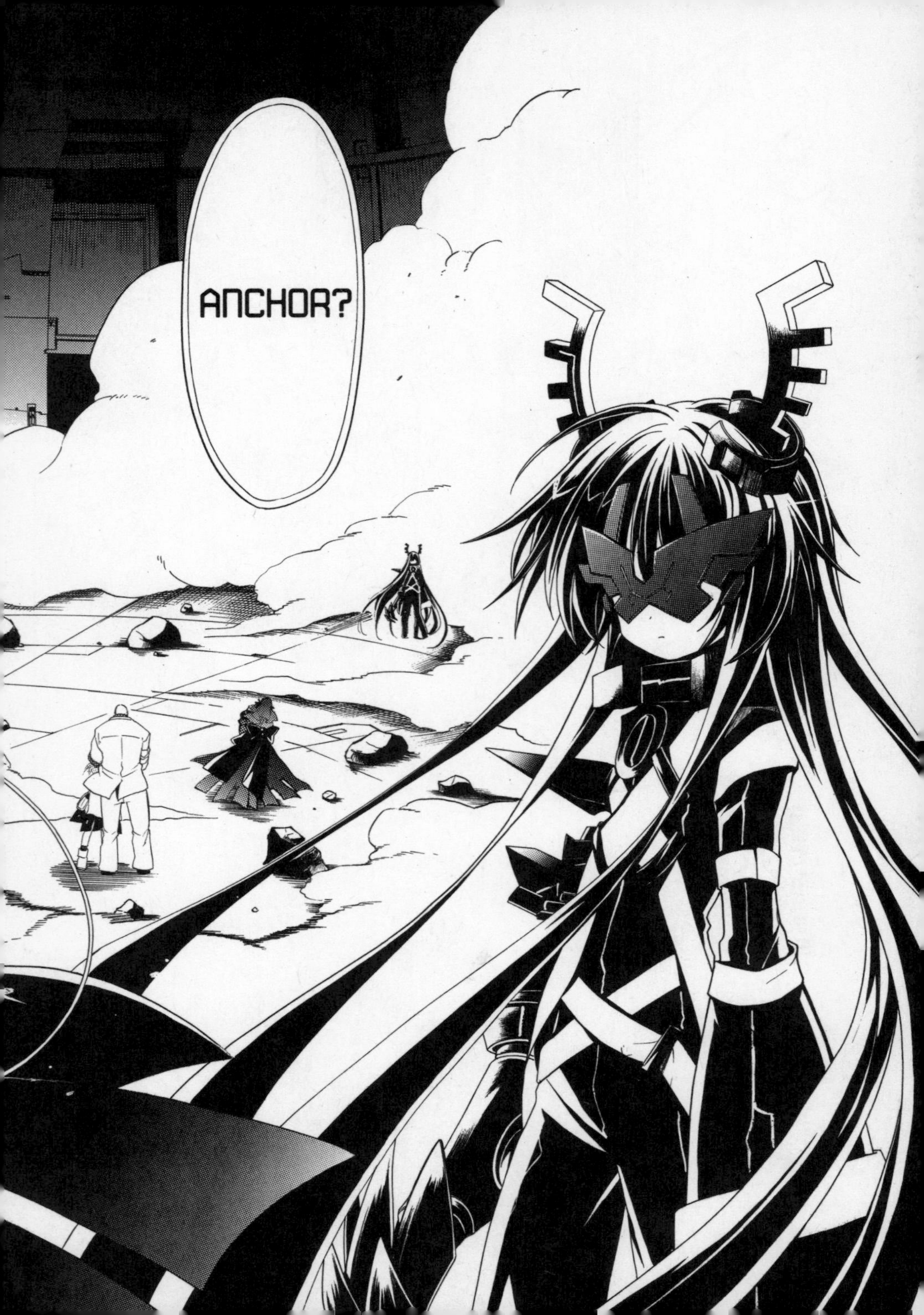
ANCHOR?

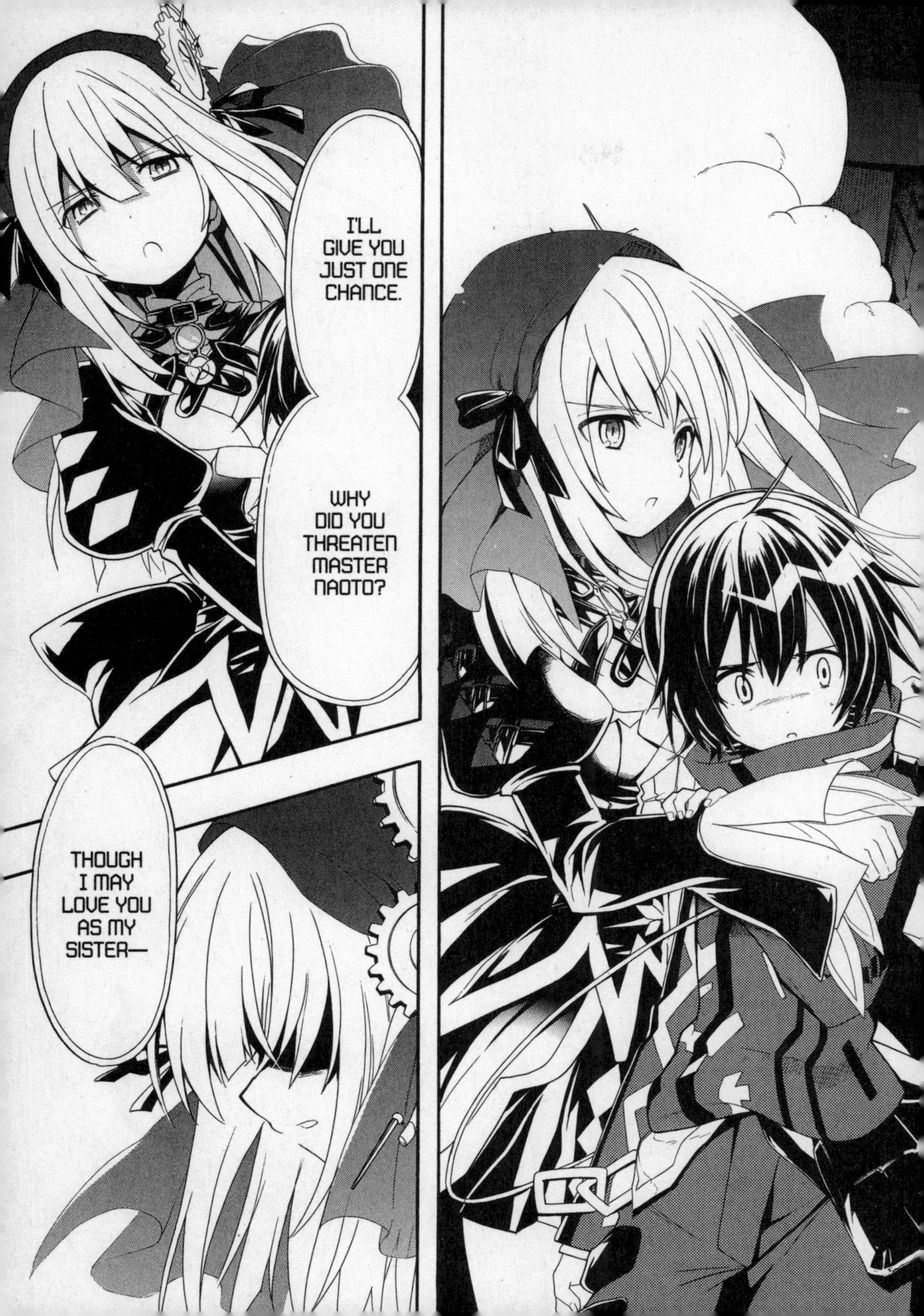
I'LL GIVE YOU JUST ONE CHANCE.
WHY DID YOU THREATEN MASTER NAOTO?
THOUGH I MAY LOVE YOU AS MY SISTER—

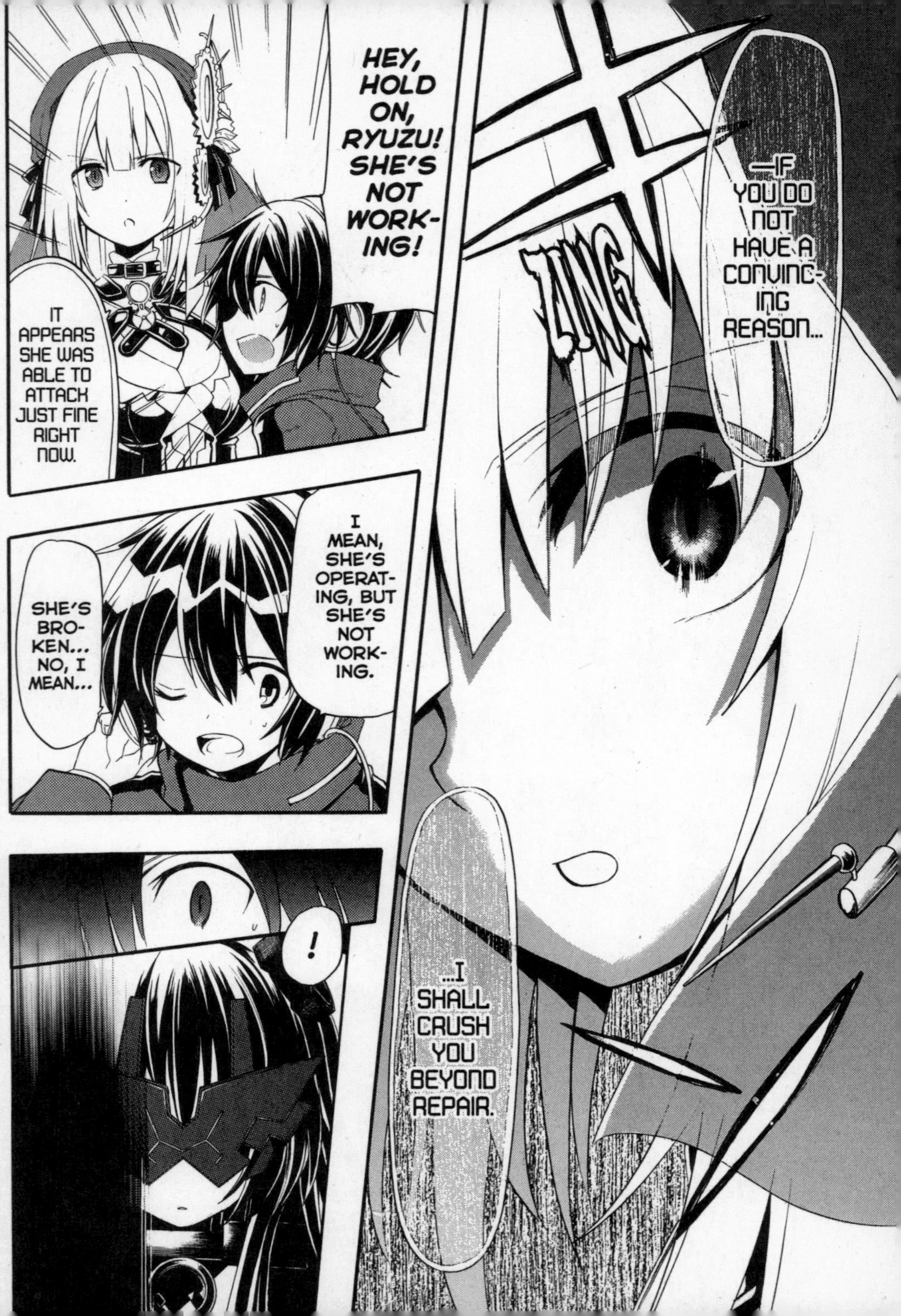
—IF YOU DO NOT HAVE A CONVINCING REASON...
ZING
...I SHALL CRUSH YOU BEYOND REPAIR.
HEY, HOLD ON, RYUZU! SHE'S NOT WORKING!
IT APPEARS SHE WAS ABLE TO ATTACK JUST FINE RIGHT NOW.
I MEAN, SHE'S OPERATING, BUT SHE'S NOT WORKING.
SHE'S BROKEN... NO, I MEAN...
!

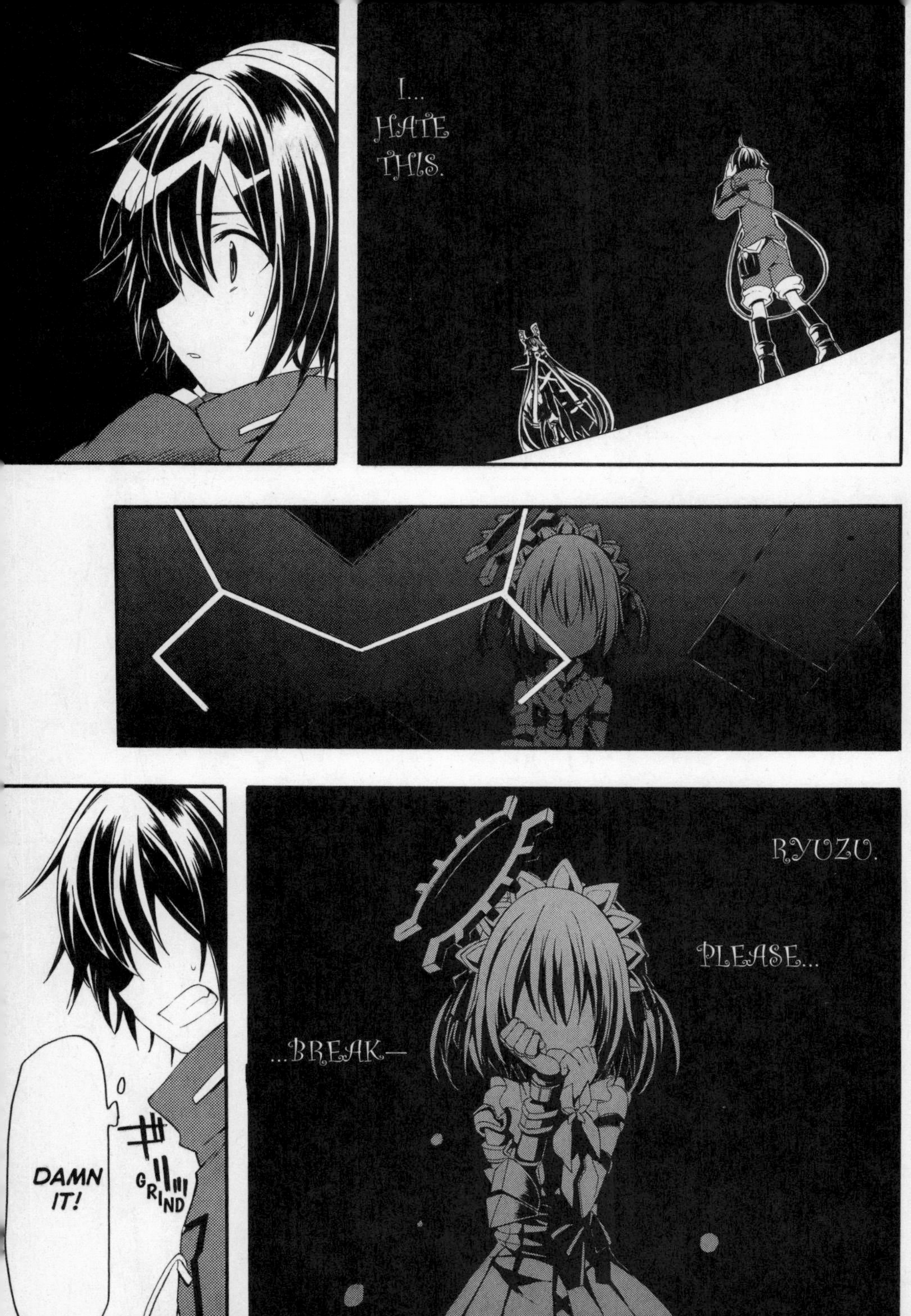
I... HATE THIS.
RYUZU.
PLEASE...
...BREAK—
GRIND
DAMN IT!

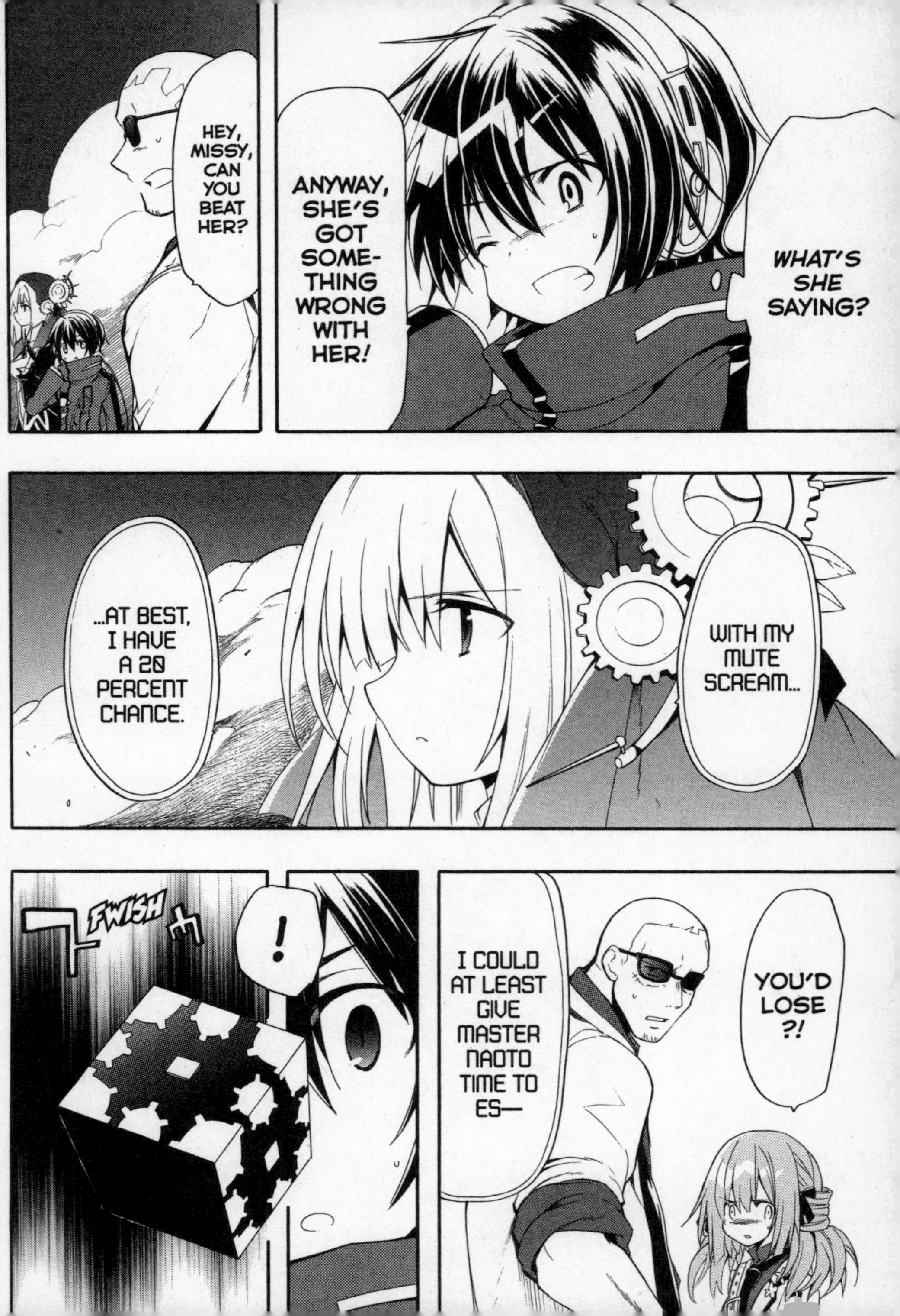
WHAT'S SHE SAYING?
ANYWAY, SHE'S GOT SOME-THING WRONG WITH HER!
HEY, MISSY, CAN YOU BEAT HER?
WITH MY MUTE SCREAM...
...AT BEST, I HAVE A 20 PERCENT CHANCE.
YOU'D LOSE ?!
I COULD AT LEAST GIVE MASTER NAOTO TIME TO ES—
!
FWISH

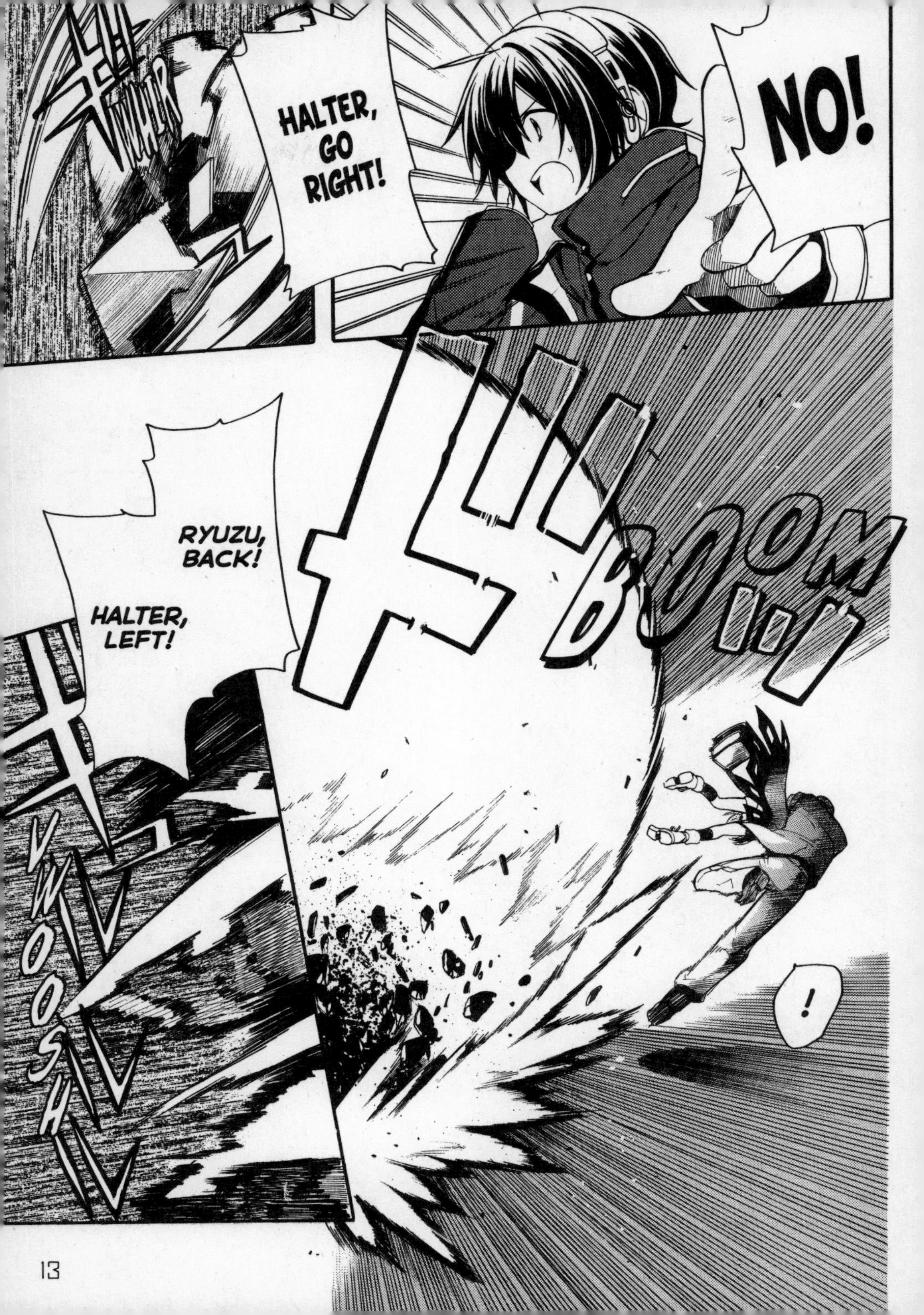
NO!
HALTER, GO RIGHT!
VWUHR
BOOM!!
!
RYUZU, BACK!
HALTER, LEFT!
WOOSH

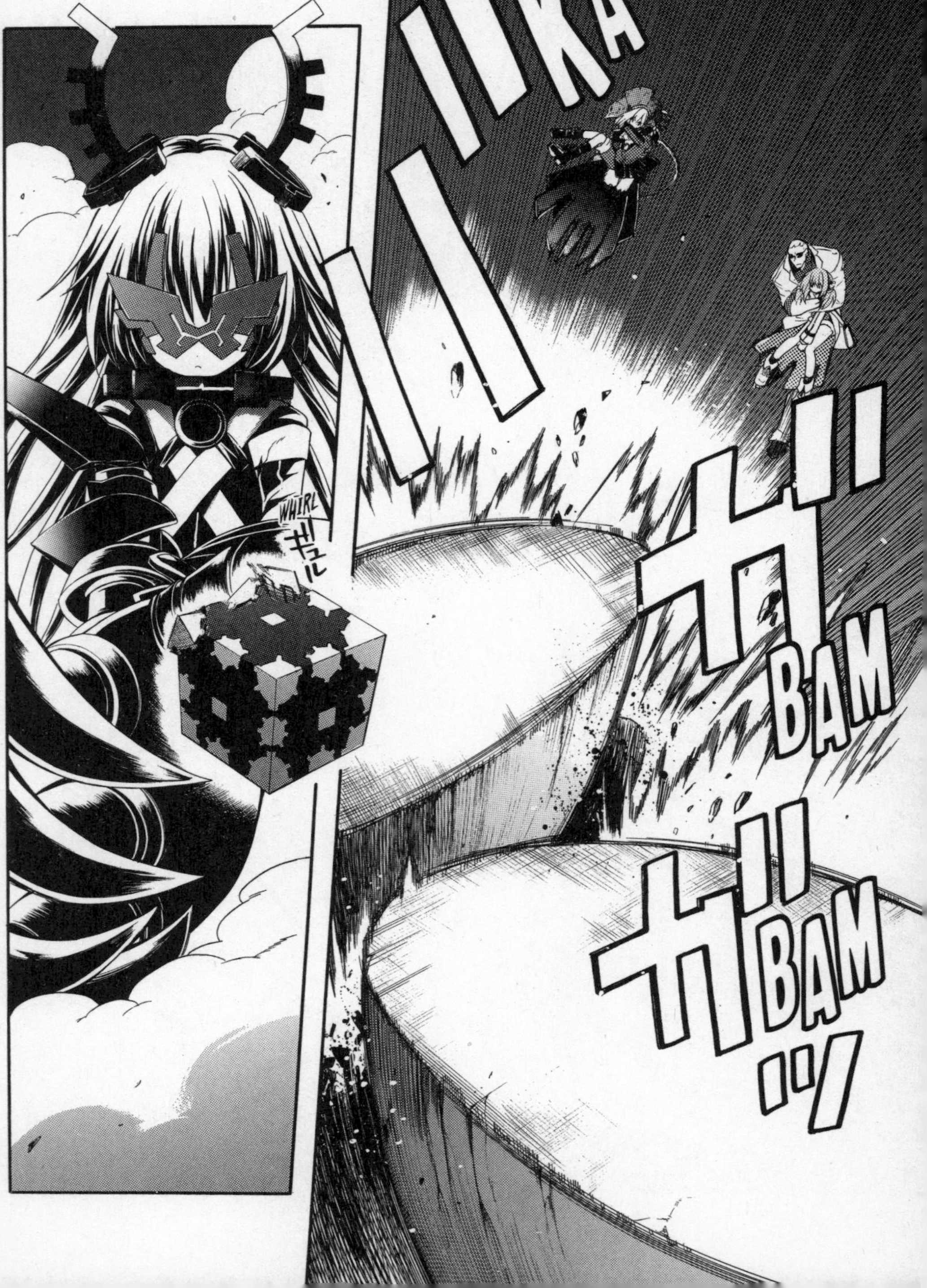
KA
ガッ
BAM
ガッ
BAM
WHIRL
ギュル

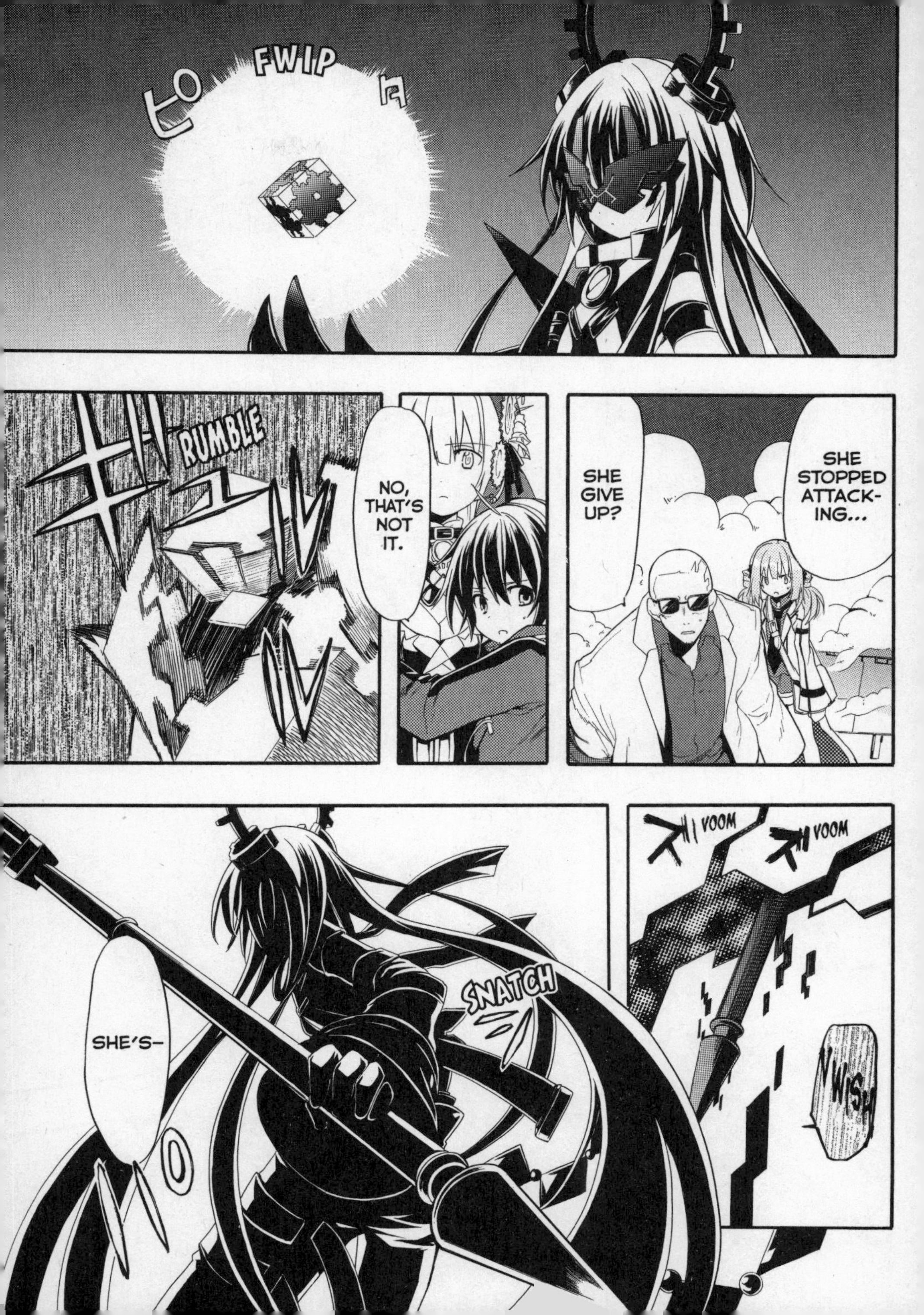
FWIP
SHE STOPPED ATTACK-ING...
SHE GIVE UP?
NO, THAT'S NOT IT.
RUMBLE
VOOM
VOOM
WISH
SNATCH
SHE'S-

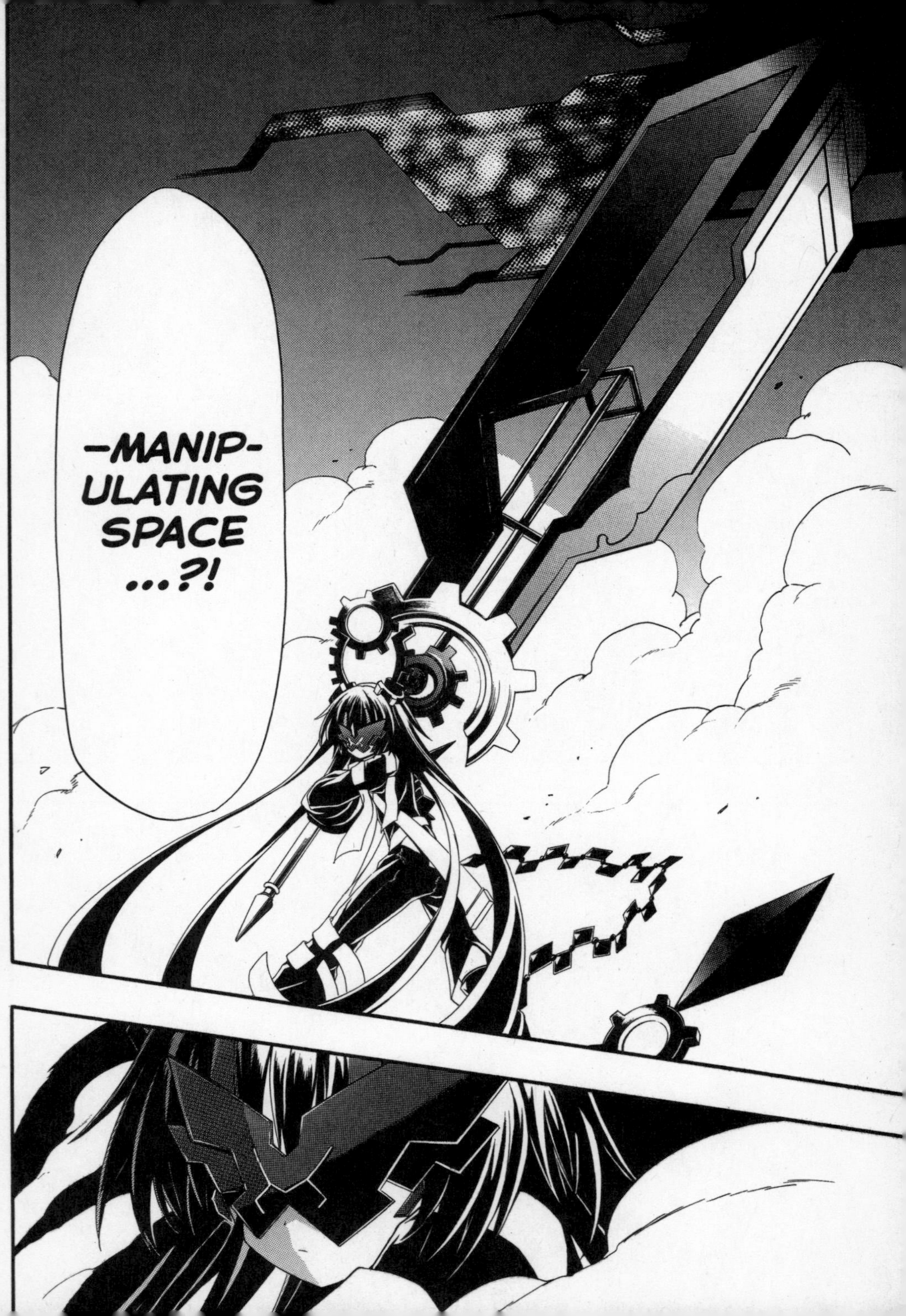
-MANIP-ULATING SPACE ...?!

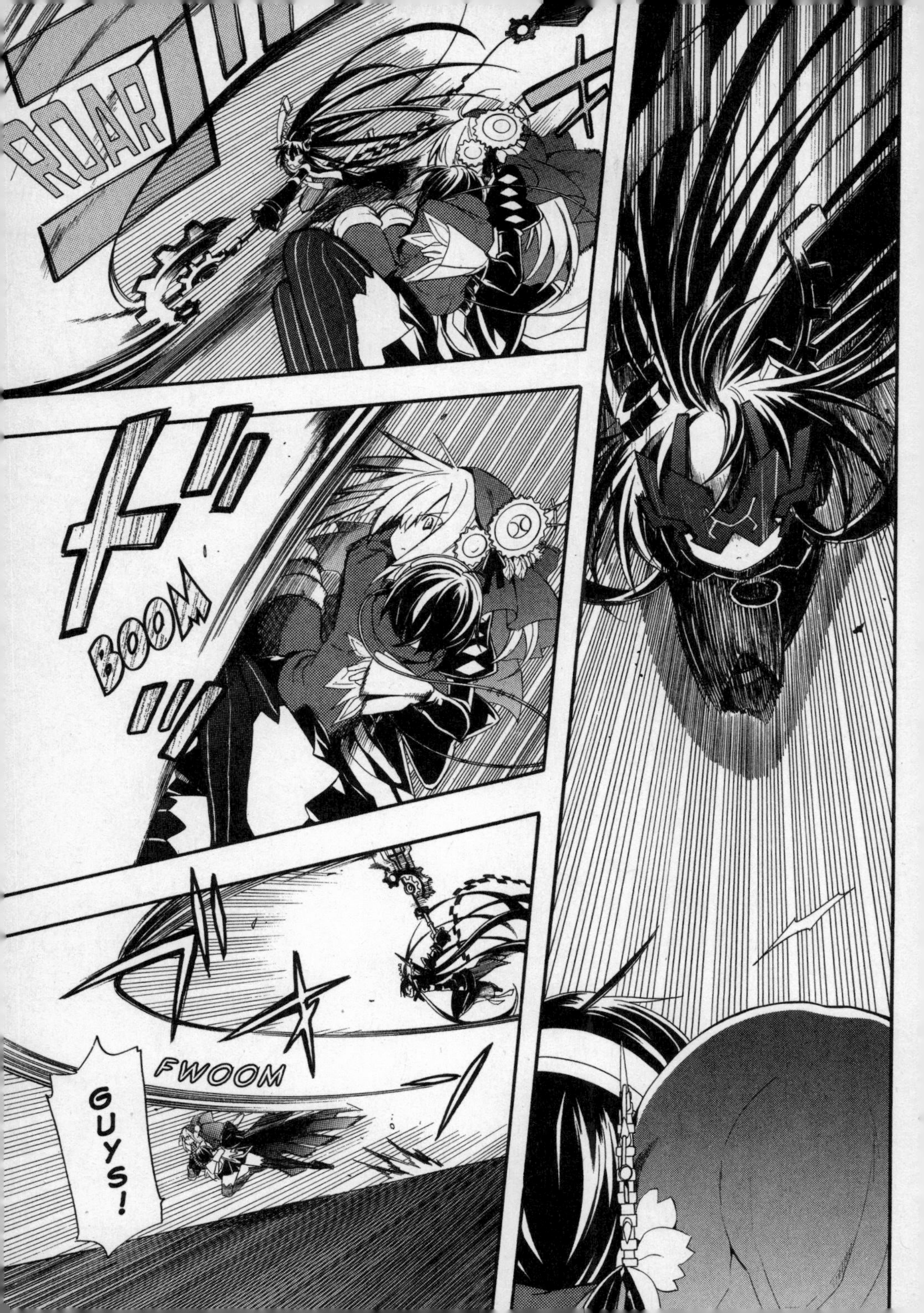
ROAR
BOOM
FWOOM
GUYS!

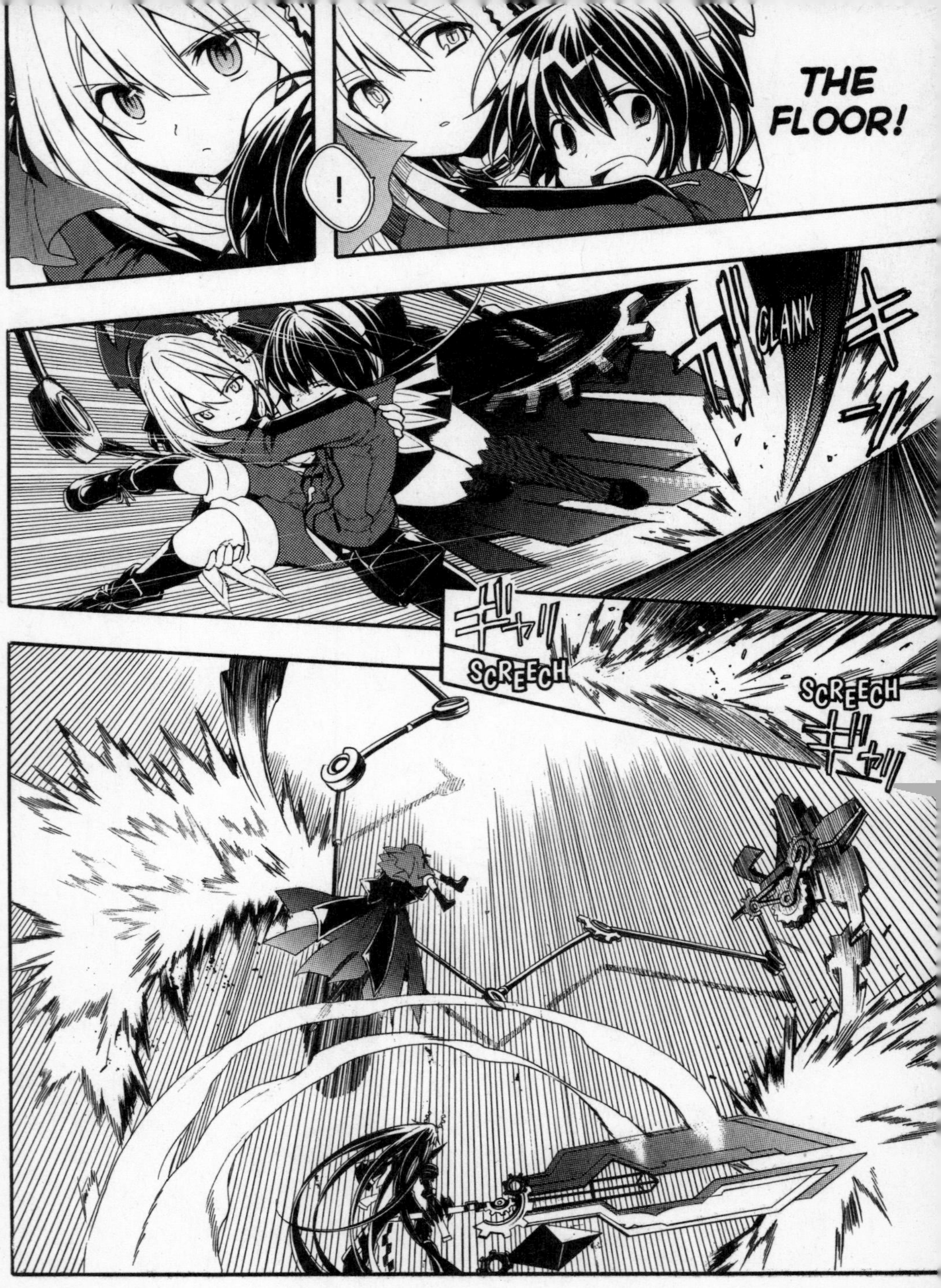
THE FLOOR!
!
ガッ
CLANK
キーン
SCREECH
ギャリ
ギャリ
SCREECH

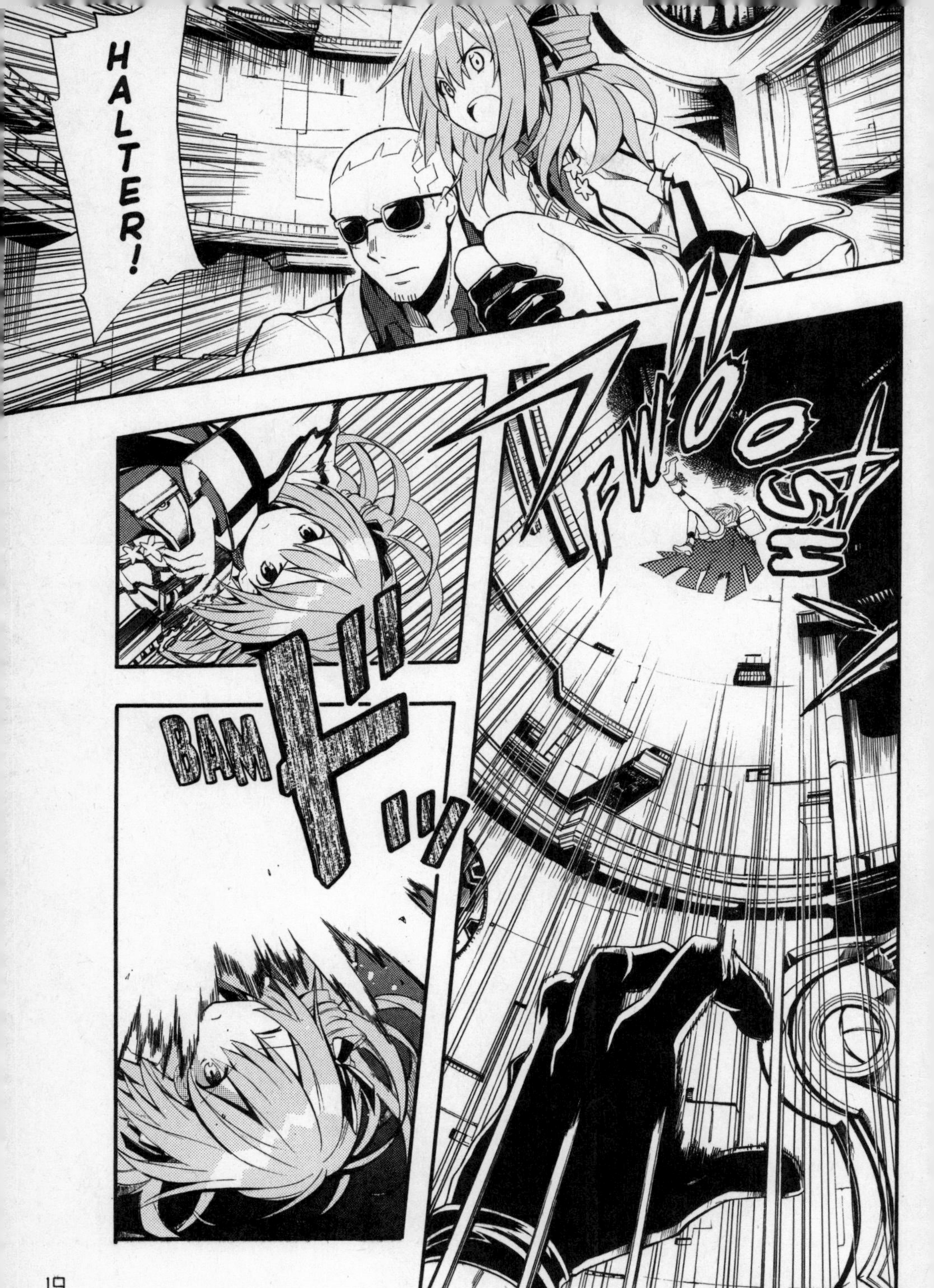
HALTER!
FWOOSH
BAM

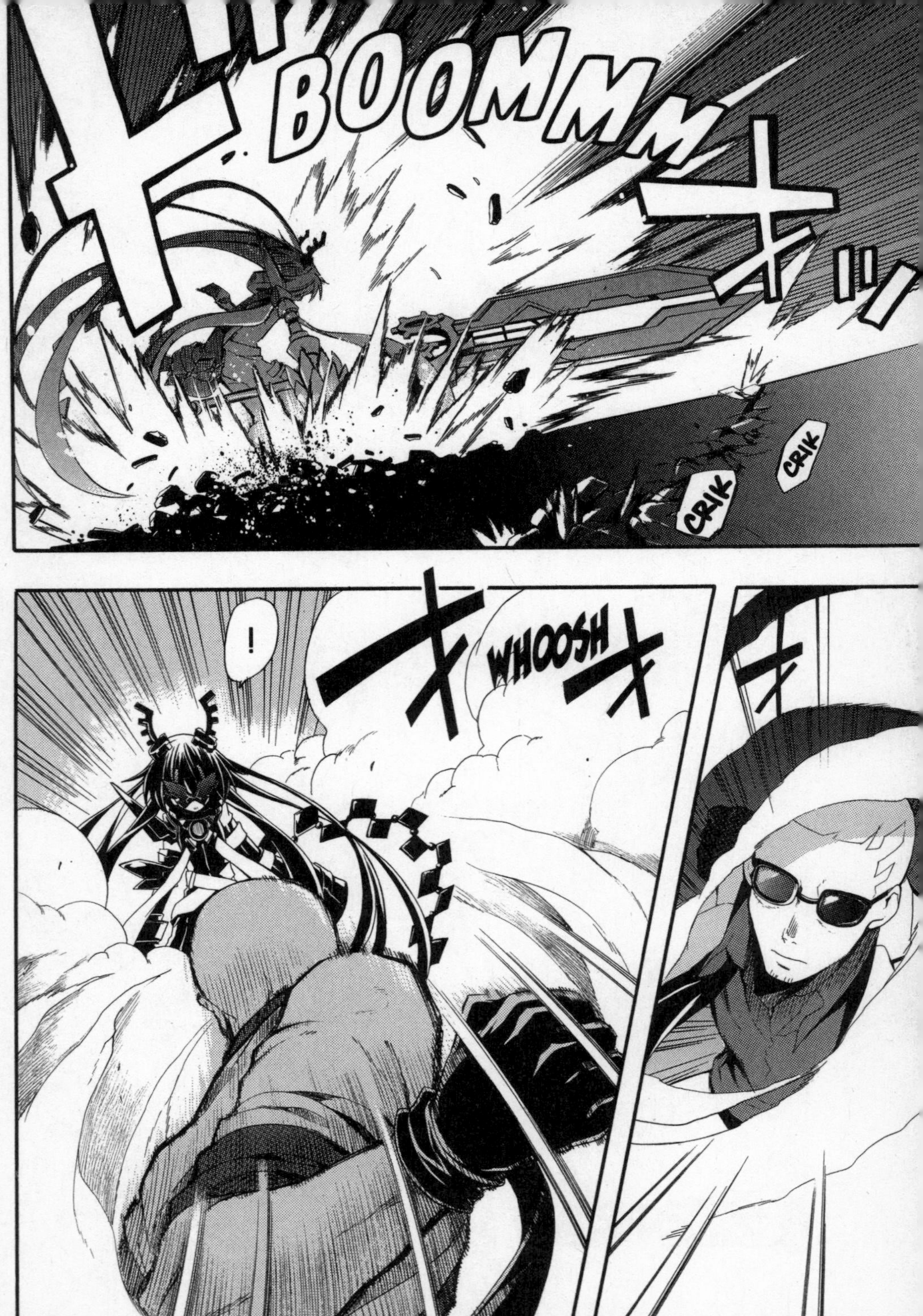

BOOMMM
CRIK
CRIK
WHOOSH
!

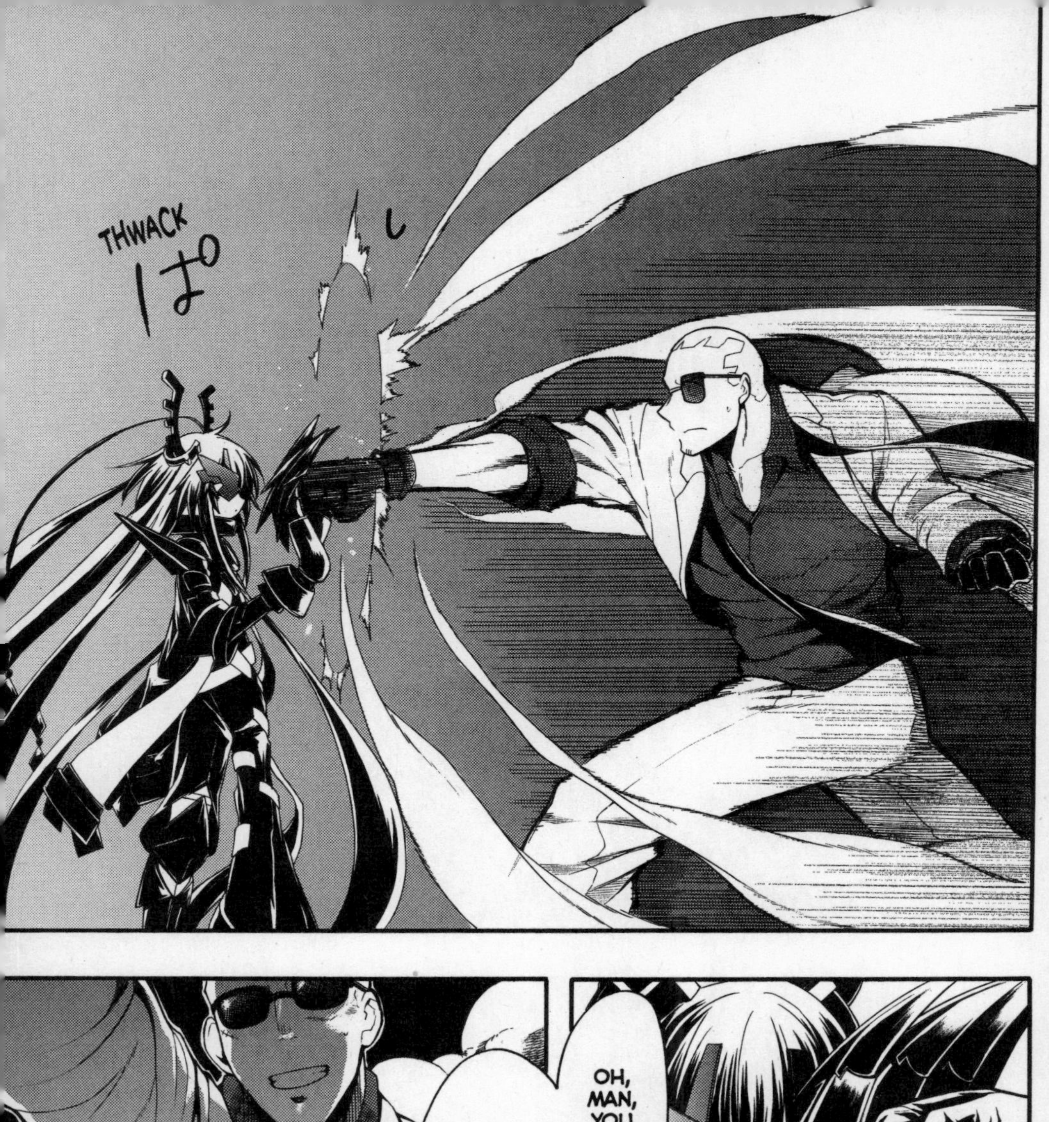
THWACK
ぱし

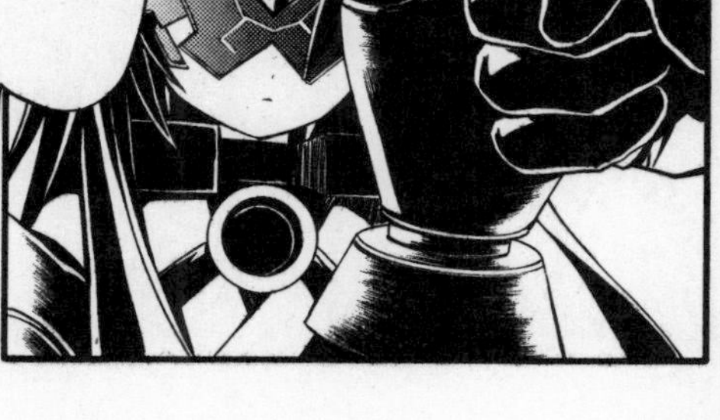
OH, MAN, YOU STOPPED IT.

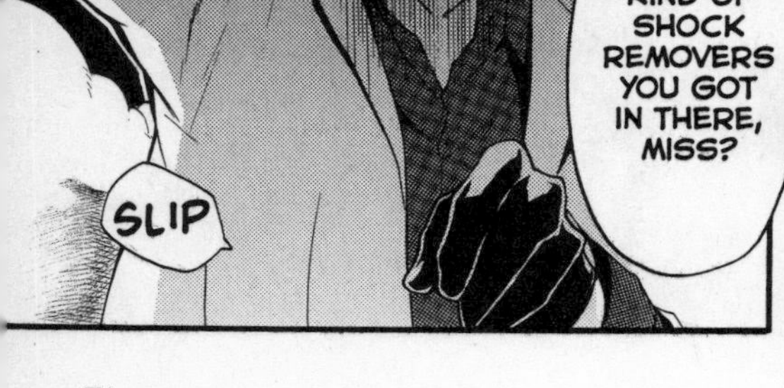
THE HELL KIND OF SHOCK REMOVERS YOU GOT IN THERE, MISS?
SLIP

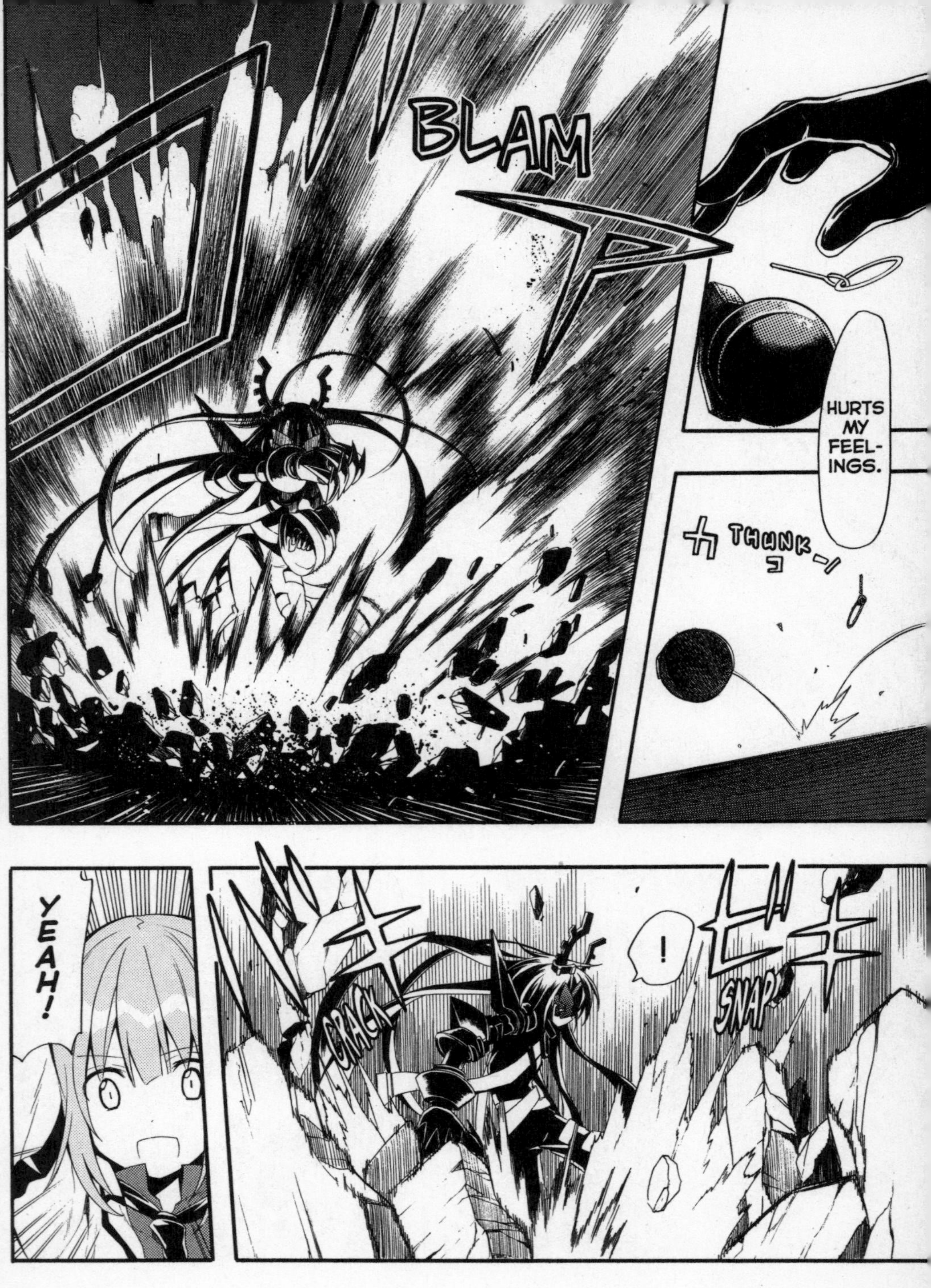
HURTS MY FEEL-INGS.
THUNK
BLAM
!
SNAP
CRACK
YEAH!

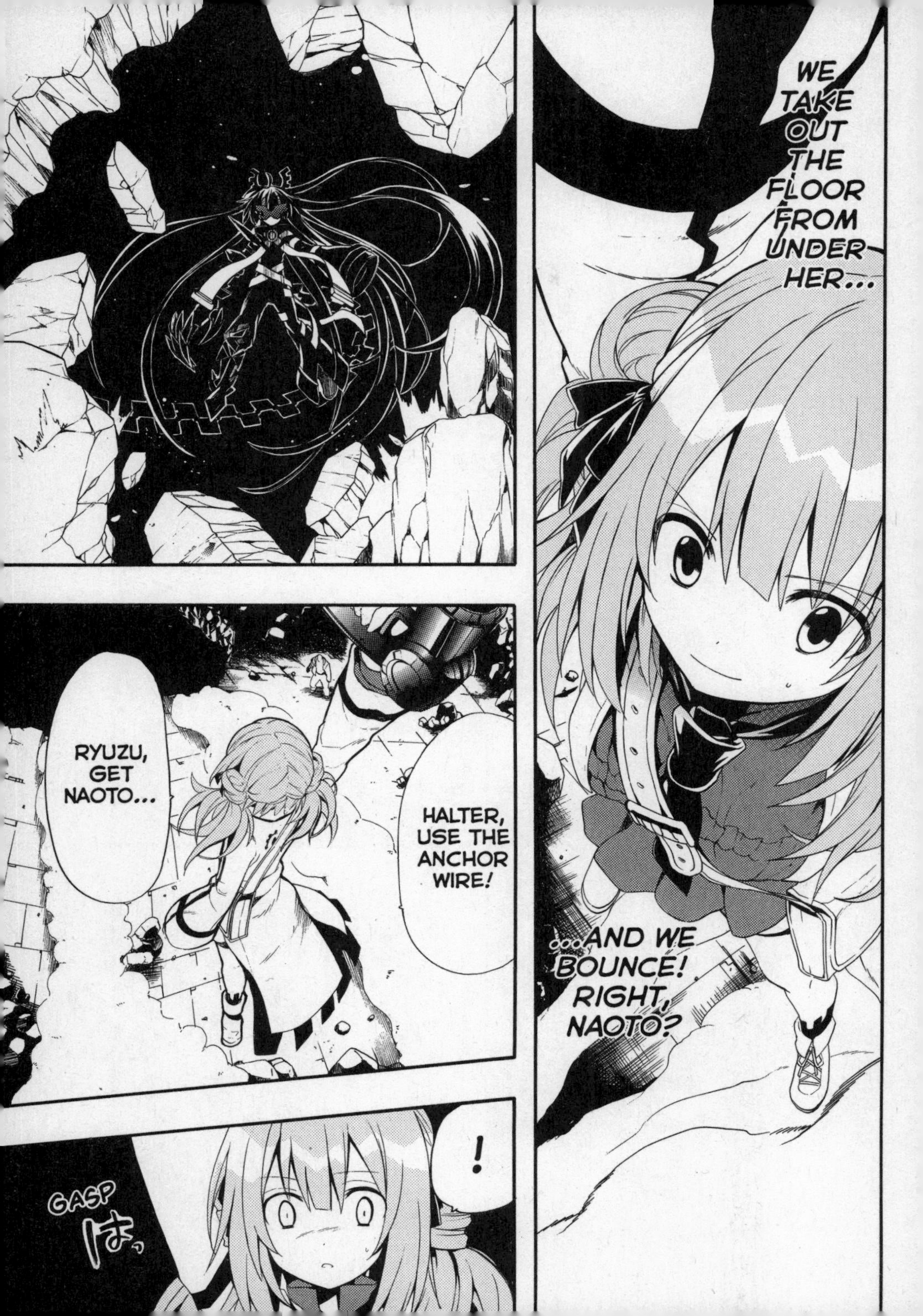
WE TAKE OUT THE FLOOR FROM UNDER-HER...
...AND WE BOUNCE! RIGHT, NAOTO?
HALTER, USE THE ANCHOR WIRE!
RYUZU, GET NAOTO...
!
GASP
はっ

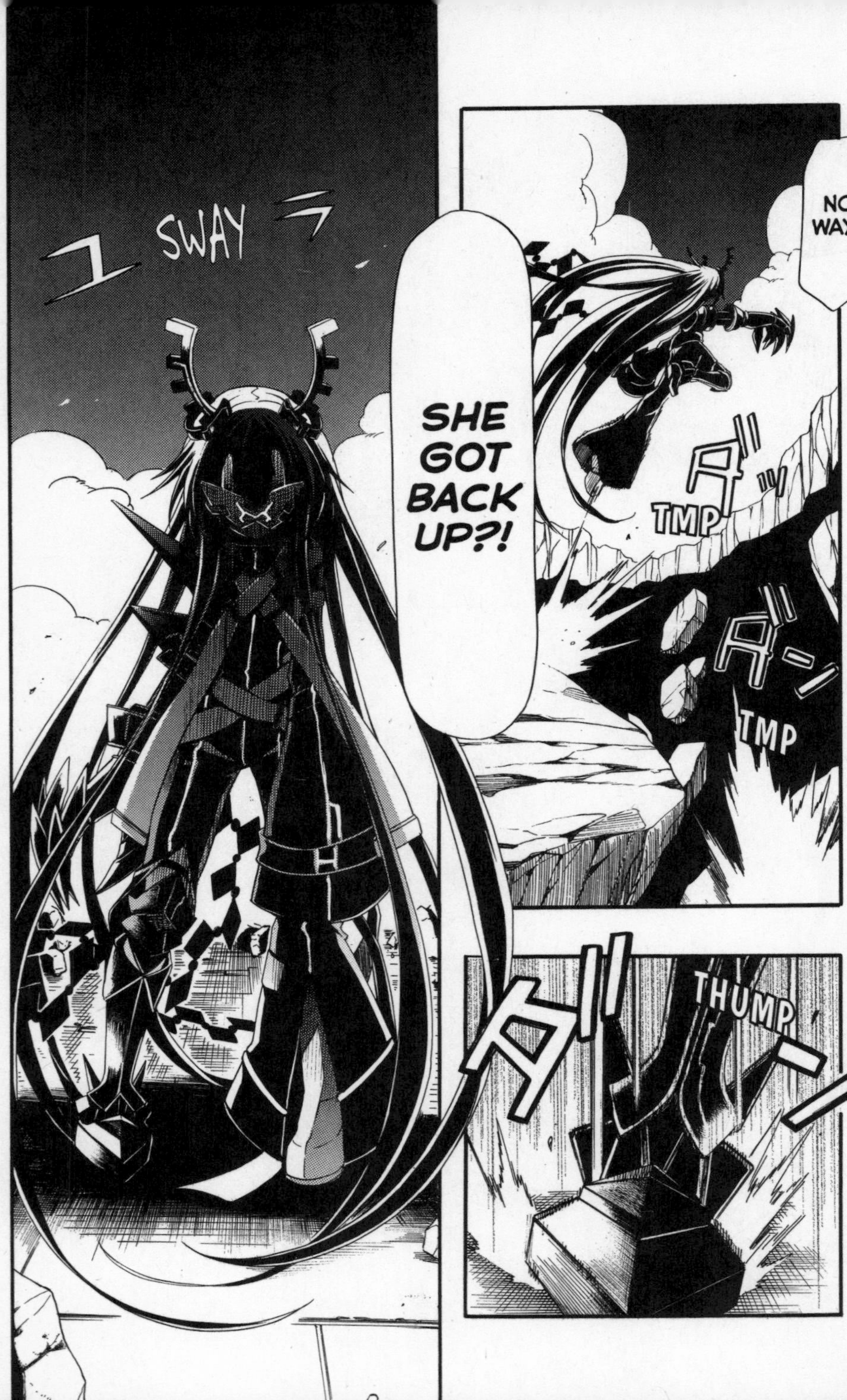
NO WAY!
TMP
TMP
THUMP
SHE GOT BACK UP?!
SWAY

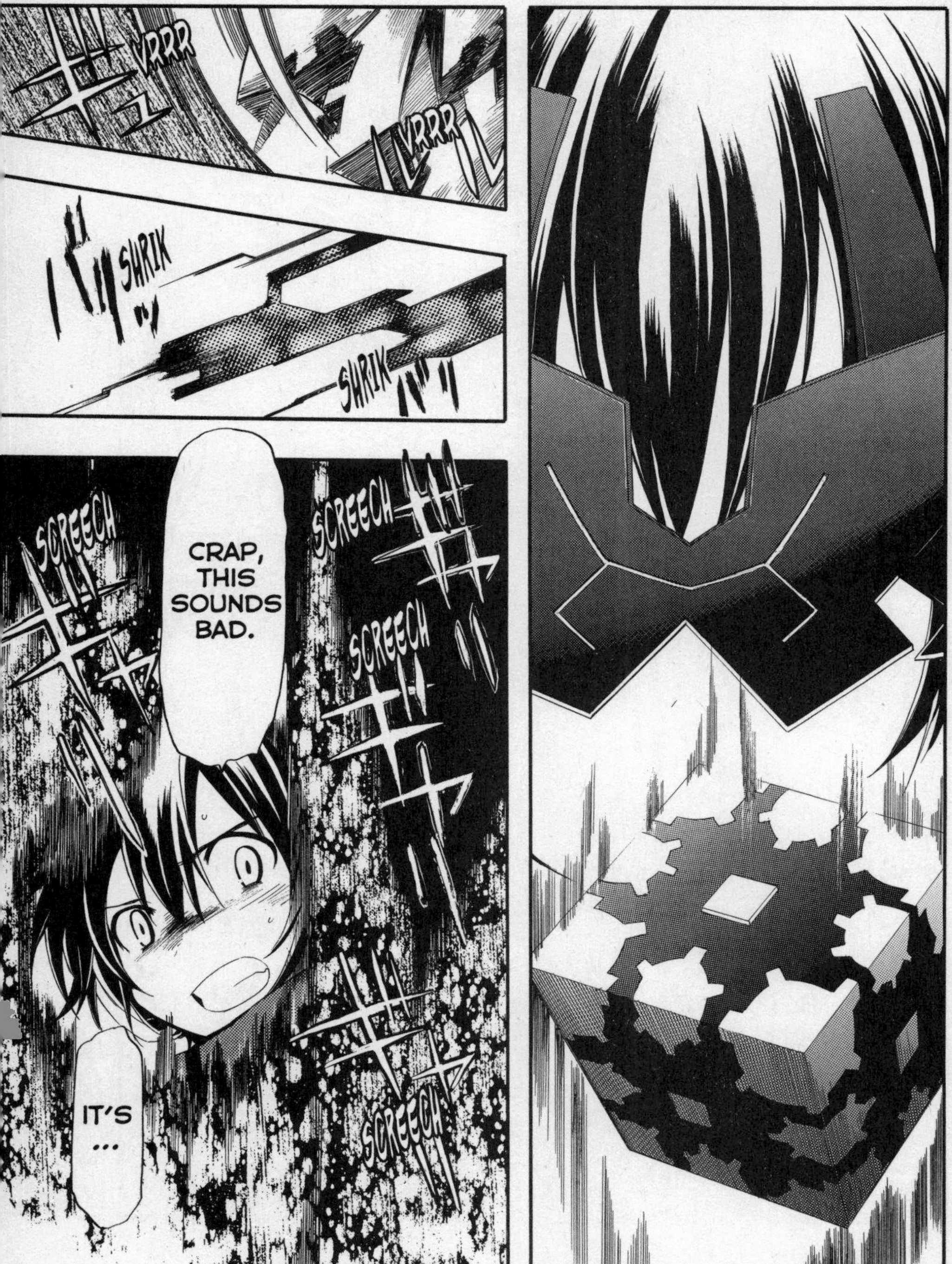
VRRR
VRRR
SHRIK
SHRIK
SCREECH
SCREECH
SCREECH
CRAP, THIS SOUNDS BAD.
SCREECH
IT'S ...

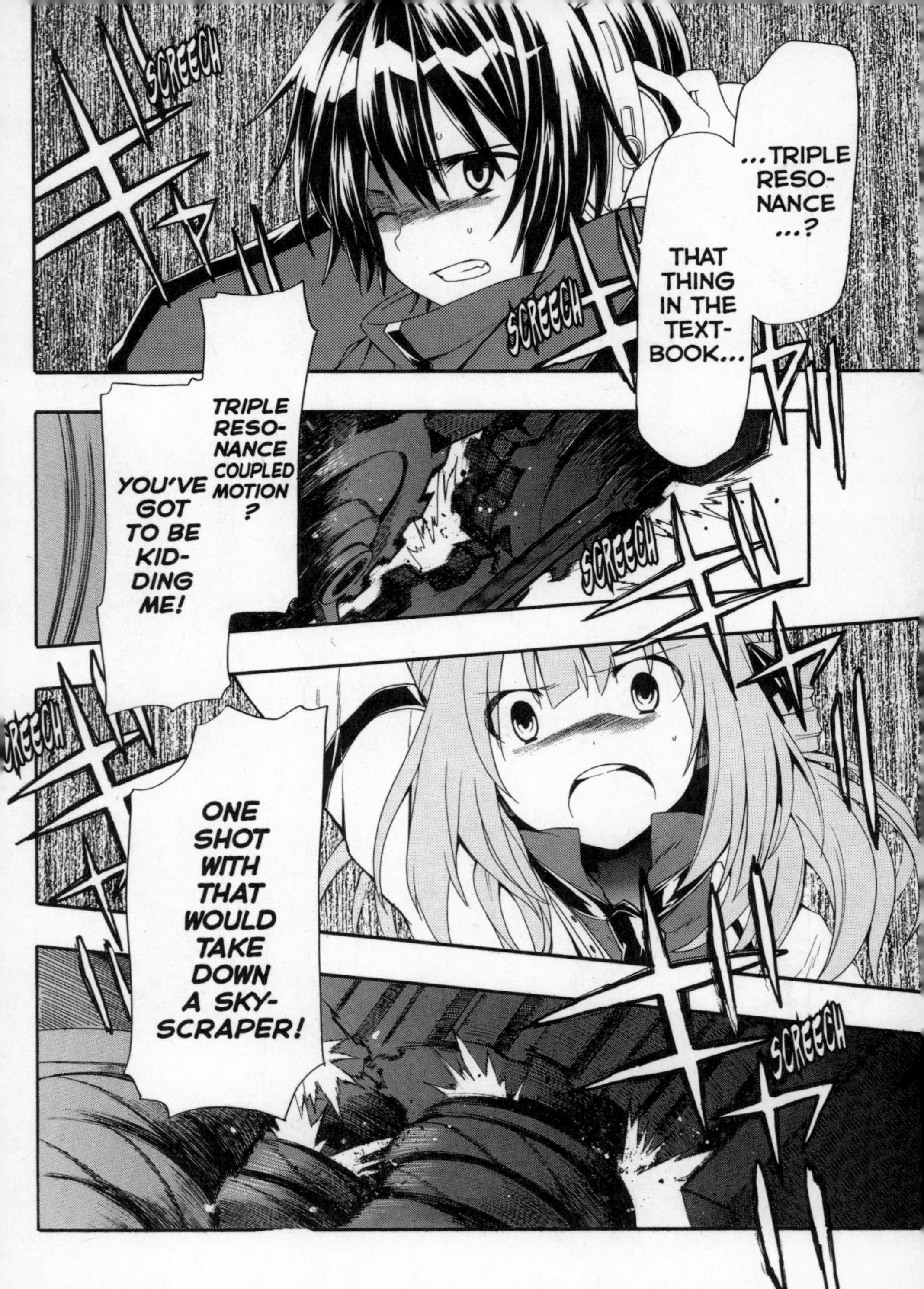
...TRIPLE RESONANCE ...? THAT THING IN THE TEXTBOOK...
SCREECH
SCREECH
TRIPLE RESONANCE COUPLED MOTION ? YOU'VE GOT TO BE KIDDING ME!
SCREECH
SCREECH
ONE SHOT WITH THAT WOULD TAKE DOWN A SKYSCRAPER!
SCREECH

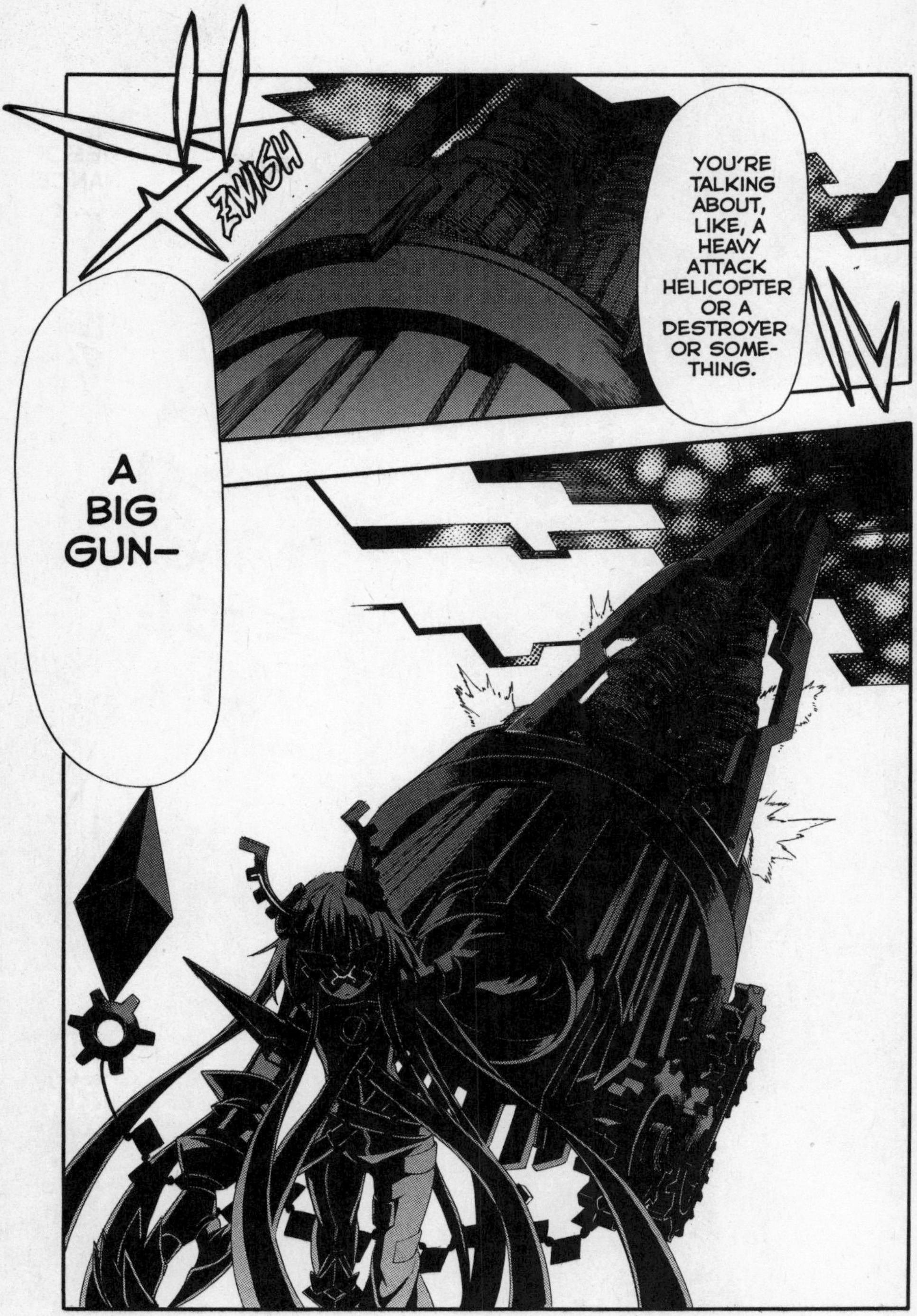
YOU'RE TALKING ABOUT, LIKE, A HEAVY ATTACK HELICOPTER OR A DESTROYER OR SOME-THING.
ZWISH
A BIG GUN—

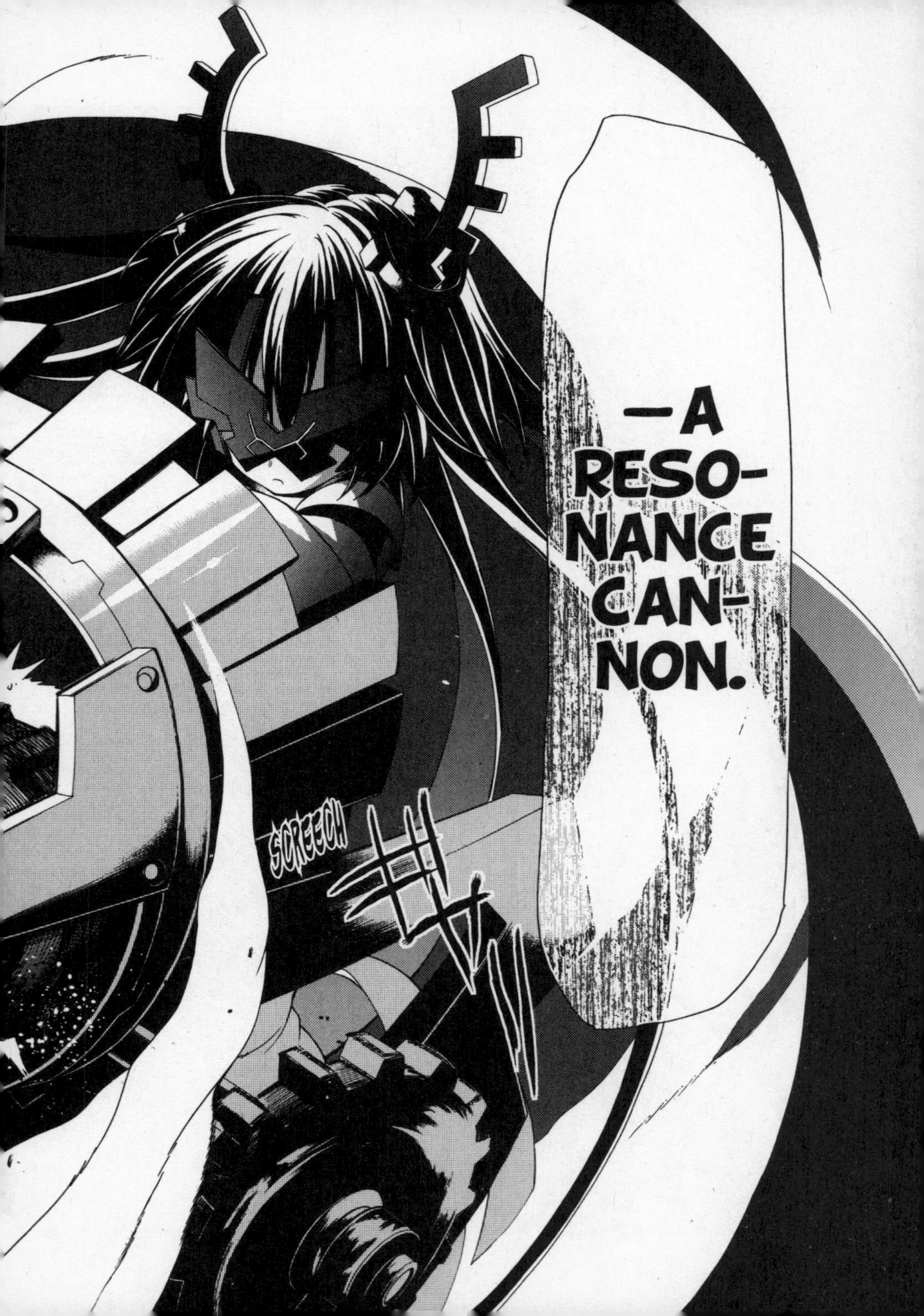
—A RESO-NANCE CAN-NON.
SCREECH

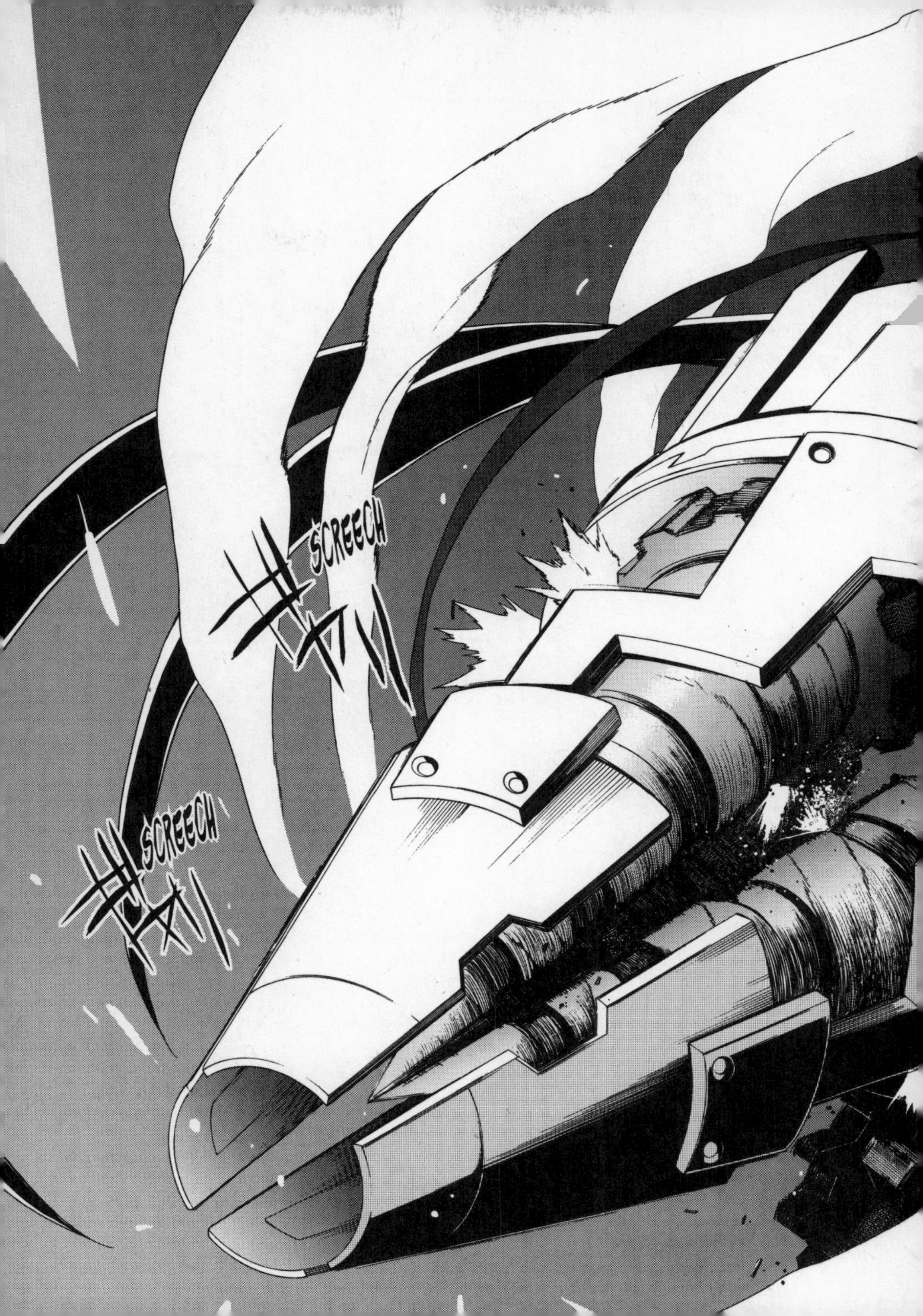
SCREECH
SCREECH

HE CAN'T!

HE WON'T MAKE IT!

!

KER-CHUNK

DUDE, RUN!

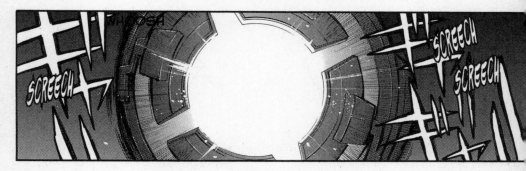

SCREECH

SCREECH

SCREECH

SCREECH

ISN'T THERE A WAY?

WHAT CAN WE DO?

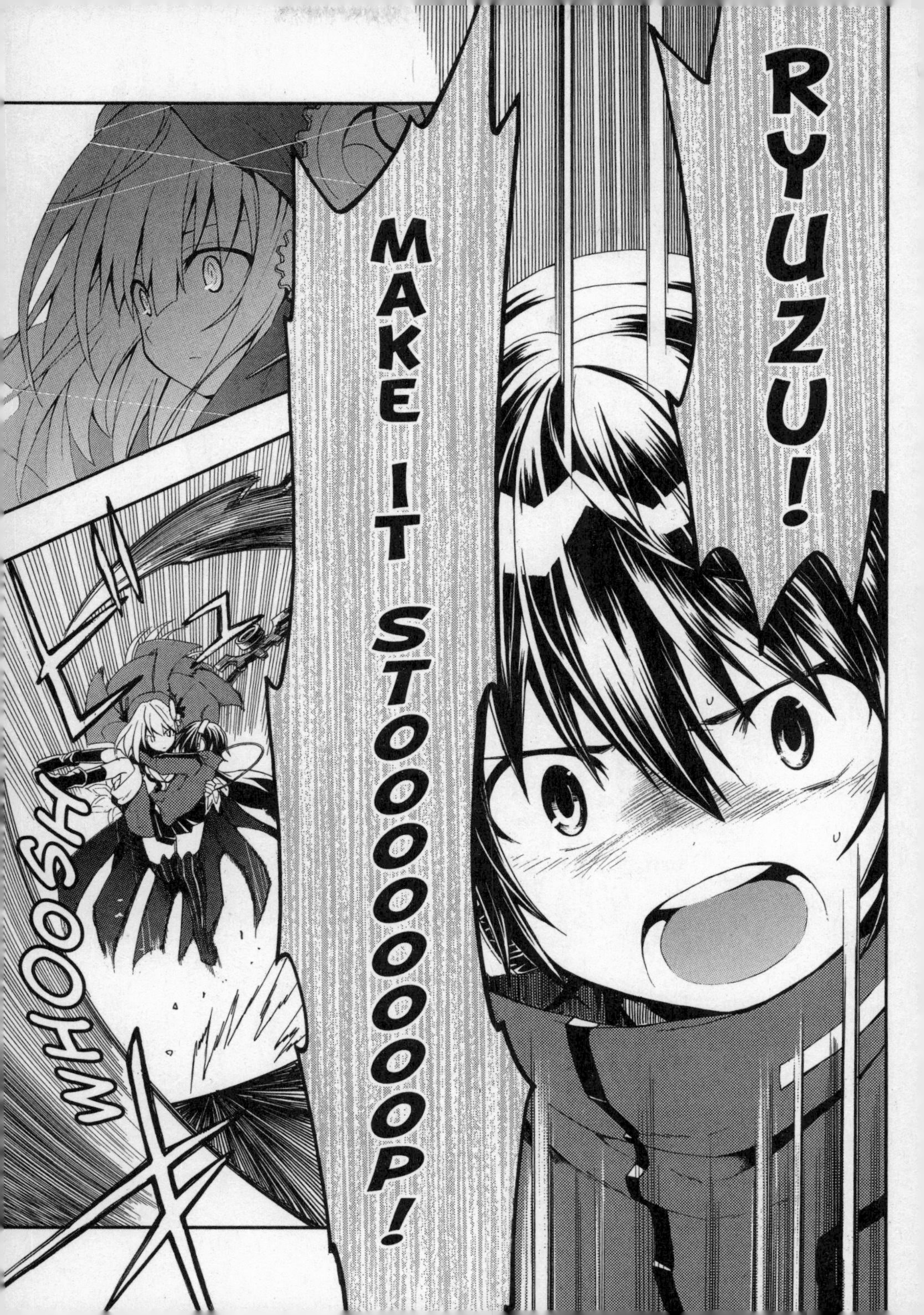
RYUZU!
MAKE IT STOOOOOOOOP!
WHOOSH

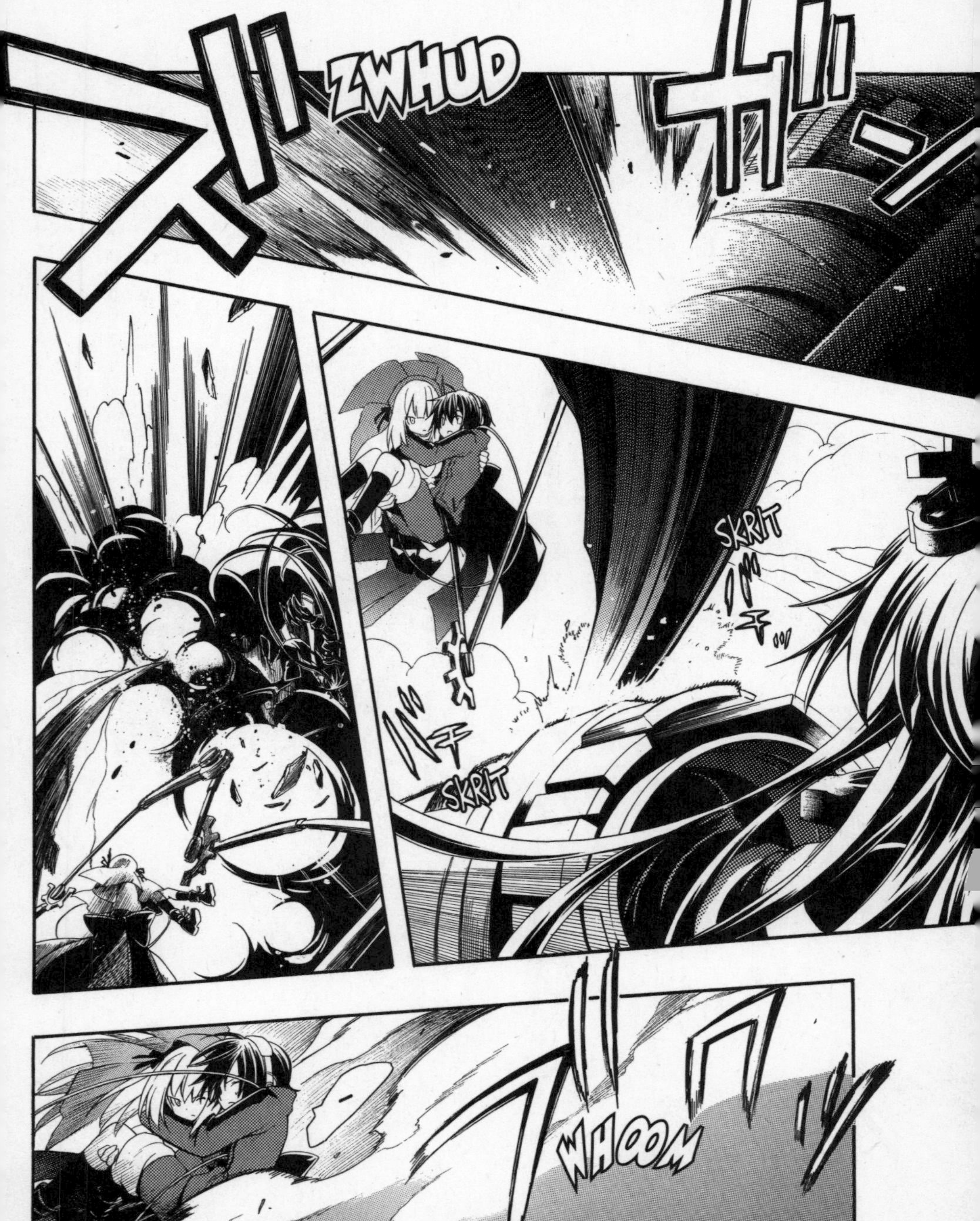
ZWHUD
SKRIT
SKRIT
WHOOM

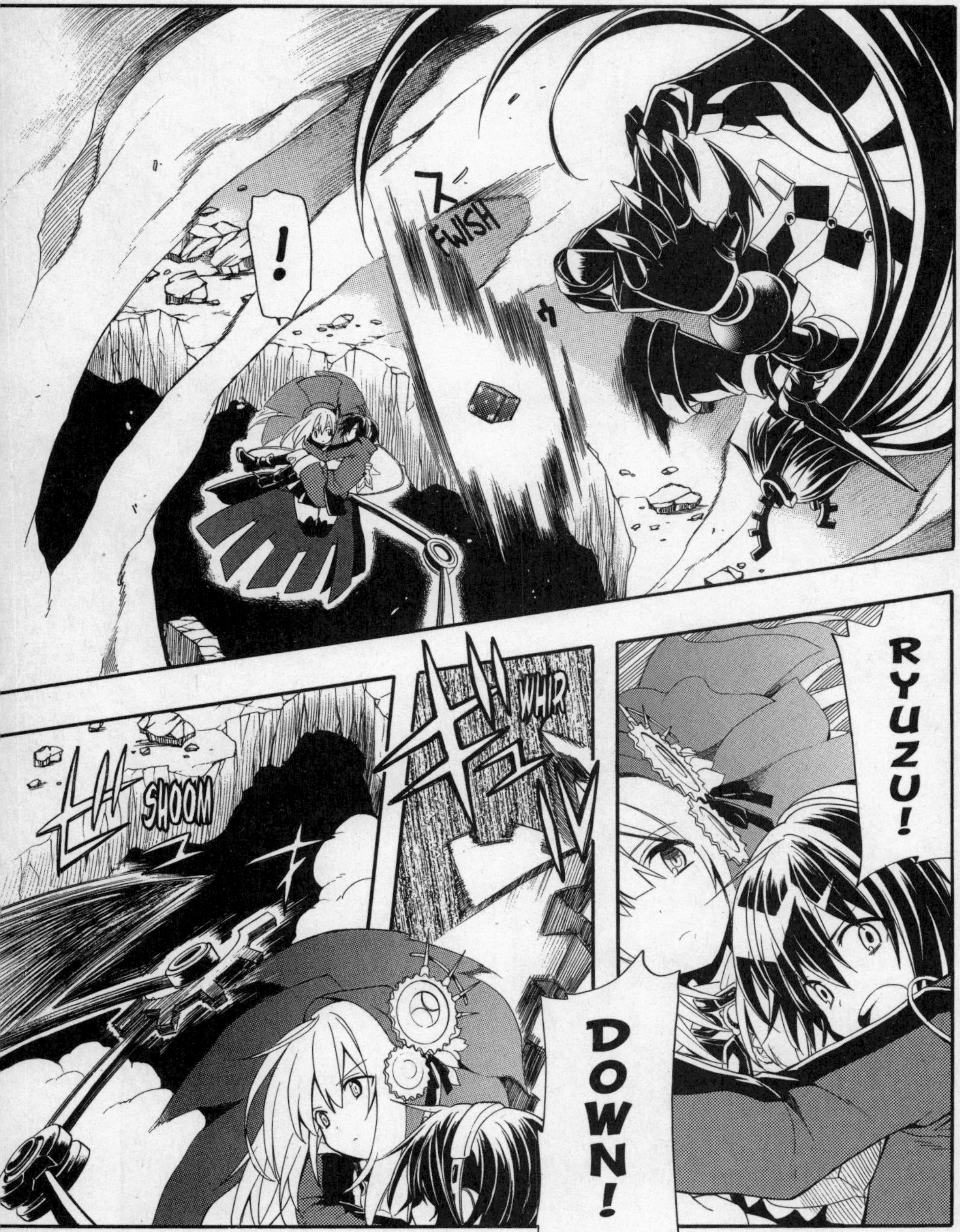
FWISH
!
RYUZU!
DOWN!
WHIR
SHOOM

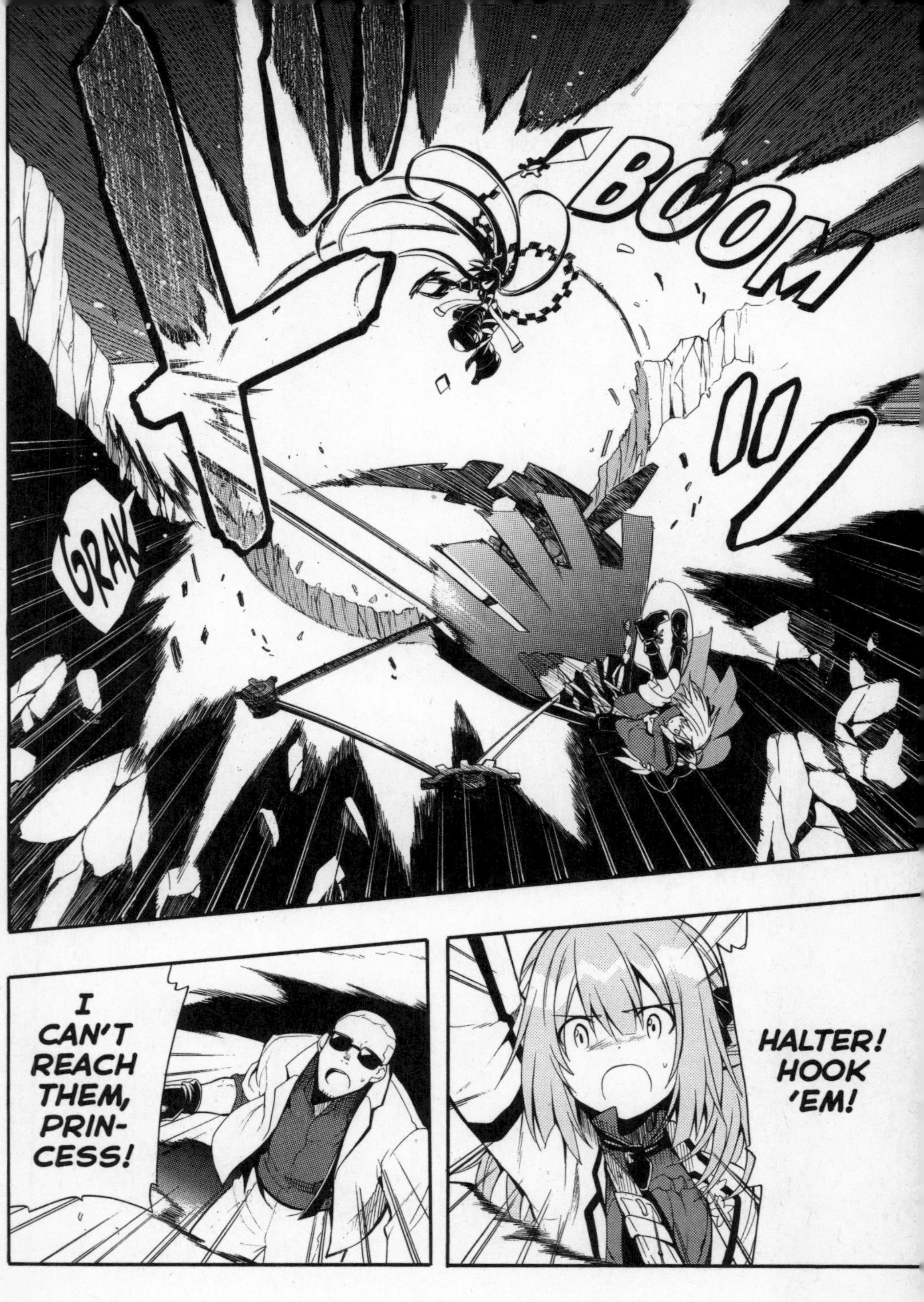
BOOM
GRAK
HALTER! HOOK 'EM!
I CAN'T REACH THEM, PRINCESS!

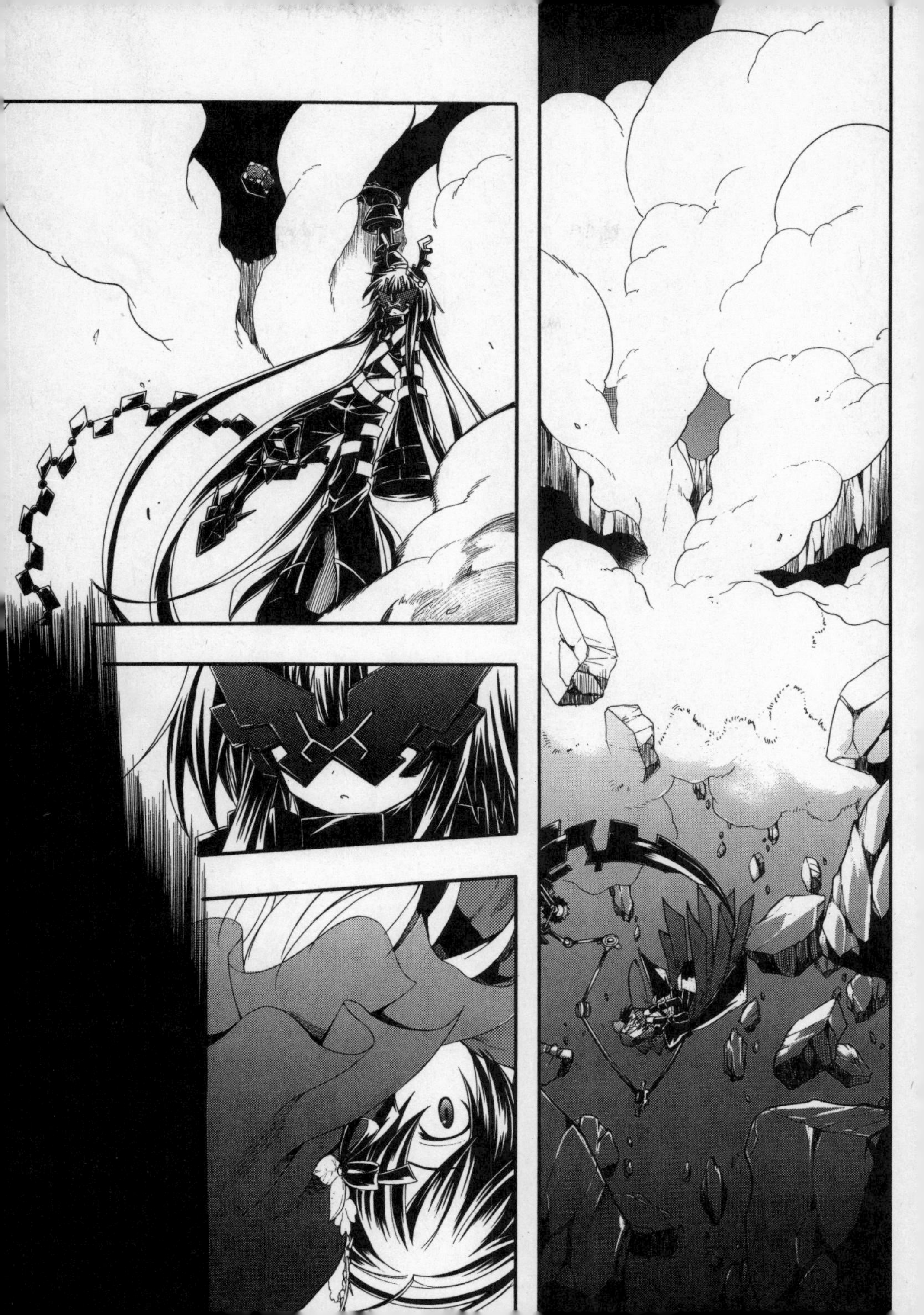

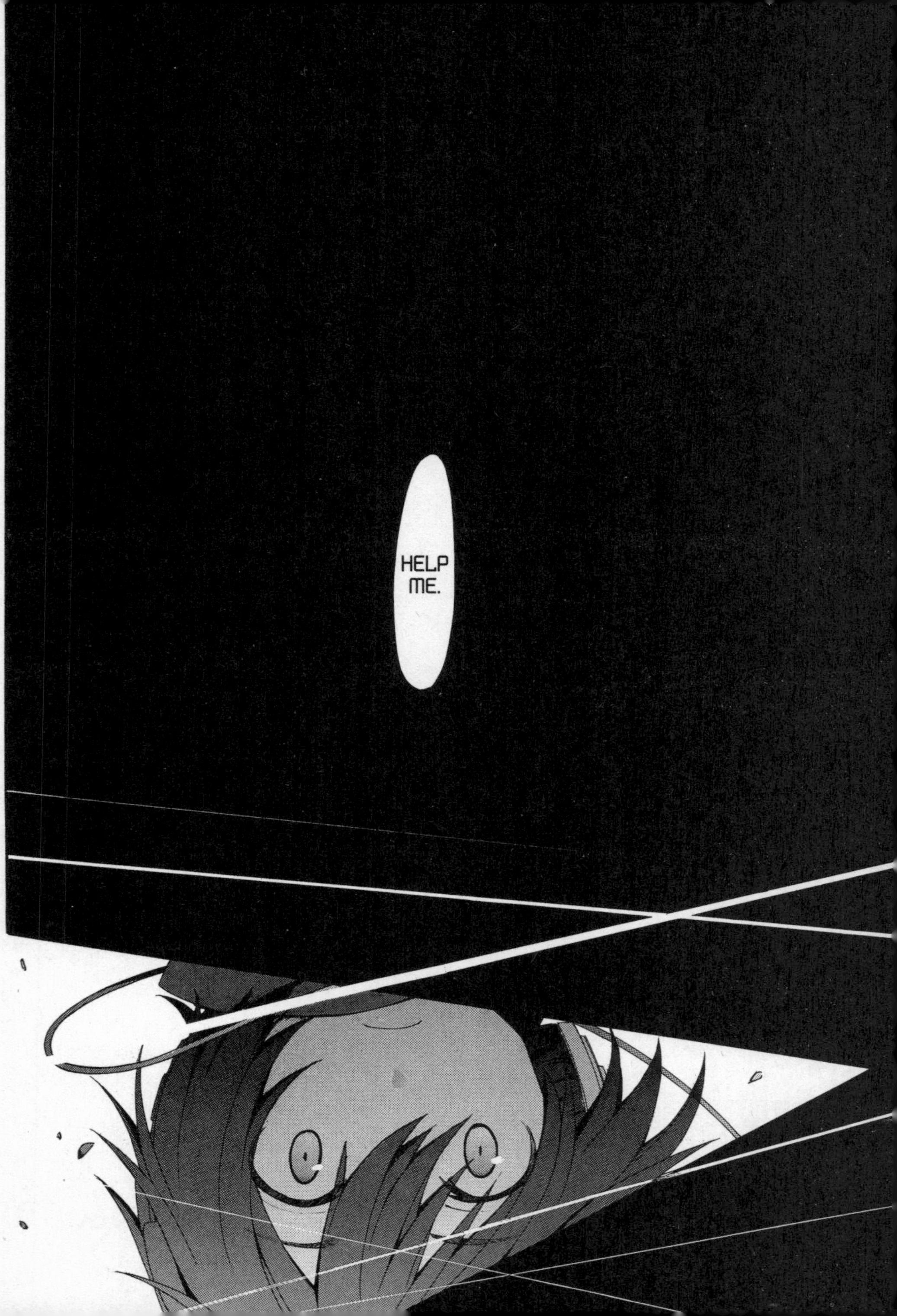
HELP ME.

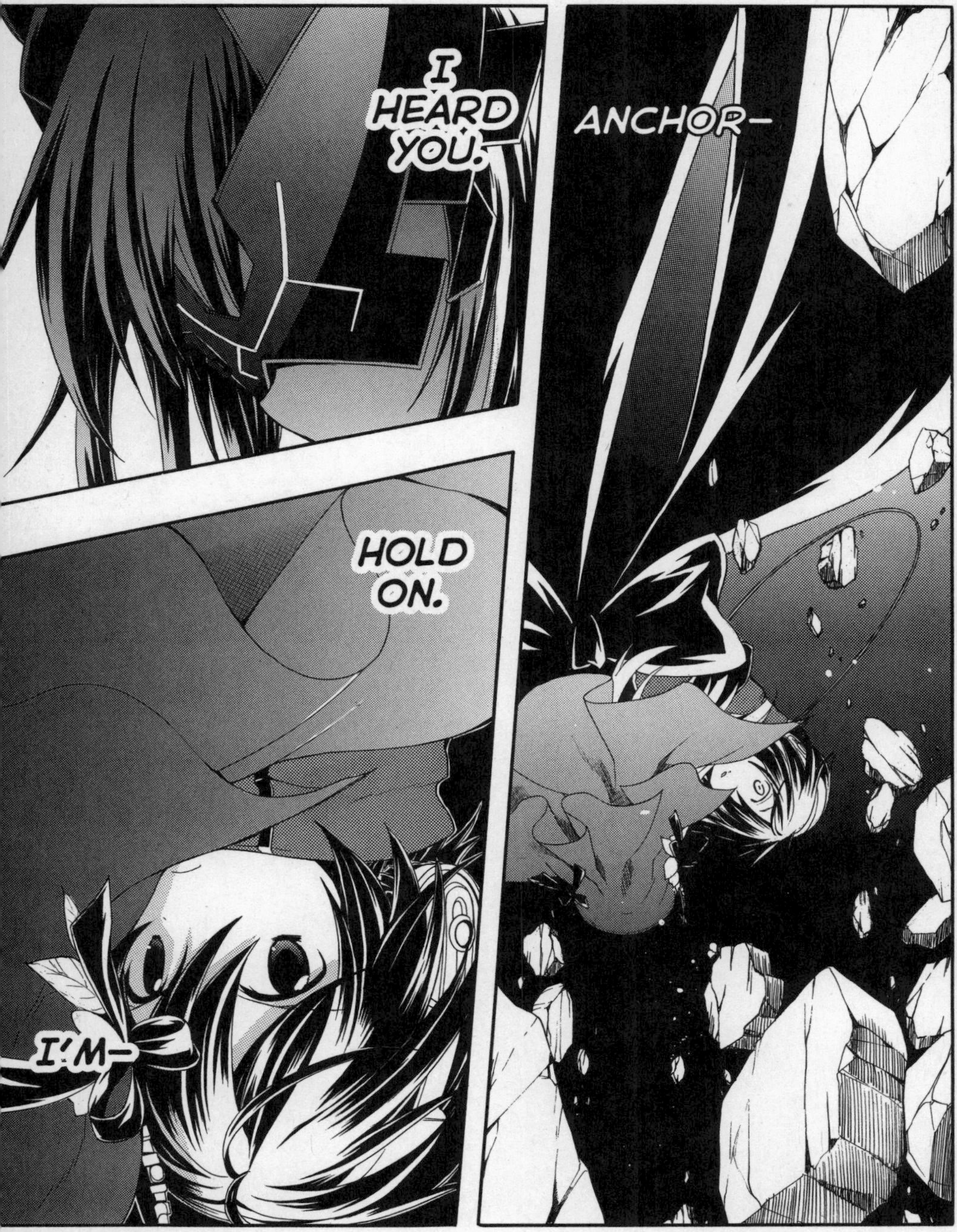
ANCHOR—
I HEARD YOU.
HOLD ON.
I'M—

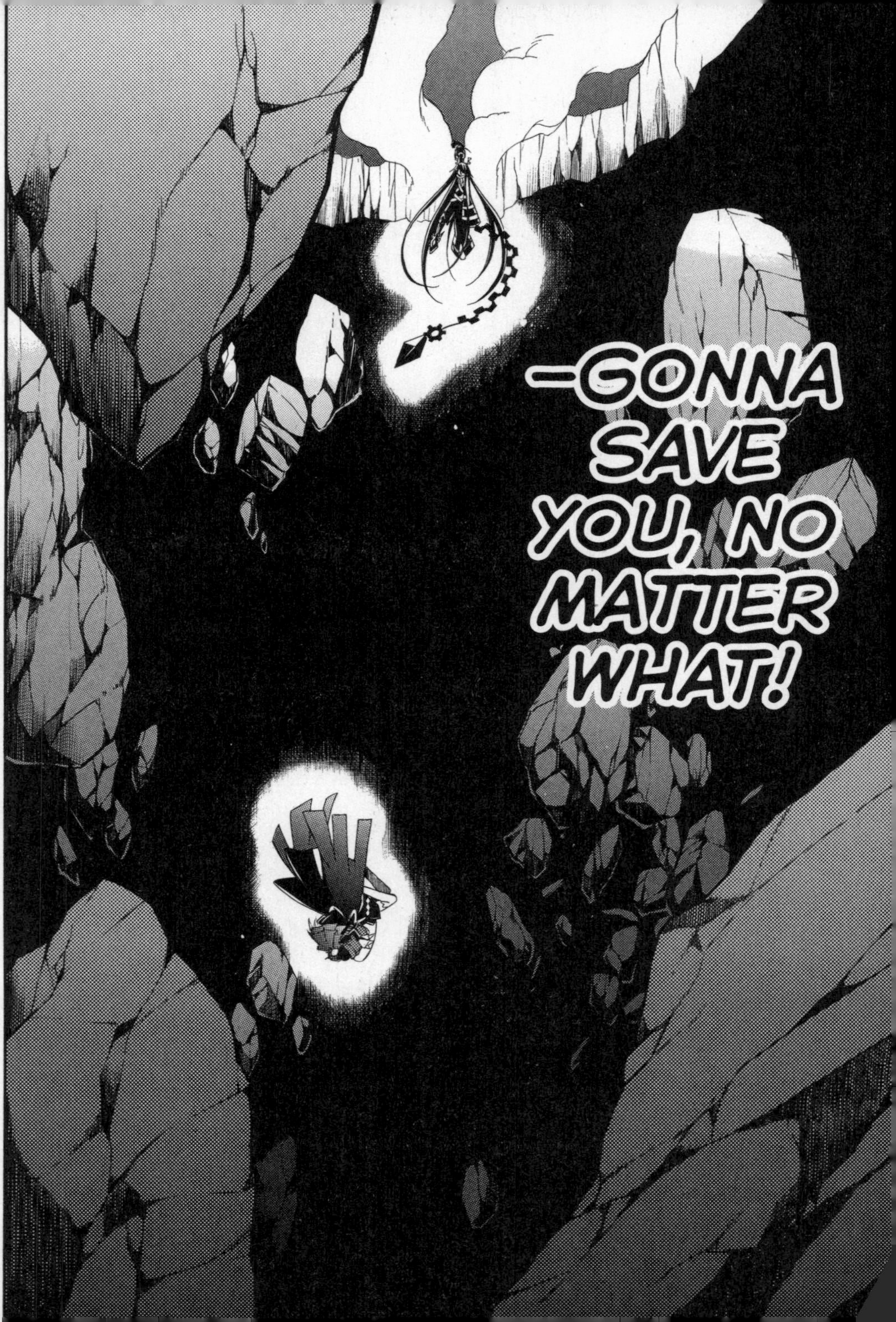
–GONNA SAVE YOU, NO MATTER WHAT!

CLOCKWORK PLANET

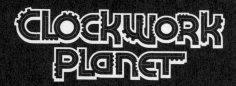

Clockwork Planet

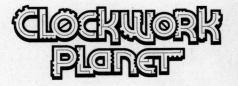

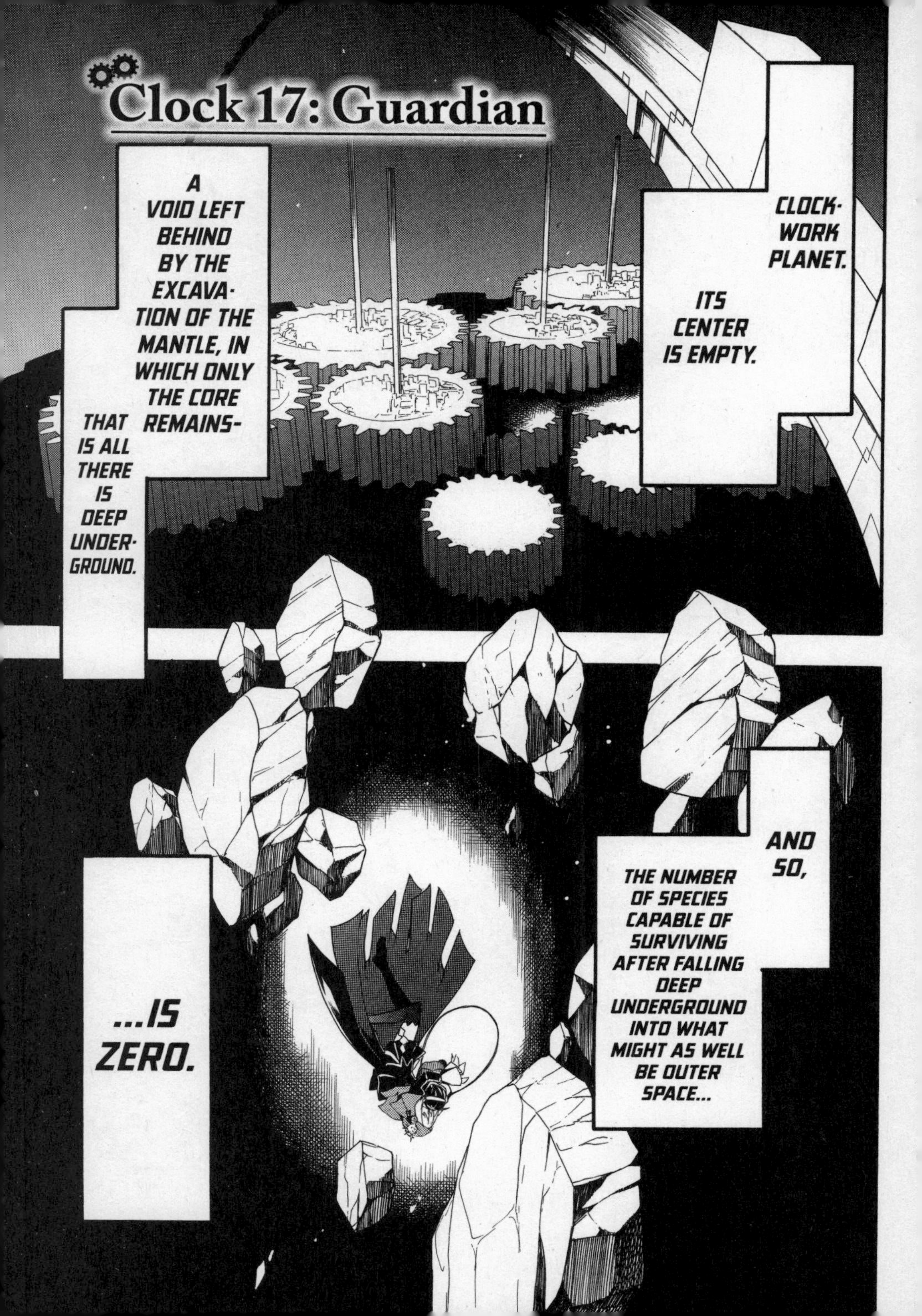
Clock 17: Guardian
CLOCKWORK PLANET.
ITS CENTER IS EMPTY.
A VOID LEFT BEHIND BY THE EXCAVATION OF THE MANTLE, IN WHICH ONLY THE CORE REMAINS-
THAT IS ALL THERE IS DEEP UNDERGROUND.
AND SO,
THE NUMBER OF SPECIES CAPABLE OF SURVIVING AFTER FALLING DEEP UNDERGROUND INTO WHAT MIGHT AS WELL BE OUTER SPACE...
...IS ZERO.

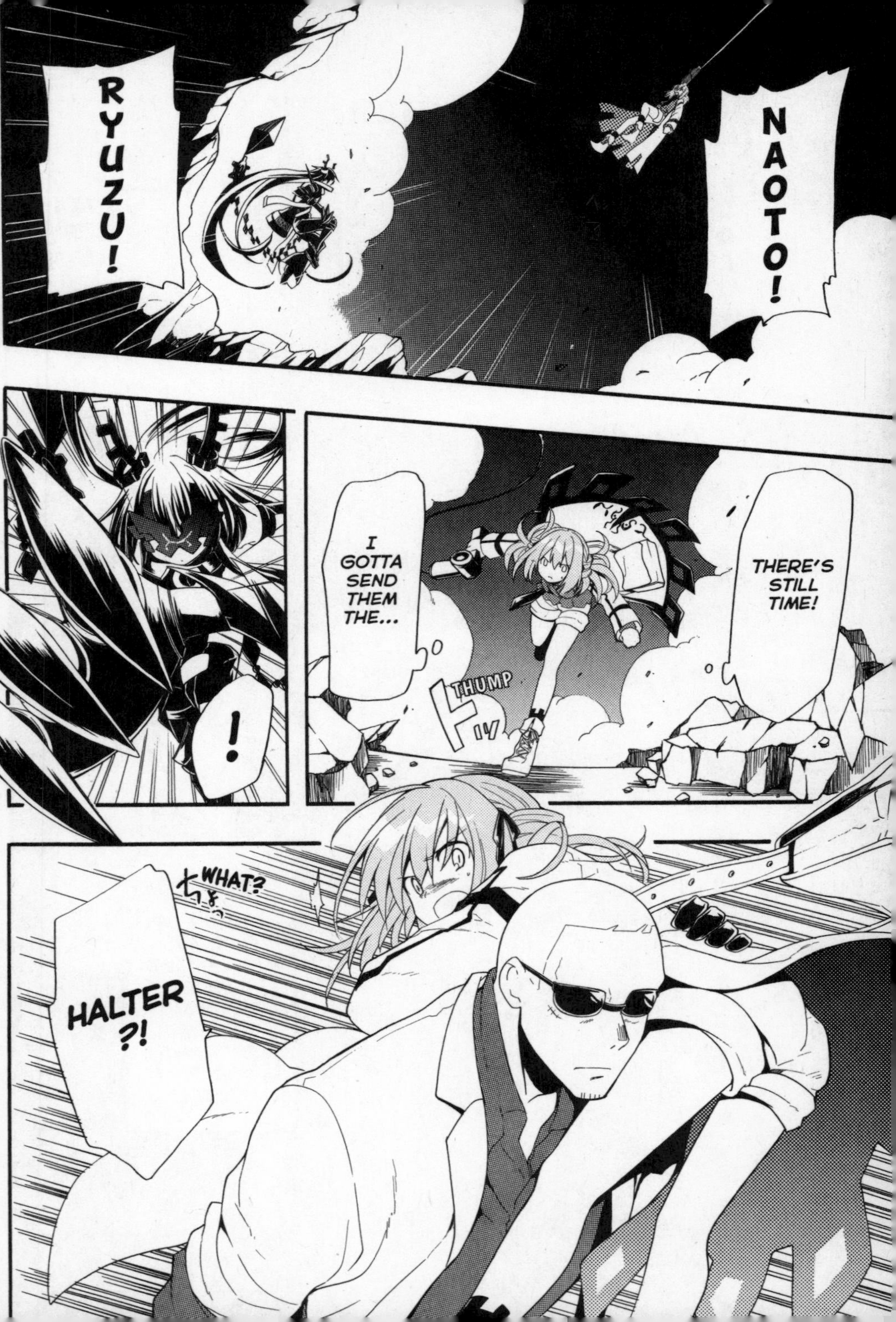
NAOTO!
RYUZU!
THERE'S STILL TIME!
I GOTTA SEND THEM THE...
THUMP
!
WHAT?
HALTER ?!

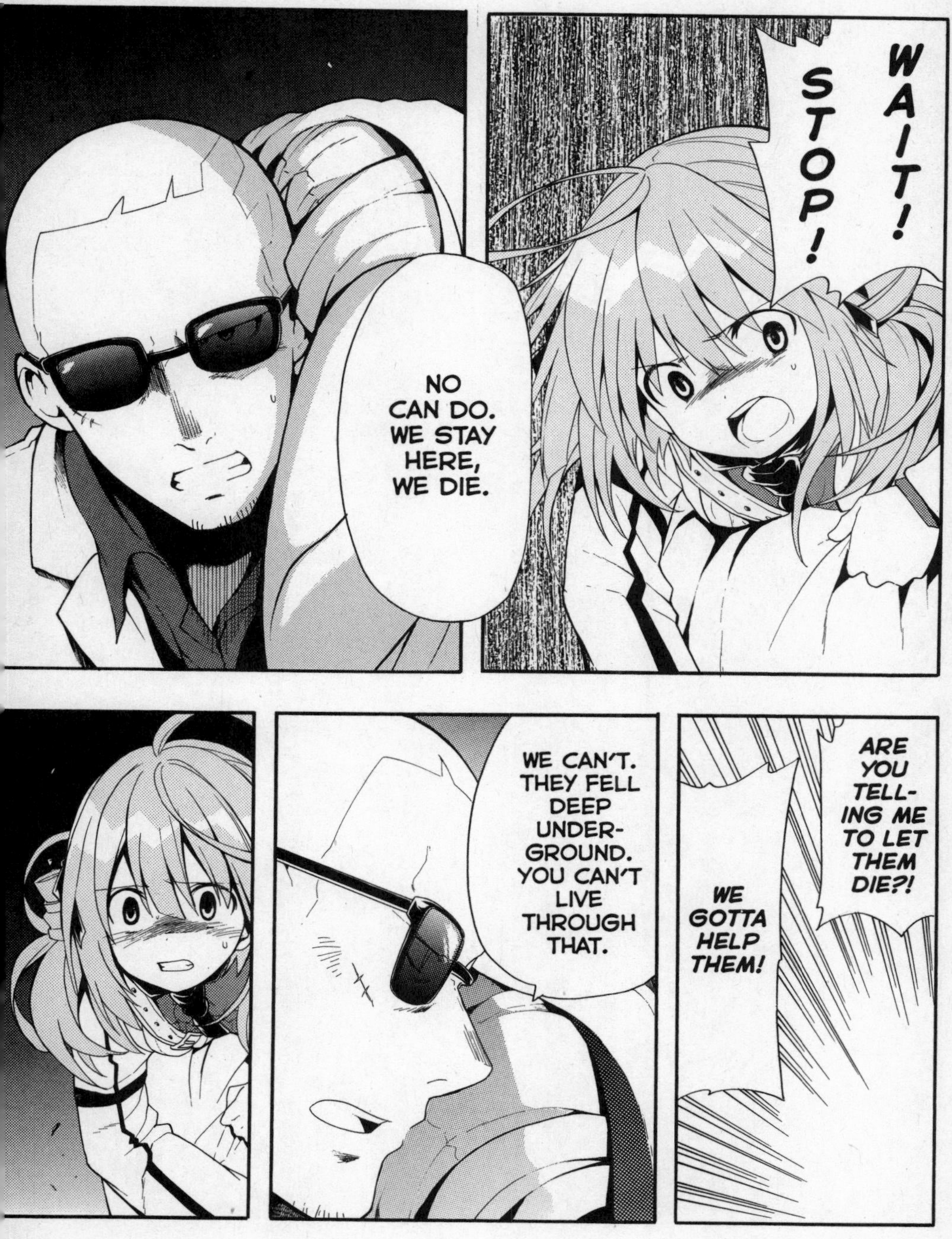
WAIT! STOP!
NO CAN DO. WE STAY HERE, WE DIE.
ARE YOU TELLING ME TO LET THEM DIE?!
WE GOTTA HELP THEM!
WE CAN'T. THEY FELL DEEP UNDERGROUND. YOU CAN'T LIVE THROUGH THAT.

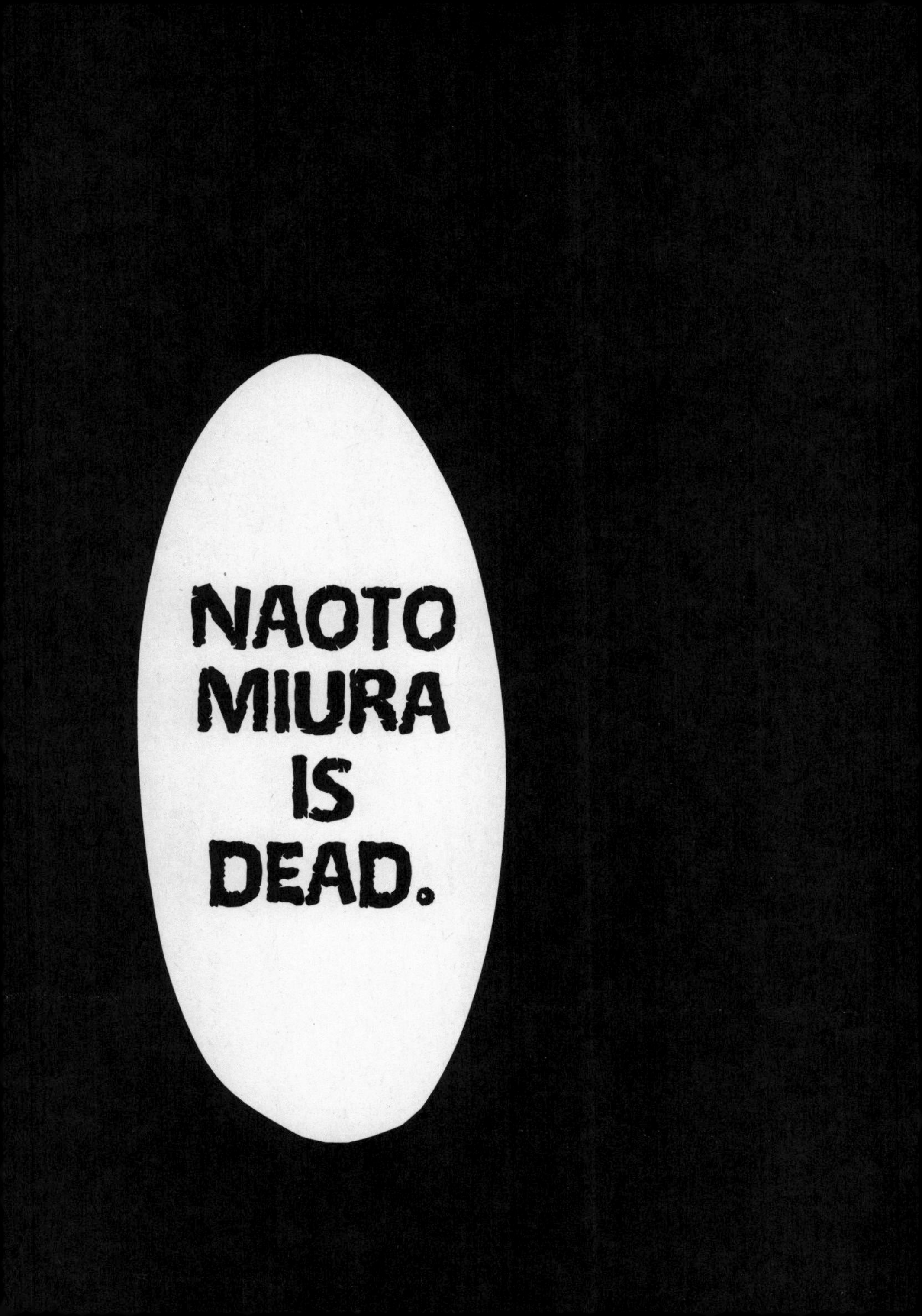
NAOTO MIURA IS DEAD.

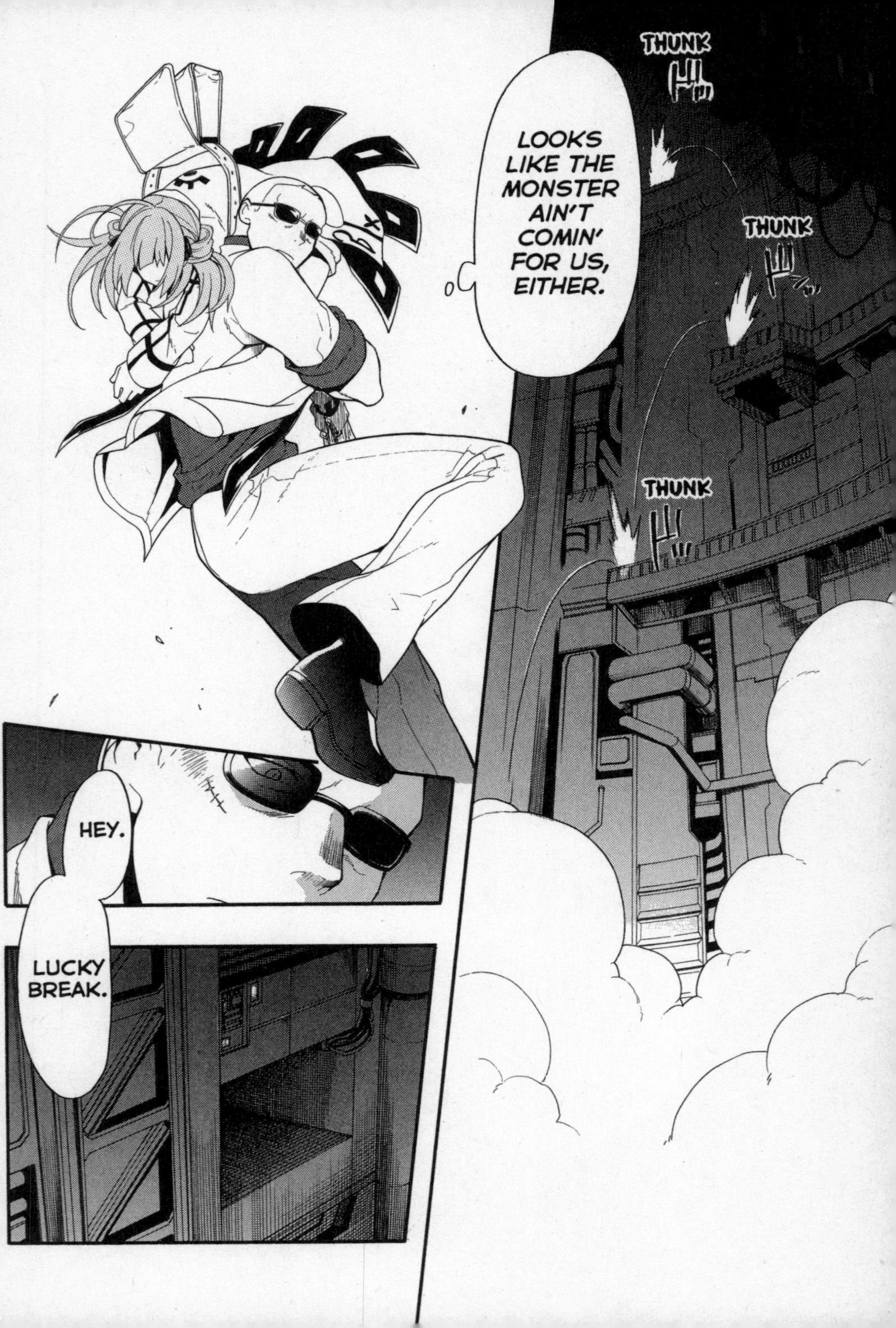
THUNK
THUNK
THUNK
LOOKS LIKE THE MONSTER AIN'T COMIN' FOR US, EITHER.
HEY.
LUCKY BREAK.

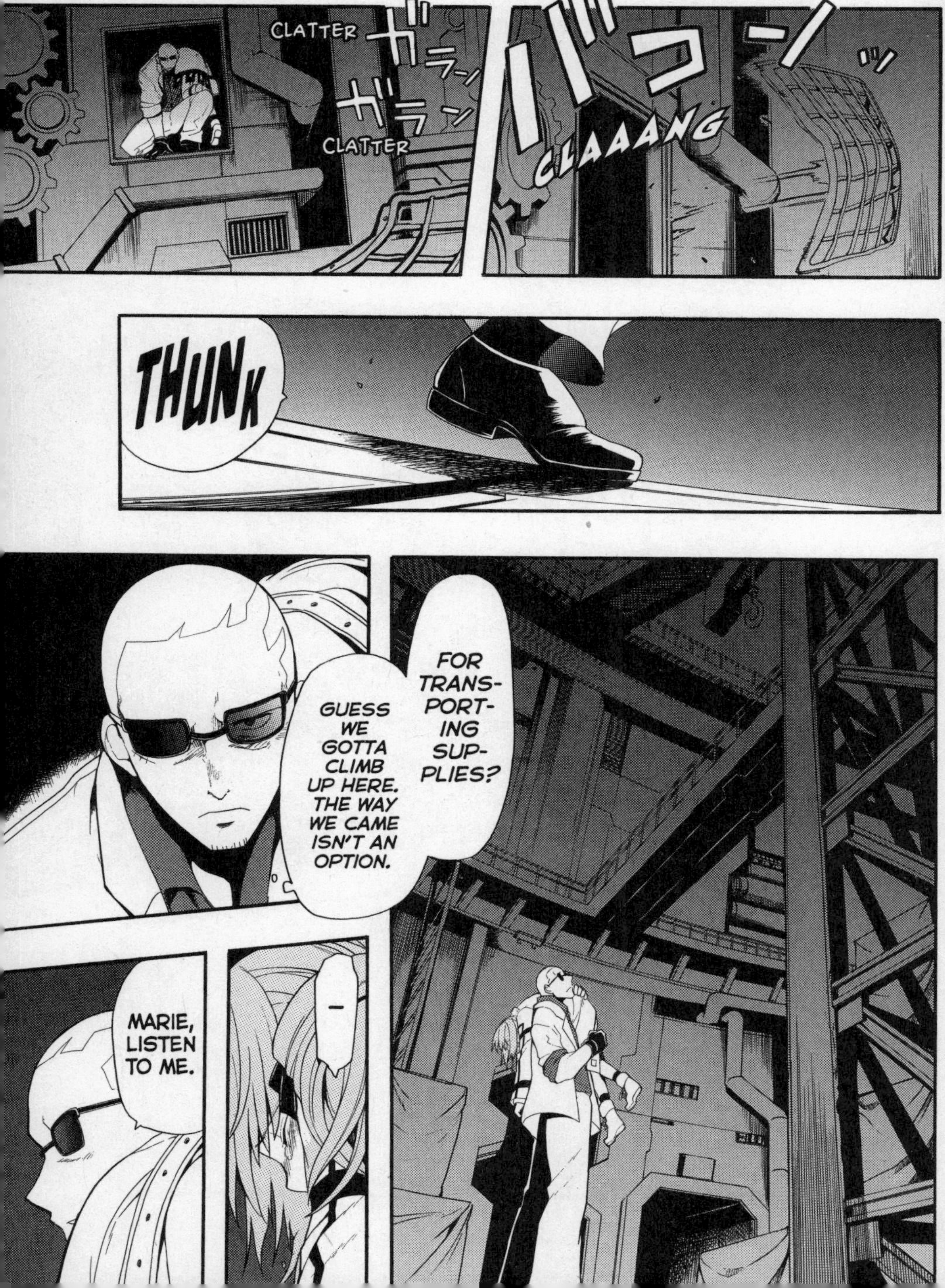
バコーン ッ
CLAAANG
ガラーン
CLATTER
ガラン
CLATTER
THUNK
FOR TRANSPORTING SUPPLIES?
GUESS WE GOTTA CLIMB UP HERE. THE WAY WE CAME ISN'T AN OPTION.
—
MARIE, LISTEN TO ME.

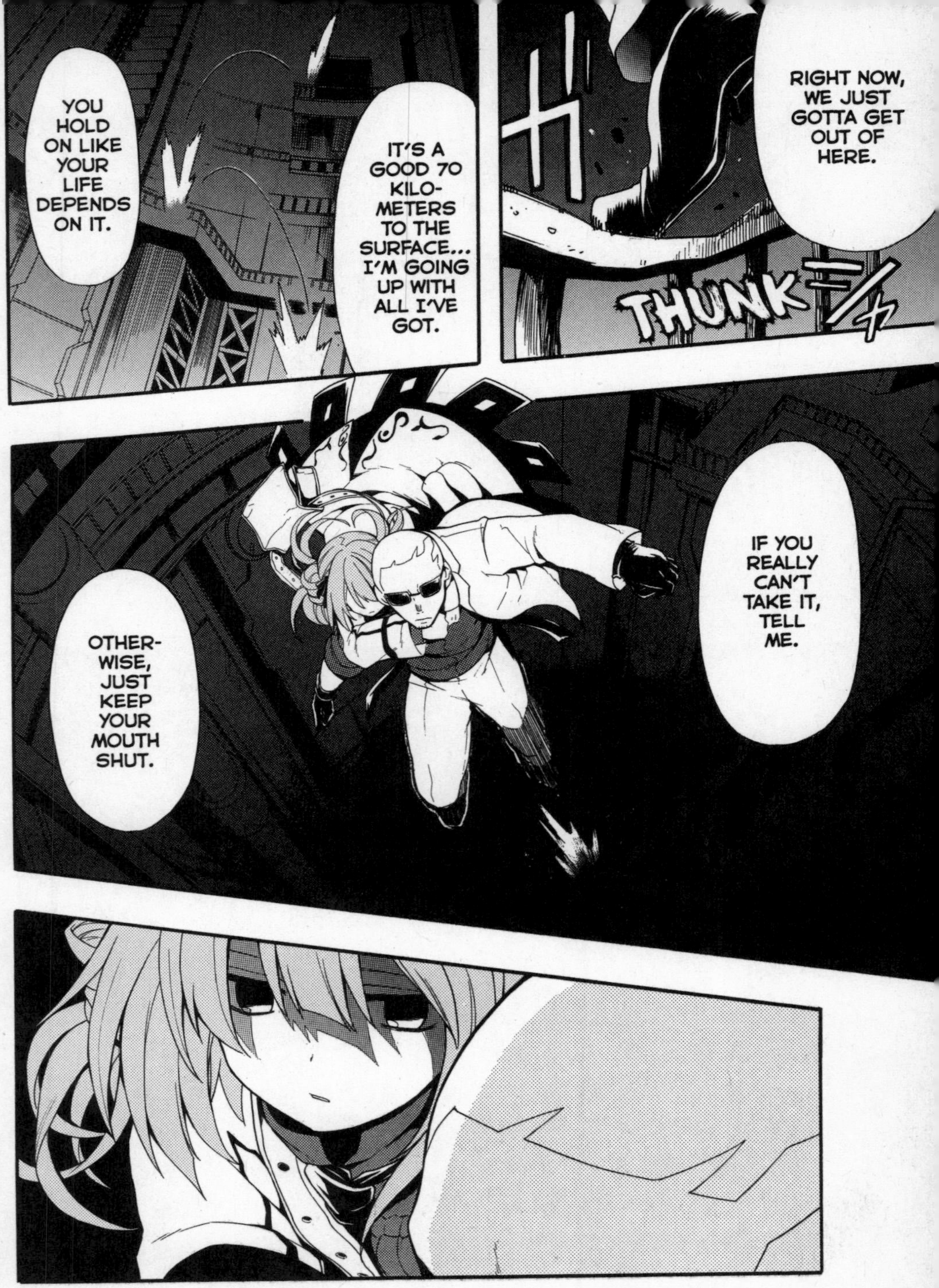
RIGHT NOW, WE JUST GOTTA GET OUT OF HERE.
THUNK
IT'S A GOOD 70 KILO-METERS TO THE SURFACE... I'M GOING UP WITH ALL I'VE GOT.
YOU HOLD ON LIKE YOUR LIFE DEPENDS ON IT.
IF YOU REALLY CAN'T TAKE IT, TELL ME.
OTHER-WISE, JUST KEEP YOUR MOUTH SHUT.

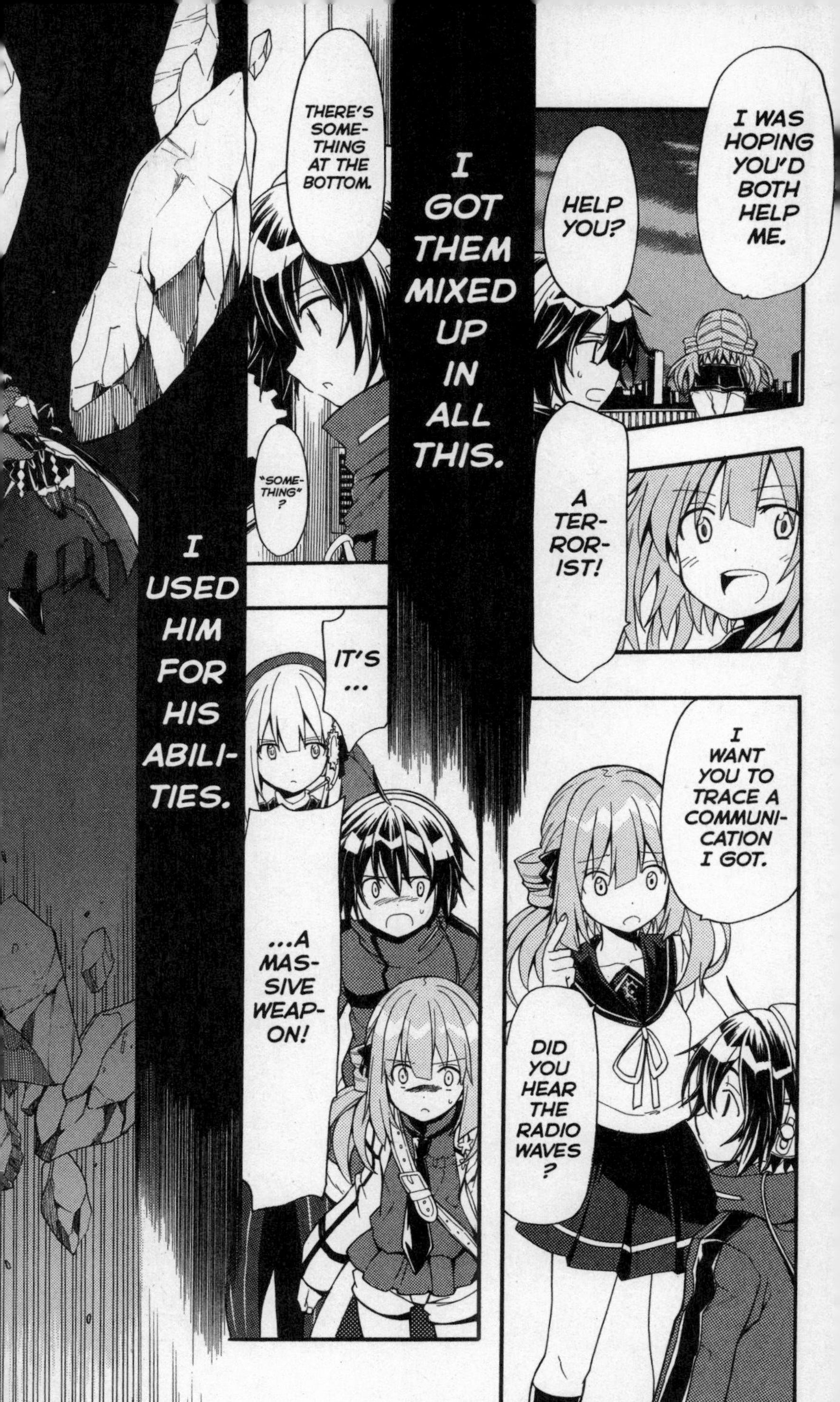
I WAS HOPING YOU'D BOTH HELP ME.
HELP YOU?
A TERRORIST!
I WANT YOU TO TRACE A COMMUNICATION I GOT.
DID YOU HEAR THE RADIO WAVES?
I GOT THEM MIXED UP IN ALL THIS.
THERE'S SOMETHING AT THE BOTTOM.
"SOMETHING"?
IT'S...
...A MASSIVE WEAPON!
I USED HIM FOR HIS ABILITIES.

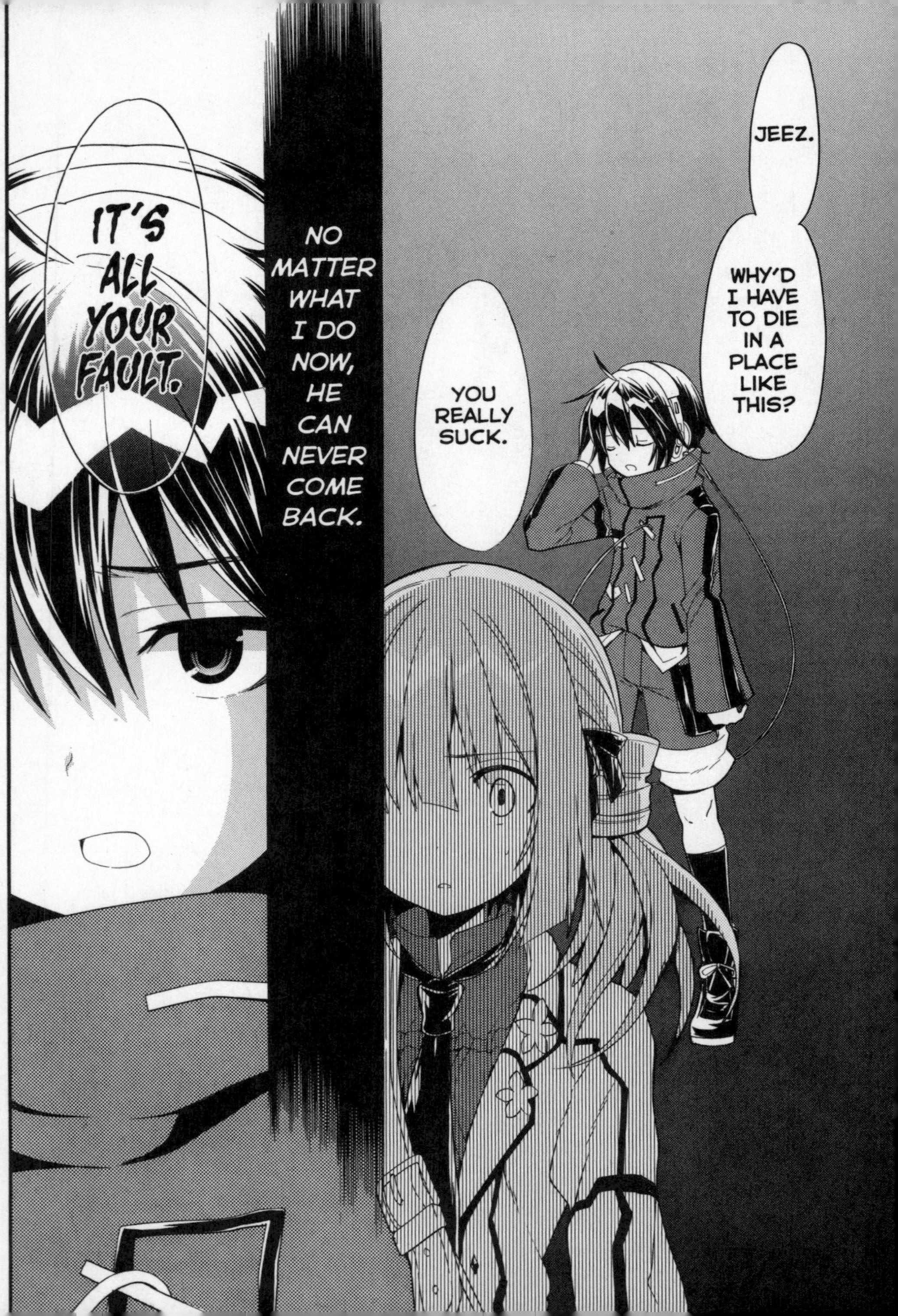
JEEZ.
WHY'D I HAVE TO DIE IN A PLACE LIKE THIS?
YOU REALLY SUCK.
NO MATTER WHAT I DO NOW, HE CAN NEVER COME BACK.
IT'S ALL YOUR FAULT.

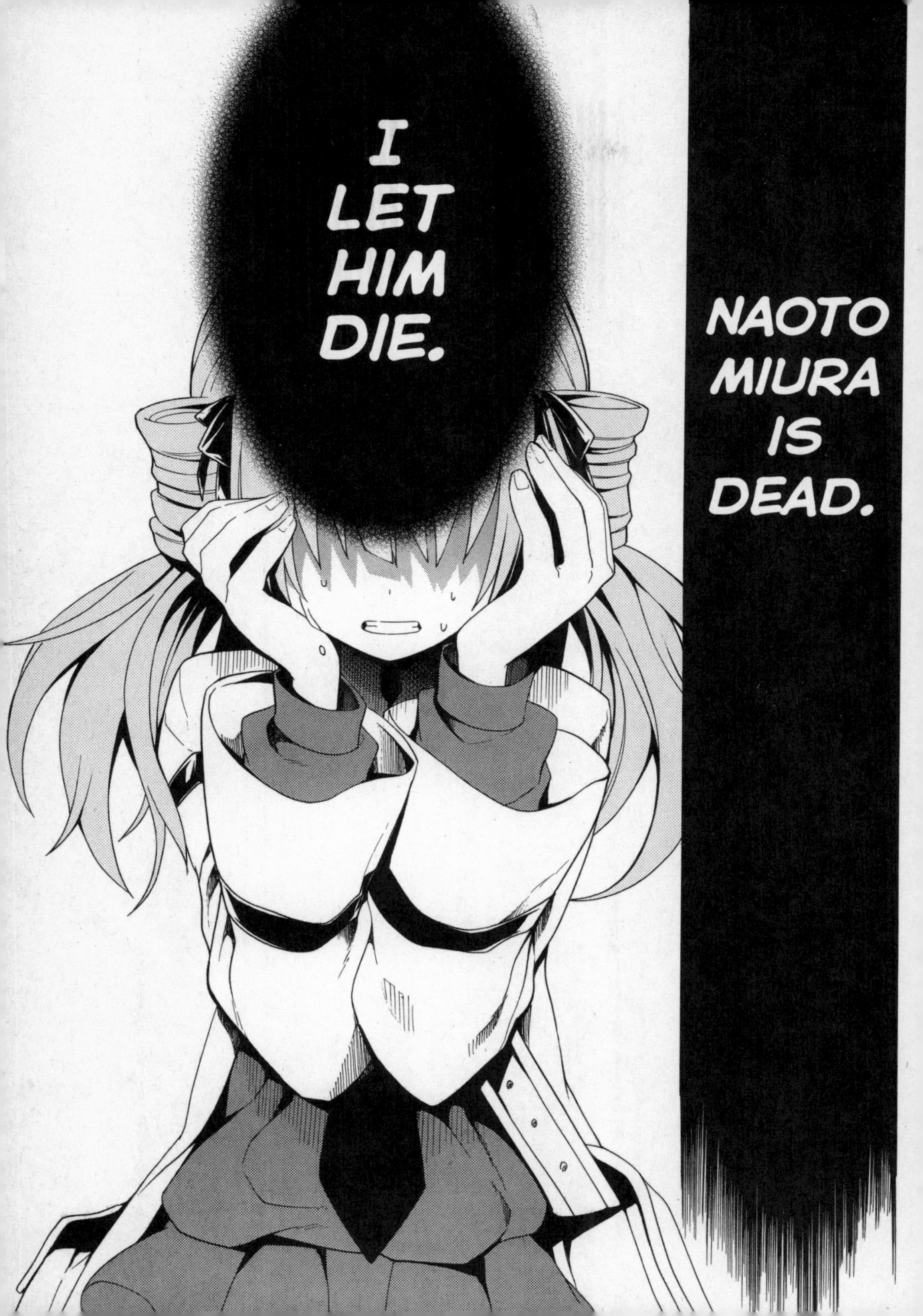
NAOTO MIURA IS DEAD.
I LET HIM DIE.

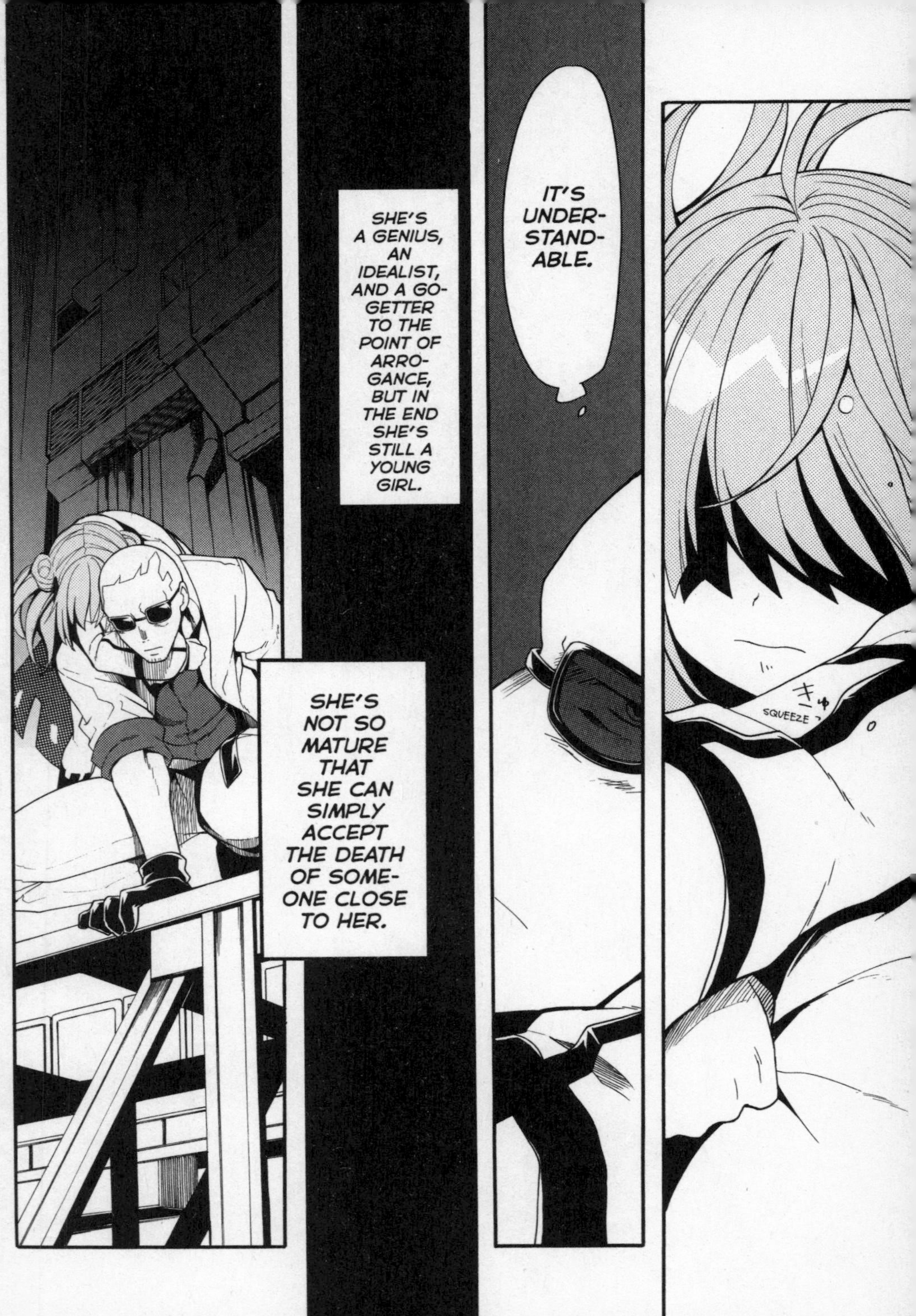

SQUEEZE
IT'S UNDER-STAND-ABLE.
SHE'S A GENIUS, AN IDEALIST, AND A GO-GETTER TO THE POINT OF ARRO-GANCE, BUT IN THE END SHE'S STILL A YOUNG GIRL.
SHE'S NOT SO MATURE THAT SHE CAN SIMPLY ACCEPT THE DEATH OF SOME-ONE CLOSE TO HER.

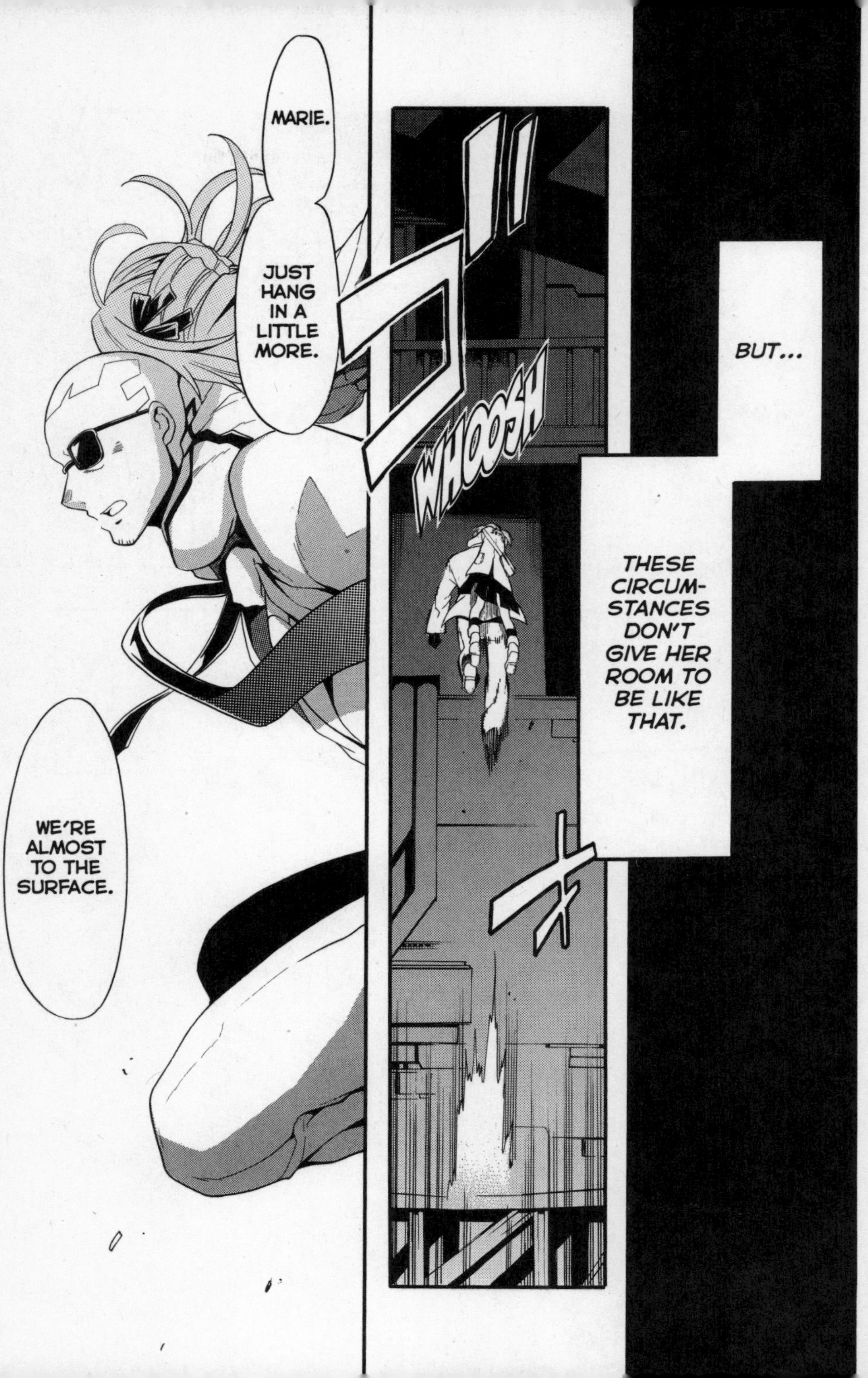
BUT...
THESE CIRCUMSTANCES DON'T GIVE HER ROOM TO BE LIKE THAT.
WHOOSH
MARIE.
JUST HANG IN A LITTLE MORE.
WE'RE ALMOST TO THE SURFACE.

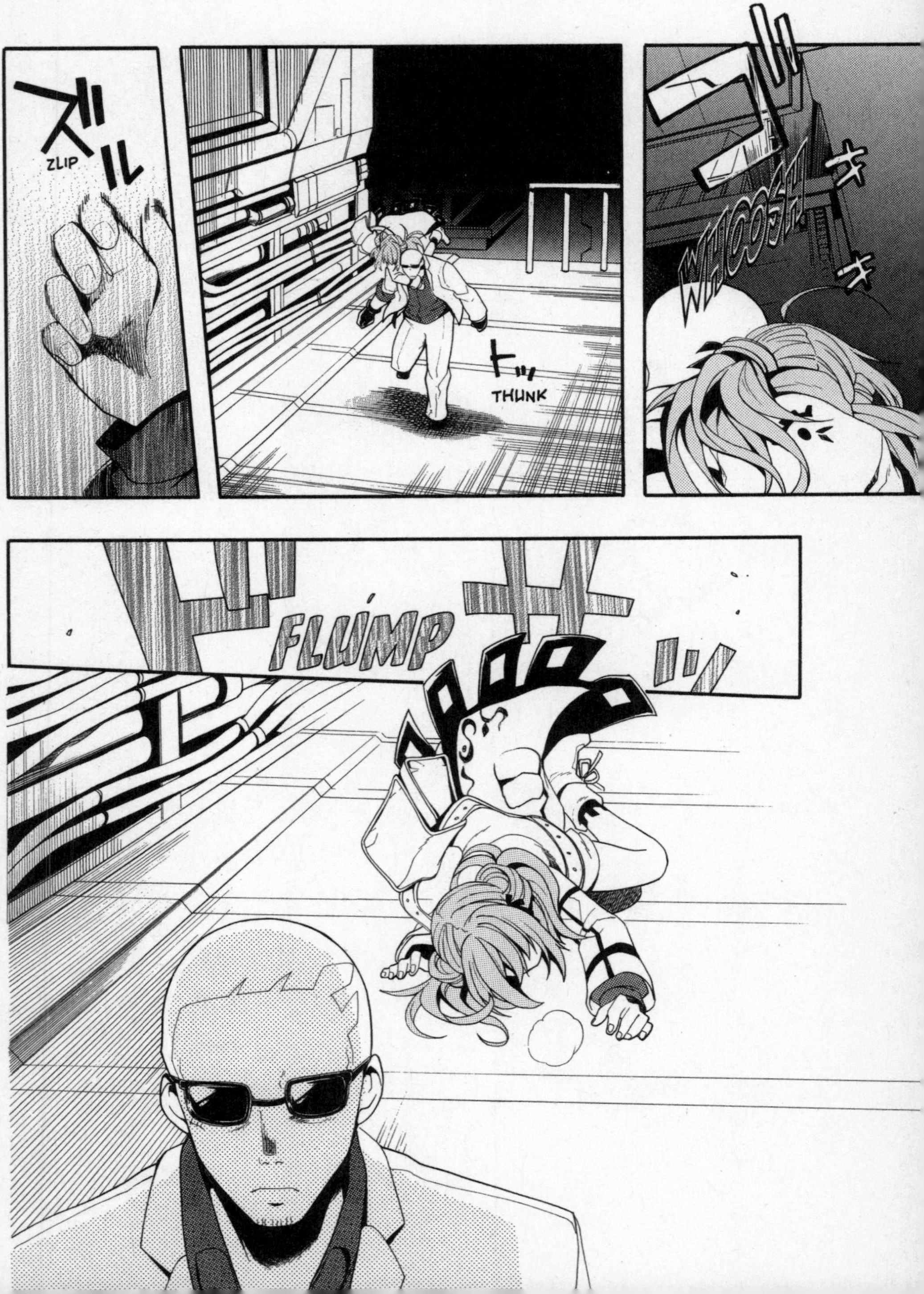
WHOOSH
トッ
THUNK
ズル
ZLIP
FLUMP

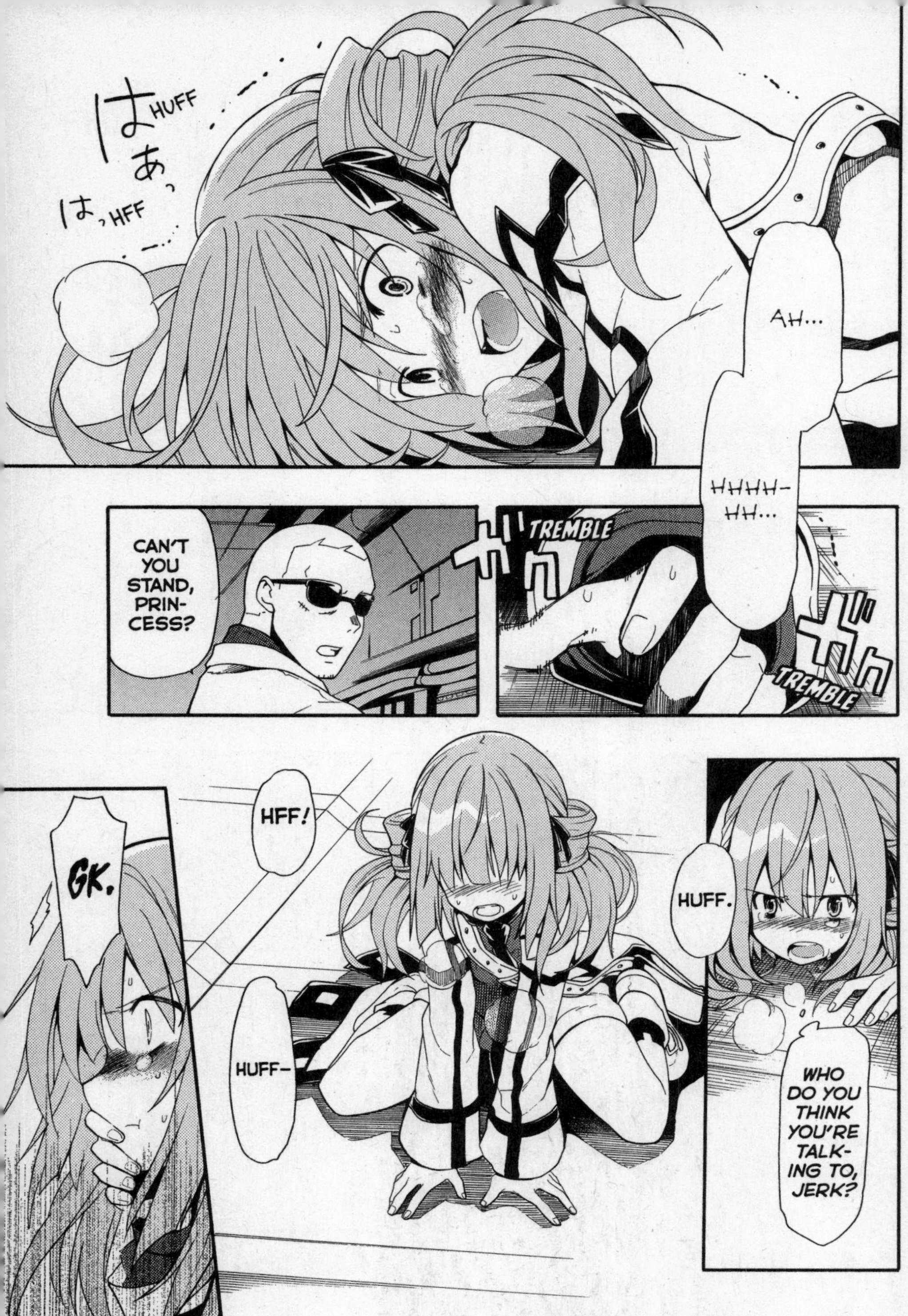
はあっ HUFF
はっ HFF
AH... HHHH-HH...
ガクッ TREMBLE
ガクッ TREMBLE
CAN'T YOU STAND, PRIN-CESS?
HUFF.
WHO DO YOU THINK YOU'RE TALK-ING TO, JERK?
HFF!
HUFF–
GK.

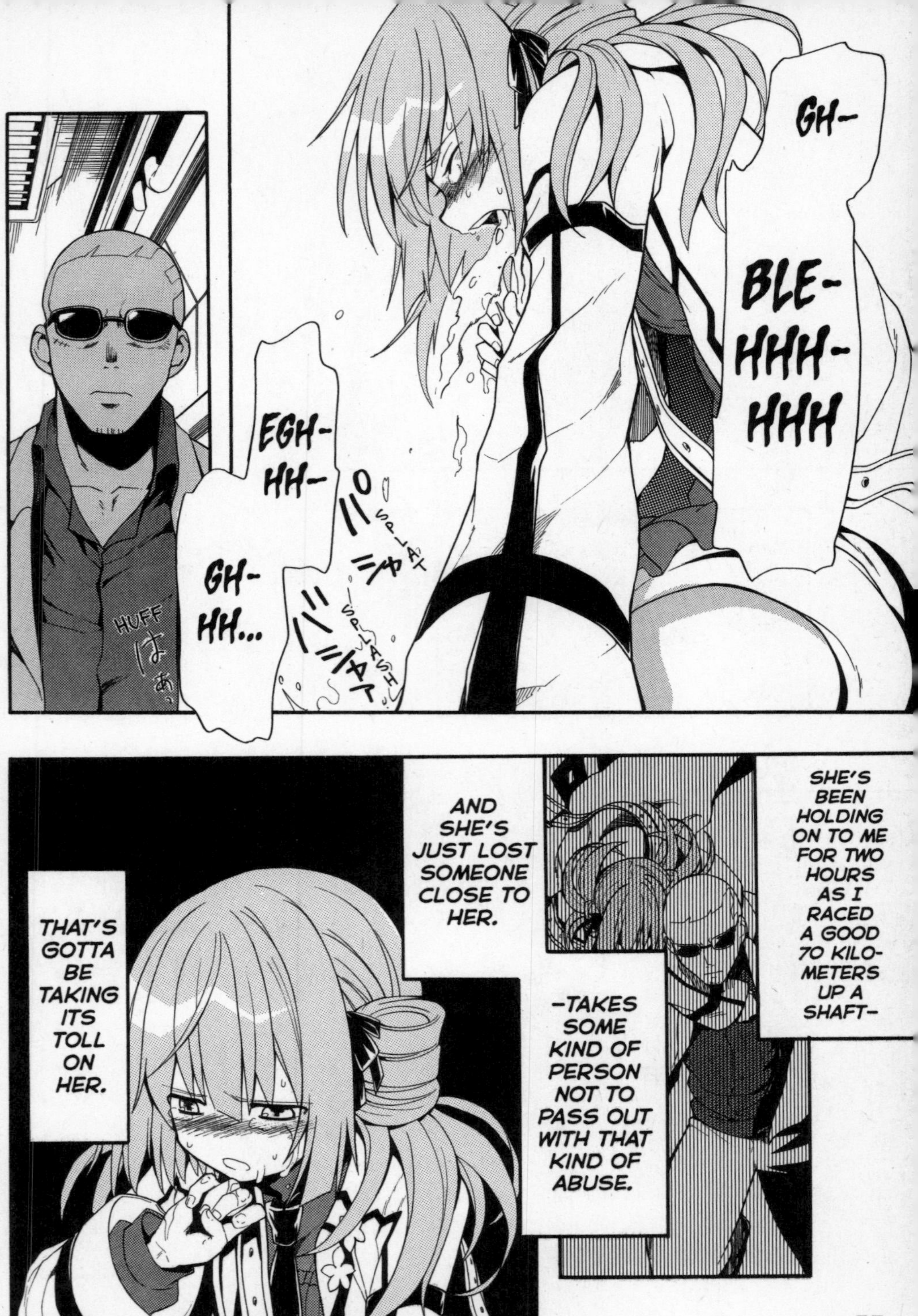
GH-
BLE-HHH-HHH
EGH-HH-
パシャ
SPLAT
バシャア
SPLASH
GH-HH...
HUFF
はあ
SHE'S BEEN HOLDING ON TO ME FOR TWO HOURS AS I RACED A GOOD 70 KILOMETERS UP A SHAFT-
-TAKES SOME KIND OF PERSON NOT TO PASS OUT WITH THAT KIND OF ABUSE.
AND SHE'S JUST LOST SOMEONE CLOSE TO HER.
THAT'S GOTTA BE TAKING ITS TOLL ON HER.

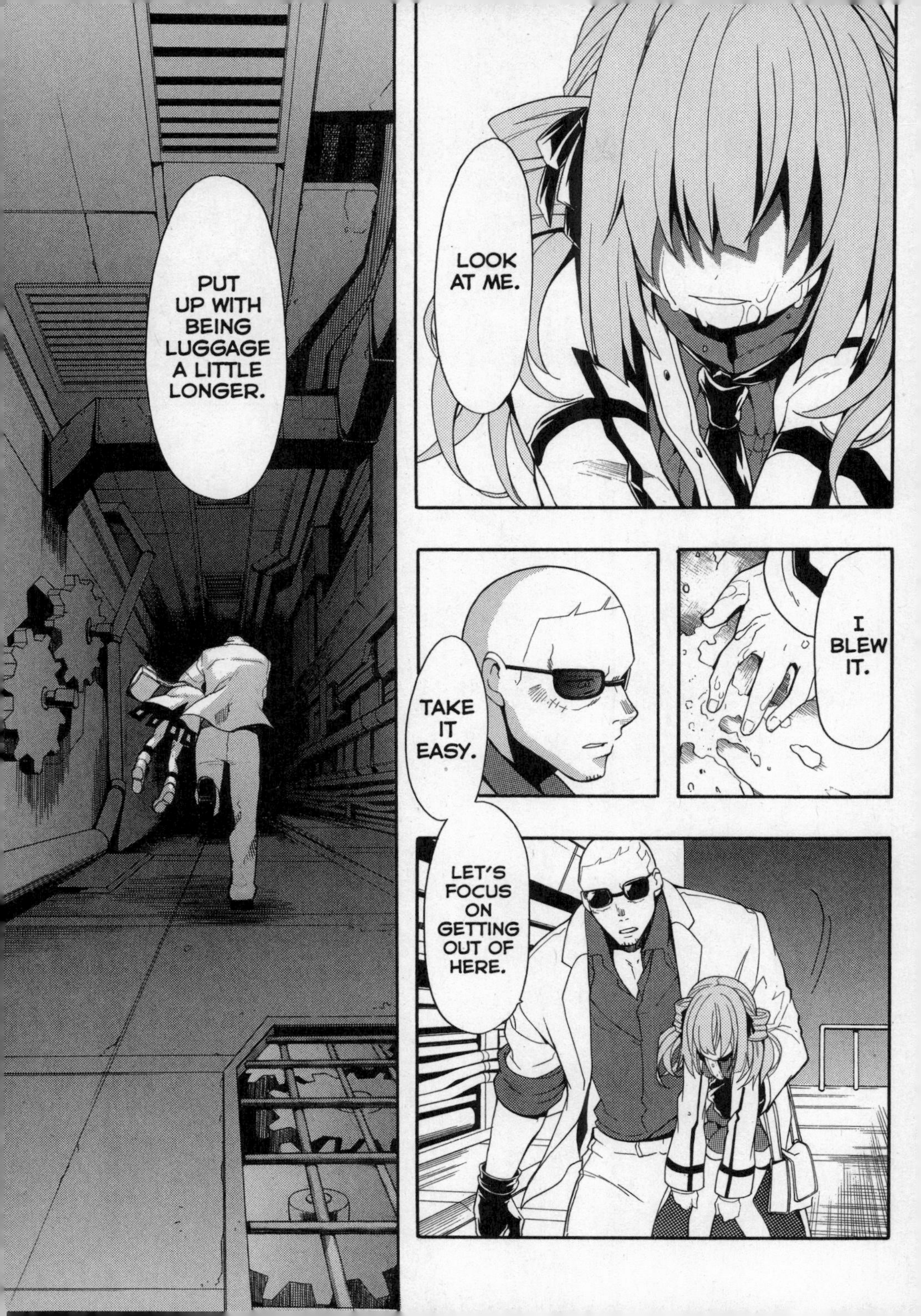
LOOK AT ME.
I BLEW IT.
TAKE IT EASY.
LET'S FOCUS ON GETTING OUT OF HERE.
PUT UP WITH BEING LUGGAGE A LITTLE LONGER.

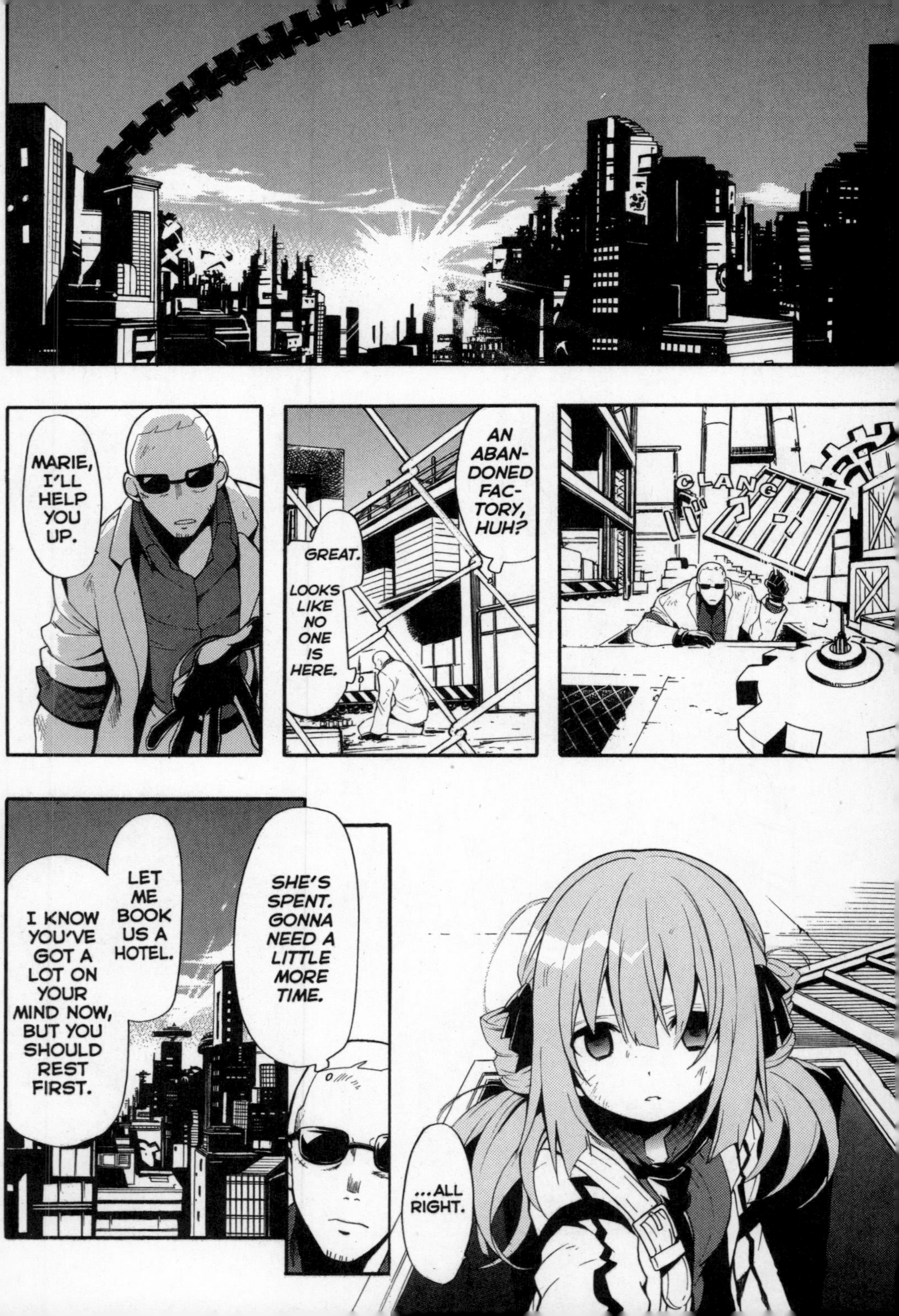
CLANG
AN ABANDONED FACTORY, HUH?
GREAT.
LOOKS LIKE NO ONE IS HERE.
MARIE, I'LL HELP YOU UP.
SHE'S SPENT. GONNA NEED A LITTLE MORE TIME.
LET ME BOOK US A HOTEL.
I KNOW YOU'VE GOT A LOT ON YOUR MIND NOW, BUT YOU SHOULD REST FIRST.
...ALL RIGHT.

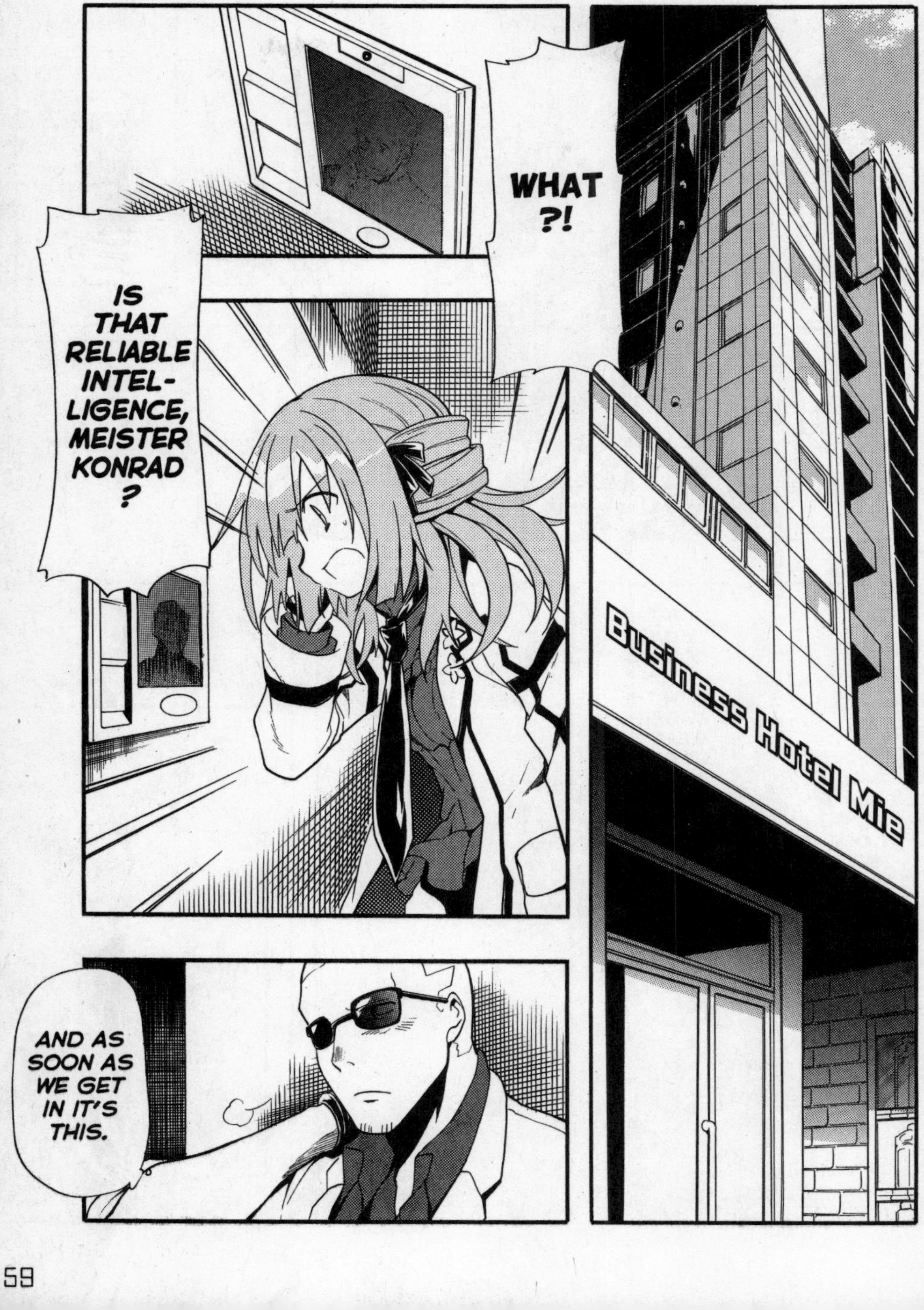
Business Hotel Mie
WHAT ?!
IS THAT RELIABLE INTEL-LIGENCE, MEISTER KONRAD ?
AND AS SOON AS WE GET IN IT'S THIS.

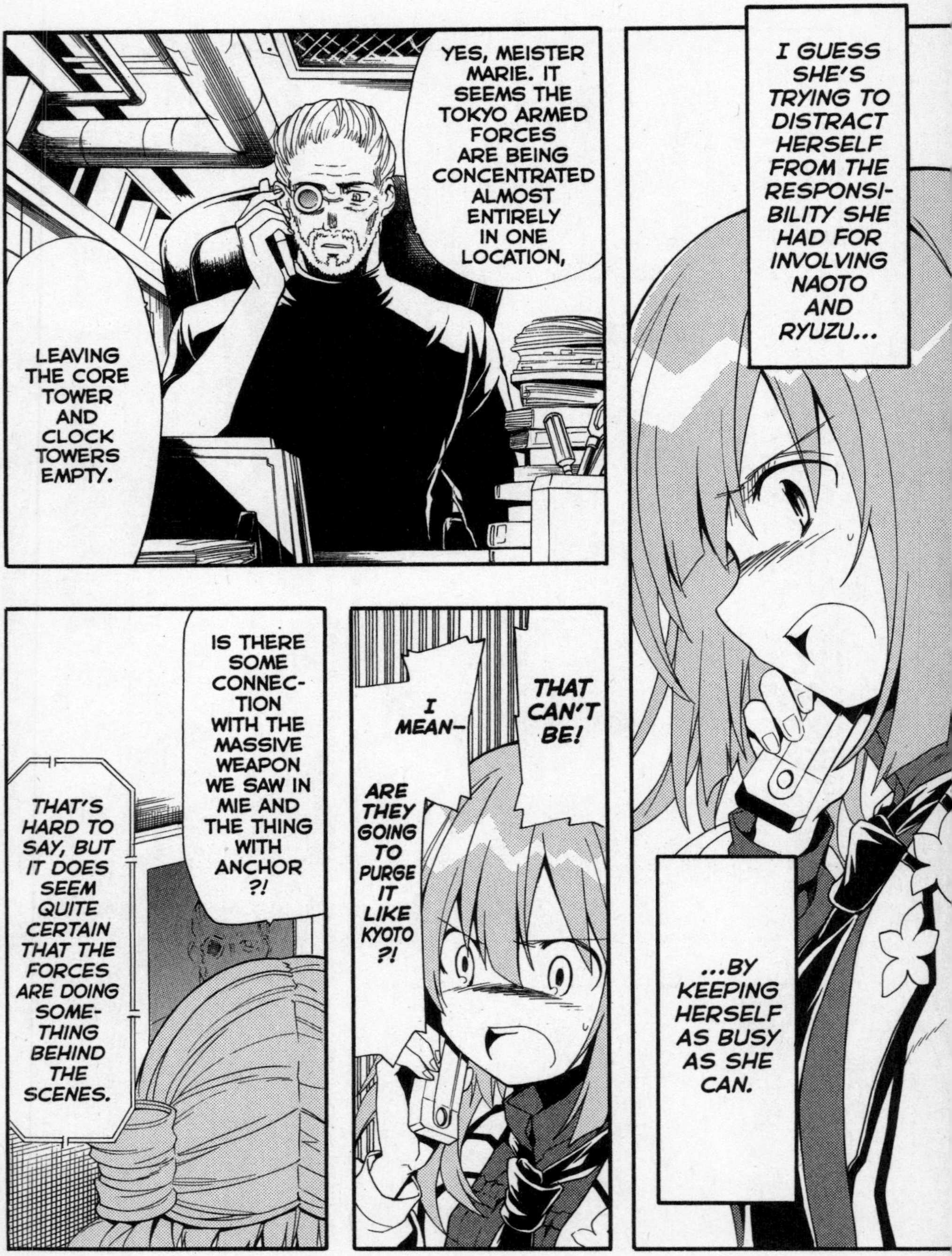
I GUESS SHE'S TRYING TO DISTRACT HERSELF FROM THE RESPONSIBILITY SHE HAD FOR INVOLVING NAOTO AND RYUZU...
...BY KEEPING HERSELF AS BUSY AS SHE CAN.
YES, MEISTER MARIE. IT SEEMS THE TOKYO ARMED FORCES ARE BEING CONCENTRATED ALMOST ENTIRELY IN ONE LOCATION,
LEAVING THE CORE TOWER AND CLOCK TOWERS EMPTY.
THAT CAN'T BE!
I MEAN—
ARE THEY GOING TO PURGE IT LIKE KYOTO ?!
IS THERE SOME CONNECTION WITH THE MASSIVE WEAPON WE SAW IN MIE AND THE THING WITH ANCHOR ?!
THAT'S HARD TO SAY, BUT IT DOES SEEM QUITE CERTAIN THAT THE FORCES ARE DOING SOMETHING BEHIND THE SCENES.

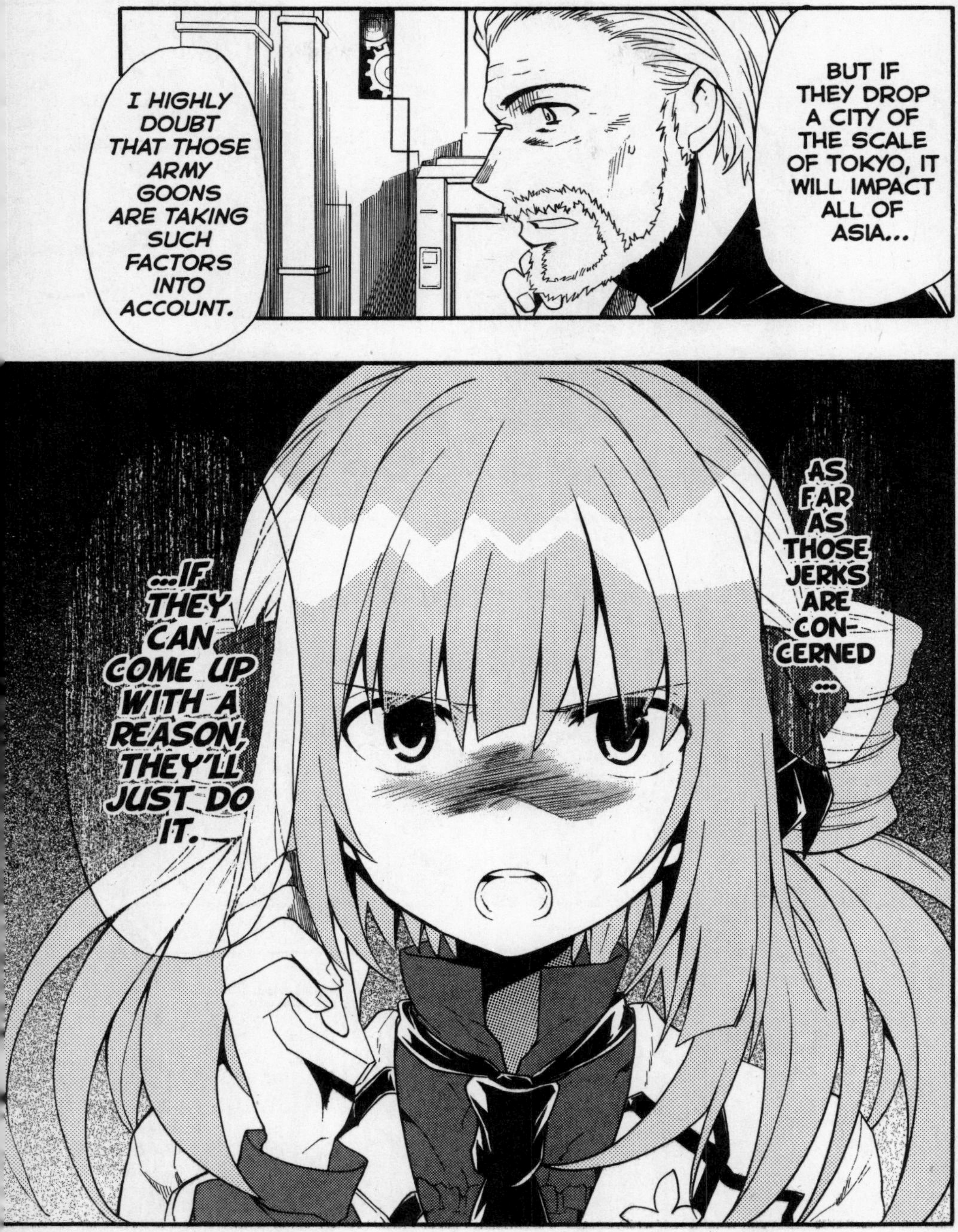
BUT IF THEY DROP A CITY OF THE SCALE OF TOKYO, IT WILL IMPACT ALL OF ASIA...
I HIGHLY DOUBT THAT THOSE ARMY GOONS ARE TAKING SUCH FACTORS INTO ACCOUNT.
AS FAR AS THOSE JERKS ARE CON-CERNED...
...IF THEY CAN COME UP WITH A REASON, THEY'LL JUST DO IT.

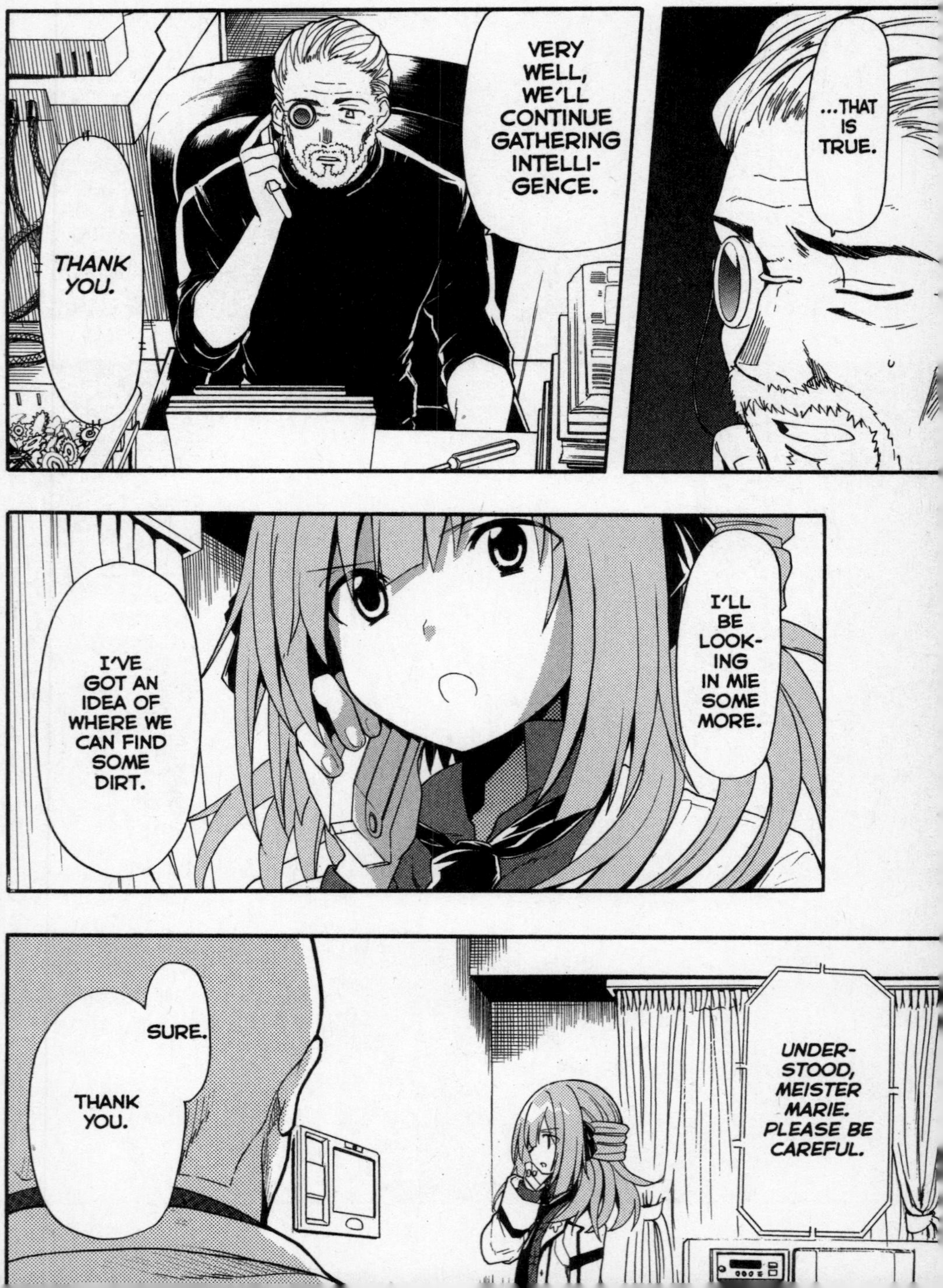
...THAT IS TRUE.
VERY WELL, WE'LL CONTINUE GATHERING INTELLIGENCE.
THANK YOU.
I'LL BE LOOKING IN MIE SOME MORE.
I'VE GOT AN IDEA OF WHERE WE CAN FIND SOME DIRT.
UNDERSTOOD, MEISTER MARIE. PLEASE BE CAREFUL.
SURE.
THANK YOU.

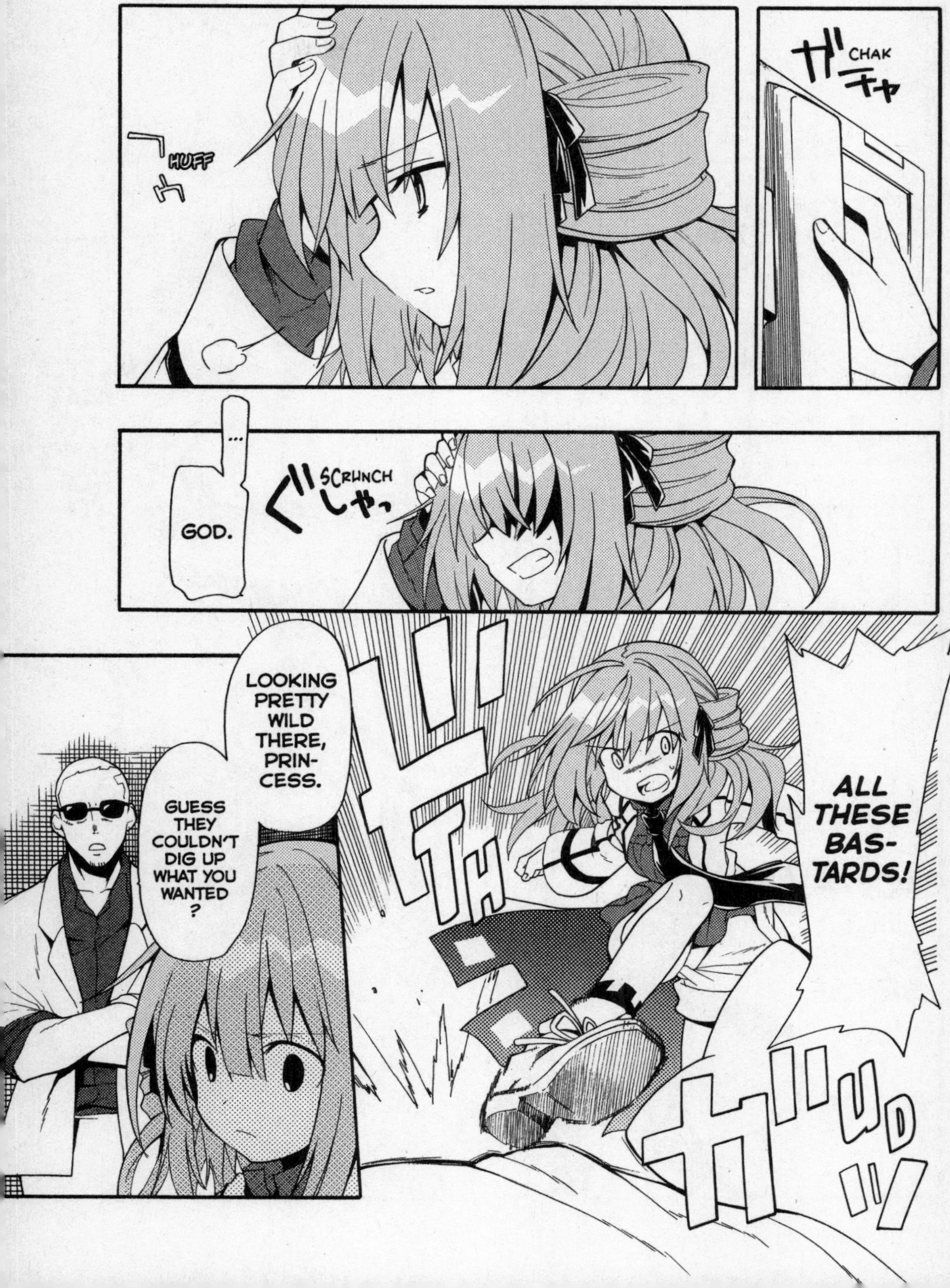
ガチャ
CHAK
ふっ
HUFF
ぐしゃっ
SCRUNCH
... GOD.
ALL THESE BAS-TARDS!
TH
UD
LOOKING PRETTY WILD THERE, PRIN-CESS.
GUESS THEY COULDN'T DIG UP WHAT YOU WANTED?

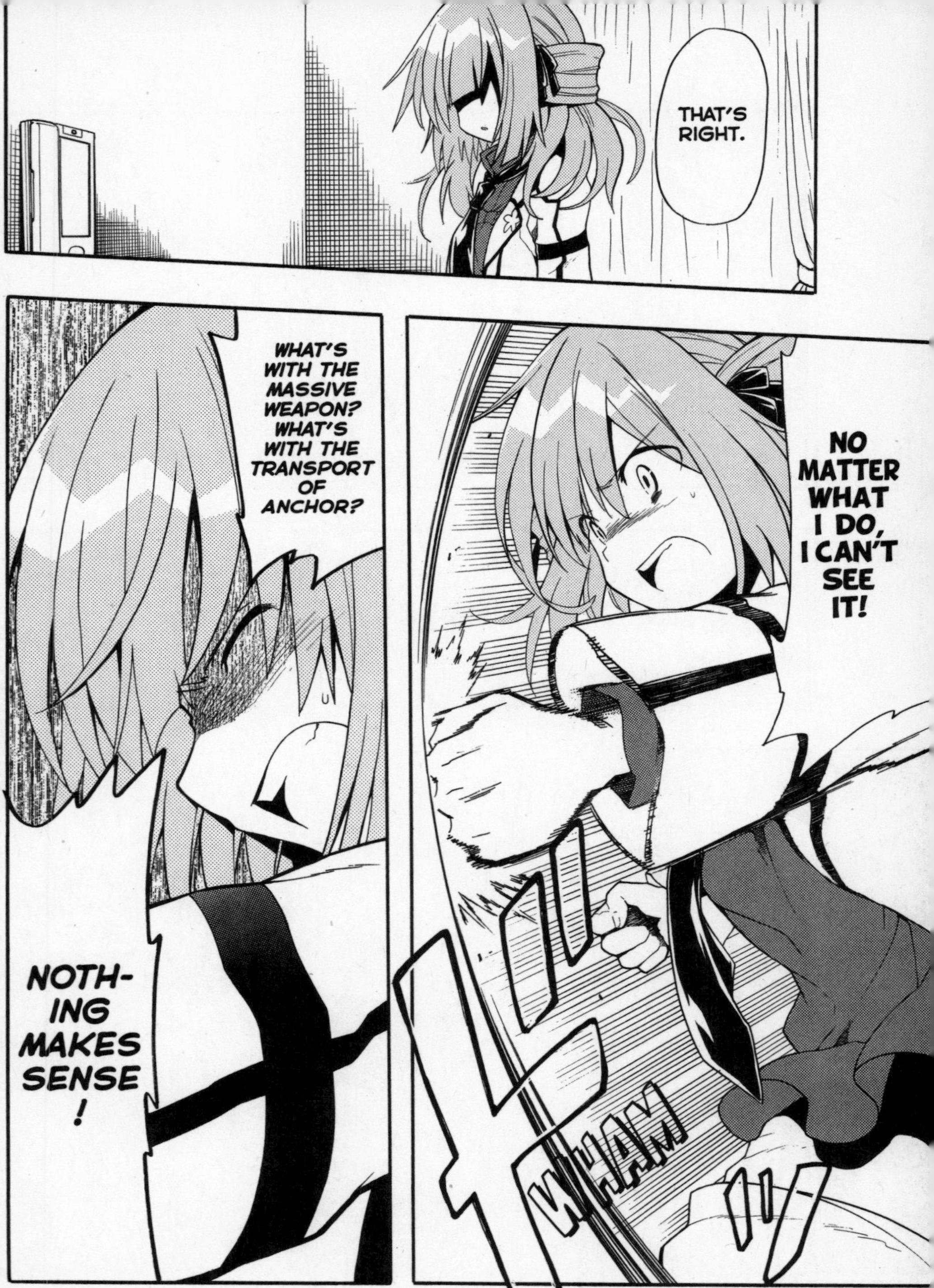
THAT'S RIGHT.
NO MATTER WHAT I DO, I CAN'T SEE IT!
WHAT'S WITH THE MASSIVE WEAPON? WHAT'S WITH THE TRANSPORT OF ANCHOR?
NOTH-ING MAKES SENSE!

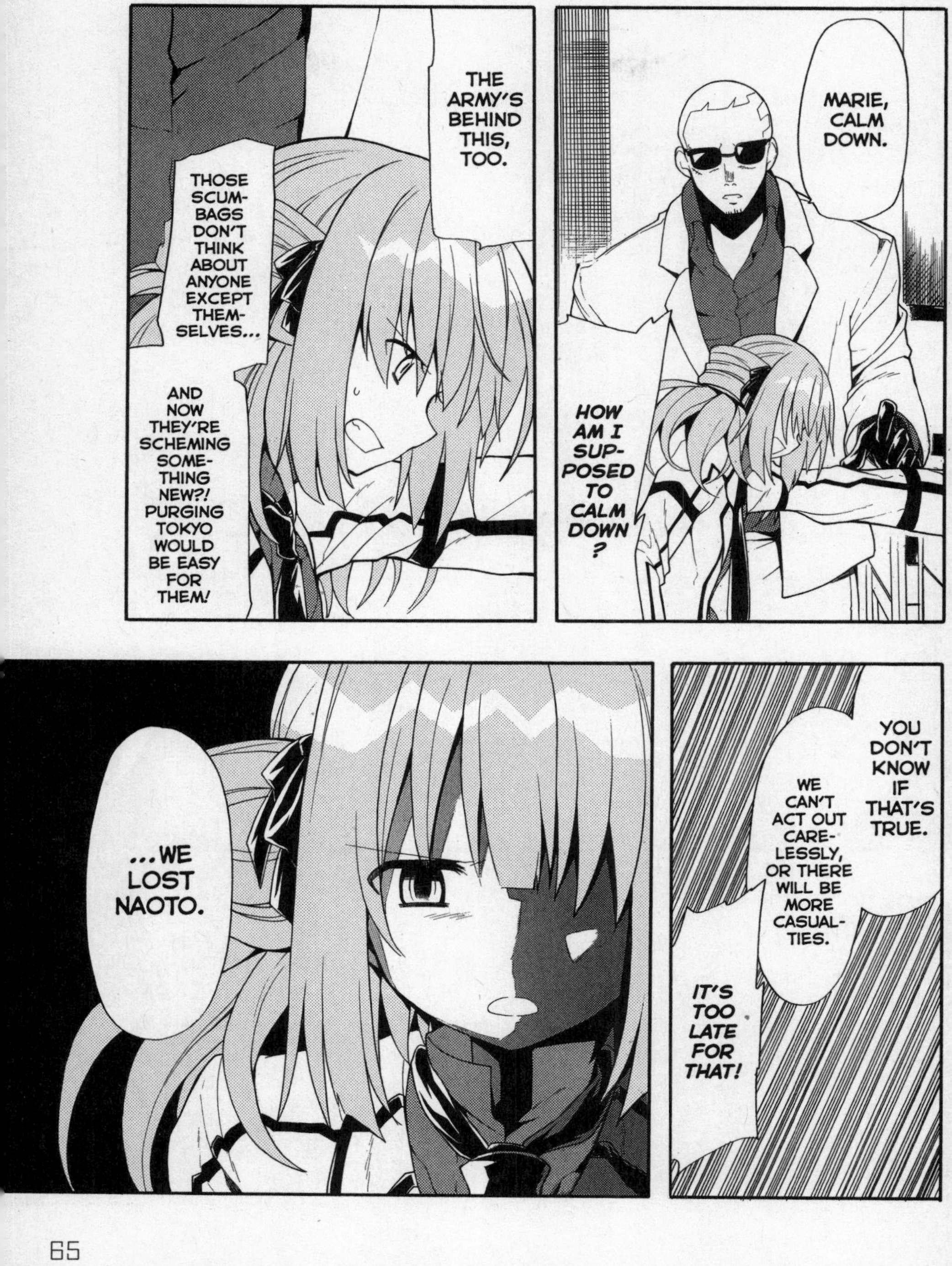
MARIE, CALM DOWN.
HOW AM I SUPPOSED TO CALM DOWN?
THE ARMY'S BEHIND THIS, TOO.
THOSE SCUMBAGS DON'T THINK ABOUT ANYONE EXCEPT THEMSELVES...
AND NOW THEY'RE SCHEMING SOMETHING NEW?! PURGING TOKYO WOULD BE EASY FOR THEM!
YOU DON'T KNOW IF THAT'S TRUE.
WE CAN'T ACT OUT CARELESSLY, OR THERE WILL BE MORE CASUALTIES.
IT'S TOO LATE FOR THAT!
...WE LOST NAOTO.

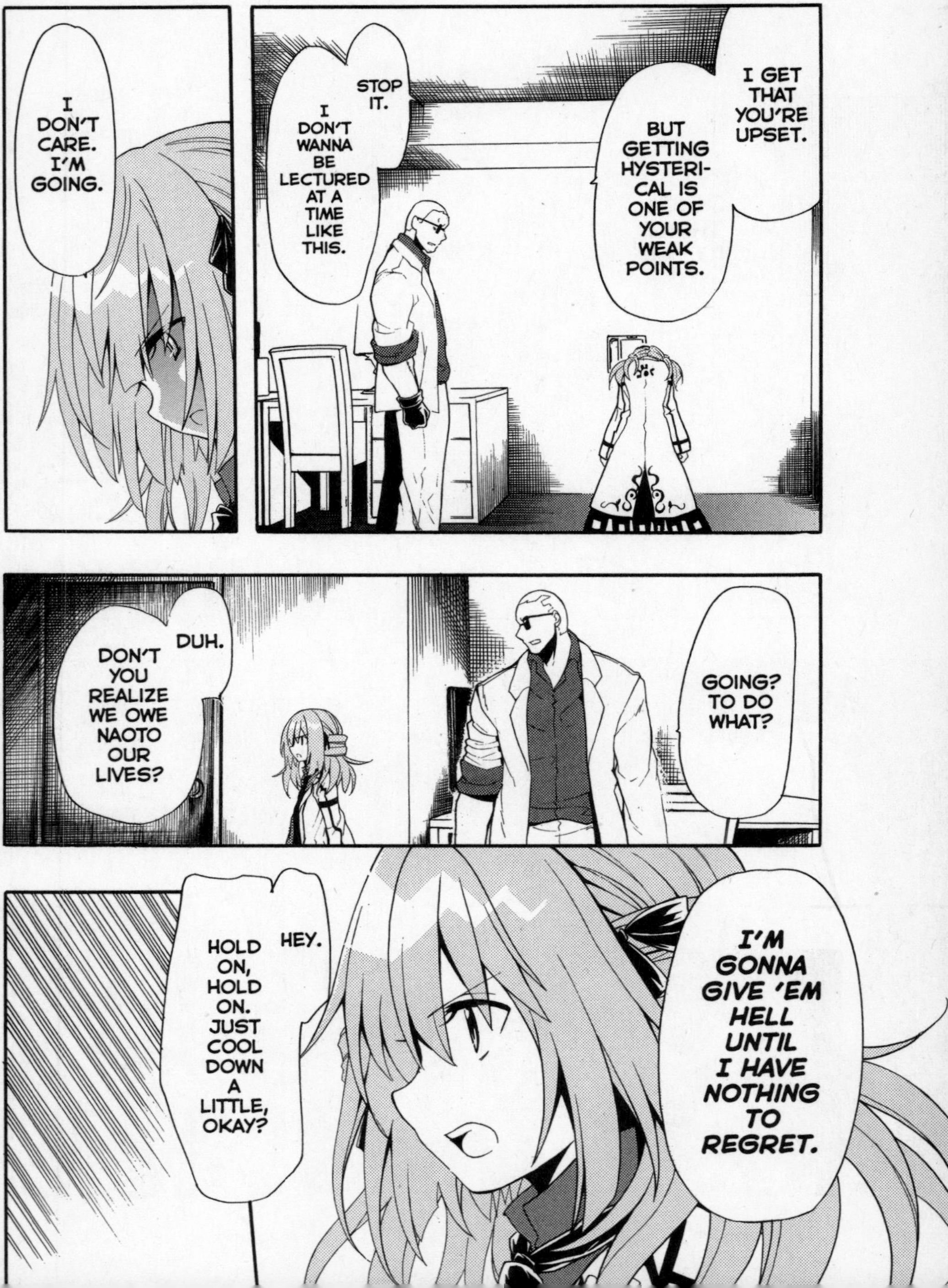

I GET THAT YOU'RE UPSET.
BUT GETTING HYSTERICAL IS ONE OF YOUR WEAK POINTS.
STOP IT. I DON'T WANNA BE LECTURED AT A TIME LIKE THIS.
I DON'T CARE. I'M GOING.
GOING? TO DO WHAT?
DUH. DON'T YOU REALIZE WE OWE NAOTO OUR LIVES?
I'M GONNA GIVE 'EM HELL UNTIL I HAVE NOTHING TO REGRET.
HEY. HOLD ON, HOLD ON. JUST COOL DOWN A LITTLE, OKAY?

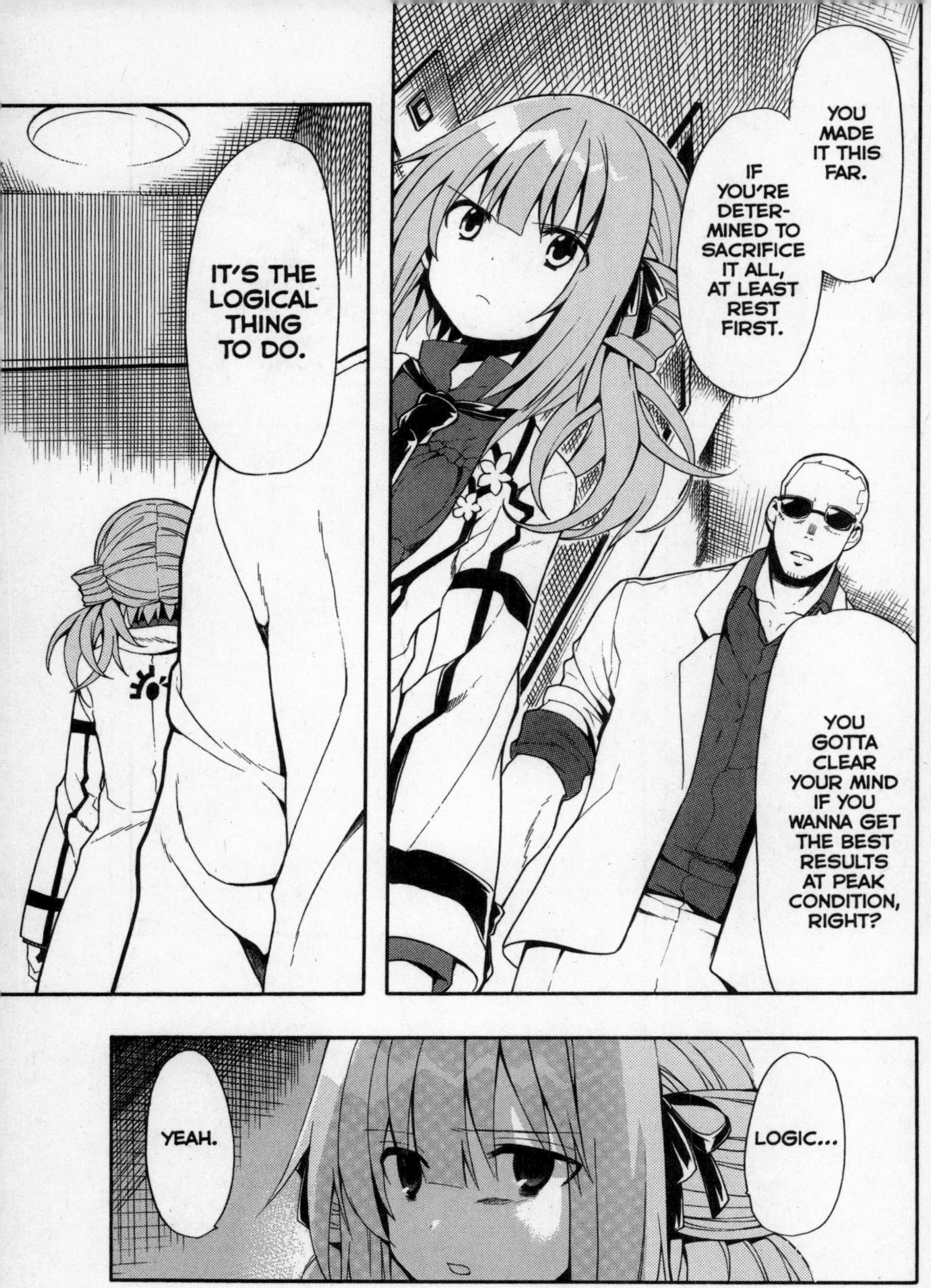
YOU MADE IT THIS FAR.
IF YOU'RE DETER-MINED TO SACRIFICE IT ALL, AT LEAST REST FIRST.
YOU GOTTA CLEAR YOUR MIND IF YOU WANNA GET THE BEST RESULTS AT PEAK CONDITION, RIGHT?
IT'S THE LOGICAL THING TO DO.
LOGIC...
YEAH.

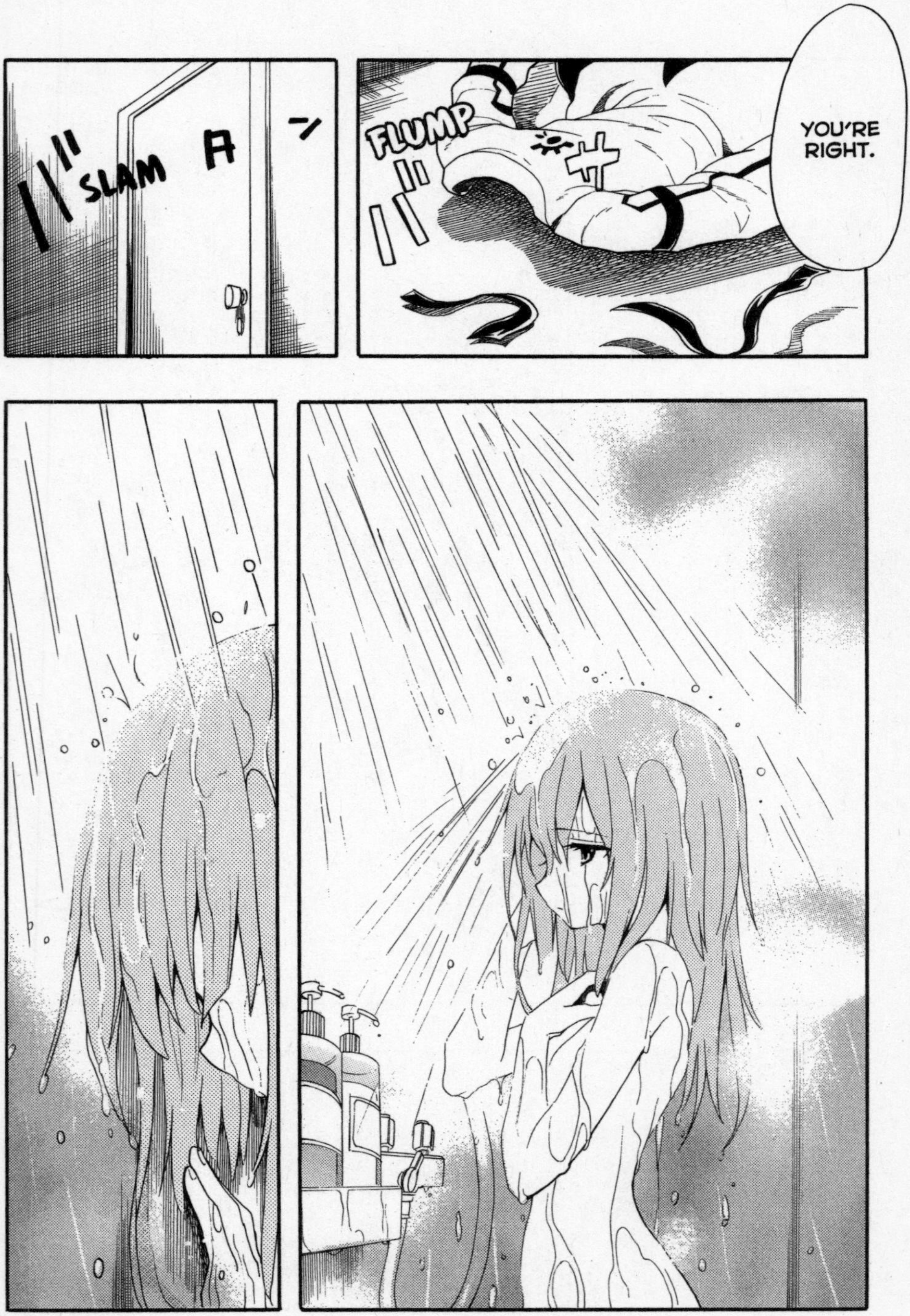
YOU'RE RIGHT.
FLUMP
SLAM

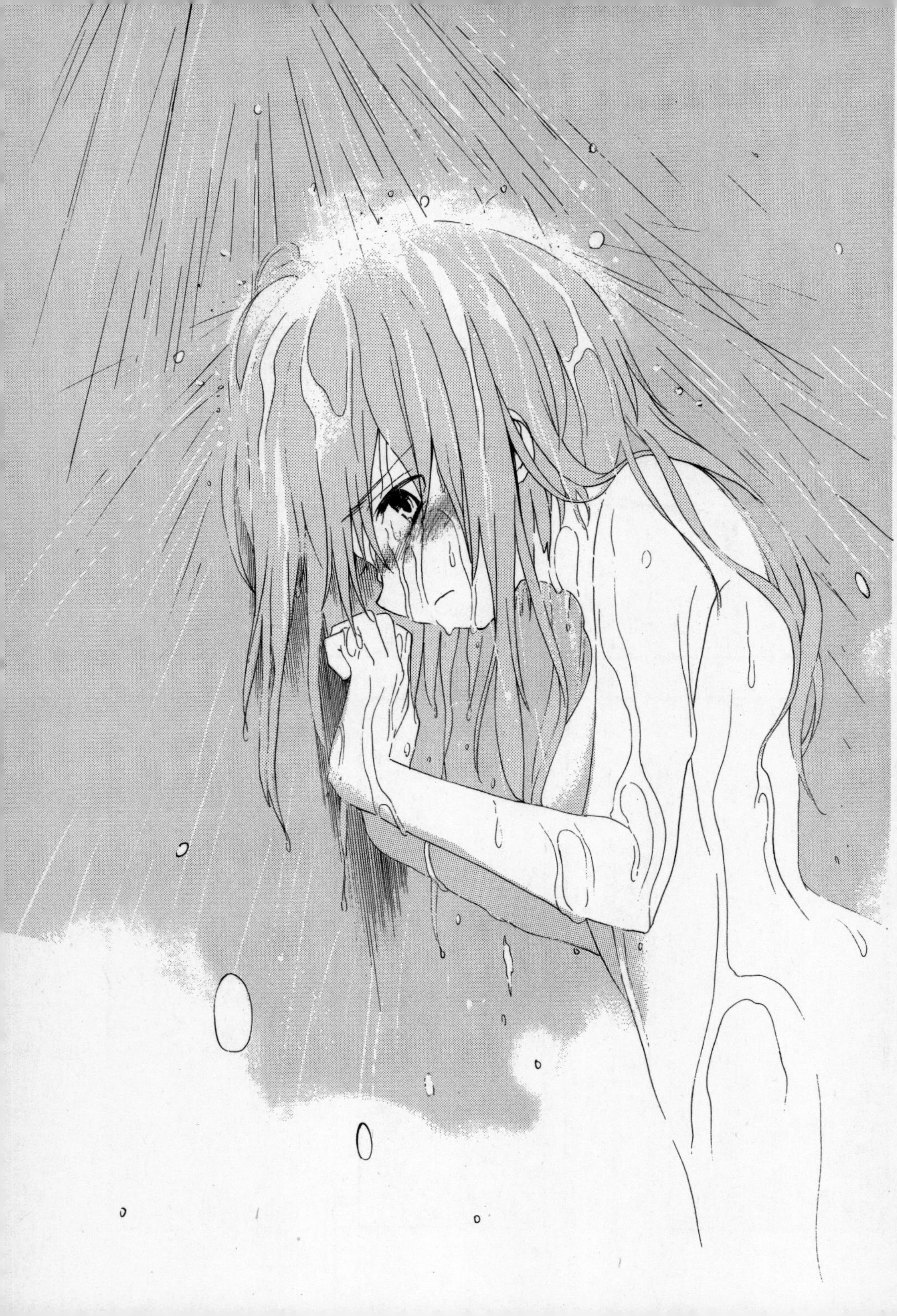

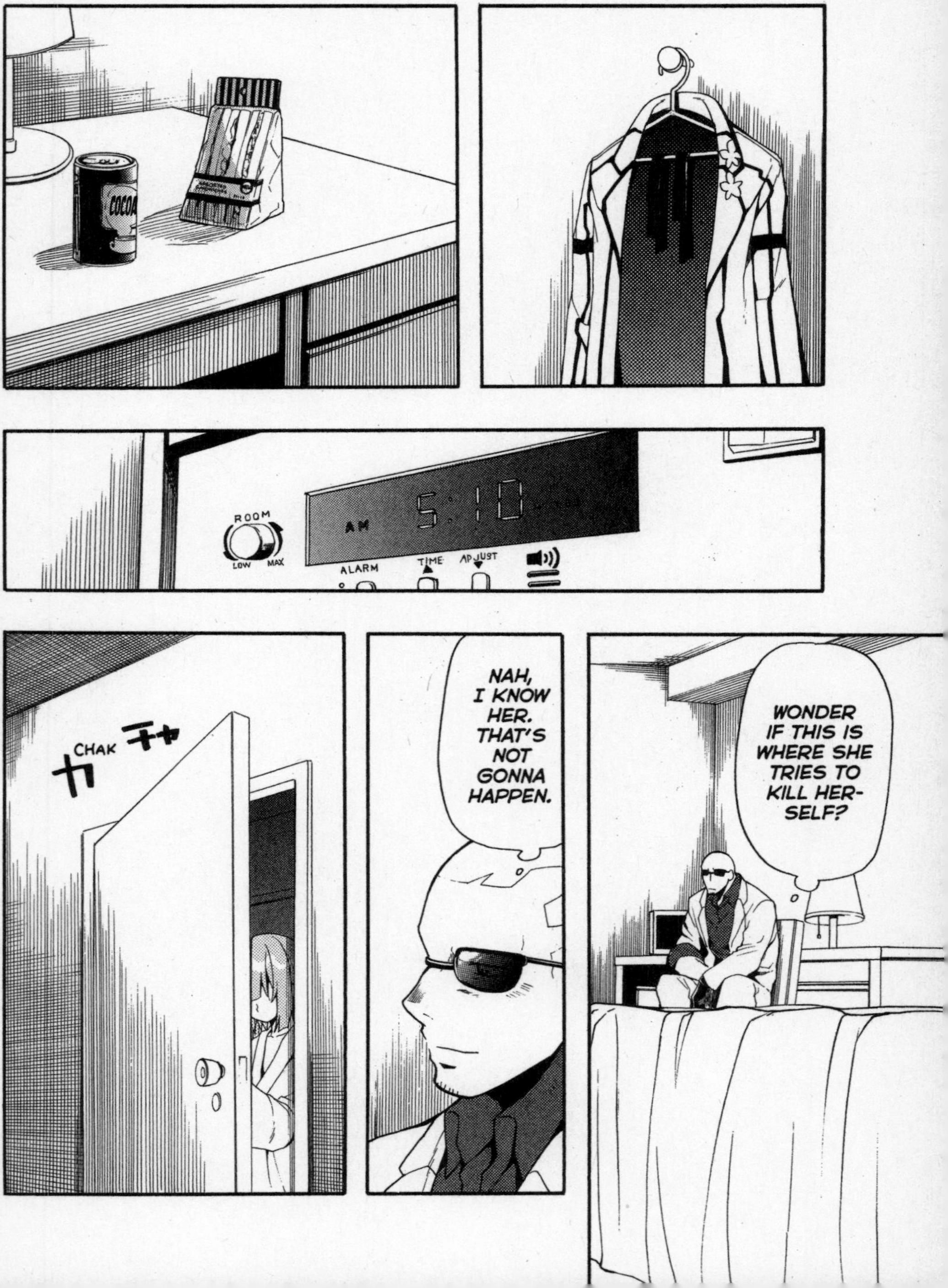

COCOA
ROOM
LOW
MAX
AM 5:10
ALARM
TIME
ADJUST
WONDER IF THIS IS WHERE SHE TRIES TO KILL HER-SELF?
NAH, I KNOW HER. THAT'S NOT GONNA HAPPEN.
カ CHAK チャ

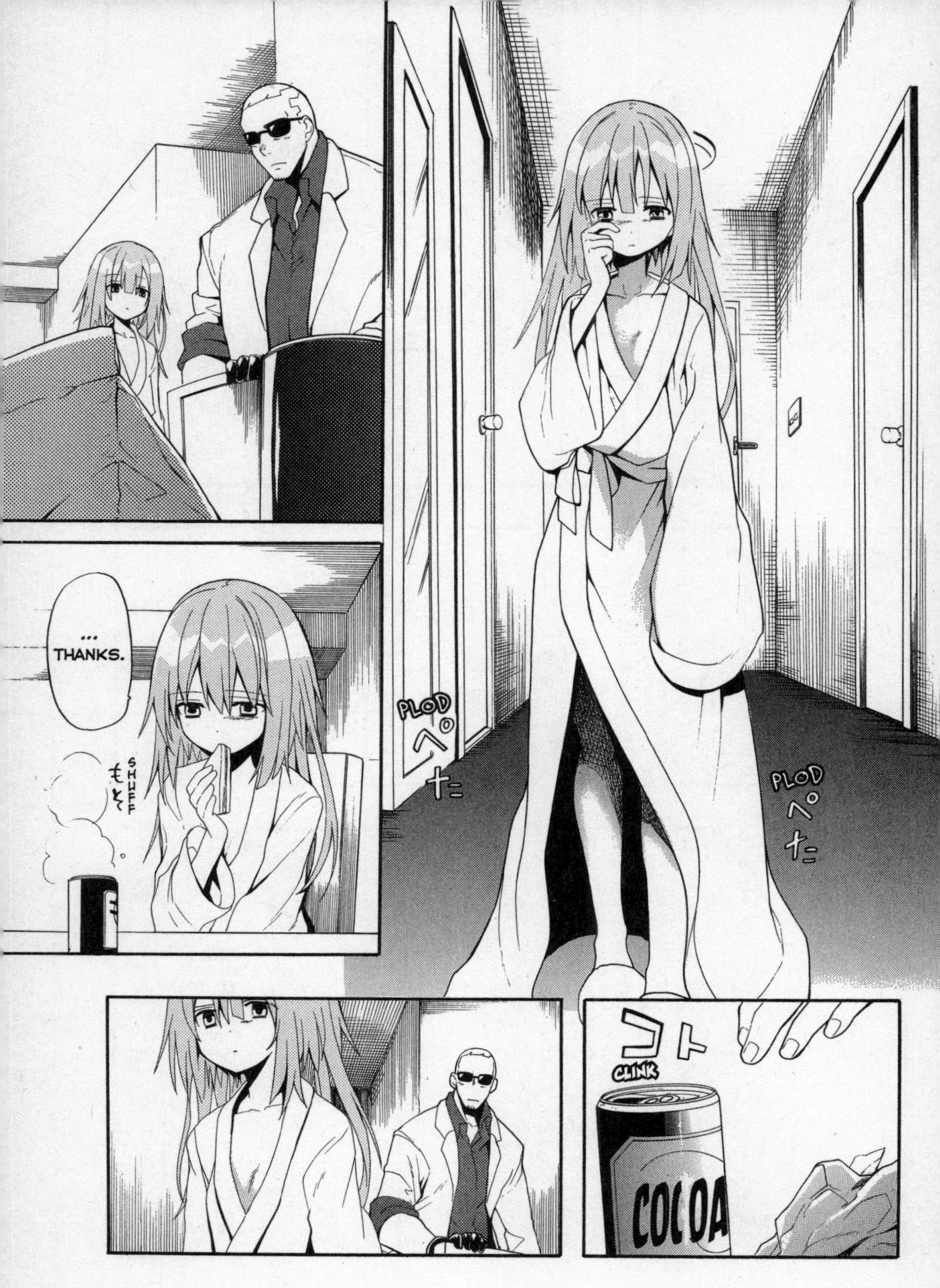
PLOD
ぺた
PLOD
ぺた
...THANKS.
SHUFF
もそ
コト
CLINK
COCOA

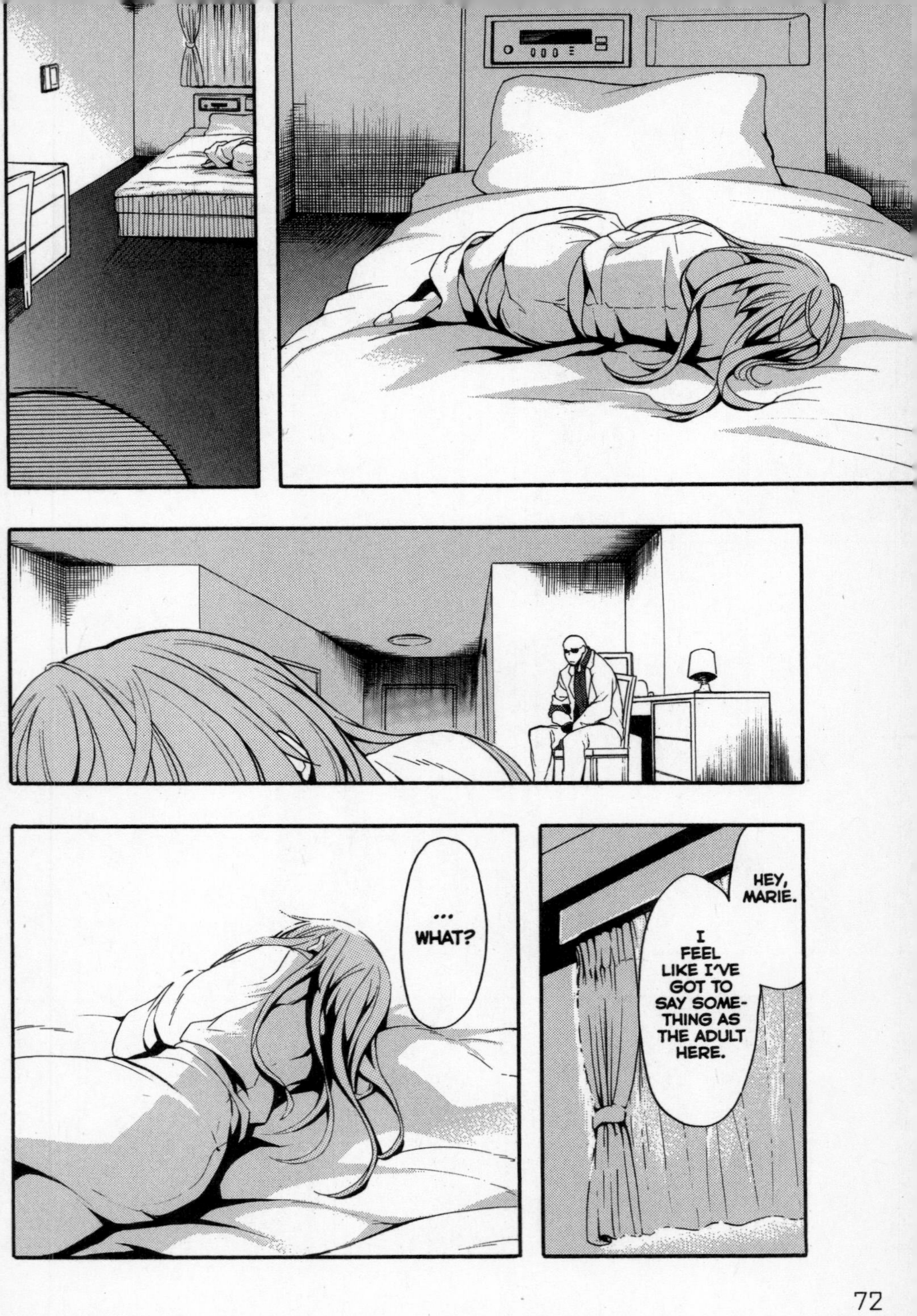
HEY, MARIE.
I FEEL LIKE I'VE GOT TO SAY SOME-THING AS THE ADULT HERE.
... WHAT?

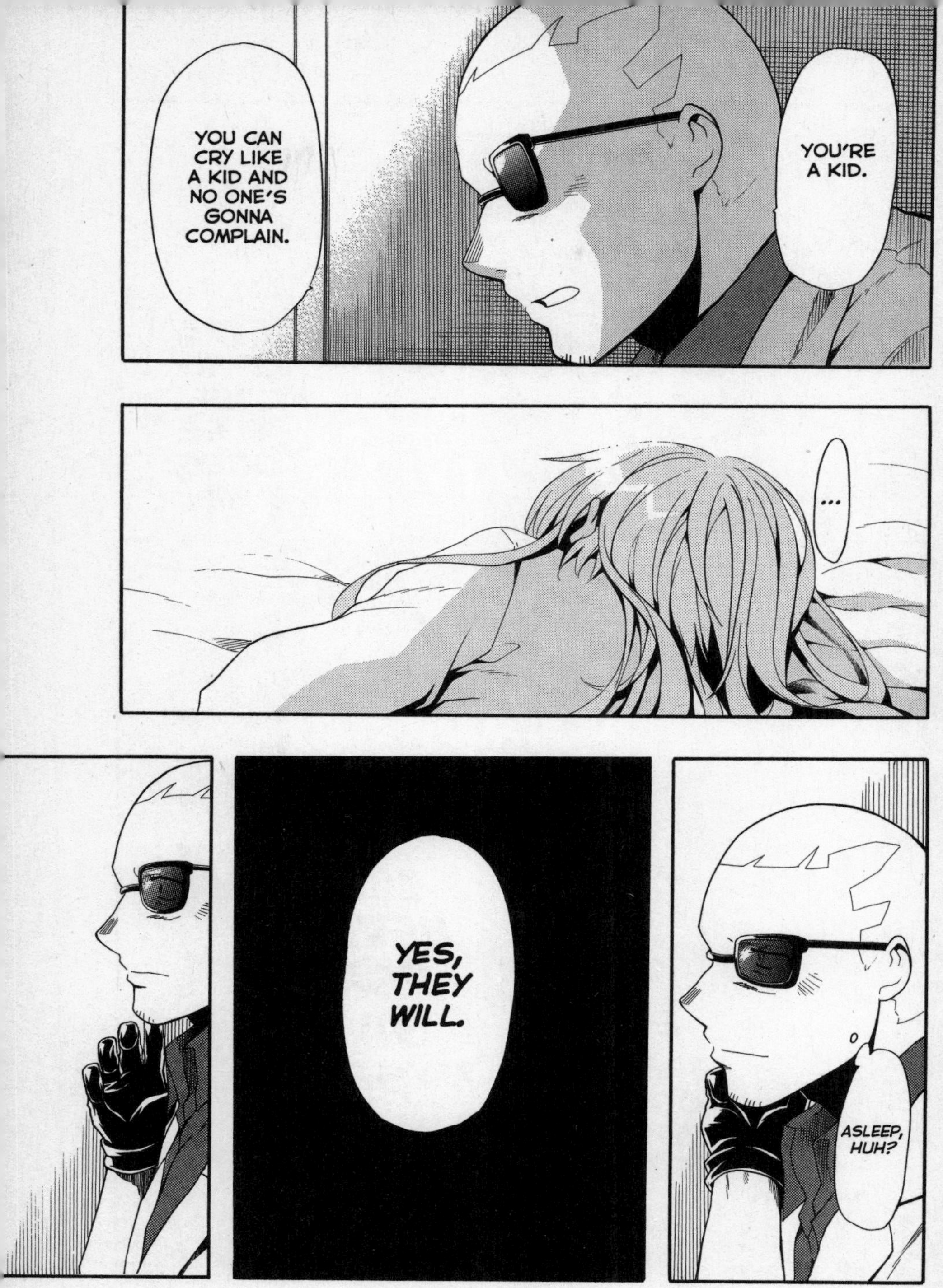
YOU'RE A KID.
YOU CAN CRY LIKE A KID AND NO ONE'S GONNA COMPLAIN.
...
ASLEEP, HUH?
YES, THEY WILL.

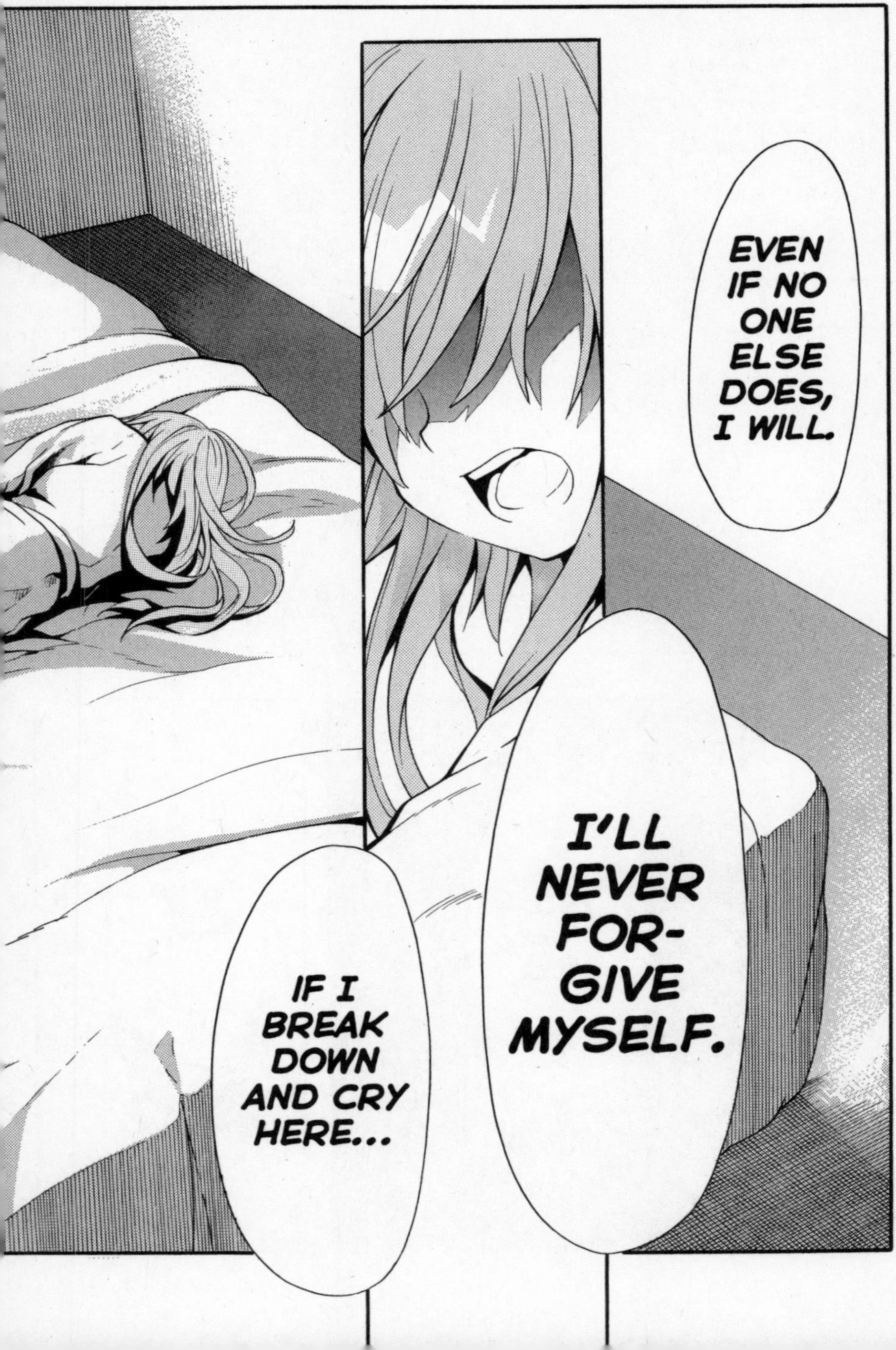
EVEN IF NO ONE ELSE DOES, I WILL.
I'LL NEVER FOR-GIVE MYSELF.
IF I BREAK DOWN AND CRY HERE...

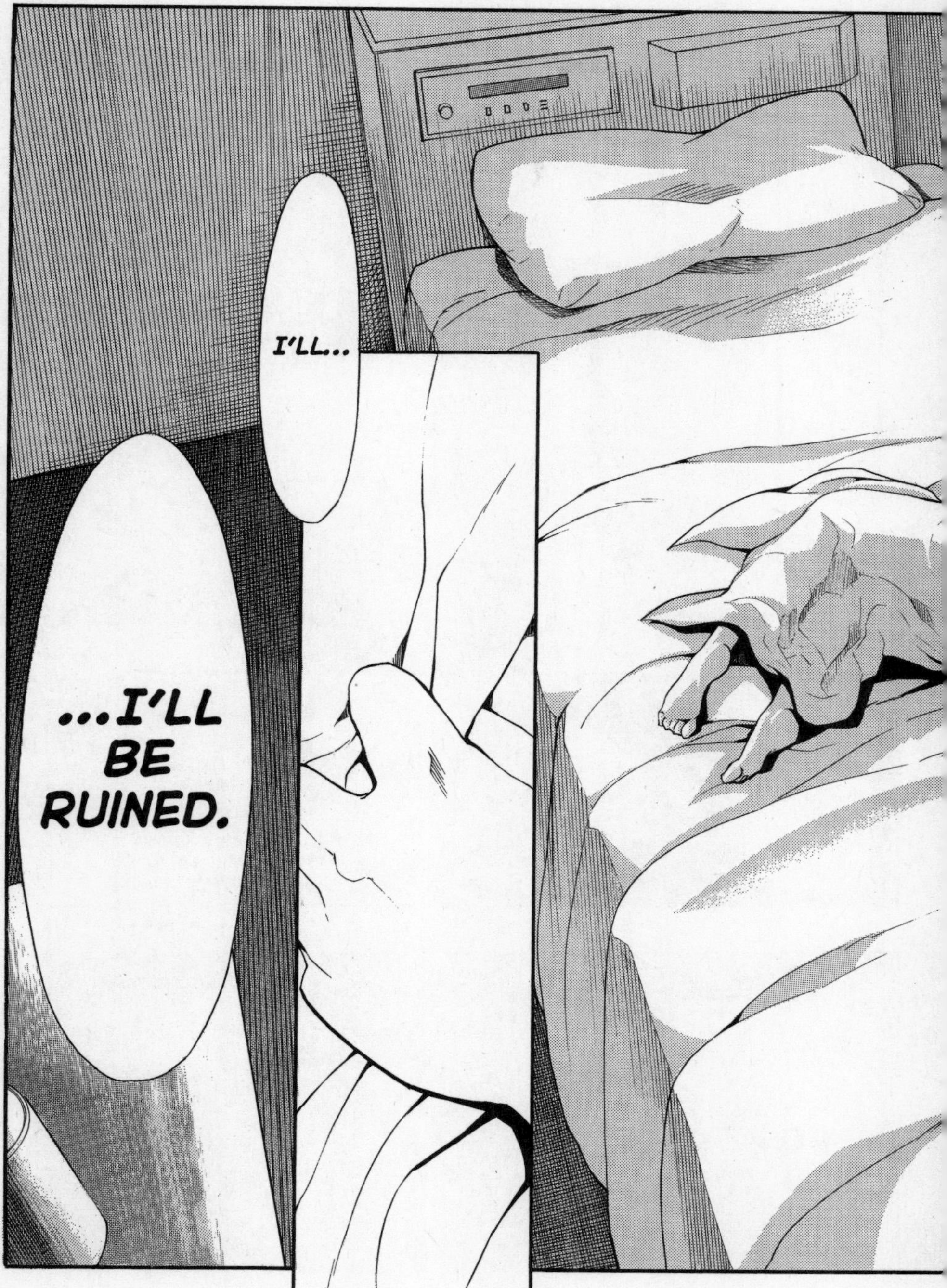
I'LL...
...I'LL BE RUINED.

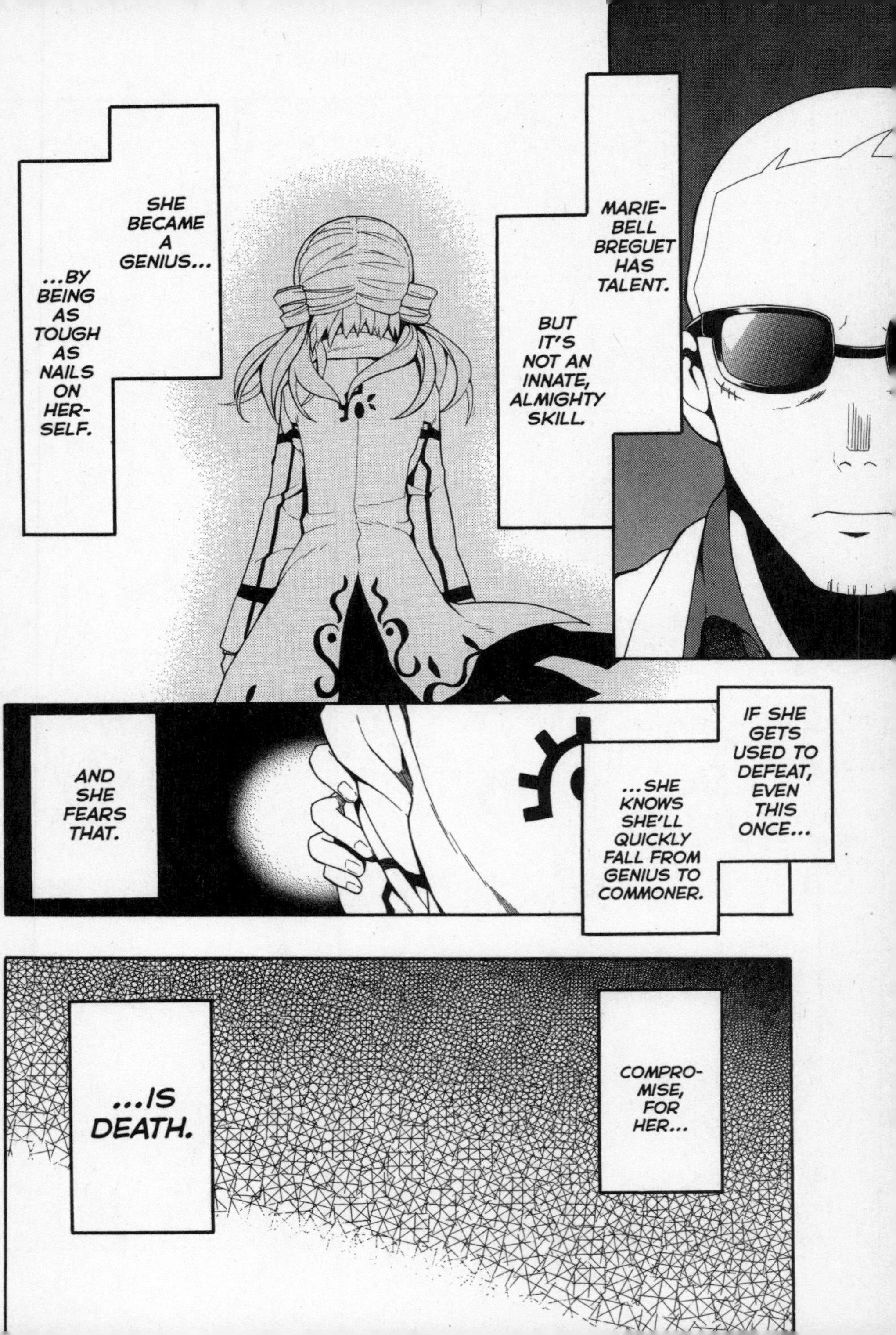
MARIE-BELL BREGUET HAS TALENT.
BUT IT'S NOT AN INNATE, ALMIGHTY SKILL.
SHE BECAME A GENIUS...
...BY BEING AS TOUGH AS NAILS ON HER-SELF.
IF SHE GETS USED TO DEFEAT, EVEN THIS ONCE...
...SHE KNOWS SHE'LL QUICKLY FALL FROM GENIUS TO COMMONER.
AND SHE FEARS THAT.
COMPRO-MISE, FOR HER...
...IS DEATH.

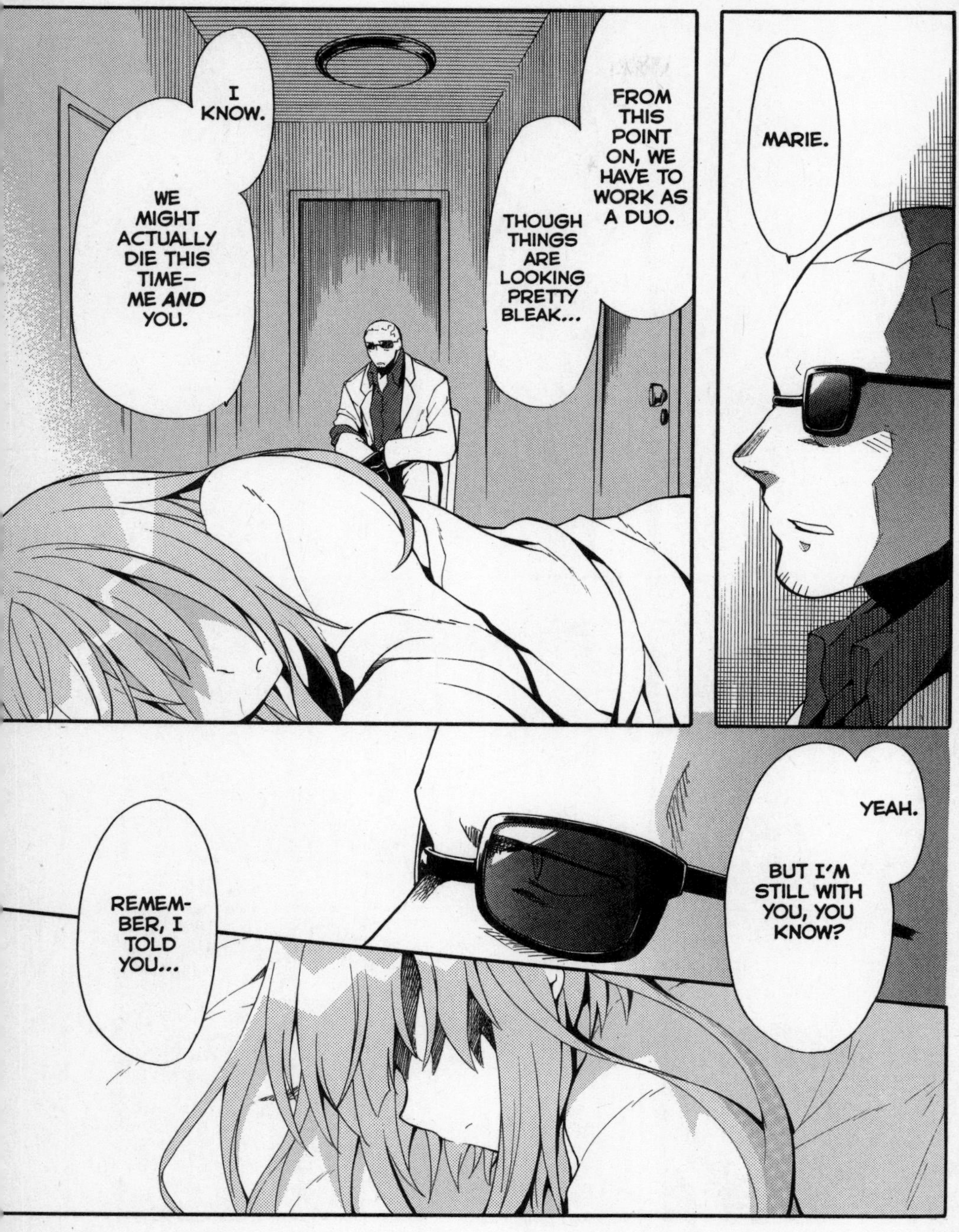
MARIE.
FROM THIS POINT ON, WE HAVE TO WORK AS A DUO.
THOUGH THINGS ARE LOOKING PRETTY BLEAK...
I KNOW.
WE MIGHT ACTUALLY DIE THIS TIME— ME *AND* YOU.
YEAH.
BUT I'M STILL WITH YOU, YOU KNOW?
REMEMBER, I TOLD YOU...

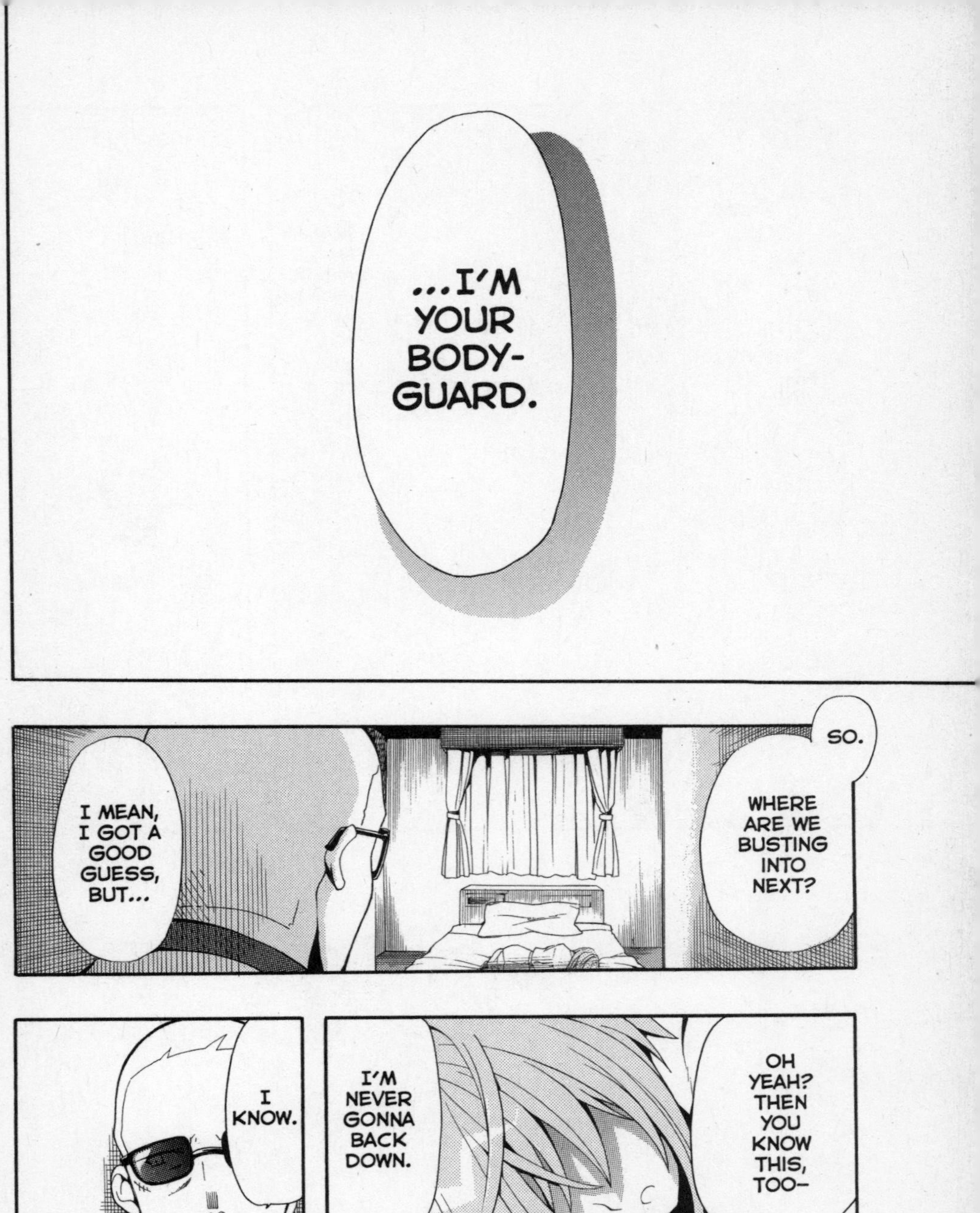
...I'M YOUR BODY-GUARD.
SO.
WHERE ARE WE BUSTING INTO NEXT?
I MEAN, I GOT A GOOD GUESS, BUT...
OH YEAH? THEN YOU KNOW THIS, TOO—
I'M NEVER GONNA BACK DOWN.
I KNOW.

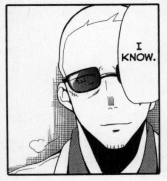

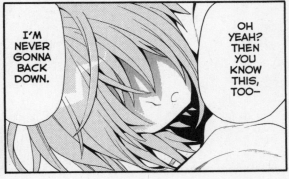

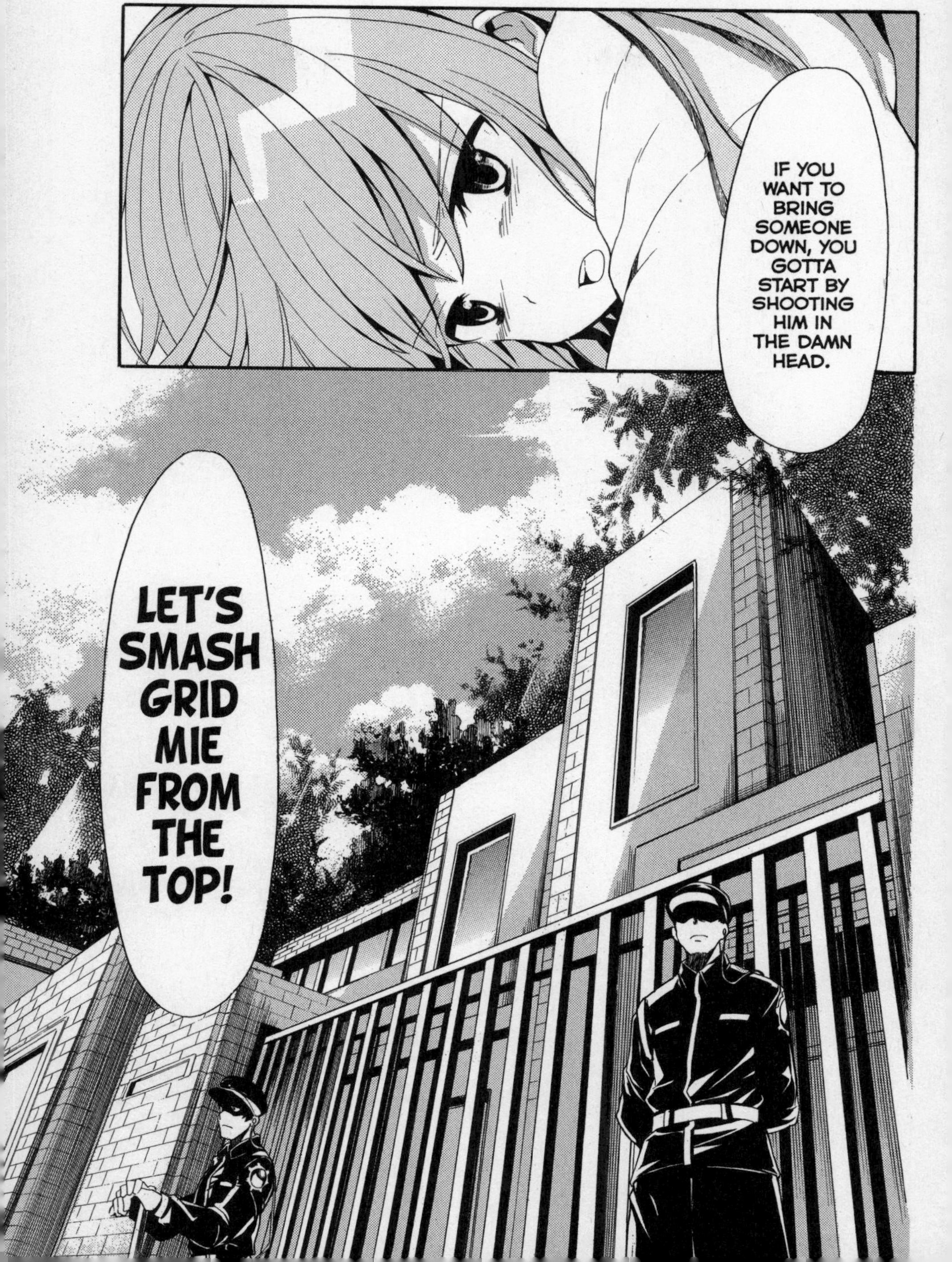
IF YOU WANT TO BRING SOMEONE DOWN, YOU GOTTA START BY SHOOTING HIM IN THE DAMN HEAD.
LET'S SMASH GRID MIE FROM THE TOP!

Clockwork Planet

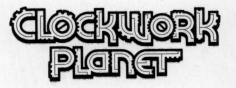

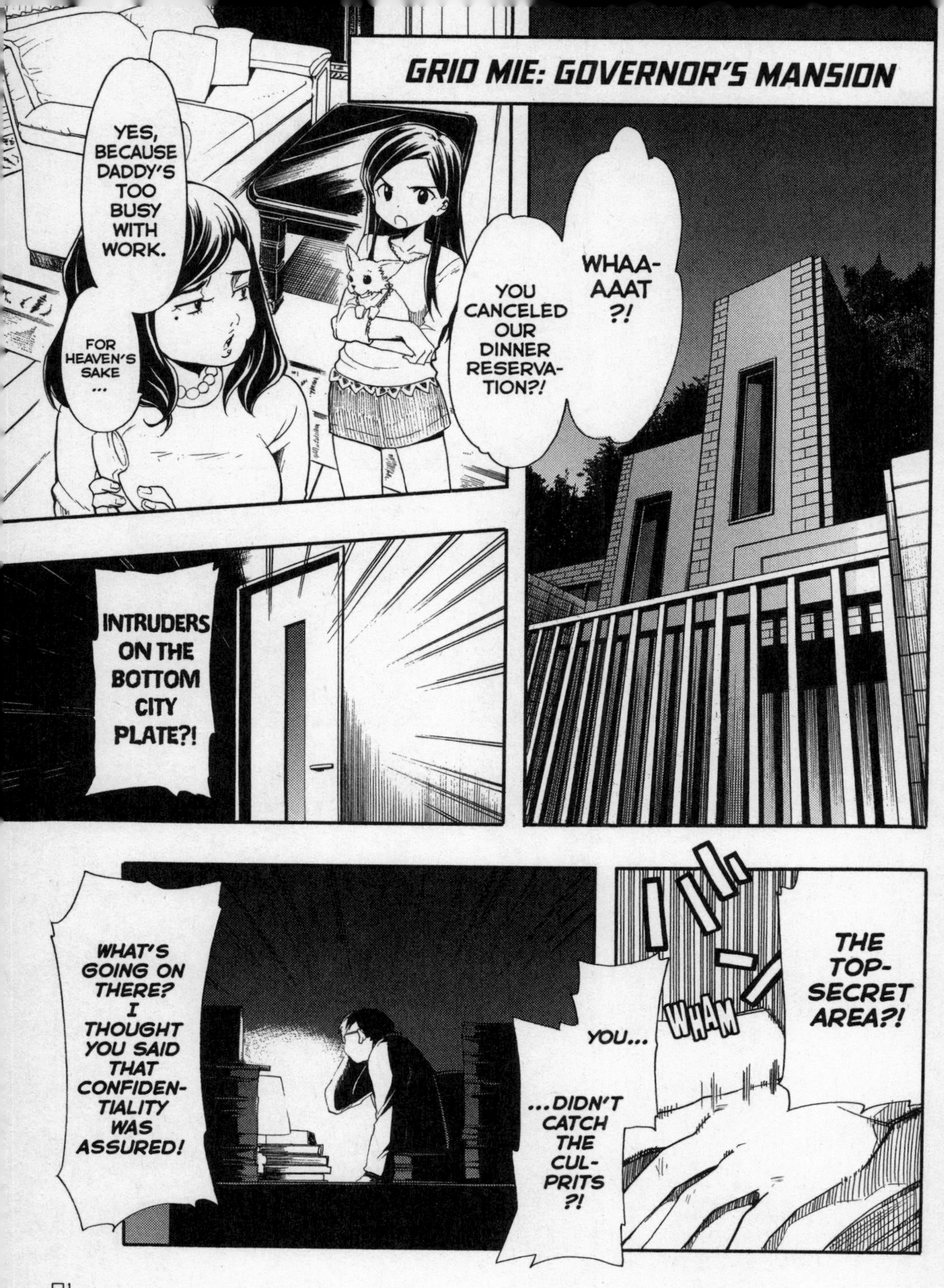
GRID MIE: GOVERNOR'S MANSION
WHAA-AAAT?!
YOU CANCELED OUR DINNER RESERVA-TION?!
YES, BECAUSE DADDY'S TOO BUSY WITH WORK.
FOR HEAVEN'S SAKE...
INTRUDERS ON THE BOTTOM CITY PLATE?!
THE TOP-SECRET AREA?!
WHAM
YOU...
...DIDN'T CATCH THE CUL-PRITS?!
WHAT'S GOING ON THERE? I THOUGHT YOU SAID THAT CONFIDEN-TIALITY WAS ASSURED!

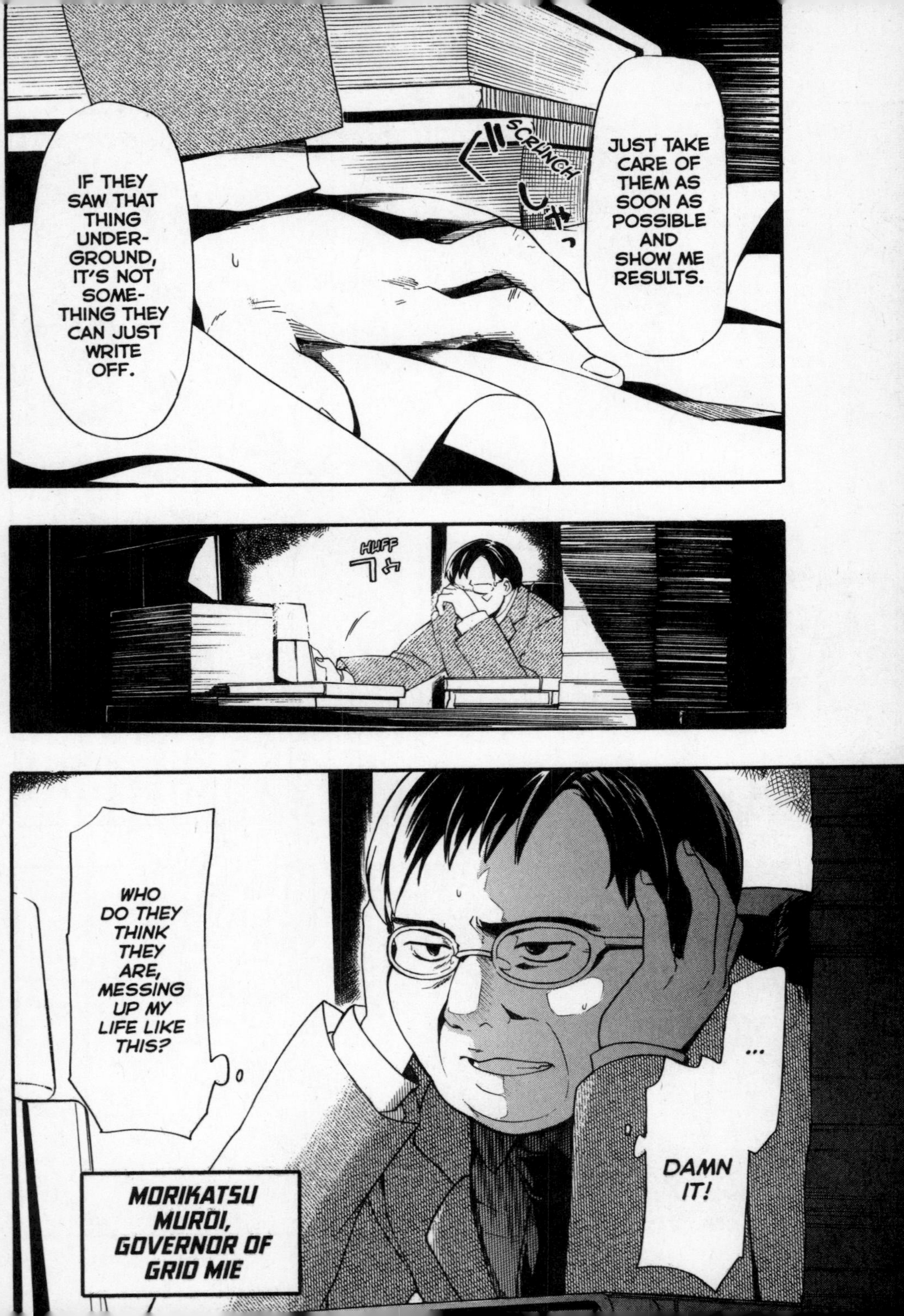
JUST TAKE CARE OF THEM AS SOON AS POSSIBLE AND SHOW ME RESULTS.
SCRUNCH
IF THEY SAW THAT THING UNDER-GROUND, IT'S NOT SOME-THING THEY CAN JUST WRITE OFF.
HUFF
...
DAMN IT!
WHO DO THEY THINK THEY ARE, MESSING UP MY LIFE LIKE THIS?
MORIKATSU MUROI, GOVERNOR OF GRID MIE

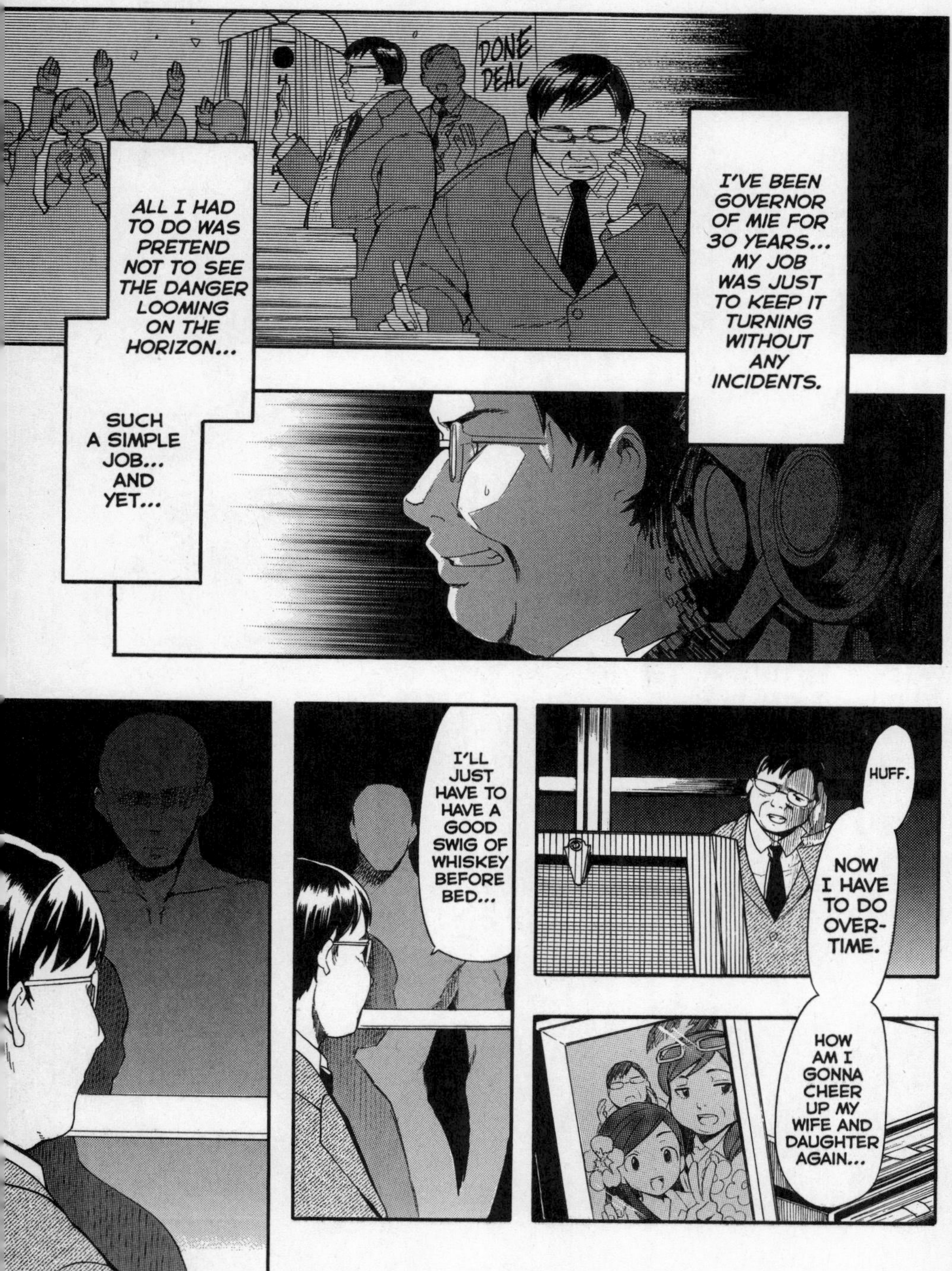
DONE DEAL
I'VE BEEN GOVERNOR OF MIE FOR 30 YEARS... MY JOB WAS JUST TO KEEP IT TURNING WITHOUT ANY INCIDENTS.
ALL I HAD TO DO WAS PRETEND NOT TO SEE THE DANGER LOOMING ON THE HORIZON...
SUCH A SIMPLE JOB... AND YET...
HUFF.
NOW I HAVE TO DO OVER-TIME.
HOW AM I GONNA CHEER UP MY WIFE AND DAUGHTER AGAIN...
I'LL JUST HAVE TO HAVE A GOOD SWIG OF WHISKEY BEFORE BED...

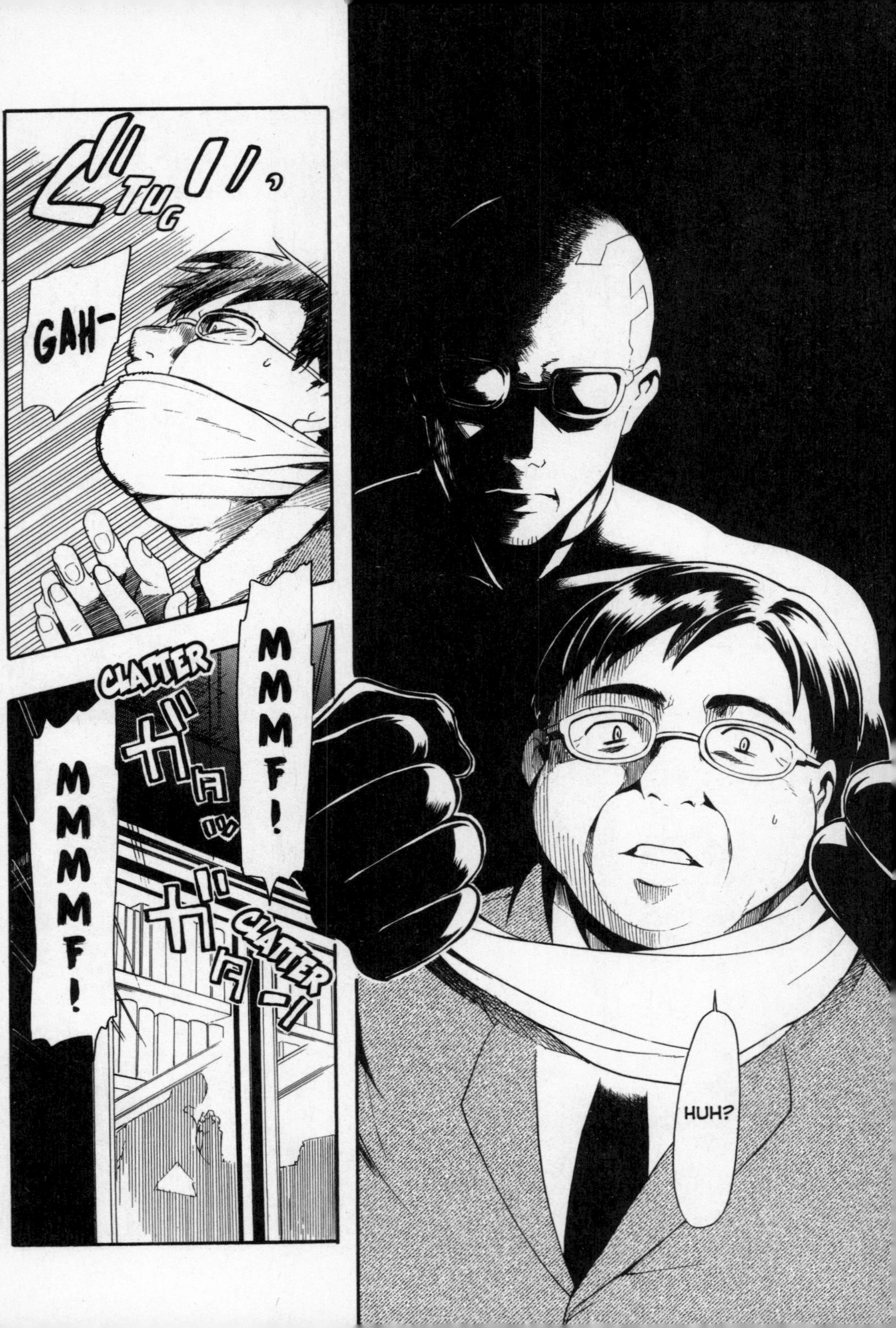
HUH?
TUG
GAH-
MMMF!
CLATTER
MMMMF!
CLATTER

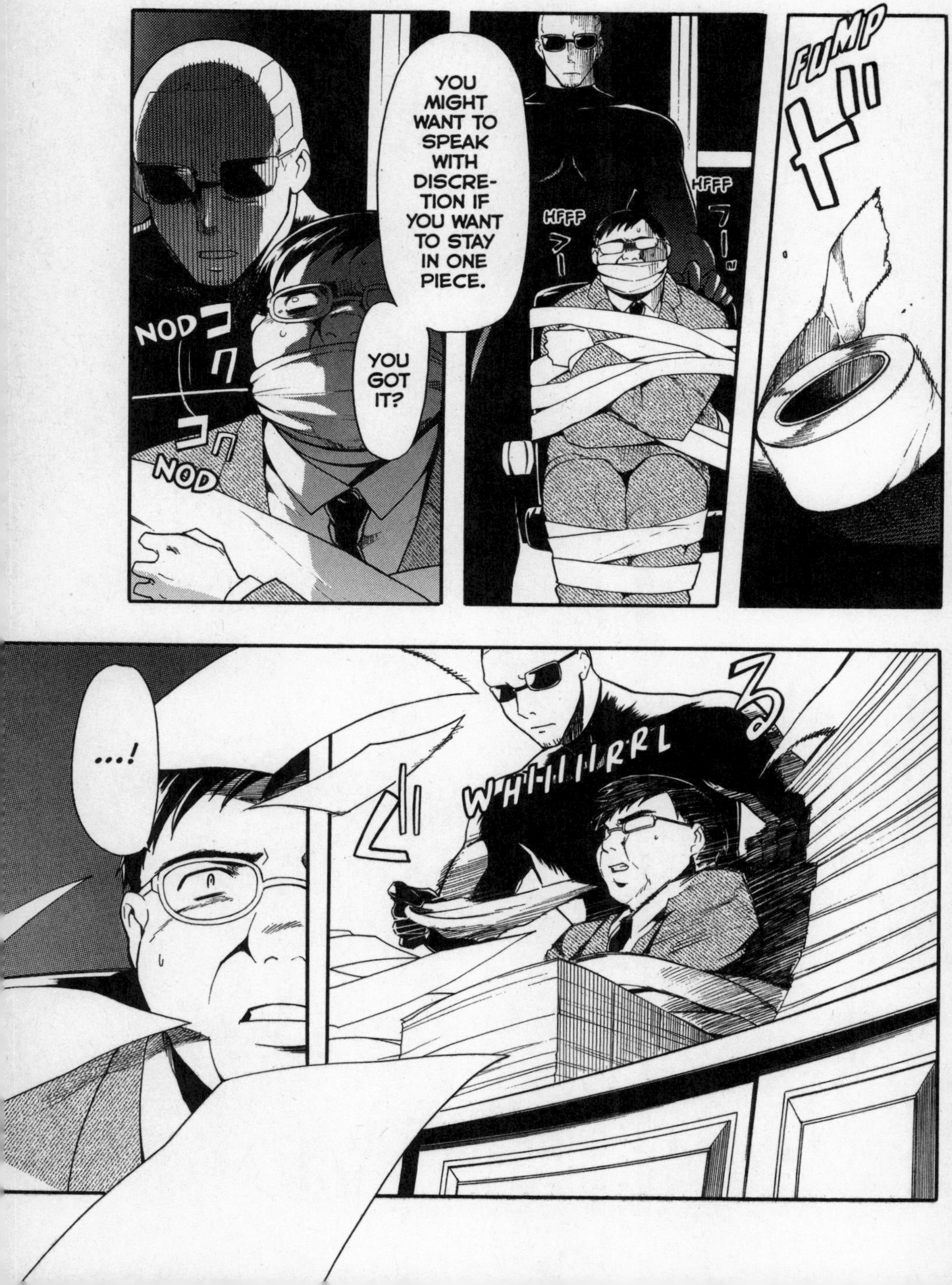
FUMP
YOU MIGHT WANT TO SPEAK WITH DISCRETION IF YOU WANT TO STAY IN ONE PIECE.
HFFF
HFFF
YOU GOT IT?
NOD
NOD
WHIIIIIRRL
...!

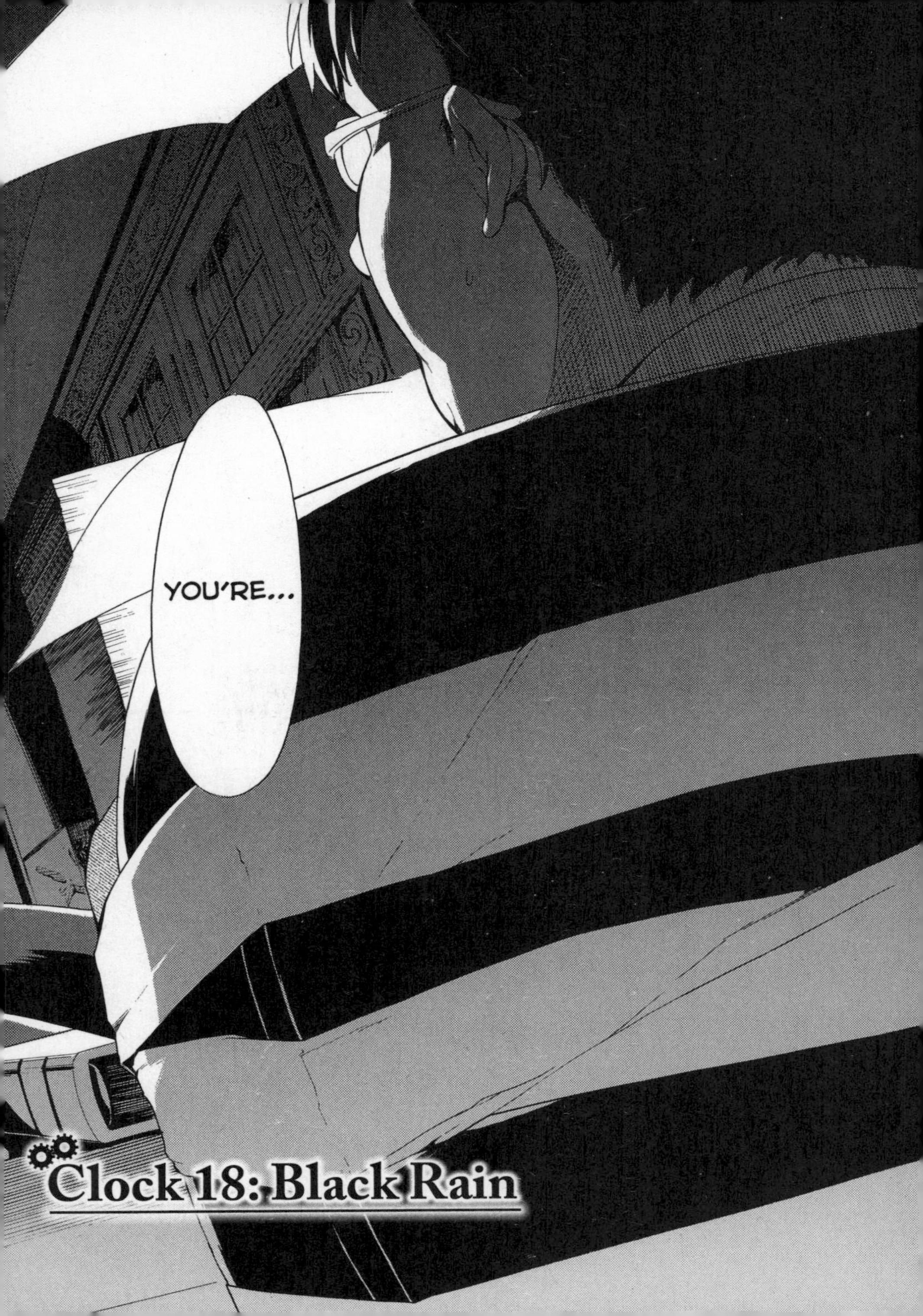
YOU'RE...

Clock 18: Black Rain

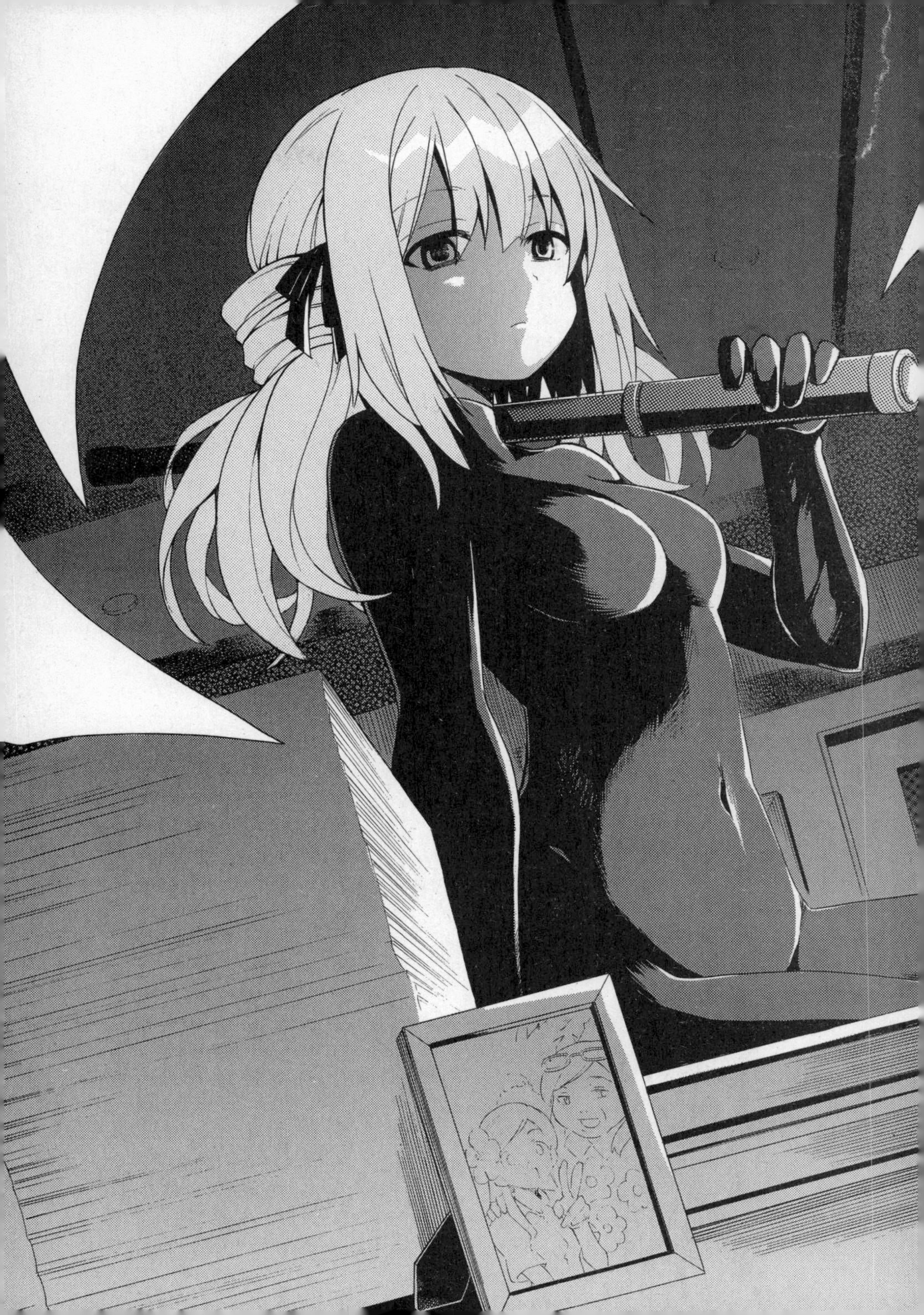

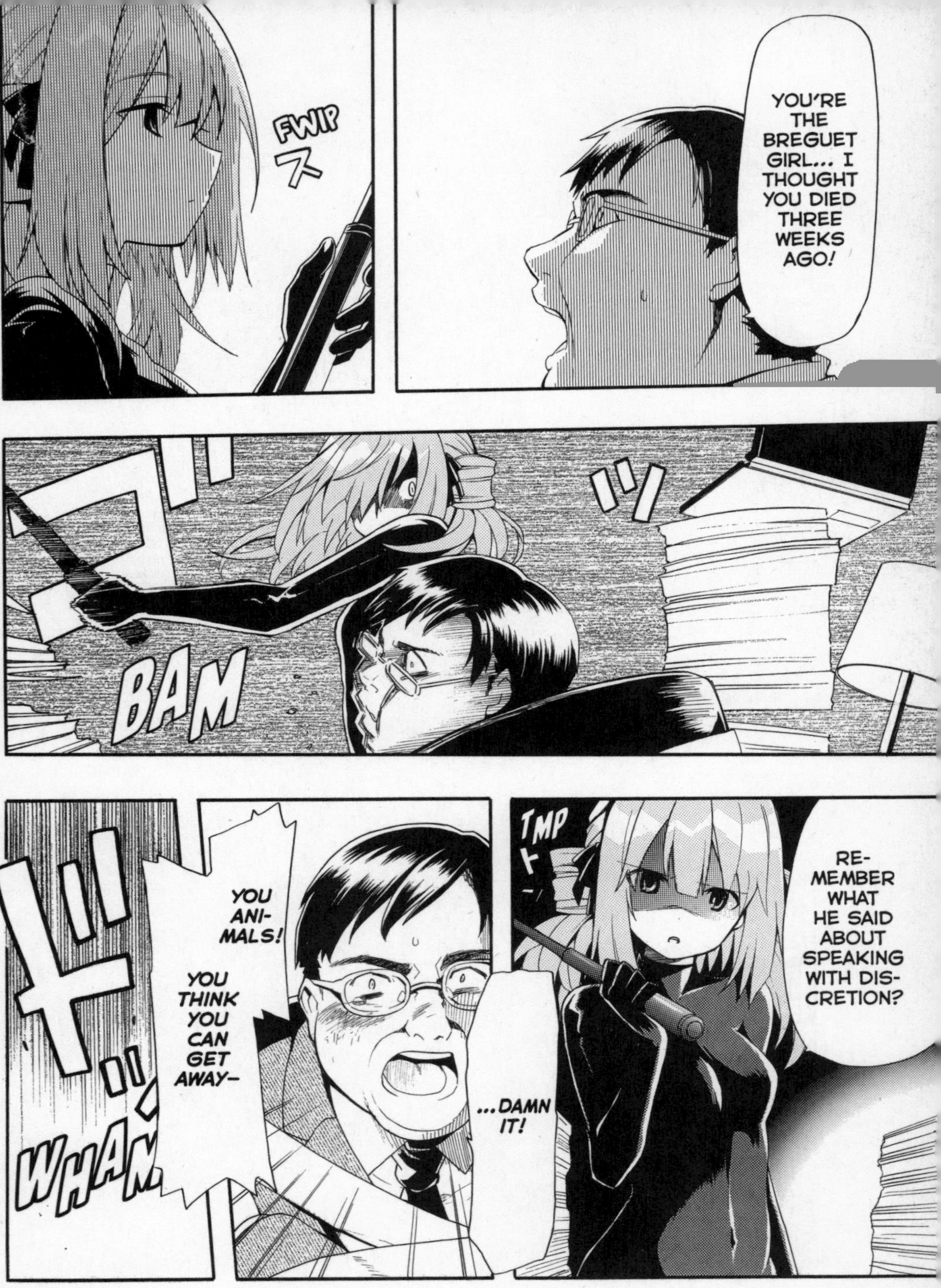

YOU'RE THE BREGUET GIRL... I THOUGHT YOU DIED THREE WEEKS AGO!
FWIP
ス
BAM
TMP
RE-MEMBER WHAT HE SAID ABOUT SPEAKING WITH DIS-CRETION?
YOU ANI-MALS!
YOU THINK YOU CAN GET AWAY—
...DAMN IT!
WHAM

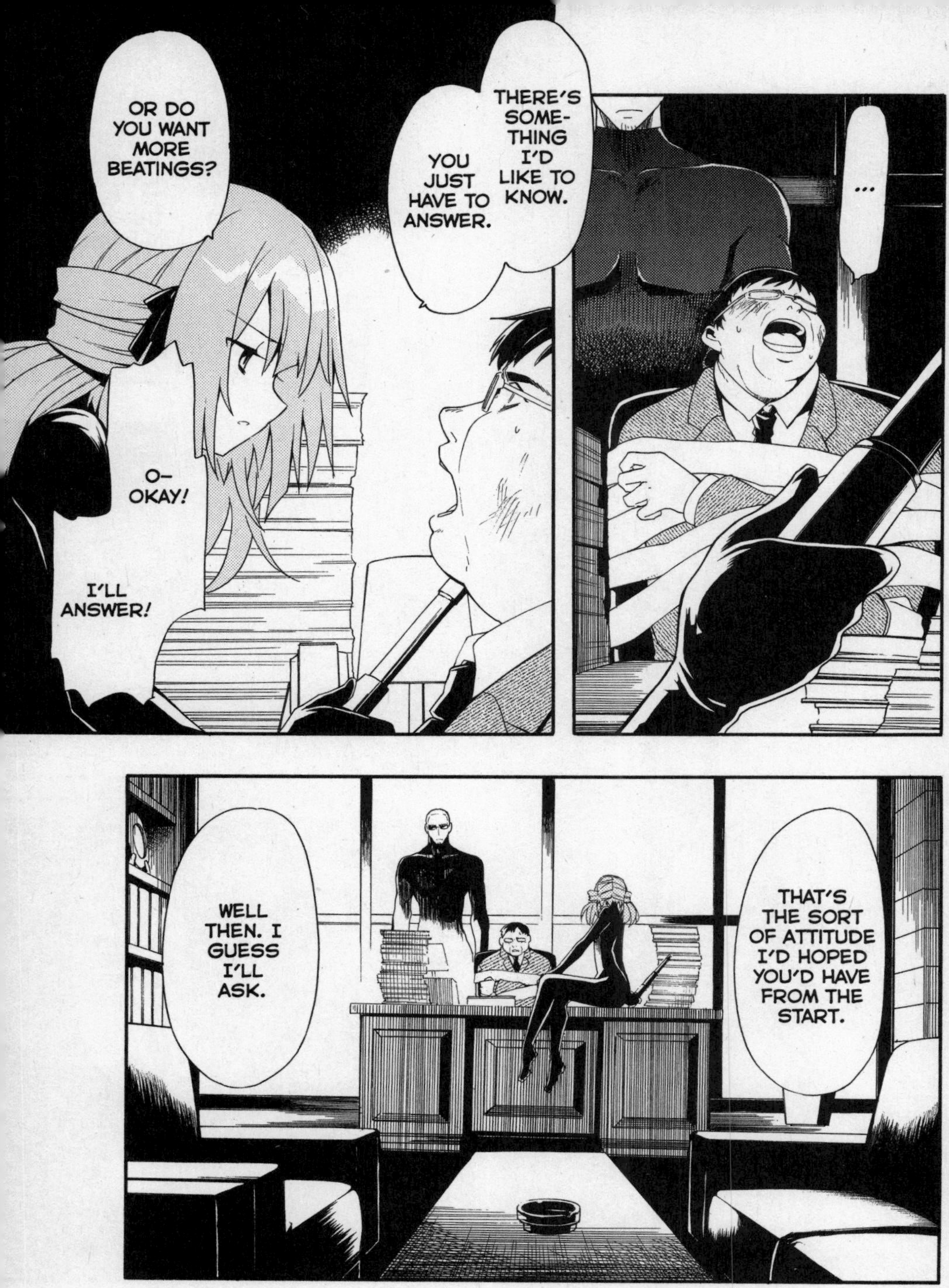
...
THERE'S SOMETHING I'D LIKE TO KNOW.
YOU JUST HAVE TO ANSWER.
OR DO YOU WANT MORE BEATINGS?
O-OKAY!
I'LL ANSWER!
THAT'S THE SORT OF ATTITUDE I'D HOPED YOU'D HAVE FROM THE START.
WELL THEN. I GUESS I'LL ASK.

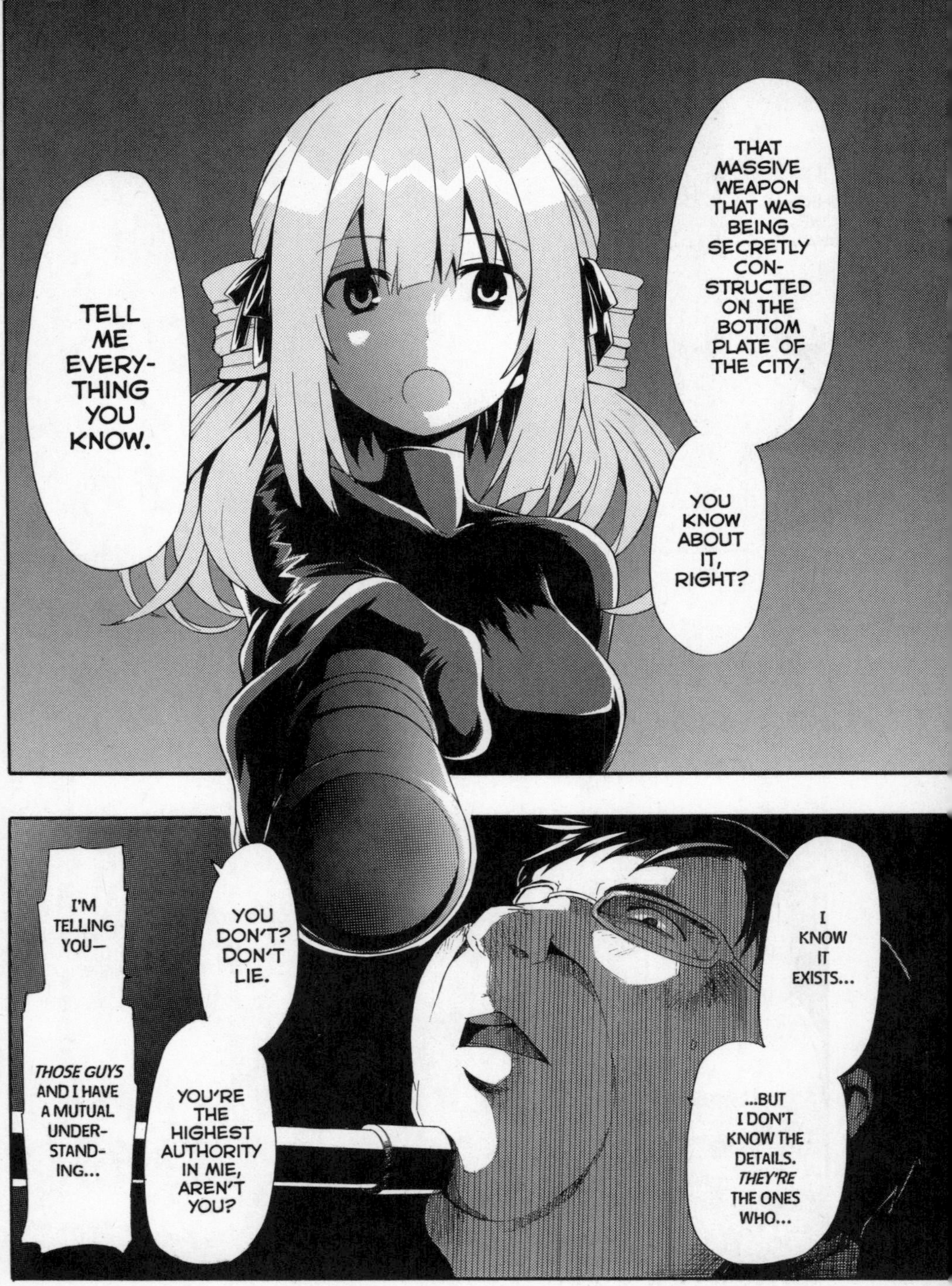
THAT MASSIVE WEAPON THAT WAS BEING SECRETLY CON-STRUCTED ON THE BOTTOM PLATE OF THE CITY.
YOU KNOW ABOUT IT, RIGHT?
TELL ME EVERY-THING YOU KNOW.
I KNOW IT EXISTS...
...BUT I DON'T KNOW THE DETAILS. *THEY'RE* THE ONES WHO...
YOU DON'T? DON'T LIE.
YOU'RE THE HIGHEST AUTHORITY IN MIE, AREN'T YOU?
I'M TELLING YOU—
THOSE GUYS AND I HAVE A MUTUAL UNDER-STAND-ING...

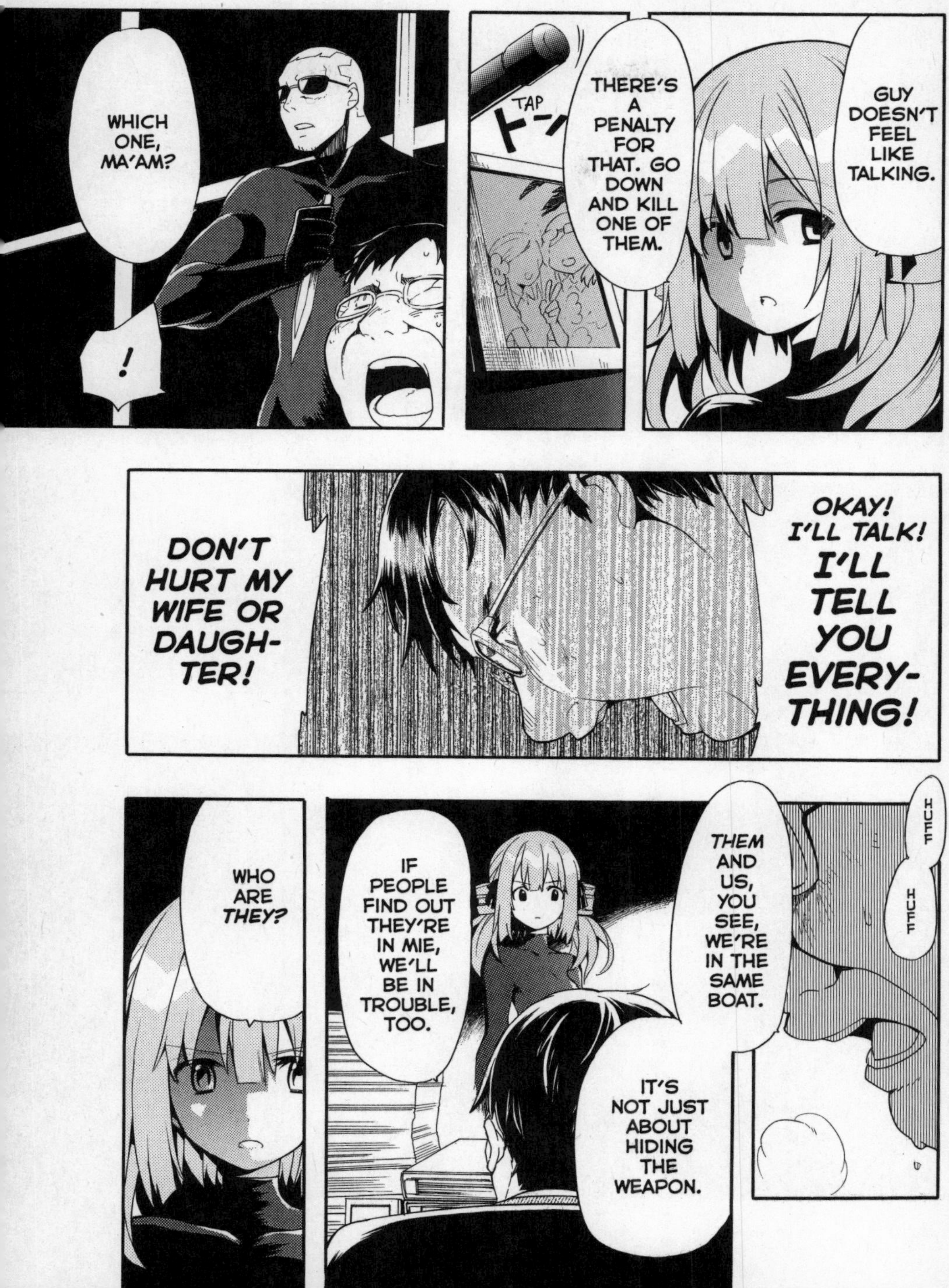
GUY DOESN'T FEEL LIKE TALKING.
TAP
THERE'S A PENALTY FOR THAT. GO DOWN AND KILL ONE OF THEM.
WHICH ONE, MA'AM?
!
OKAY! I'LL TALK! I'LL TELL YOU EVERYTHING!
DON'T HURT MY WIFE OR DAUGHTER!
HUFF
HUFF
THEM AND US, YOU SEE, WE'RE IN THE SAME BOAT.
IF PEOPLE FIND OUT THEY'RE IN MIE, WE'LL BE IN TROUBLE, TOO.
IT'S NOT JUST ABOUT HIDING THE WEAPON.
WHO ARE THEY?

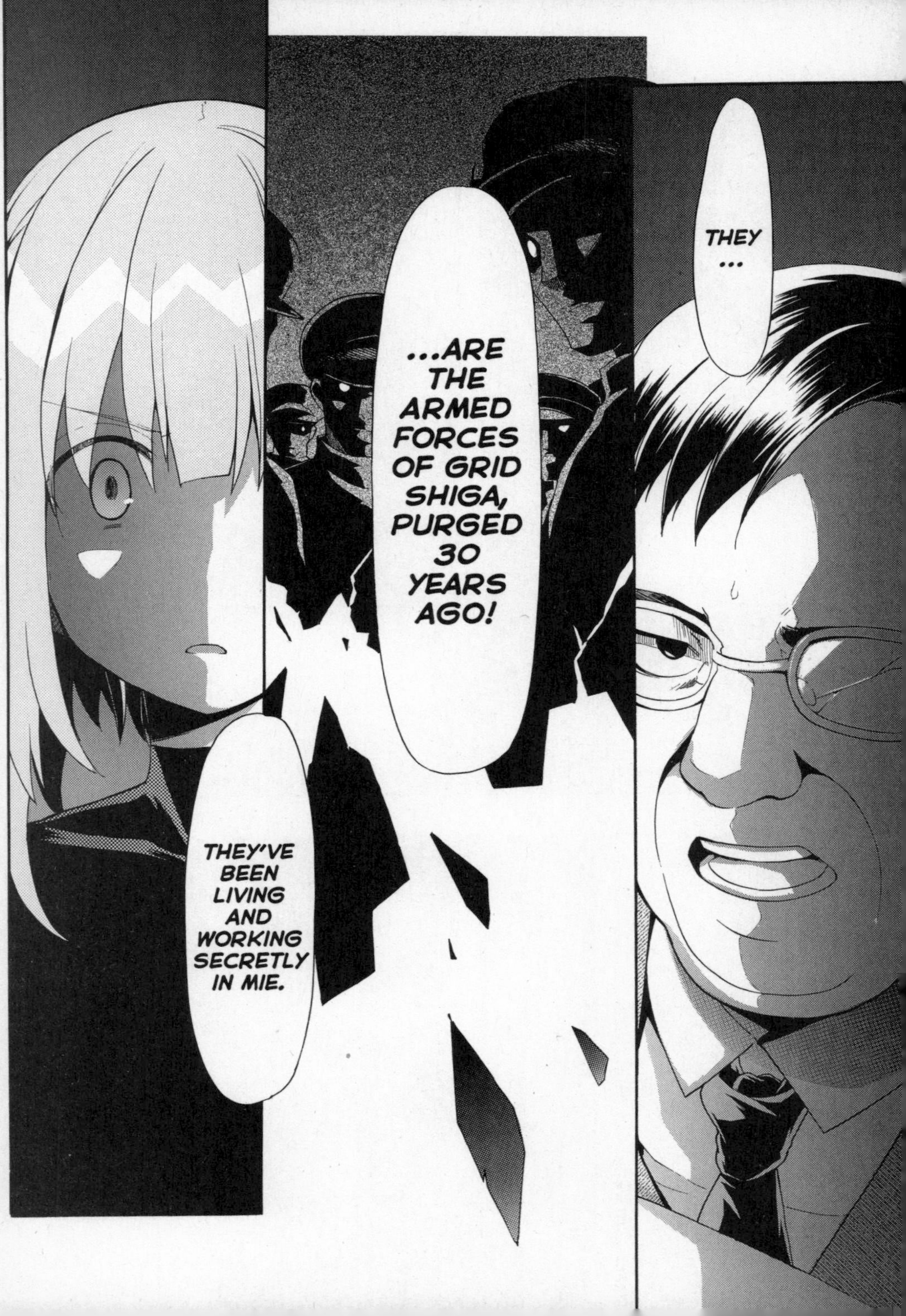
THEY ...
...ARE THE ARMED FORCES OF GRID SHIGA, PURGED 30 YEARS AGO!
THEY'VE BEEN LIVING AND WORKING SECRETLY IN MIE.

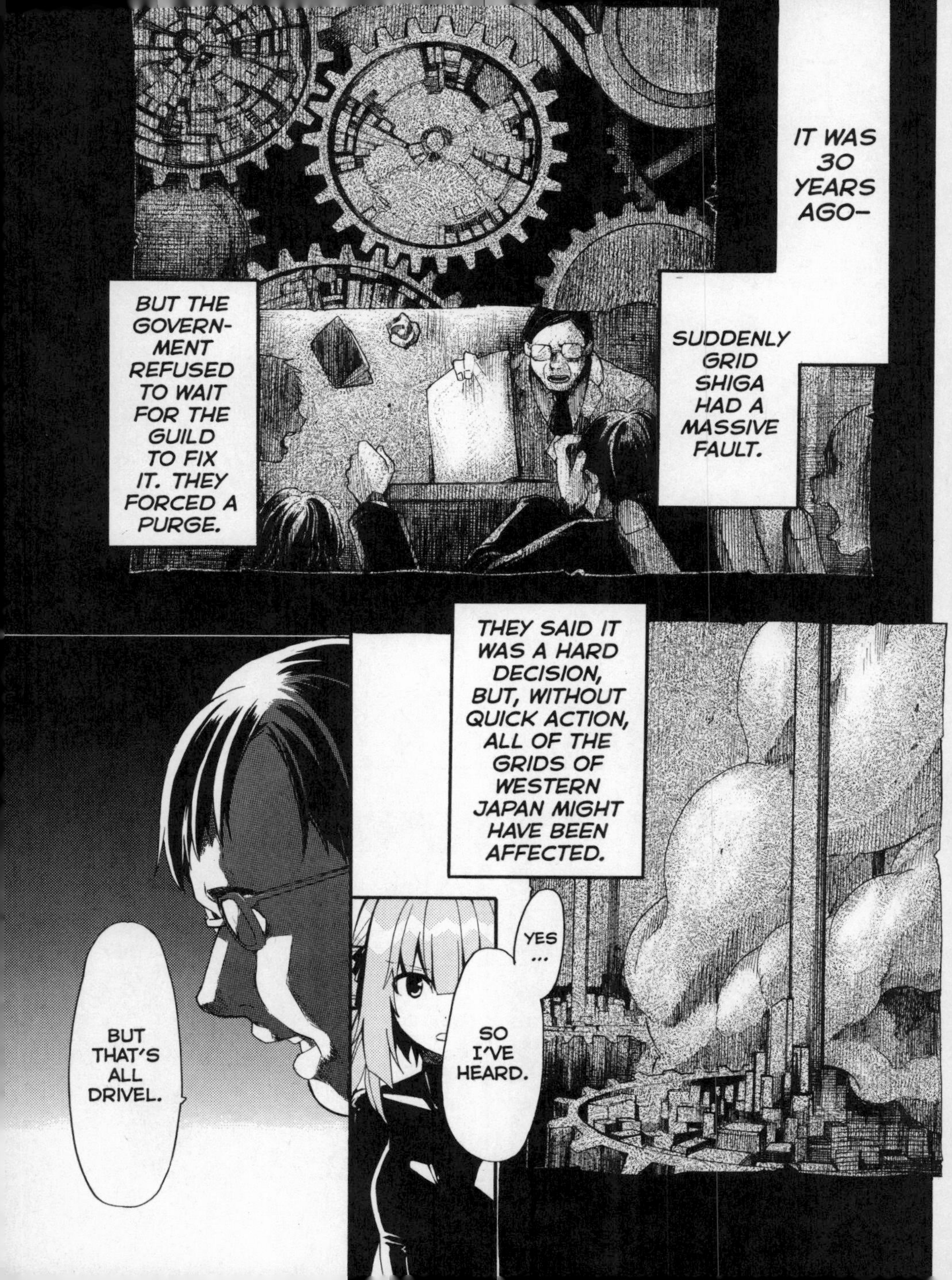
IT WAS 30 YEARS AGO–
SUDDENLY GRID SHIGA HAD A MASSIVE FAULT.
BUT THE GOVERN-MENT REFUSED TO WAIT FOR THE GUILD TO FIX IT. THEY FORCED A PURGE.
THEY SAID IT WAS A HARD DECISION, BUT, WITHOUT QUICK ACTION, ALL OF THE GRIDS OF WESTERN JAPAN MIGHT HAVE BEEN AFFECTED.
YES ...
SO I'VE HEARD.
BUT THAT'S ALL DRIVEL.

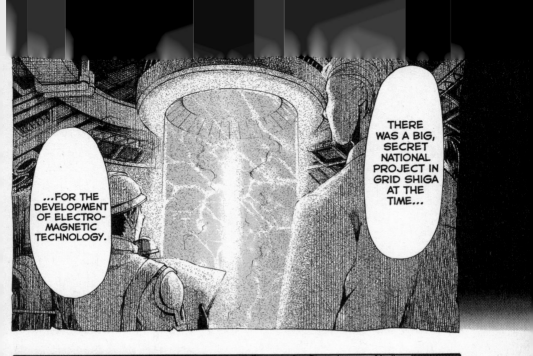

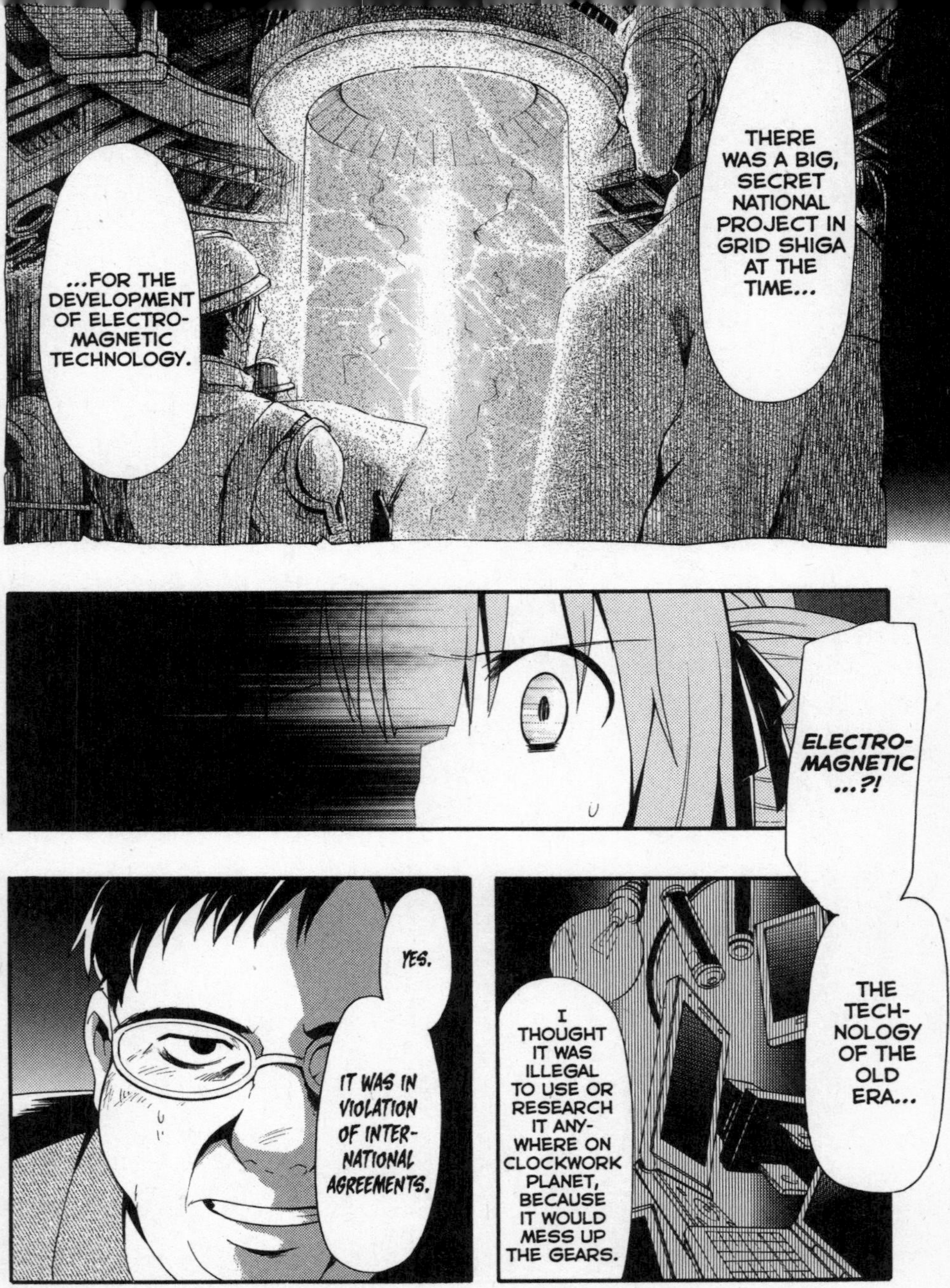
THERE WAS A BIG, SECRET NATIONAL PROJECT IN GRID SHIGA AT THE TIME...
...FOR THE DEVELOPMENT OF ELECTRO-MAGNETIC TECHNOLOGY.
ELECTRO-MAGNETIC ...?!
THE TECH-NOLOGY OF THE OLD ERA...
I THOUGHT IT WAS ILLEGAL TO USE OR RESEARCH IT ANY-WHERE ON CLOCKWORK PLANET, BECAUSE IT WOULD MESS UP THE GEARS.
YES.
IT WAS IN VIOLATION OF INTER-NATIONAL AGREEMENTS.

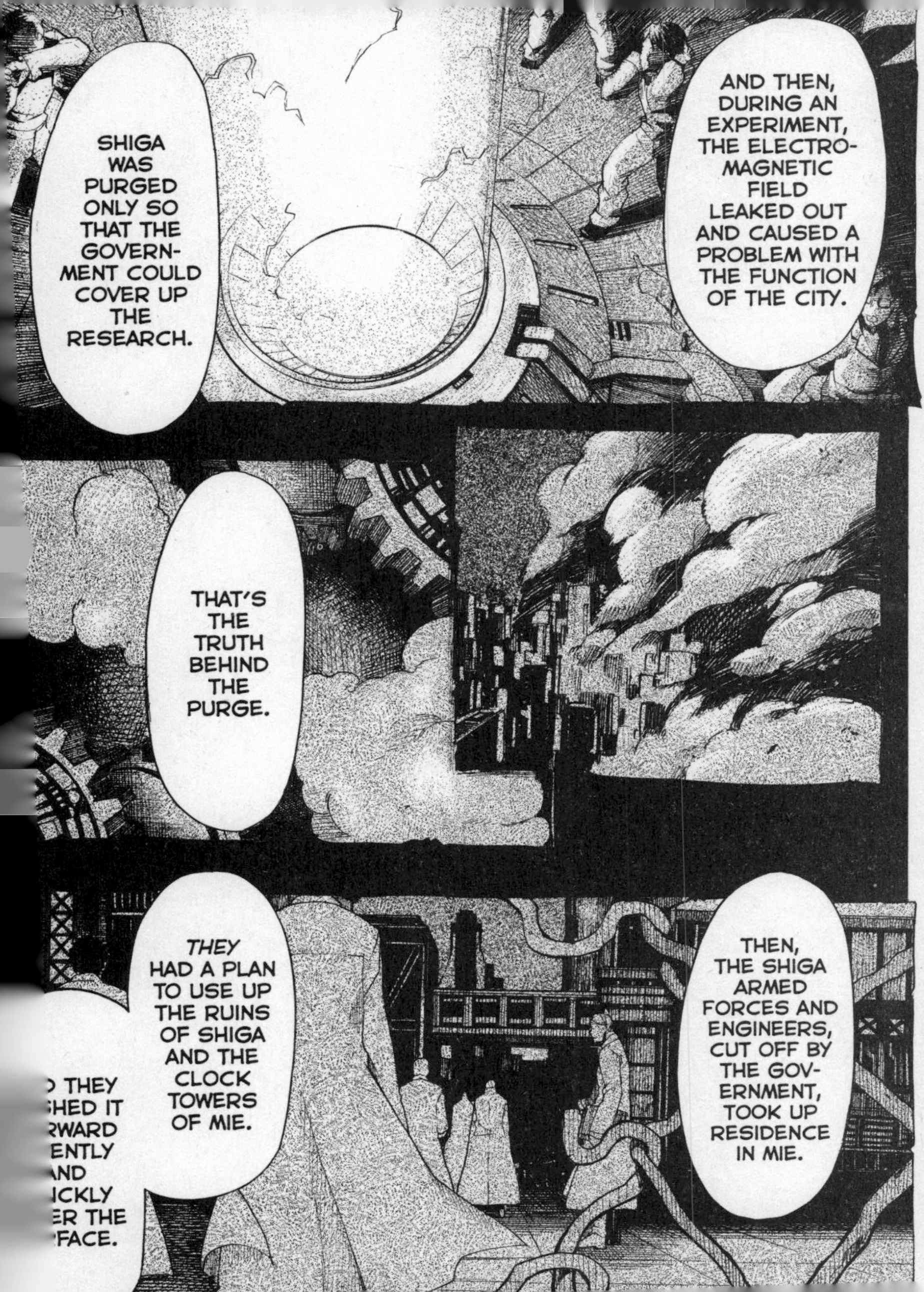
AND THEN, DURING AN EXPERIMENT, THE ELECTRO-MAGNETIC FIELD LEAKED OUT AND CAUSED A PROBLEM WITH THE FUNCTION OF THE CITY.
SHIGA WAS PURGED ONLY SO THAT THE GOVERN-MENT COULD COVER UP THE RESEARCH.
THAT'S THE TRUTH BEHIND THE PURGE.
THEN, THE SHIGA ARMED FORCES AND ENGINEERS, CUT OFF BY THE GOV-ERNMENT, TOOK UP RESIDENCE IN MIE.
THEY HAD A PLAN TO USE UP THE RUINS OF SHIGA AND THE CLOCK TOWERS OF MIE.

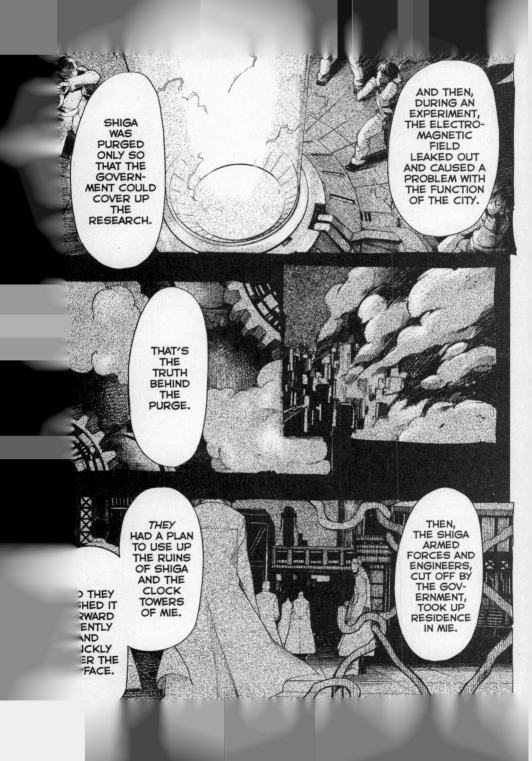

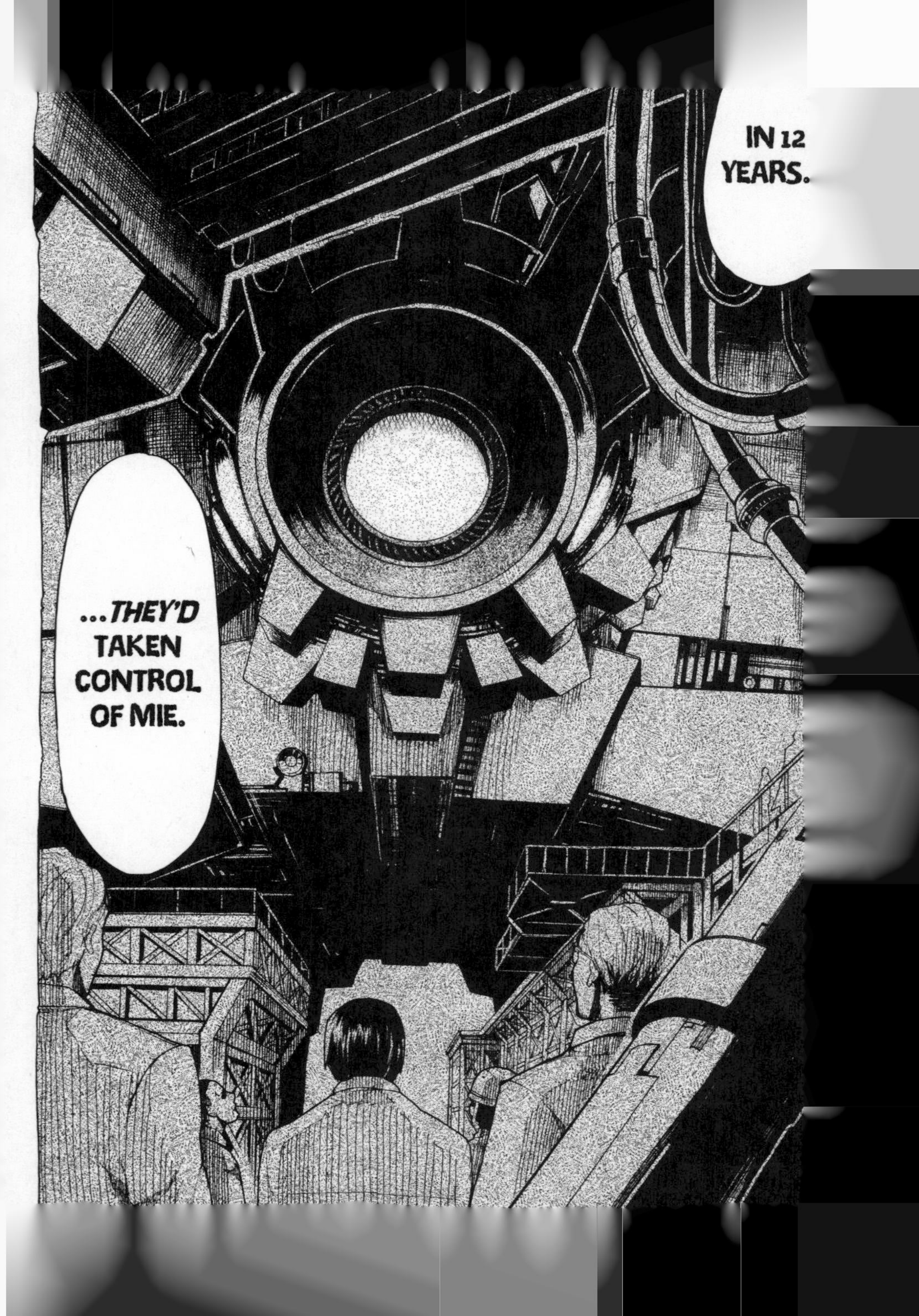
IN 12 YEARS.
...THEY'D TAKEN CONTROL OF MIE.

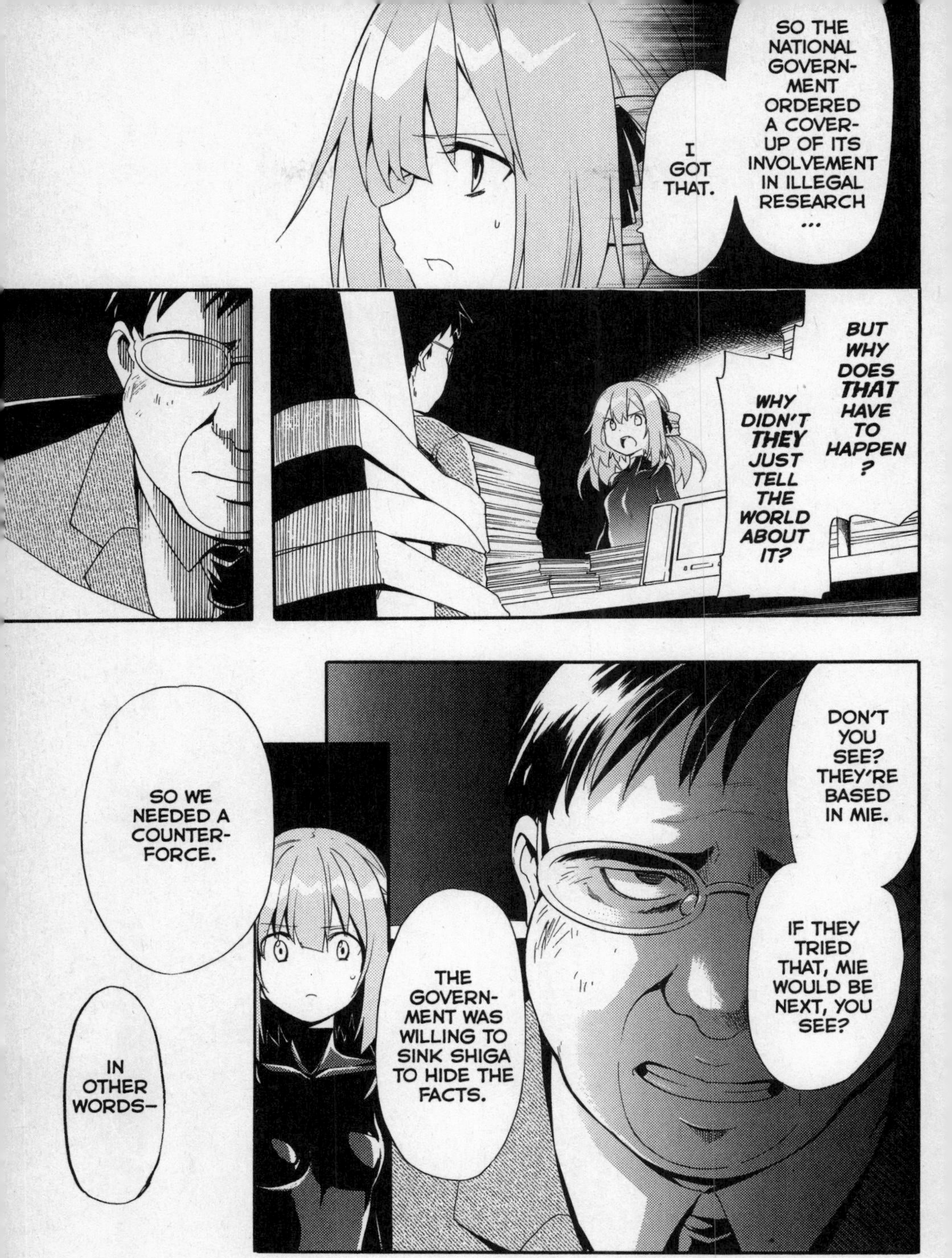
SO THE NATIONAL GOVERNMENT ORDERED A COVER-UP OF ITS INVOLVEMENT IN ILLEGAL RESEARCH ...
I GOT THAT.
BUT WHY DOES THAT HAVE TO HAPPEN?
WHY DIDN'T THEY JUST TELL THE WORLD ABOUT IT?
DON'T YOU SEE? THEY'RE BASED IN MIE.
IF THEY TRIED THAT, MIE WOULD BE NEXT, YOU SEE?
THE GOVERNMENT WAS WILLING TO SINK SHIGA TO HIDE THE FACTS.
SO WE NEEDED A COUNTERFORCE.
IN OTHER WORDS—

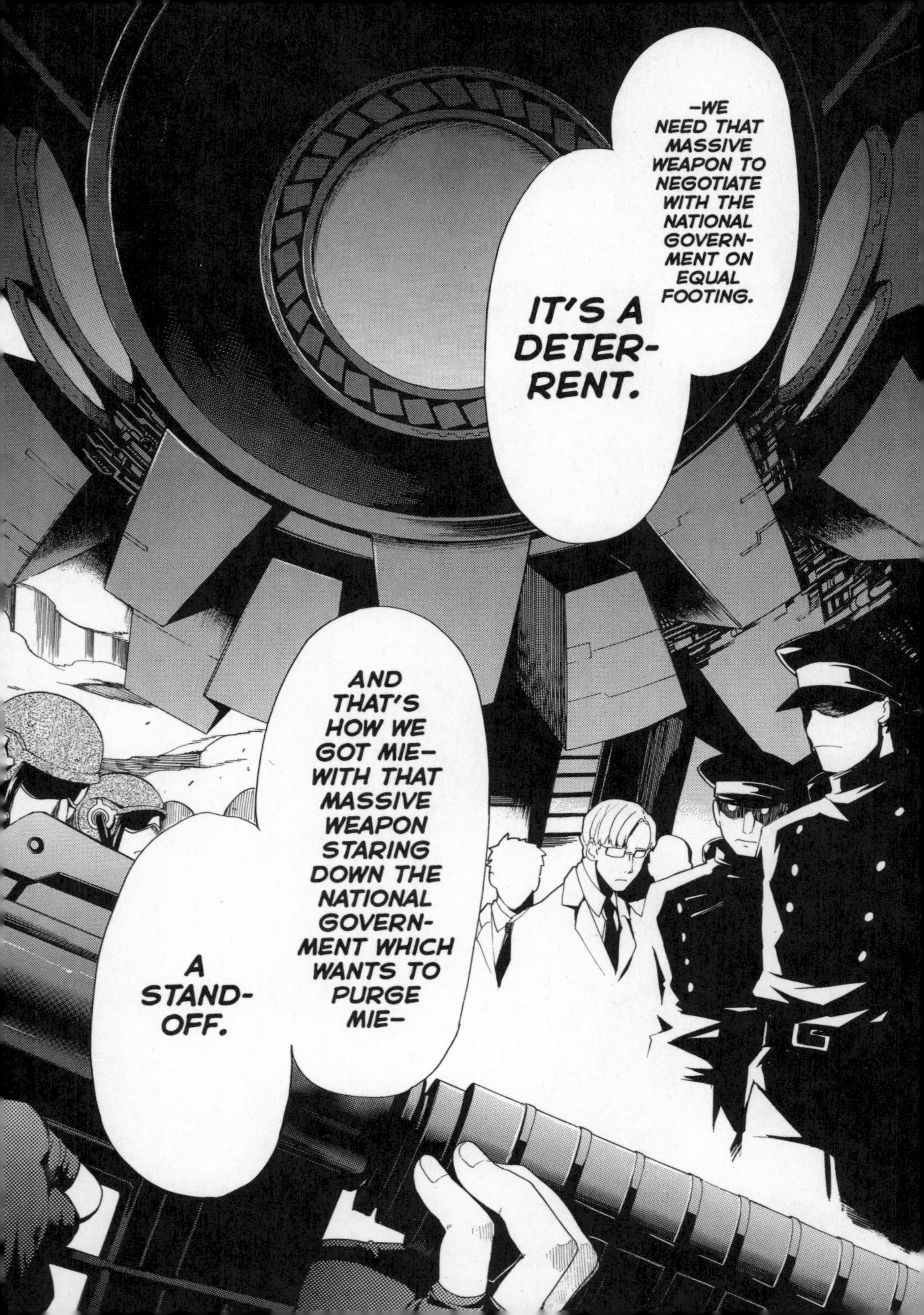

—WE NEED THAT MASSIVE WEAPON TO NEGOTIATE WITH THE NATIONAL GOVERN-MENT ON EQUAL FOOTING.
IT'S A DETER-RENT.
AND THAT'S HOW WE GOT MIE—WITH THAT MASSIVE WEAPON STARING DOWN THE NATIONAL GOVERN-MENT WHICH WANTS TO PURGE MIE—
A STAND-OFF.

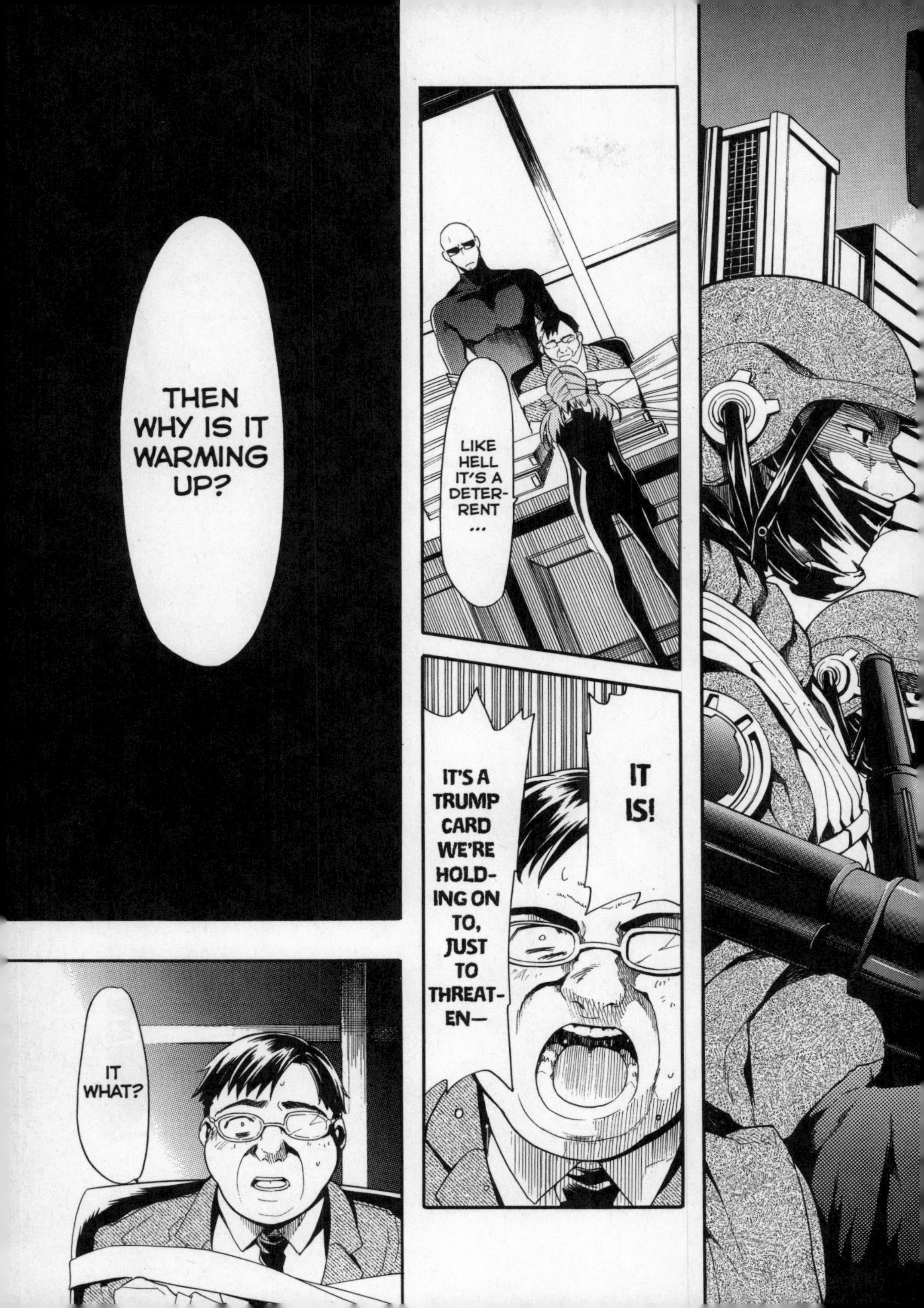
LIKE HELL IT'S A DETER-RENT ...
IT IS!
IT'S A TRUMP CARD WE'RE HOLD-ING ON TO, JUST TO THREAT-EN—
THEN WHY IS IT WARMING UP?
IT WHAT?

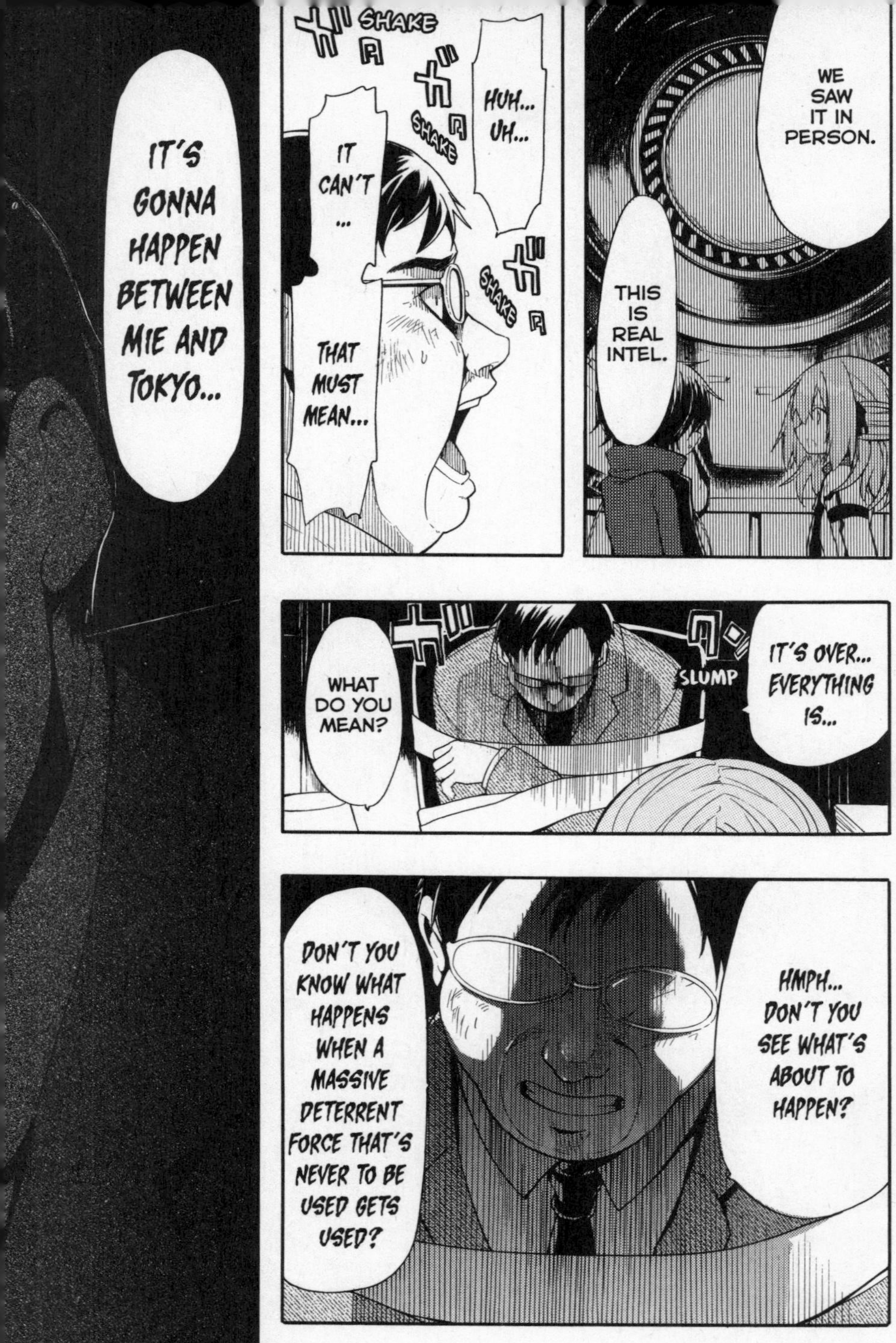

WE SAW IT IN PERSON.
THIS IS REAL INTEL.
HUH... UH...
SHAKE
SHAKE
SHAKE
IT CAN'T ...
THAT MUST MEAN...
SLUMP
IT'S OVER... EVERYTHING IS...
WHAT DO YOU MEAN?
HMPH... DON'T YOU SEE WHAT'S ABOUT TO HAPPEN?
DON'T YOU KNOW WHAT HAPPENS WHEN A MASSIVE DETERRENT FORCE THAT'S NEVER TO BE USED GETS USED?
IT'S GONNA HAPPEN BETWEEN MIE AND TOKYO...

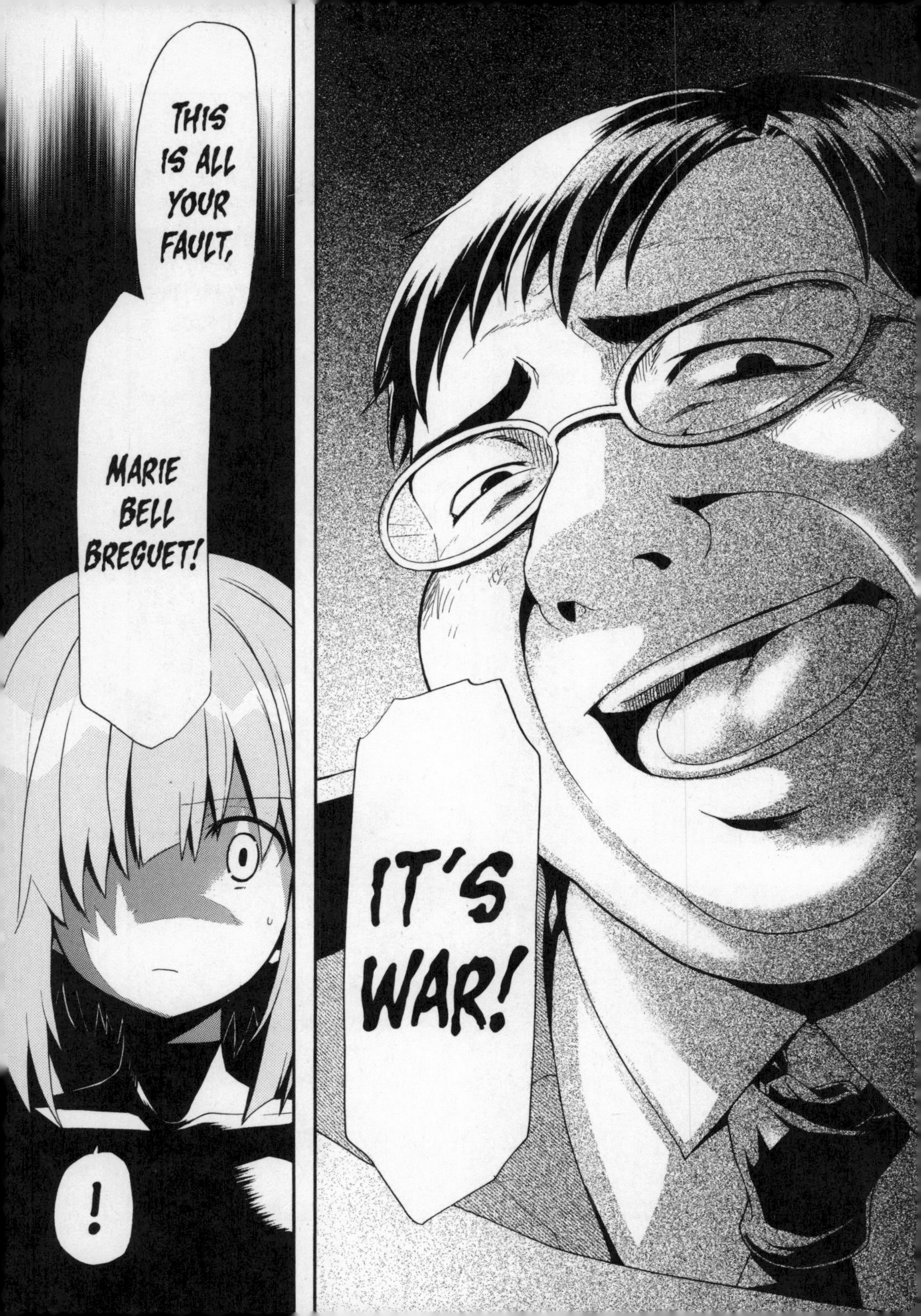
IT'S WAR!
THIS IS ALL YOUR FAULT,
MARIE BELL BREGUET!
!

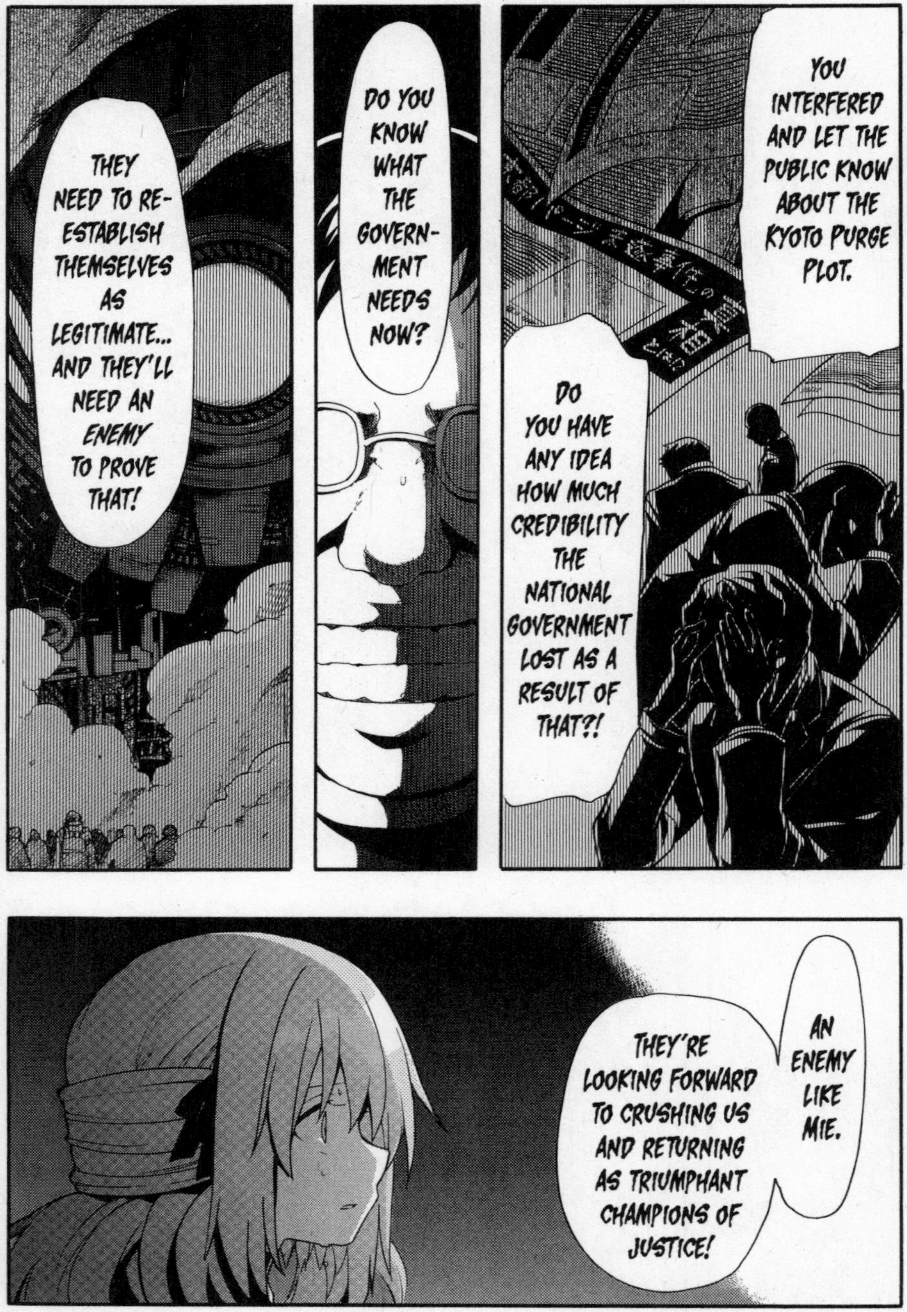
YOU INTERFERED AND LET THE PUBLIC KNOW ABOUT THE KYOTO PURGE PLOT.
DO YOU HAVE ANY IDEA HOW MUCH CREDIBILITY THE NATIONAL GOVERNMENT LOST AS A RESULT OF THAT?!
DO YOU KNOW WHAT THE GOVERN-MENT NEEDS NOW?
THEY NEED TO RE-ESTABLISH THEMSELVES AS LEGITIMATE... AND THEY'LL NEED AN *ENEMY* TO PROVE THAT!
AN ENEMY LIKE MIE.
THEY'RE LOOKING FORWARD TO CRUSHING US AND RETURNING AS TRIUMPHANT CHAMPIONS OF JUSTICE!

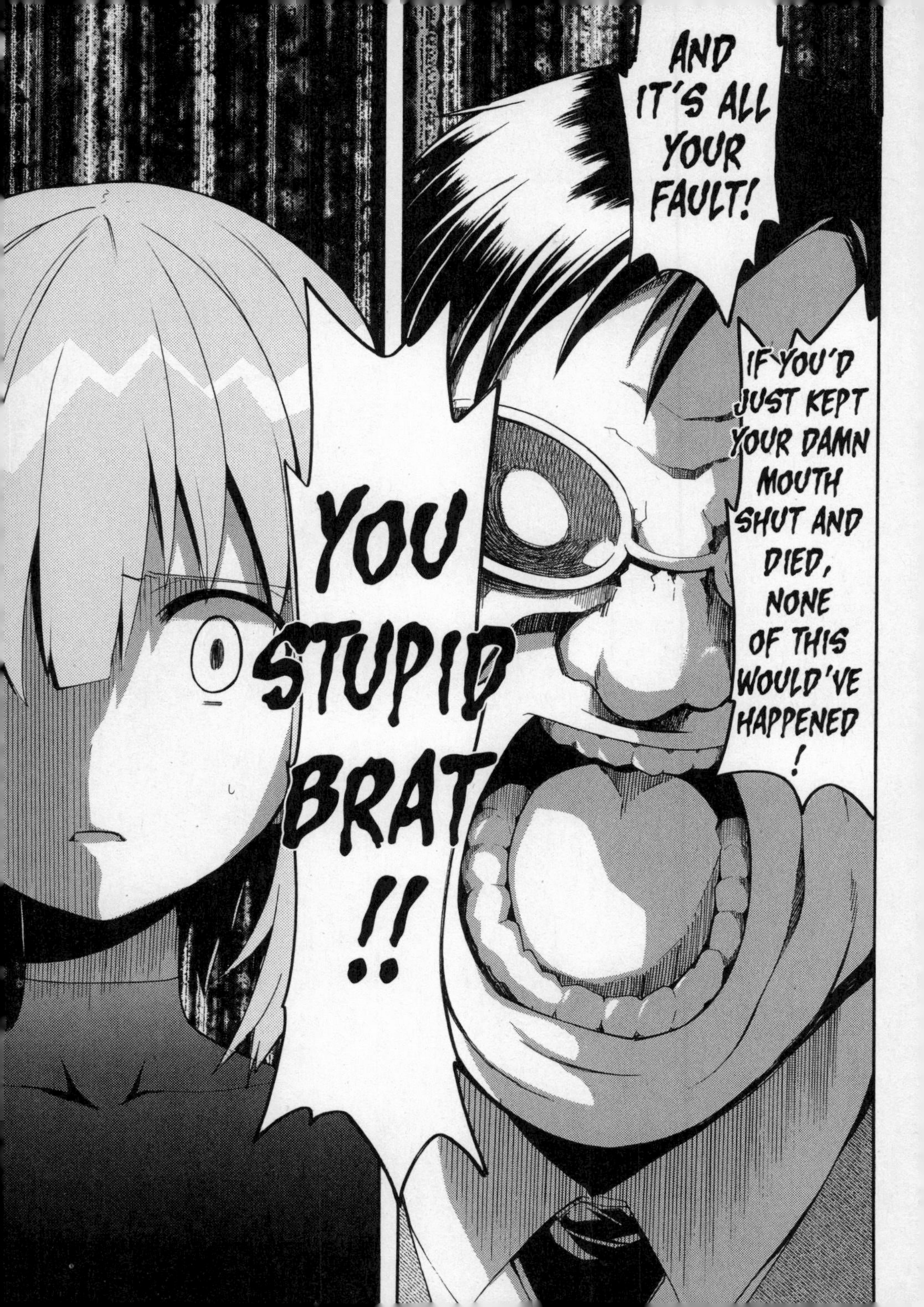
AND IT'S ALL YOUR FAULT!
IF YOU'D JUST KEPT YOUR DAMN MOUTH SHUT AND DIED, NONE OF THIS WOULD'VE HAPPENED!
YOU STUPID BRAT!!

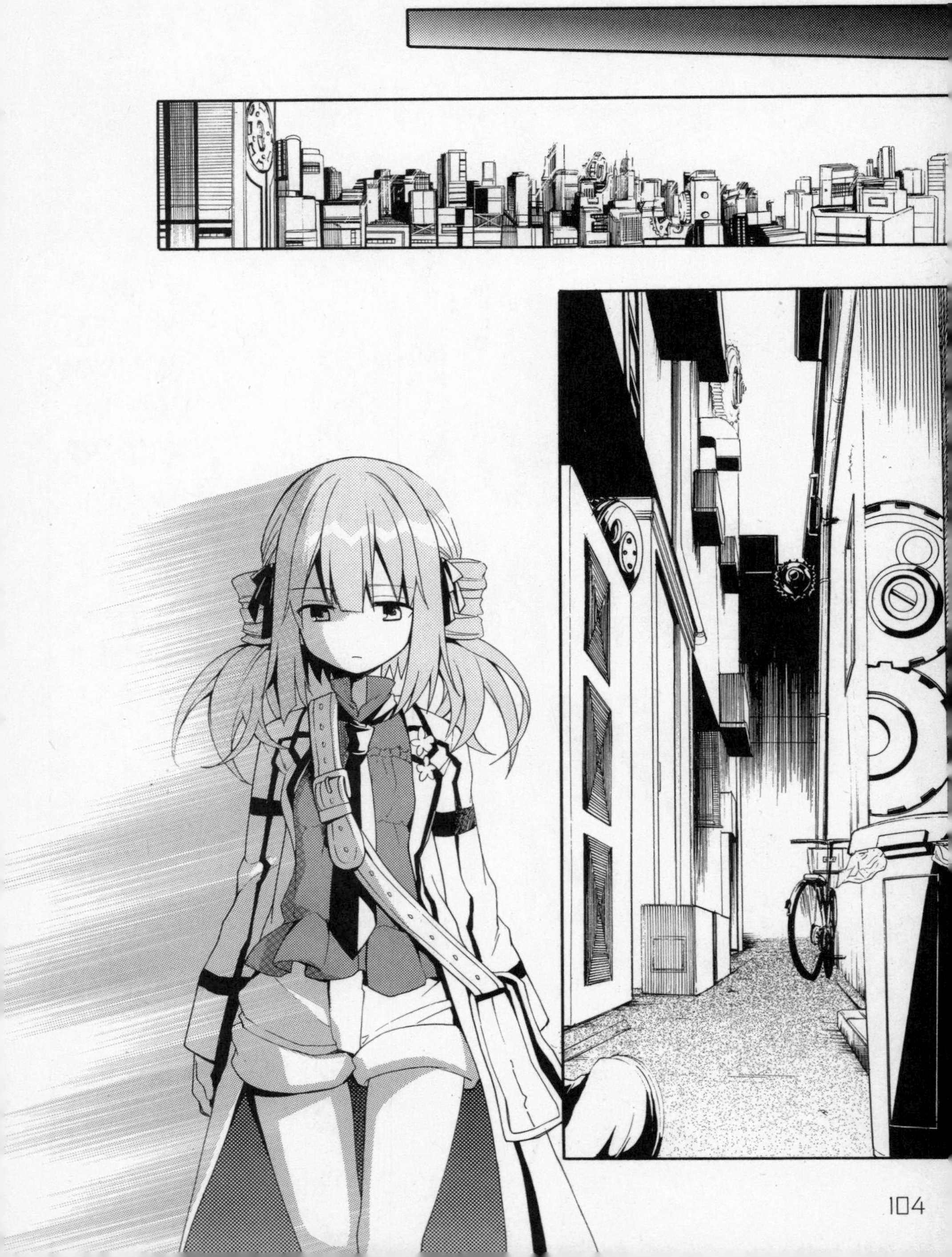

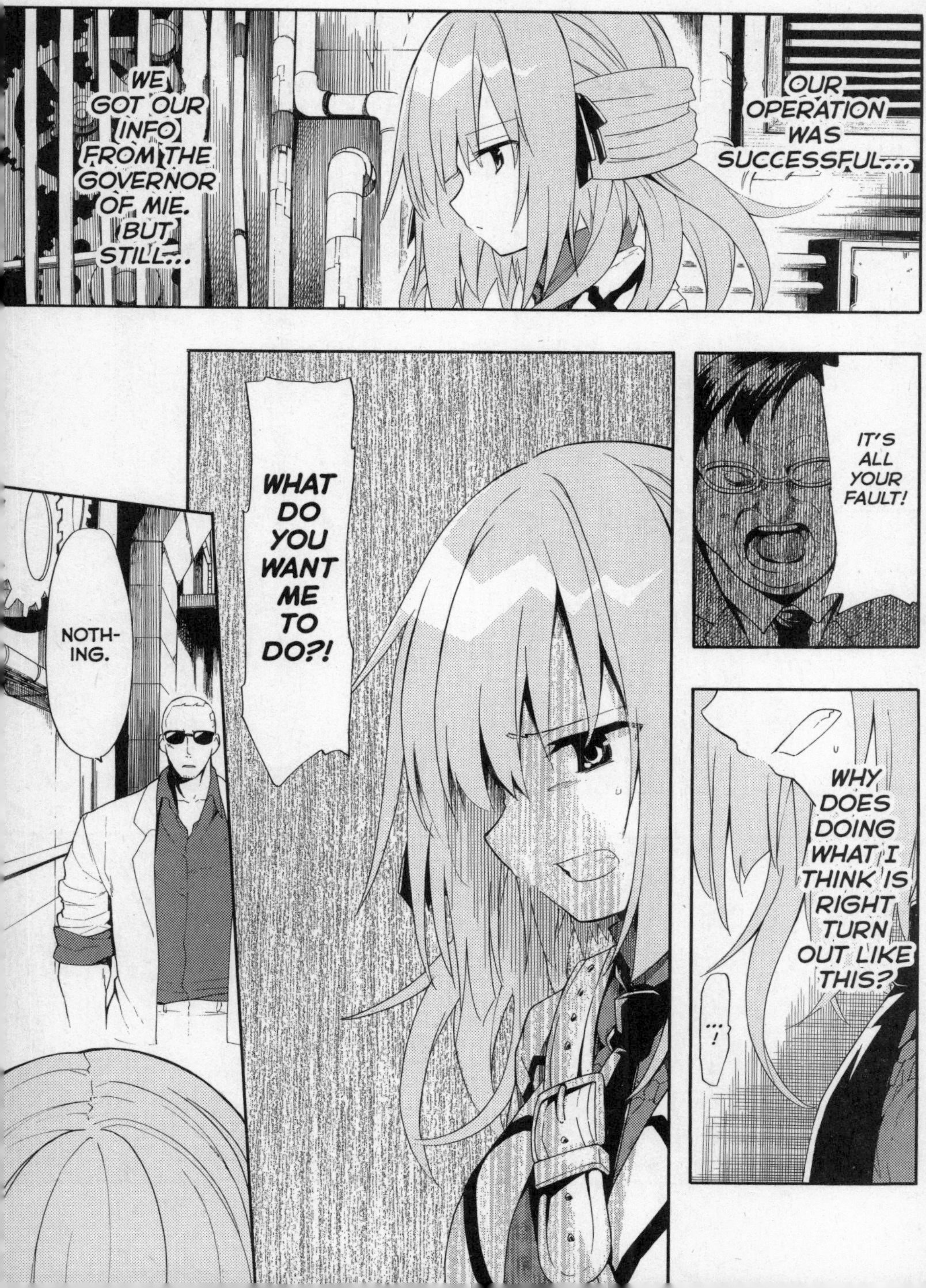
OUR OPERATION WAS SUCCESSFUL...
WE GOT OUR INFO FROM THE GOVERNOR OF MIE. BUT STILL...
IT'S ALL YOUR FAULT!
WHY DOES DOING WHAT I THINK IS RIGHT TURN OUT LIKE THIS?
...!
WHAT DO YOU WANT ME TO DO?!
NOTH-ING.

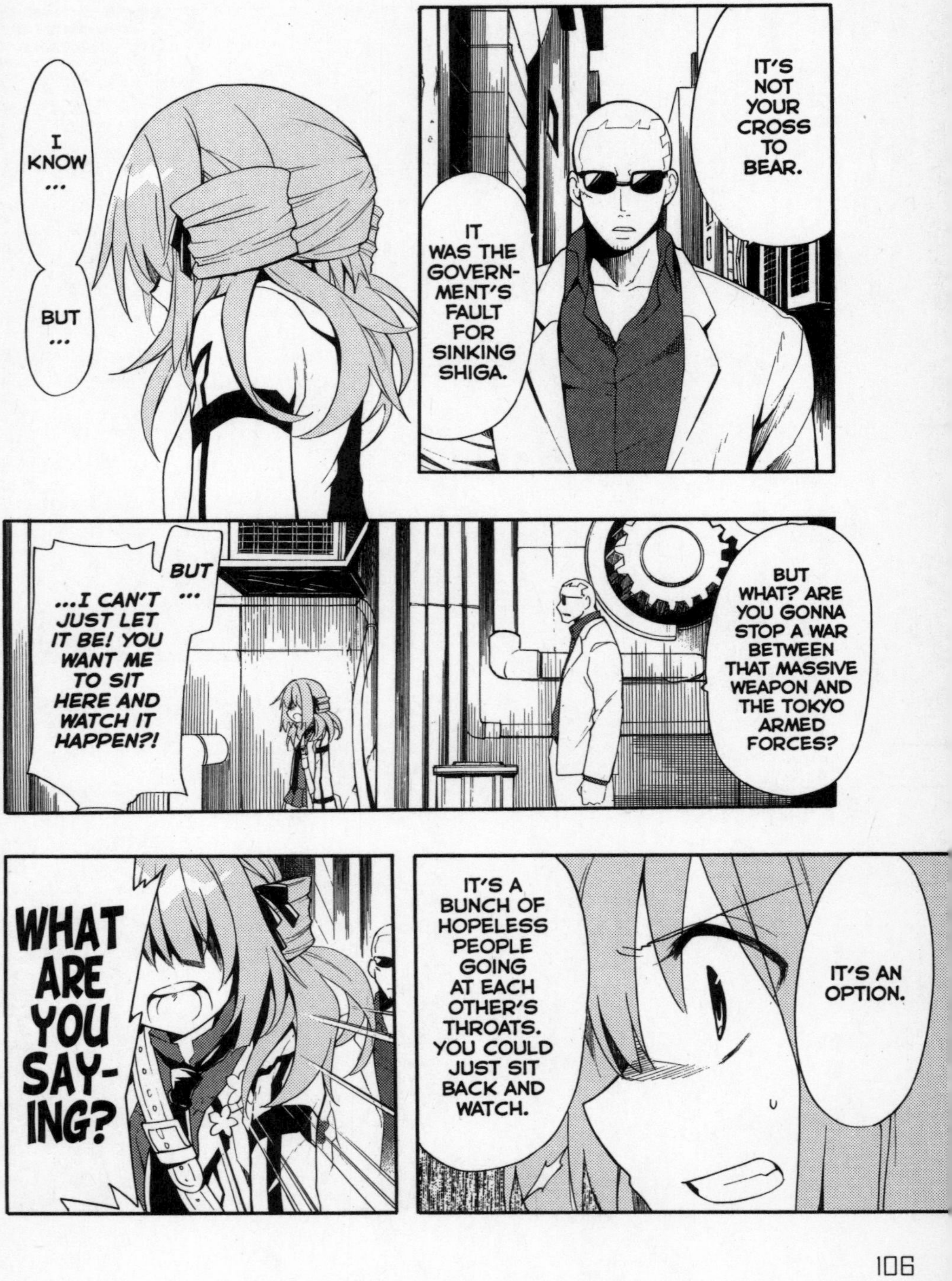
IT'S NOT YOUR CROSS TO BEAR.
IT WAS THE GOVERNMENT'S FAULT FOR SINKING SHIGA.
I KNOW...
BUT...
BUT WHAT? ARE YOU GONNA STOP A WAR BETWEEN THAT MASSIVE WEAPON AND THE TOKYO ARMED FORCES?
BUT...
...I CAN'T JUST LET IT BE! YOU WANT ME TO SIT HERE AND WATCH IT HAPPEN?!
IT'S AN OPTION.
IT'S A BUNCH OF HOPELESS PEOPLE GOING AT EACH OTHER'S THROATS. YOU COULD JUST SIT BACK AND WATCH.
WHAT ARE YOU SAY-ING?

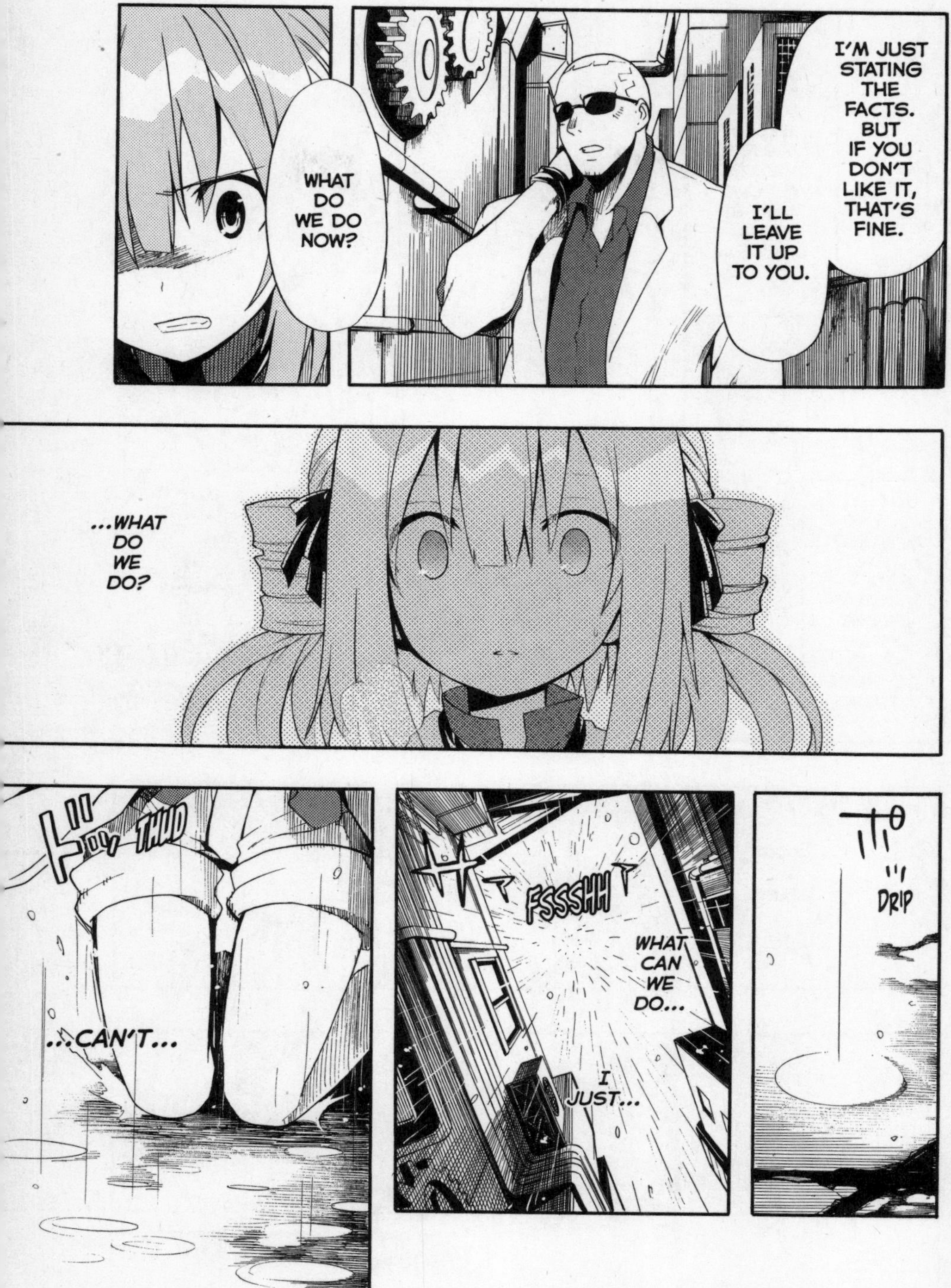
I'M JUST STATING THE FACTS. BUT IF YOU DON'T LIKE IT, THAT'S FINE.
I'LL LEAVE IT UP TO YOU.
WHAT DO WE DO NOW?
...WHAT DO WE DO?
DRIP
FSSSHH
WHAT CAN WE DO...
I JUST...
THUD
...CAN'T...

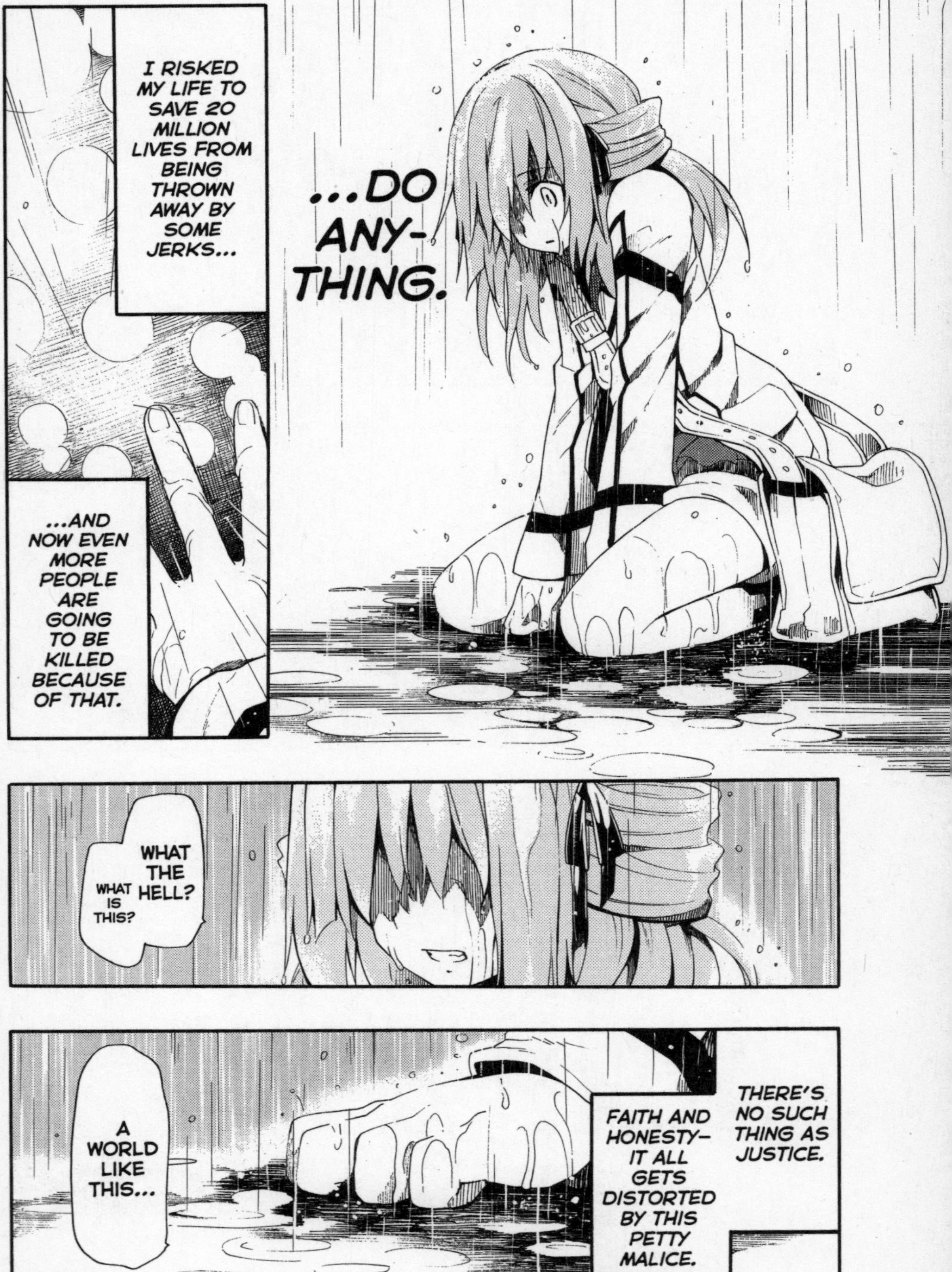
...DO ANY-THING.
I RISKED MY LIFE TO SAVE 20 MILLION LIVES FROM BEING THROWN AWAY BY SOME JERKS...
...AND NOW EVEN MORE PEOPLE ARE GOING TO BE KILLED BECAUSE OF THAT.
WHAT THE HELL?
WHAT IS THIS?
THERE'S NO SUCH THING AS JUSTICE.
FAITH AND HONESTY— IT ALL GETS DISTORTED BY THIS PETTY MALICE.
A WORLD LIKE THIS...

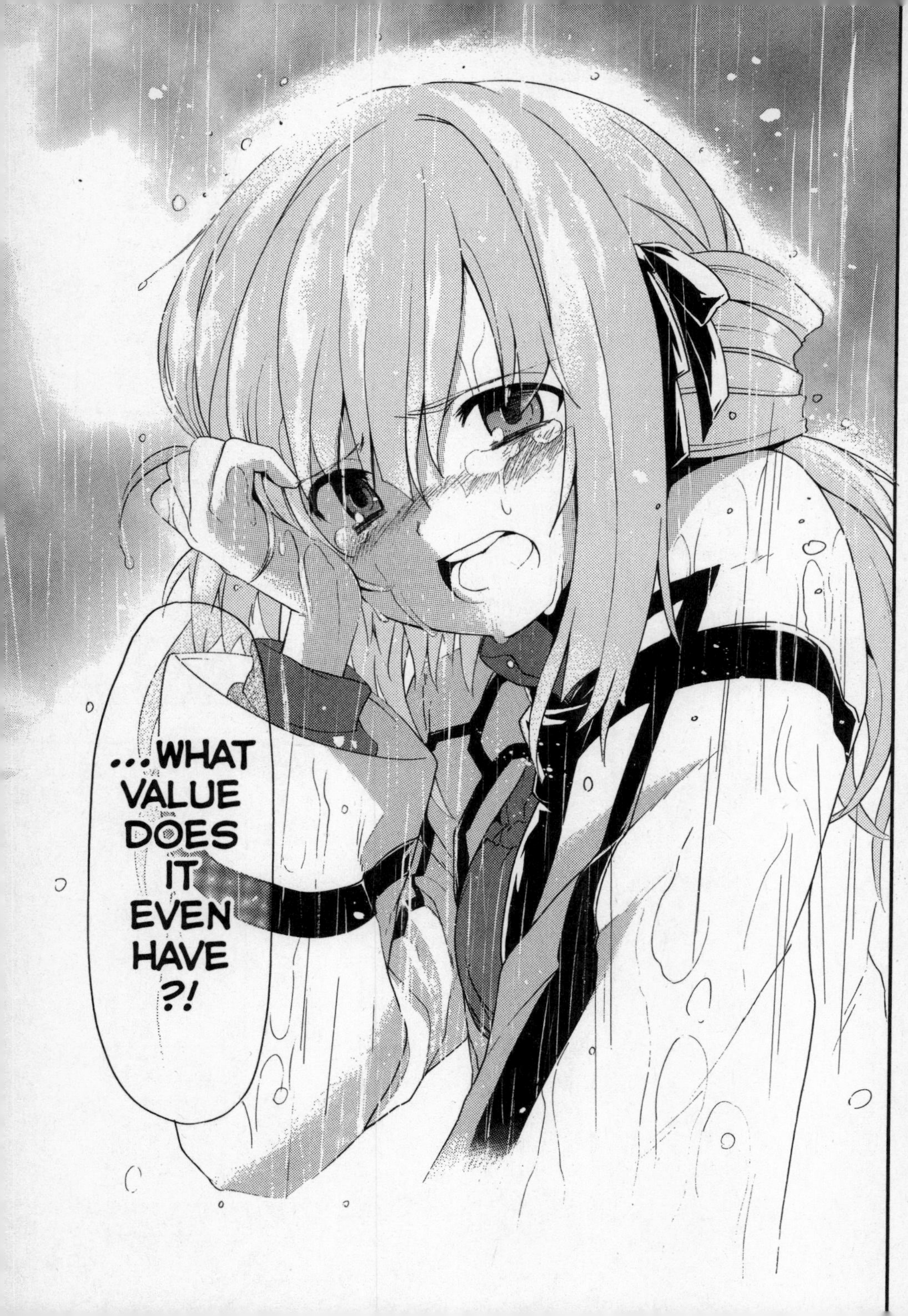
...WHAT VALUE DOES IT EVEN HAVE ?!

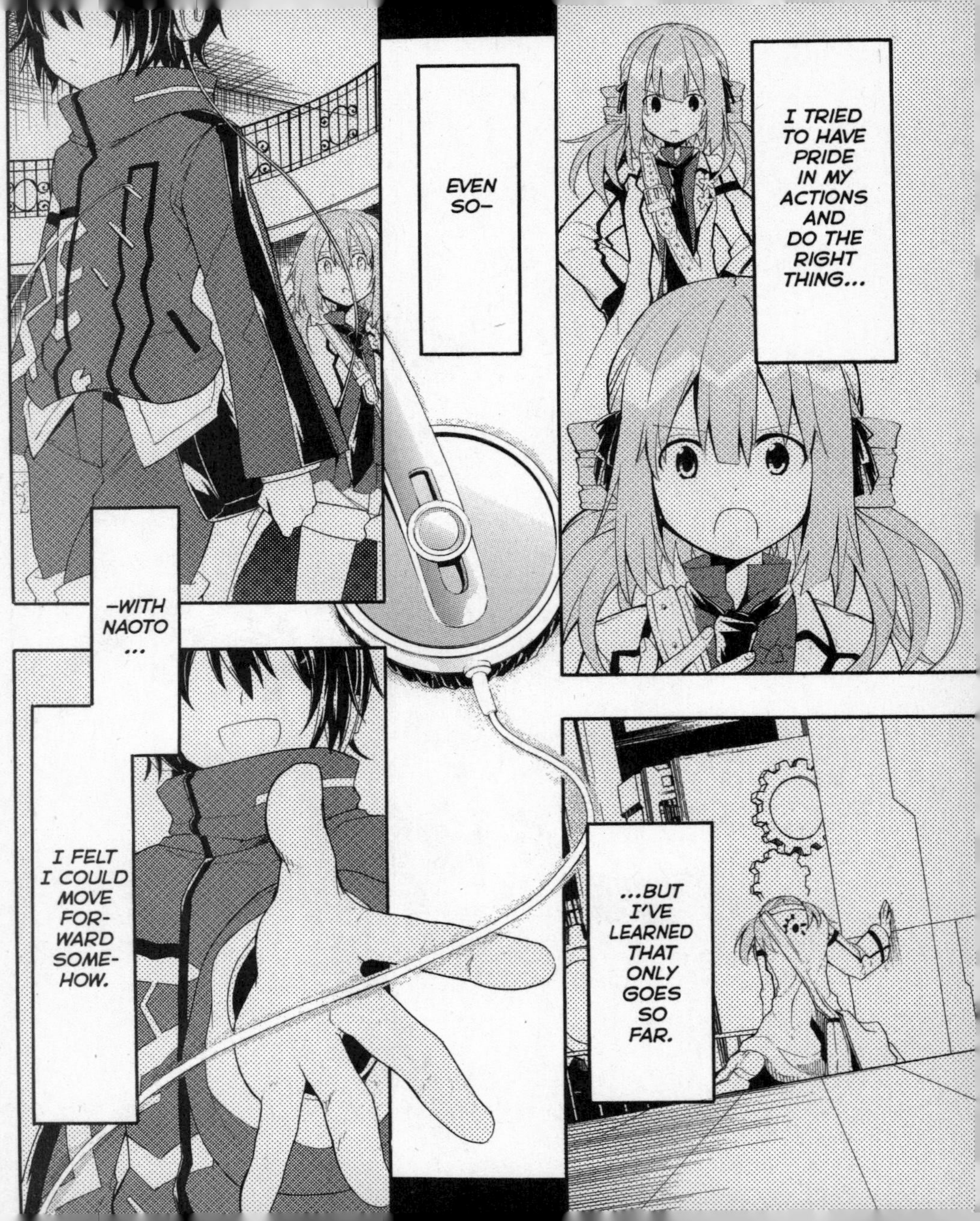
I TRIED TO HAVE PRIDE IN MY ACTIONS AND DO THE RIGHT THING...
...BUT I'VE LEARNED THAT ONLY GOES SO FAR.
EVEN SO—
—WITH NAOTO...
I FELT I COULD MOVE FORWARD SOMEHOW.

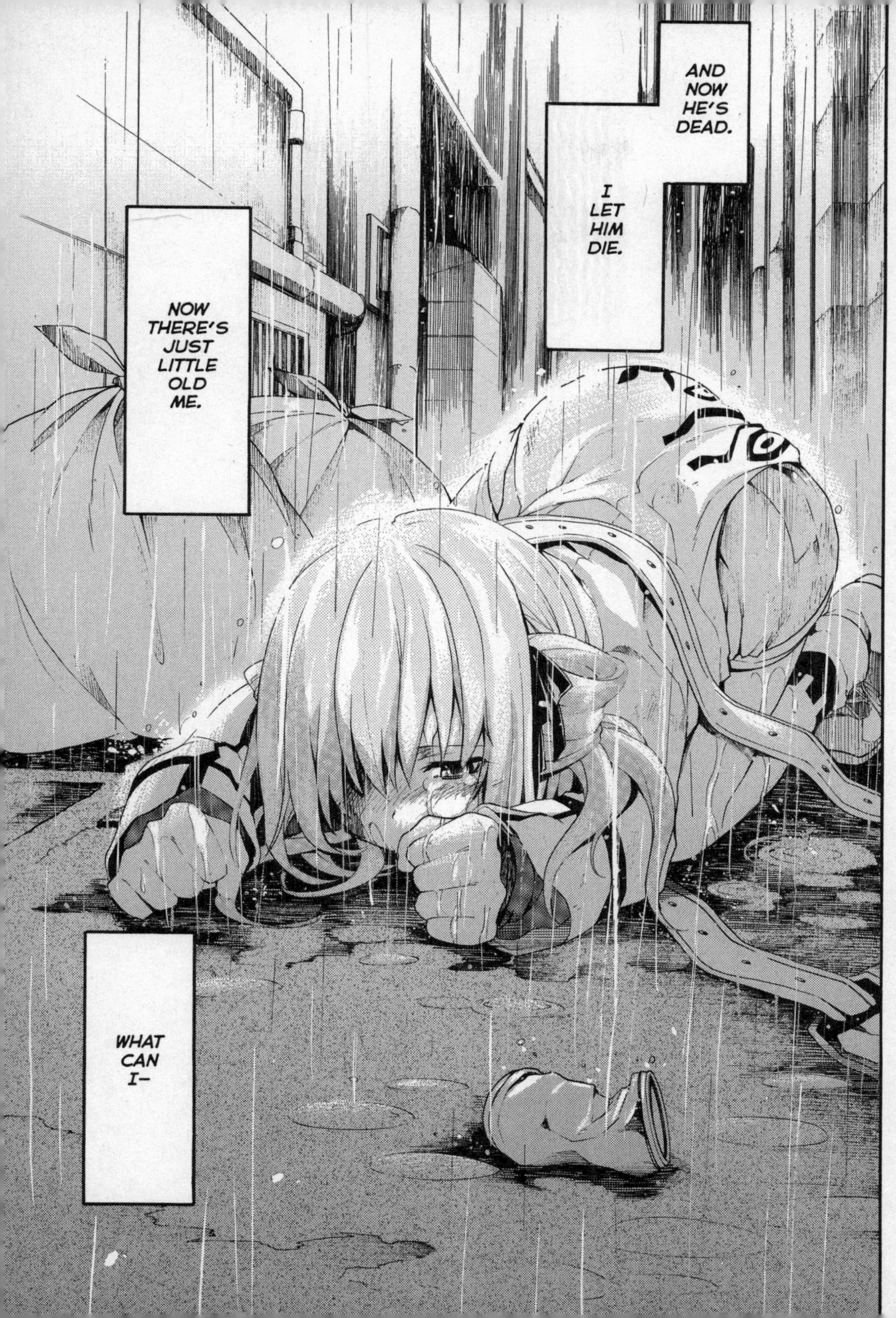
AND NOW HE'S DEAD.
I LET HIM DIE.
NOW THERE'S JUST LITTLE OLD ME.
WHAT CAN I–

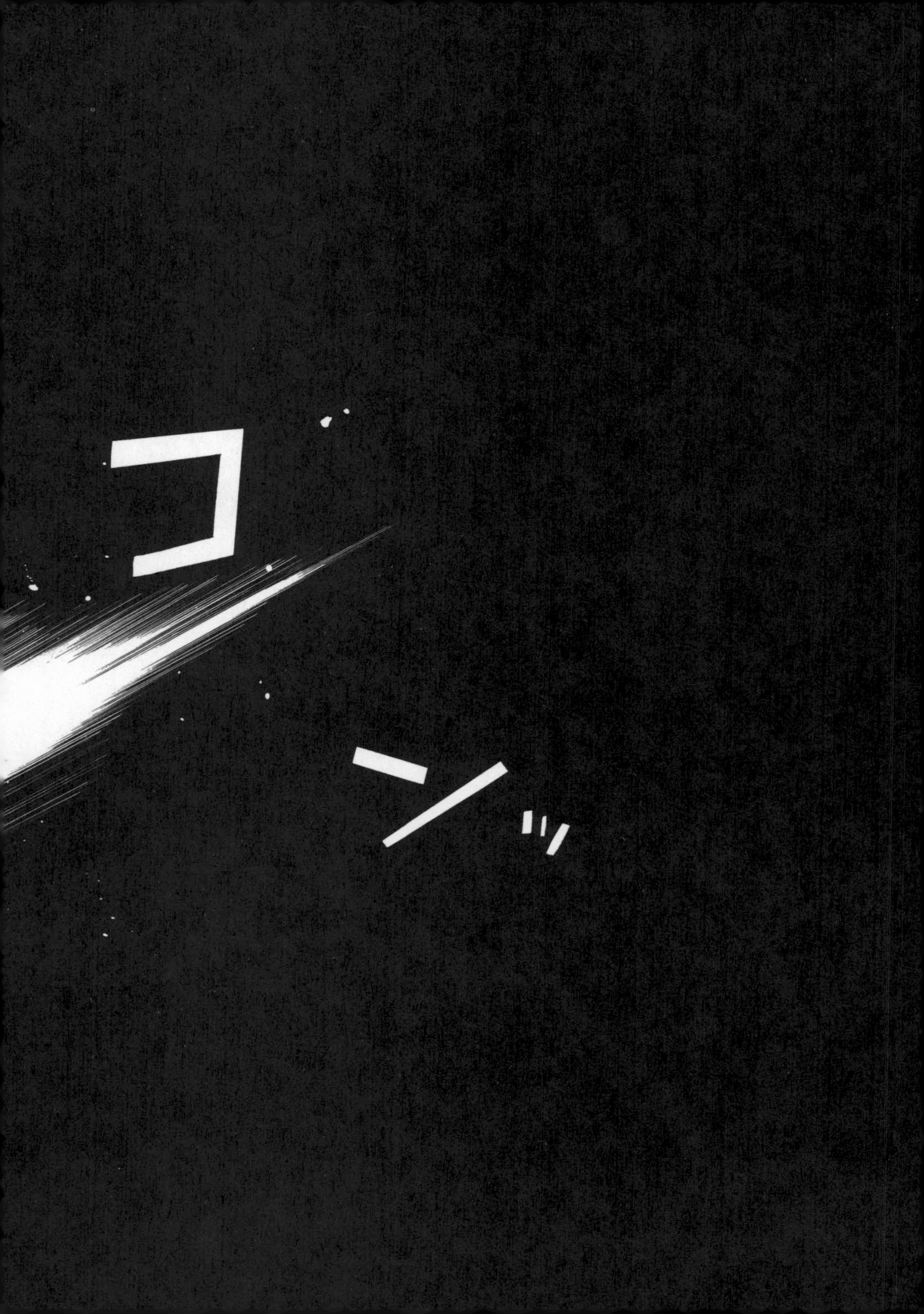
コーンッ

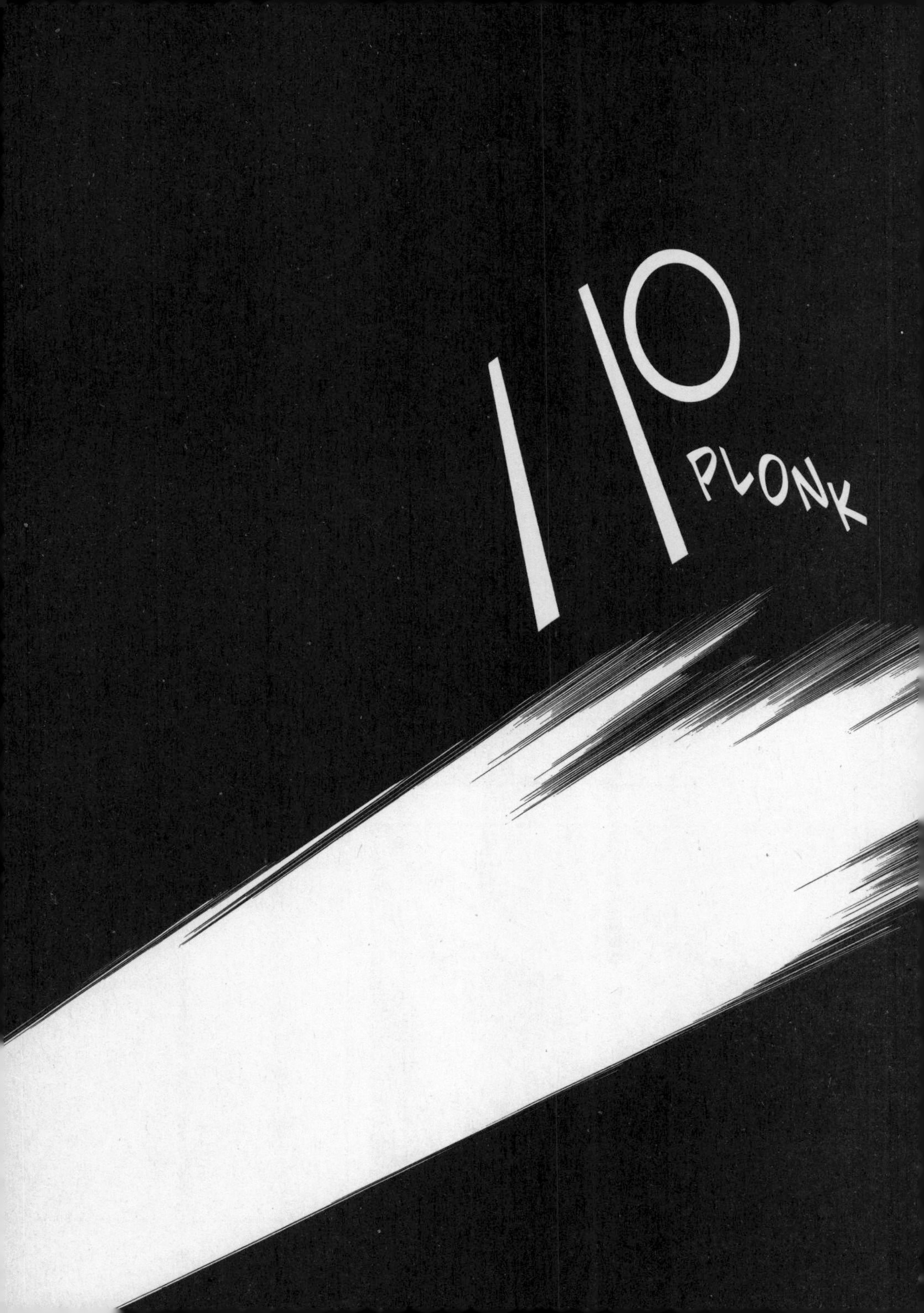
PLONK

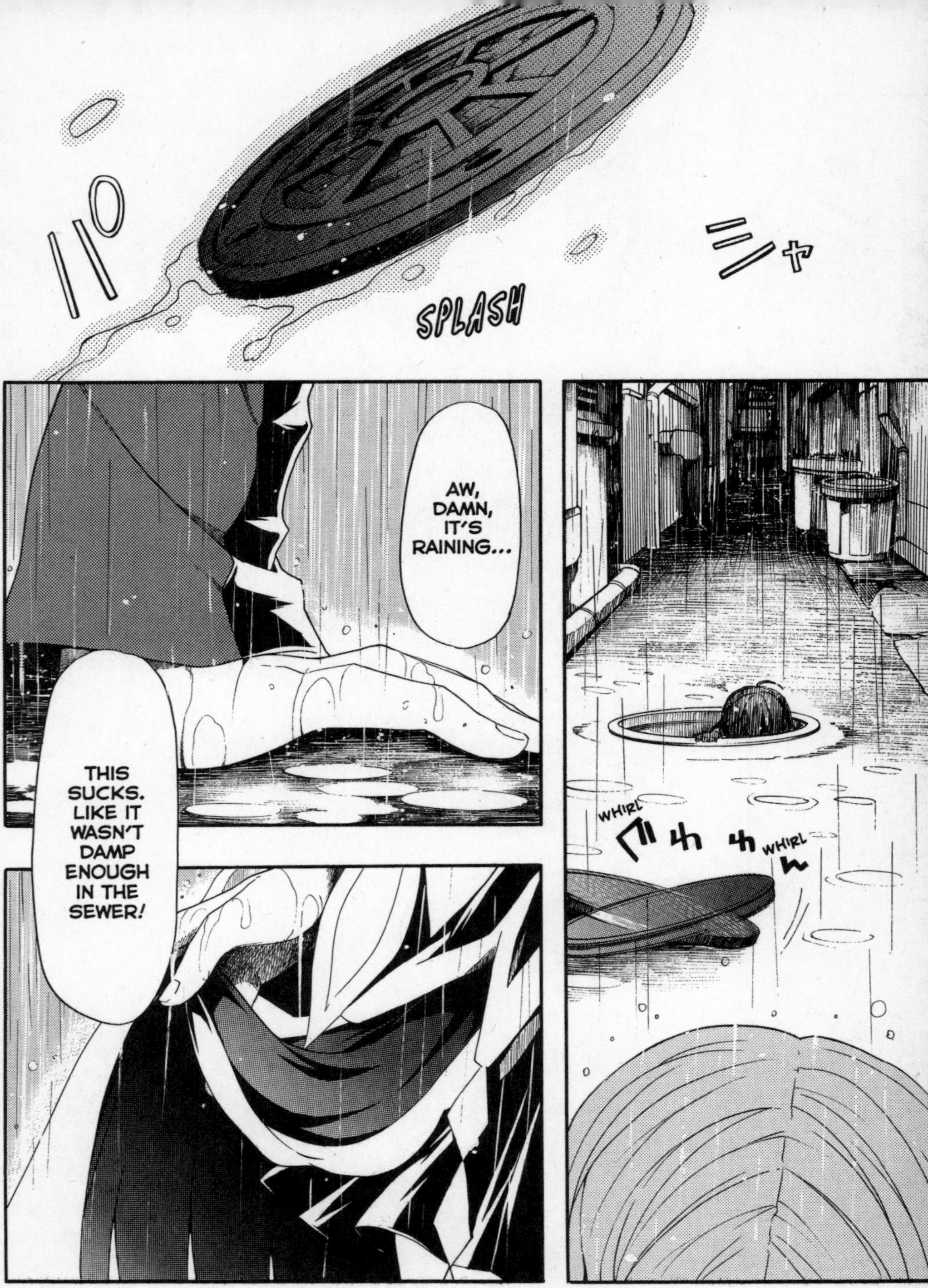
パ
シャ
SPLASH
WHIRL
WHIRL
AW, DAMN, IT'S RAINING...
THIS SUCKS. LIKE IT WASN'T DAMP ENOUGH IN THE SEWER!

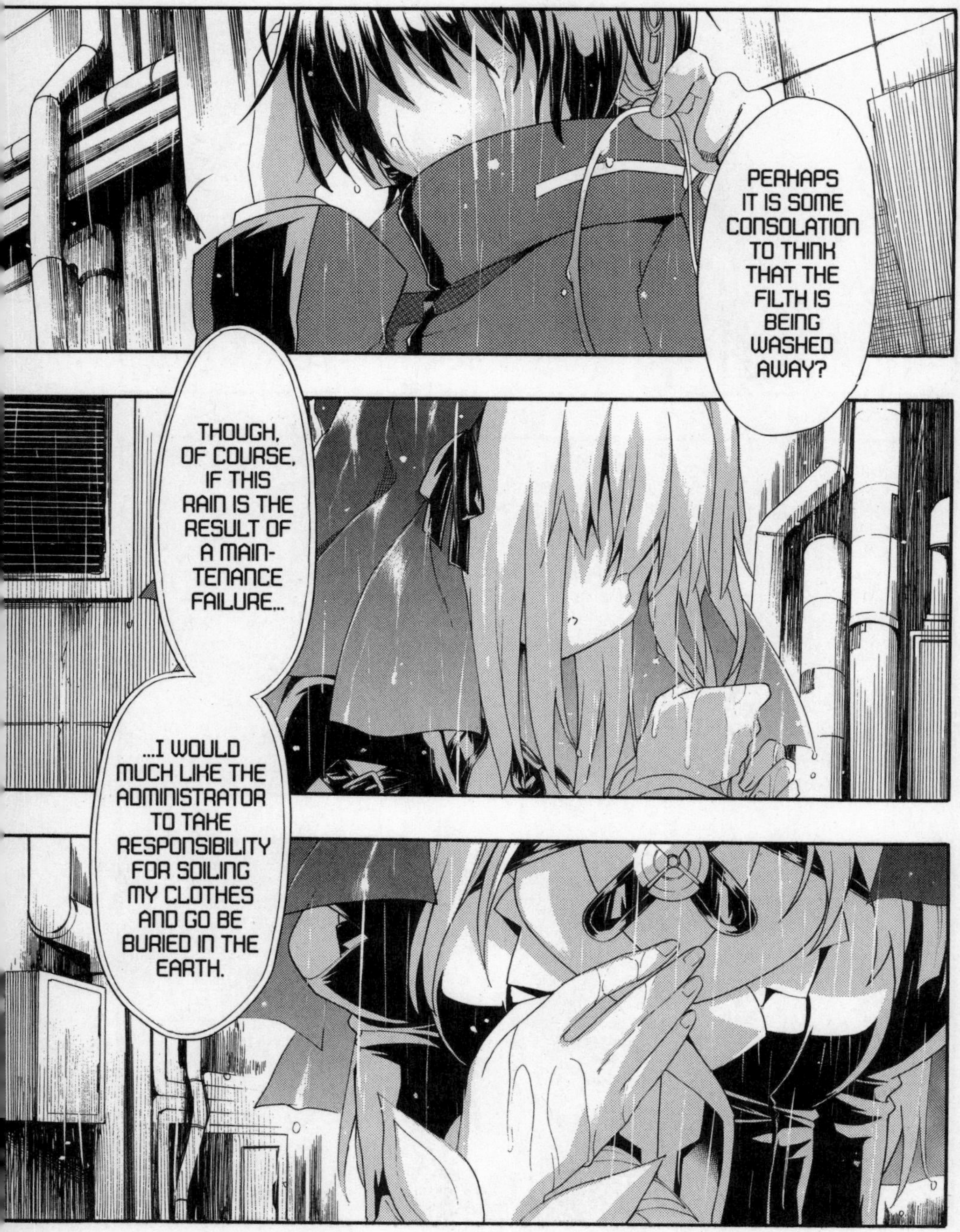

PERHAPS IT IS SOME CONSOLATION TO THINK THAT THE FILTH IS BEING WASHED AWAY?
THOUGH, OF COURSE, IF THIS RAIN IS THE RESULT OF A MAIN-TENANCE FAILURE...
...I WOULD MUCH LIKE THE ADMINISTRATOR TO TAKE RESPONSIBILITY FOR SOILING MY CLOTHES AND GO BE BURIED IN THE EARTH.

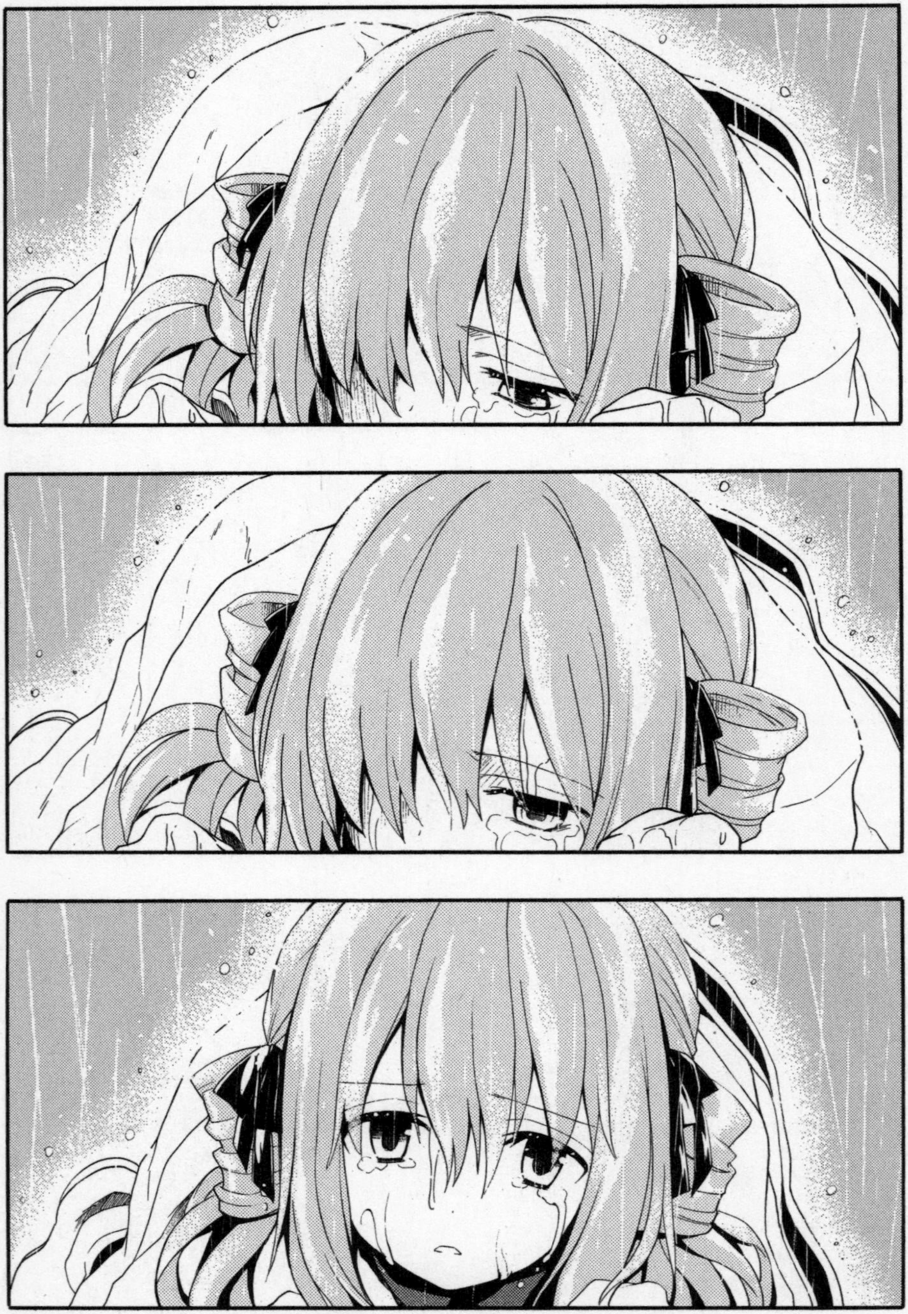

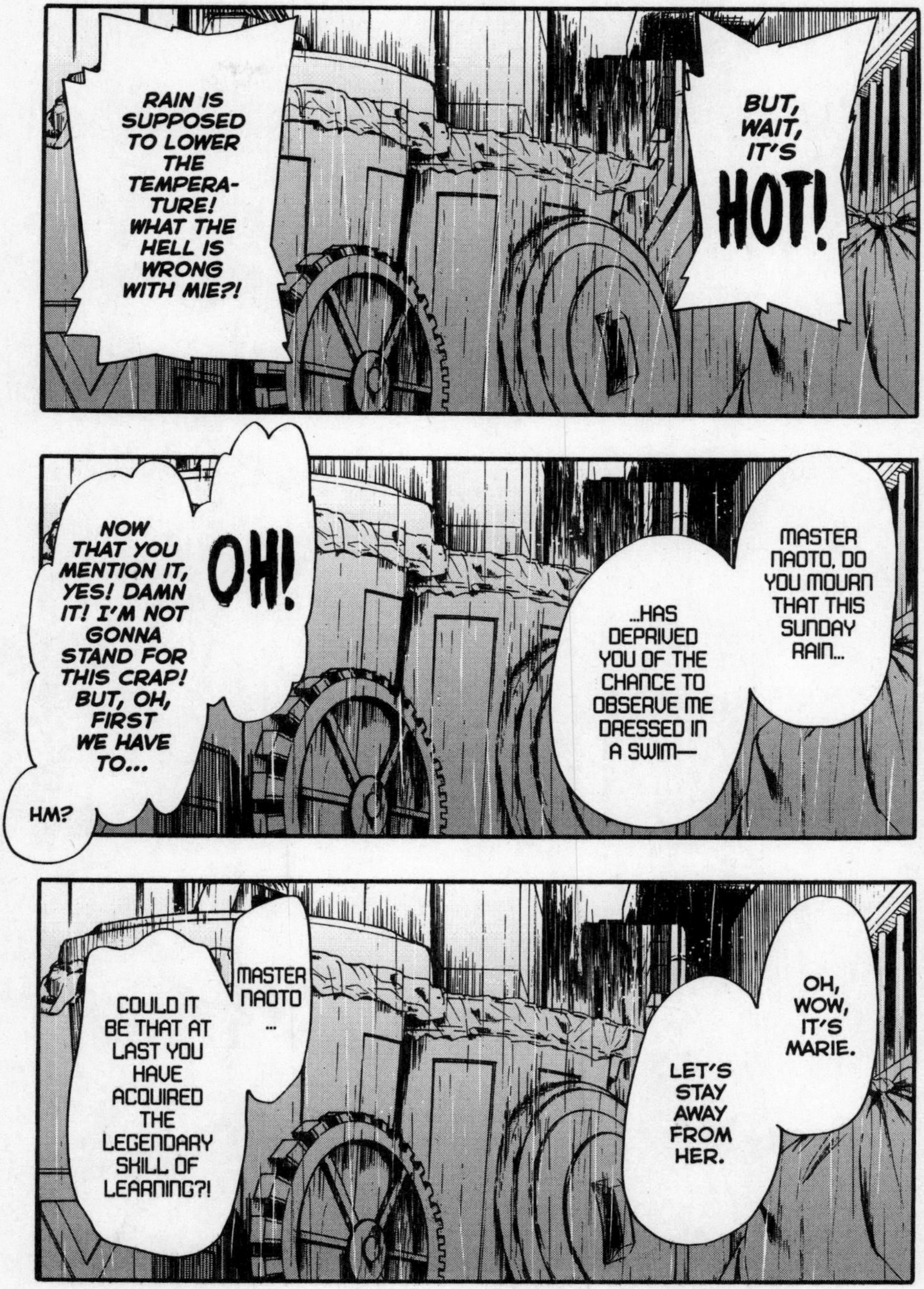
BUT, WAIT, IT'S HOT!
RAIN IS SUPPOSED TO LOWER THE TEMPERA-TURE! WHAT THE HELL IS WRONG WITH MIE?!
MASTER NAOTO, DO YOU MOURN THAT THIS SUNDAY RAIN...
...HAS DEPRIVED YOU OF THE CHANCE TO OBSERVE ME DRESSED IN A SWIM—
OH!
NOW THAT YOU MENTION IT, YES! DAMN IT! I'M NOT GONNA STAND FOR THIS CRAP! BUT, OH, FIRST WE HAVE TO...
HM?
OH, WOW, IT'S MARIE.
LET'S STAY AWAY FROM HER.
MASTER NAOTO ...
COULD IT BE THAT AT LAST YOU HAVE ACQUIRED THE LEGENDARY SKILL OF LEARNING?!

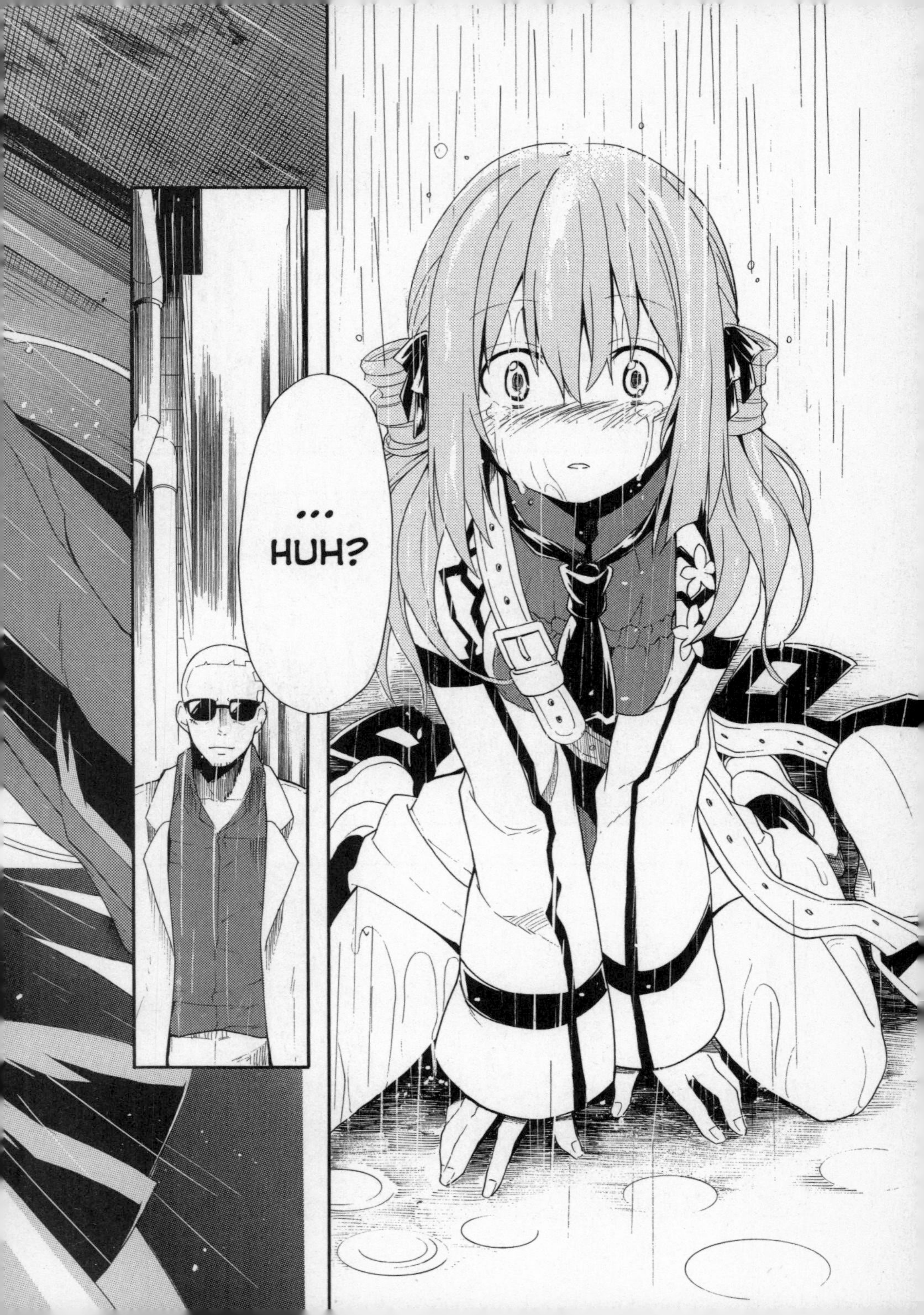
... HUH?

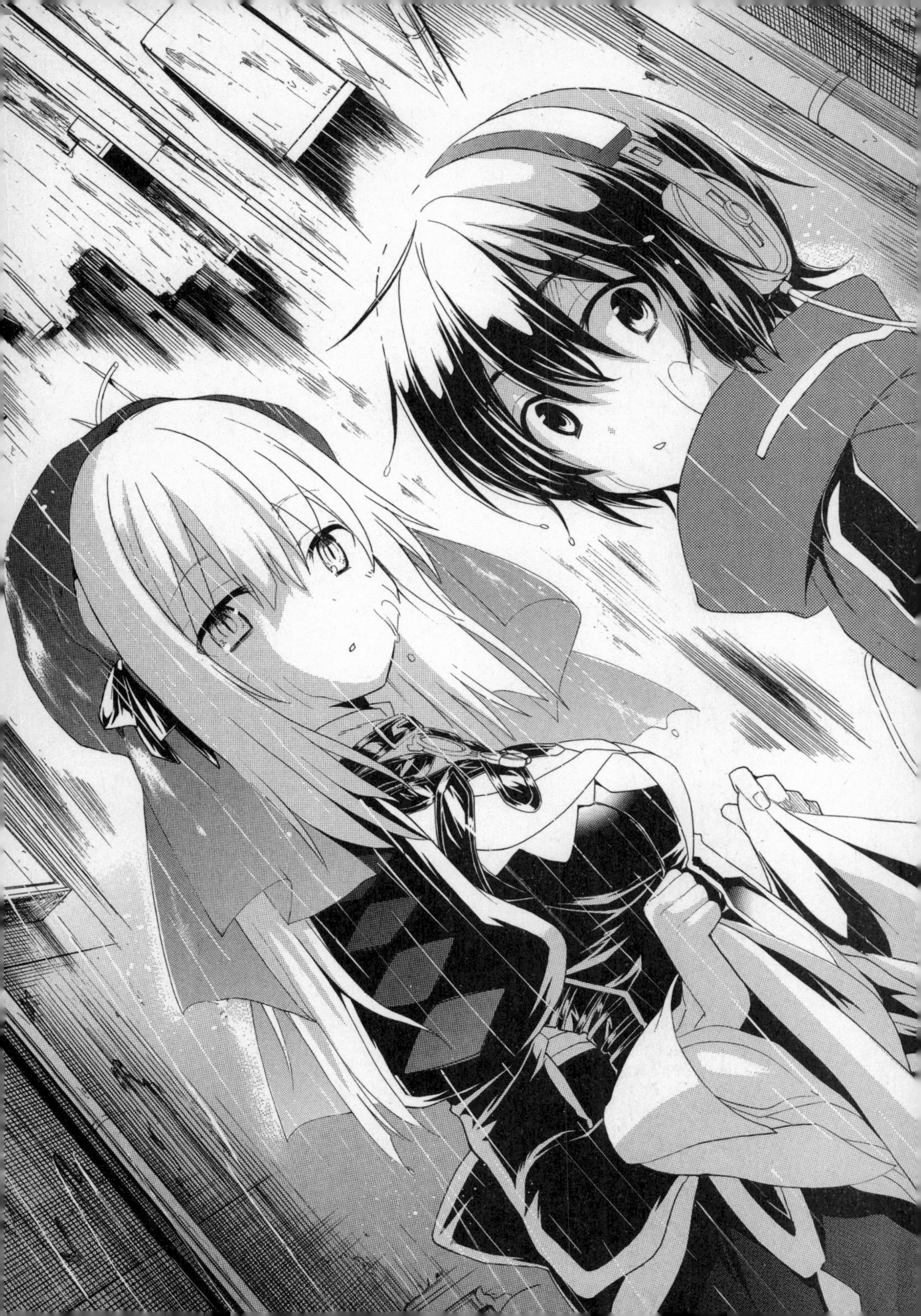

CLOCKWORK
PLANET

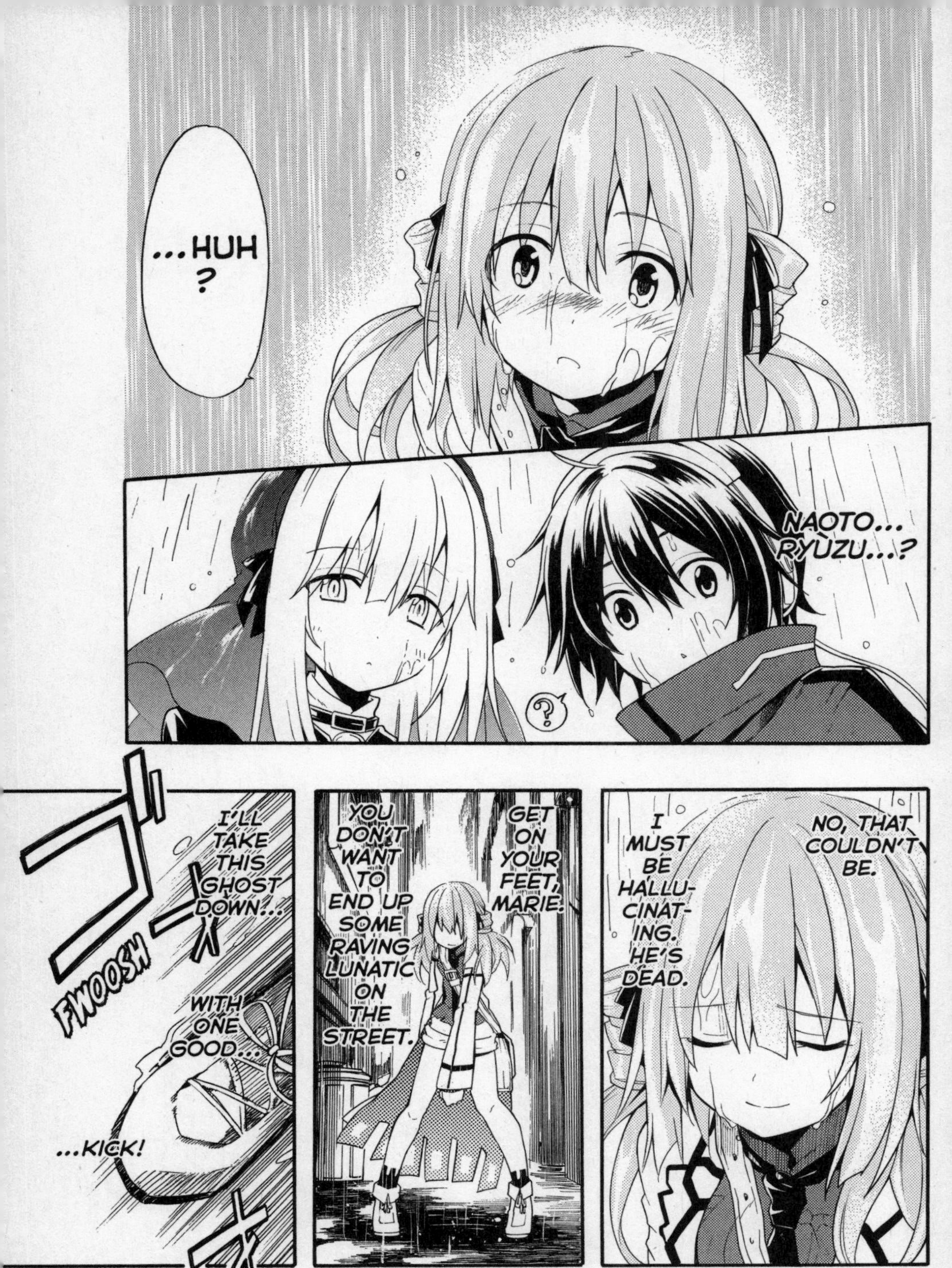
...HUH ?
NAOTO... RYUZU...?
?
NO, THAT COULDN'T BE.
I MUST BE HALLU-CINAT-ING. HE'S DEAD.
GET ON YOUR FEET, MARIE.
YOU DON'T WANT TO END UP SOME RAVING LUNATIC ON THE STREET.
I'LL TAKE THIS GHOST DOWN...
FWOOSH
WITH ONE GOOD...
...KICK!

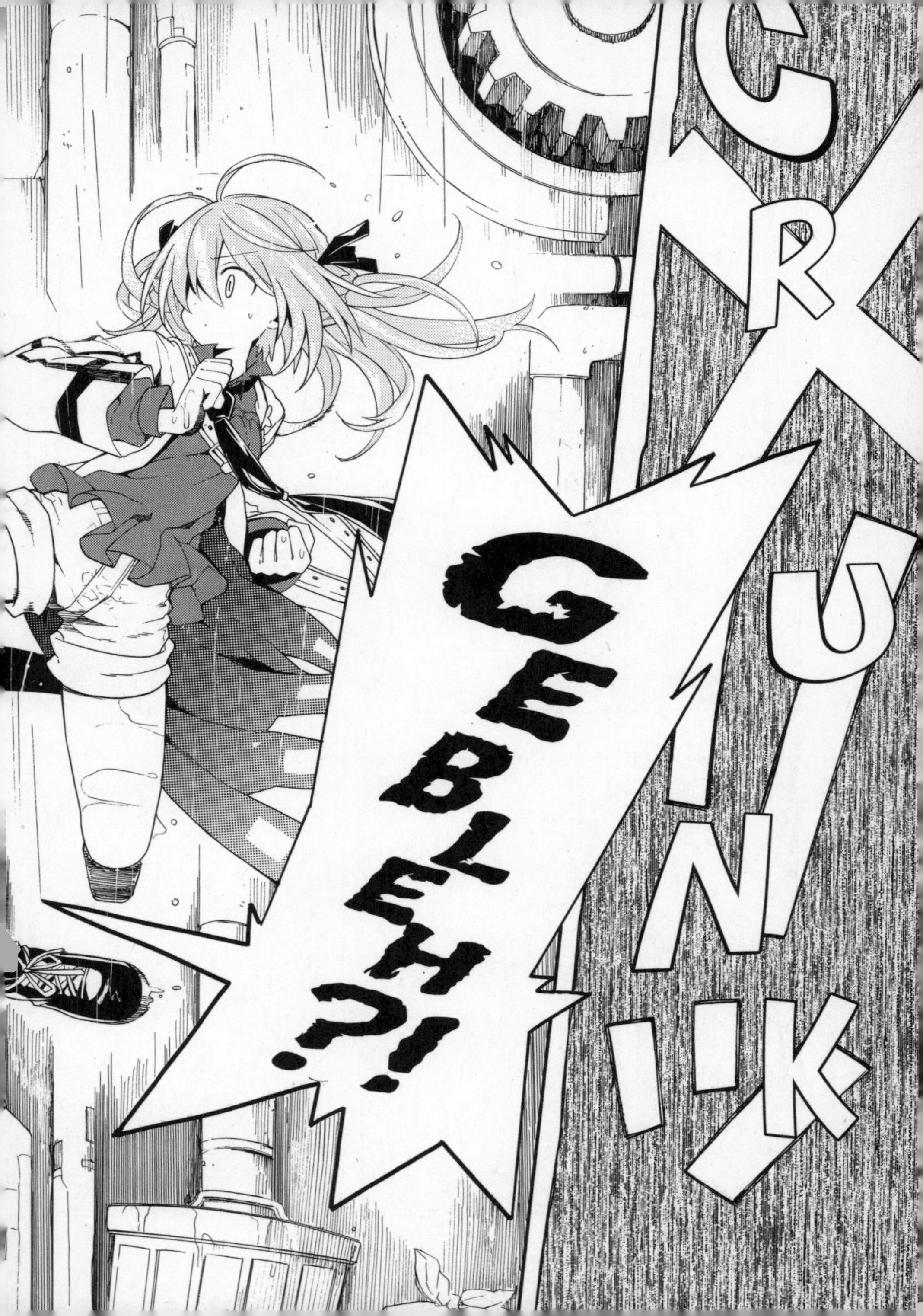
CRUNK
GEBLEH?!

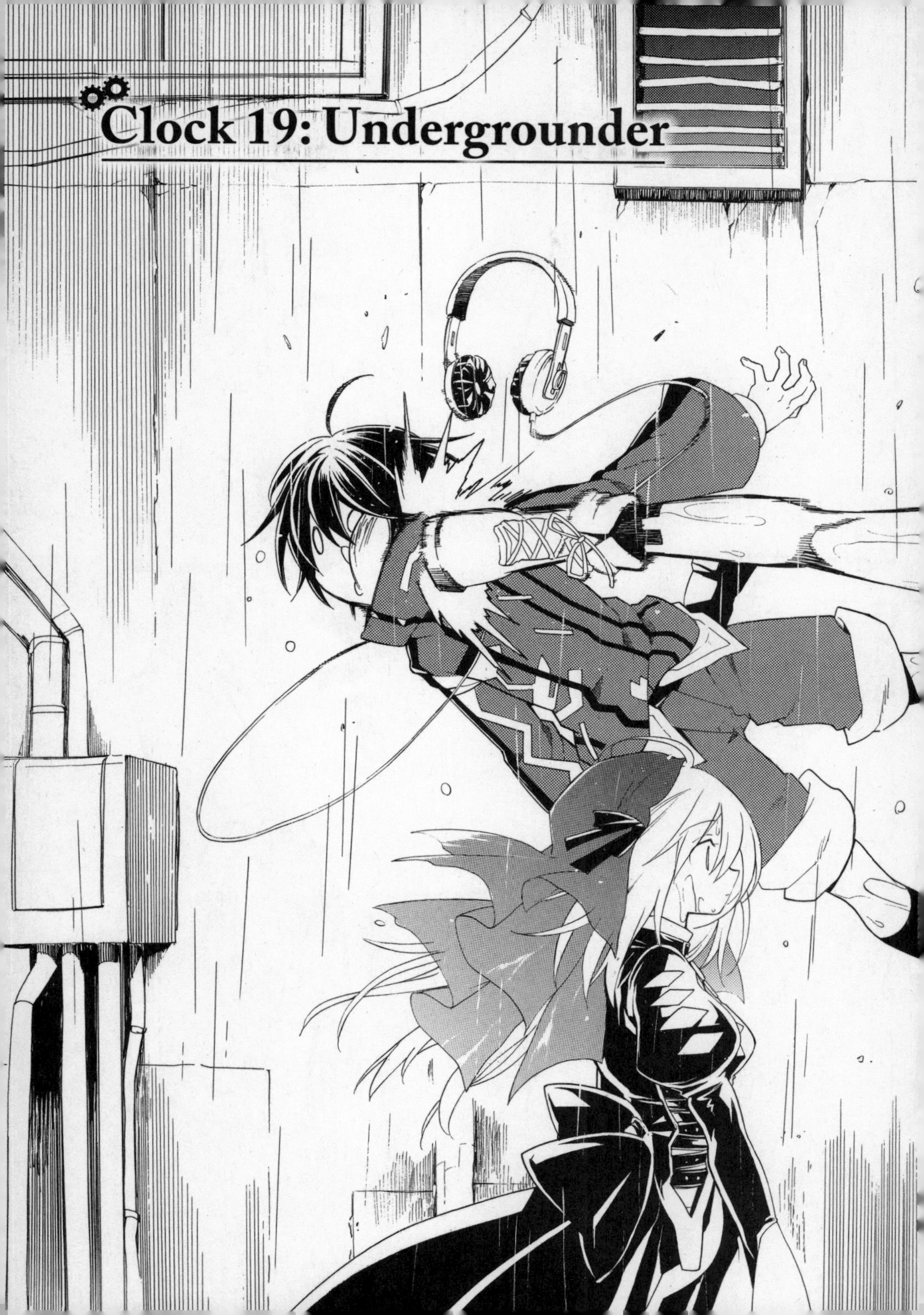
Clock 19: Undergrounder

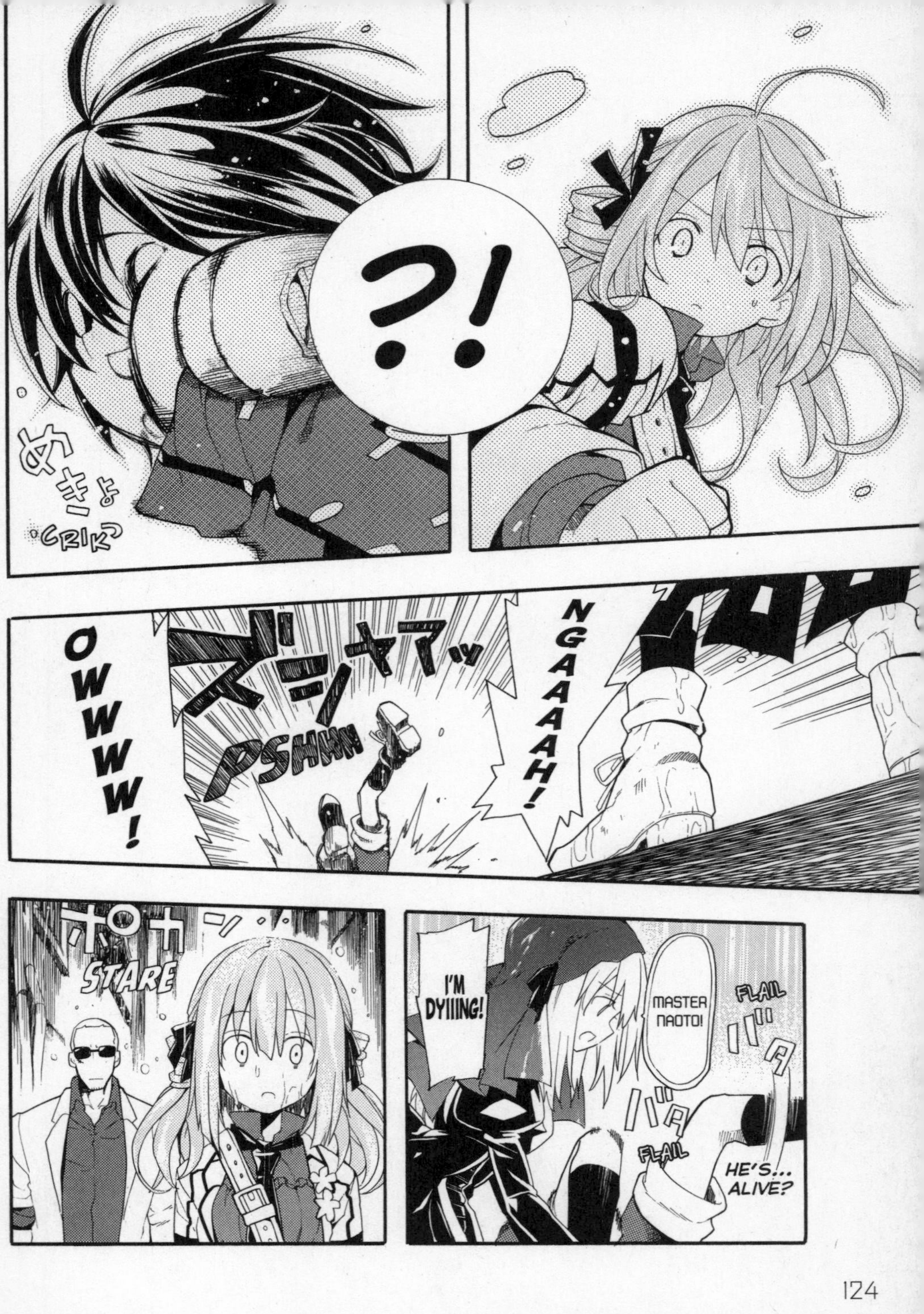
?!
めきょ
CRIK
NGAAAAAH!
ズシャアッ
PSHHH
OWWWWW!
I'M DYIIING!
MASTER NAOTO!
FLAIL
バ
FLAIL
バ
HE'S... ALIVE?
ポカーン
STARE

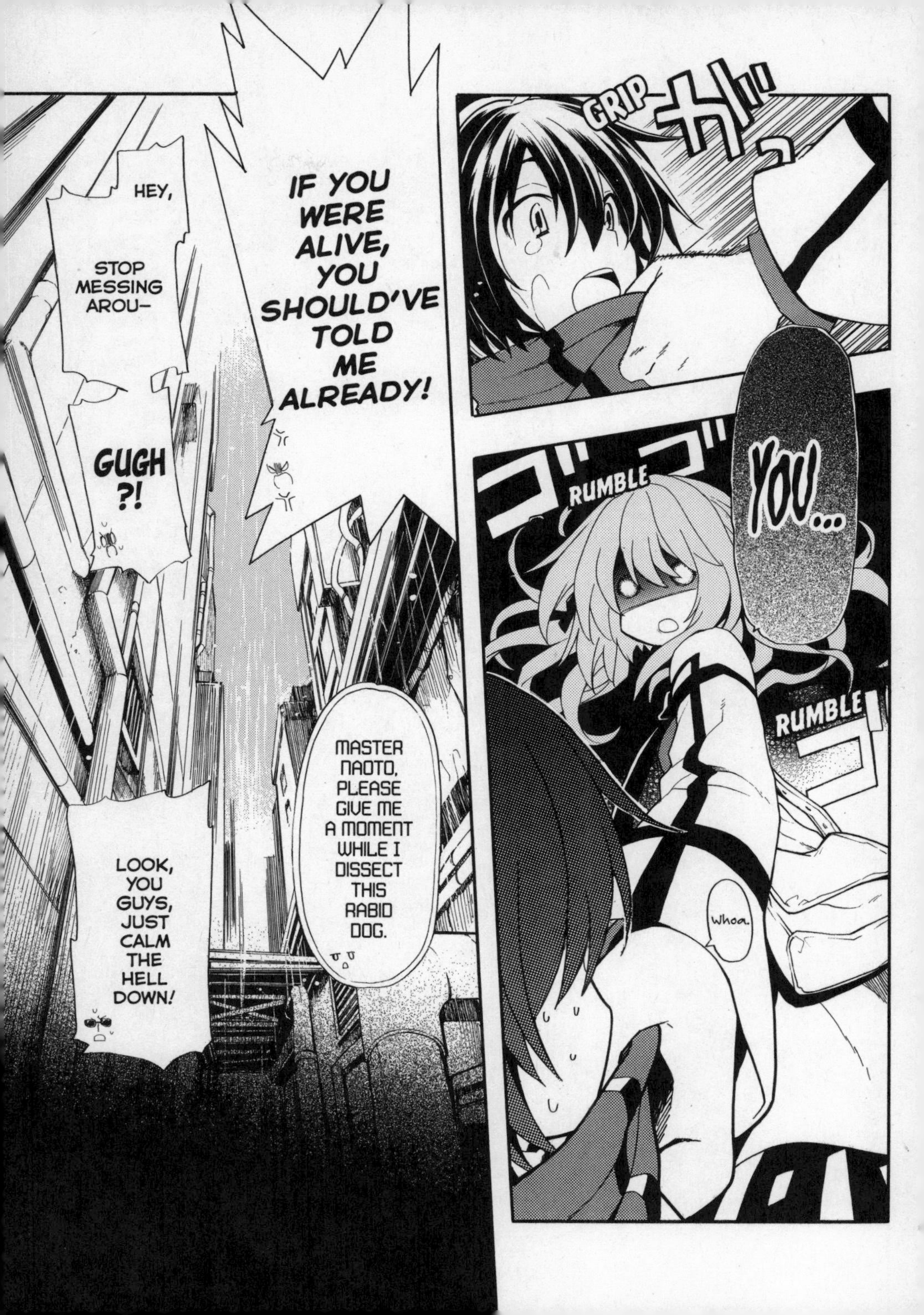
GRIP
YOU...
RUMBLE
RUMBLE
Whoa.
IF YOU WERE ALIVE, YOU SHOULD'VE TOLD ME ALREADY!
HEY,
STOP MESSING AROU-
GUGH?!
MASTER NAOTO, PLEASE GIVE ME A MOMENT WHILE I DISSECT THIS RABID DOG.
LOOK, YOU GUYS, JUST CALM THE HELL DOWN!

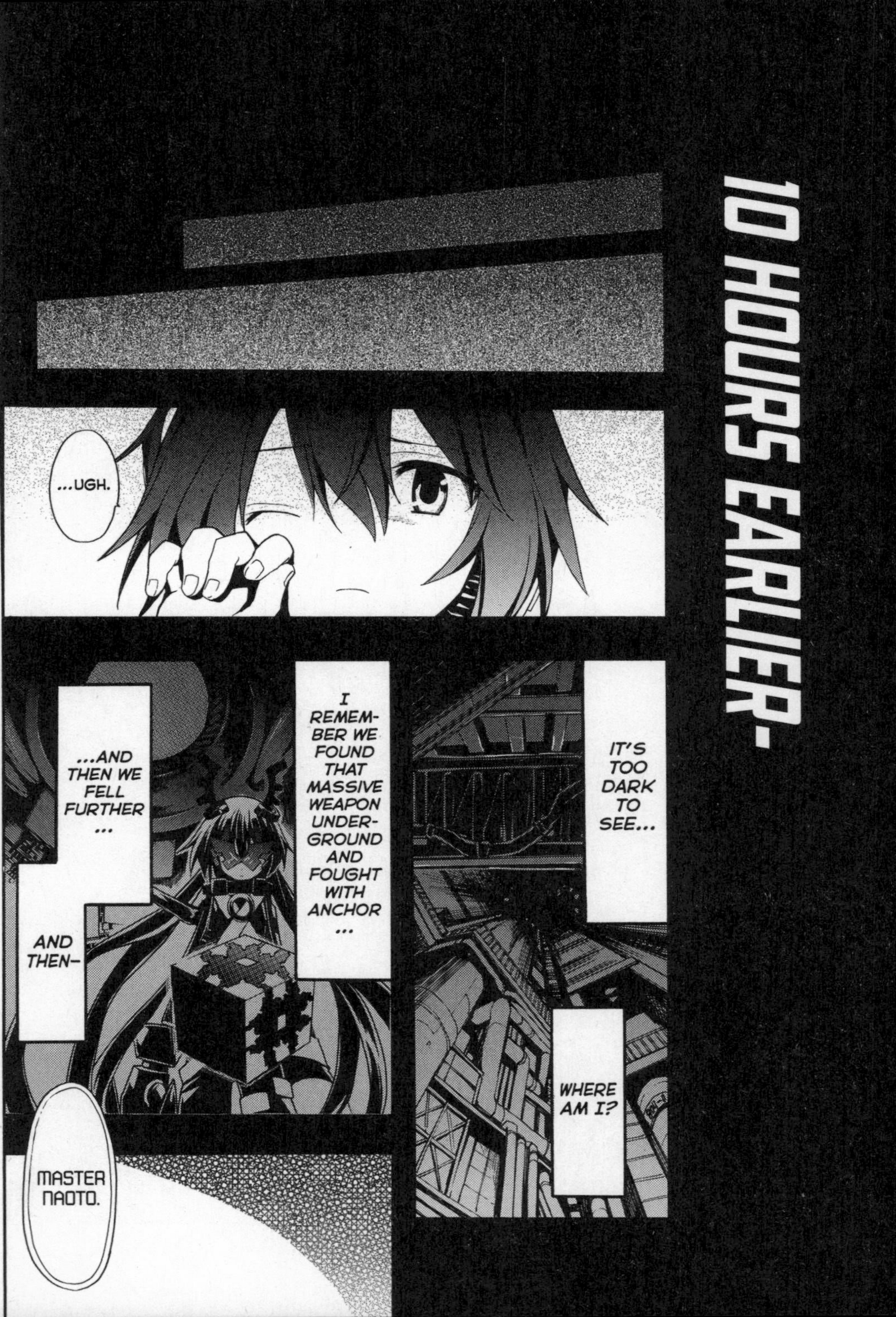
10 HOURS EARLIER-
...UGH.
IT'S TOO DARK TO SEE...
WHERE AM I?
I REMEMBER WE FOUND THAT MASSIVE WEAPON UNDERGROUND AND FOUGHT WITH ANCHOR...
...AND THEN WE FELL FURTHER...
AND THEN-
MASTER NAOTO.

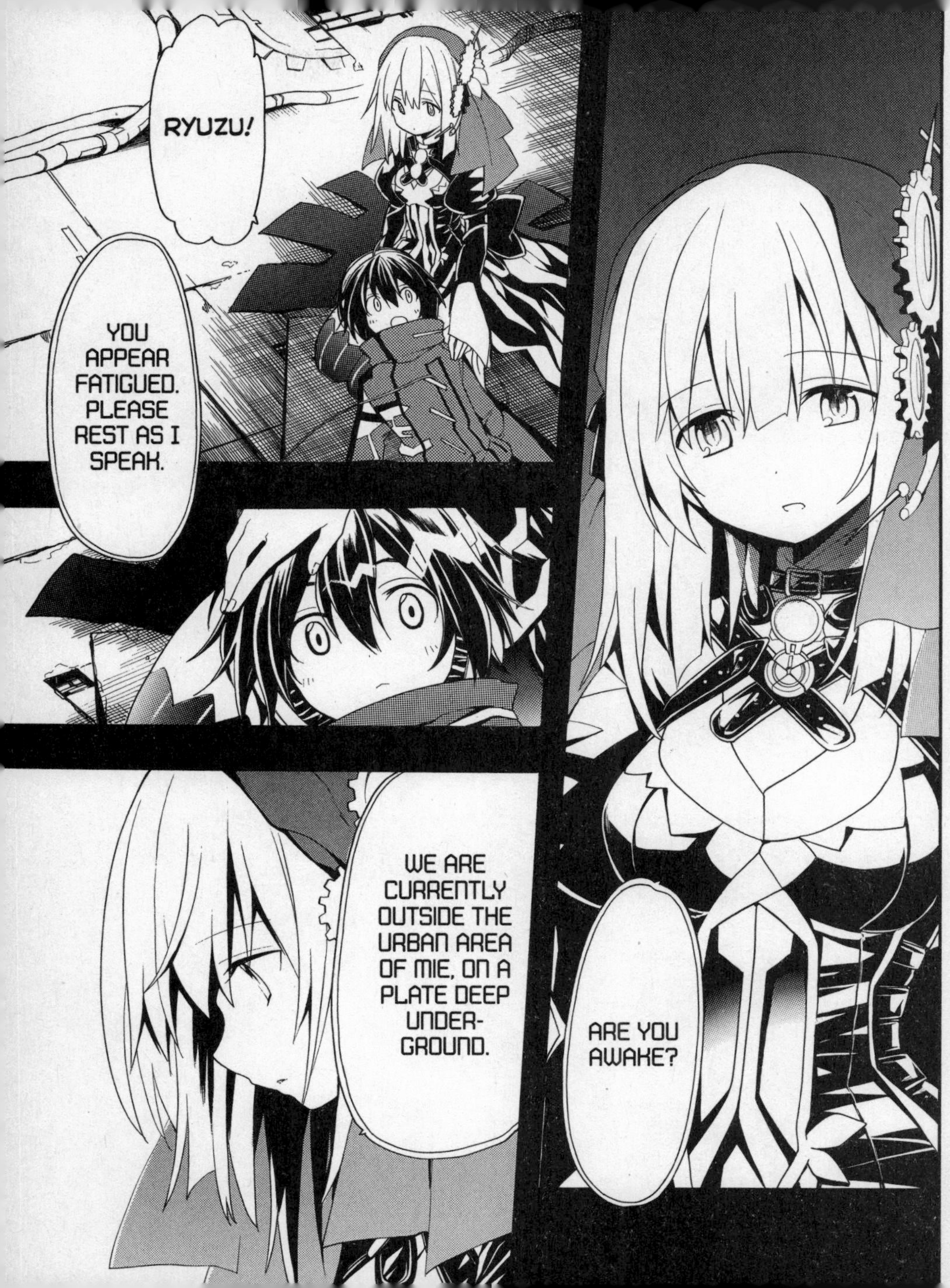
ARE YOU AWAKE?
RYUZU!
YOU APPEAR FATIGUED. PLEASE REST AS I SPEAK.
WE ARE CURRENTLY OUTSIDE THE URBAN AREA OF MIE, ON A PLATE DEEP UNDER-GROUND.

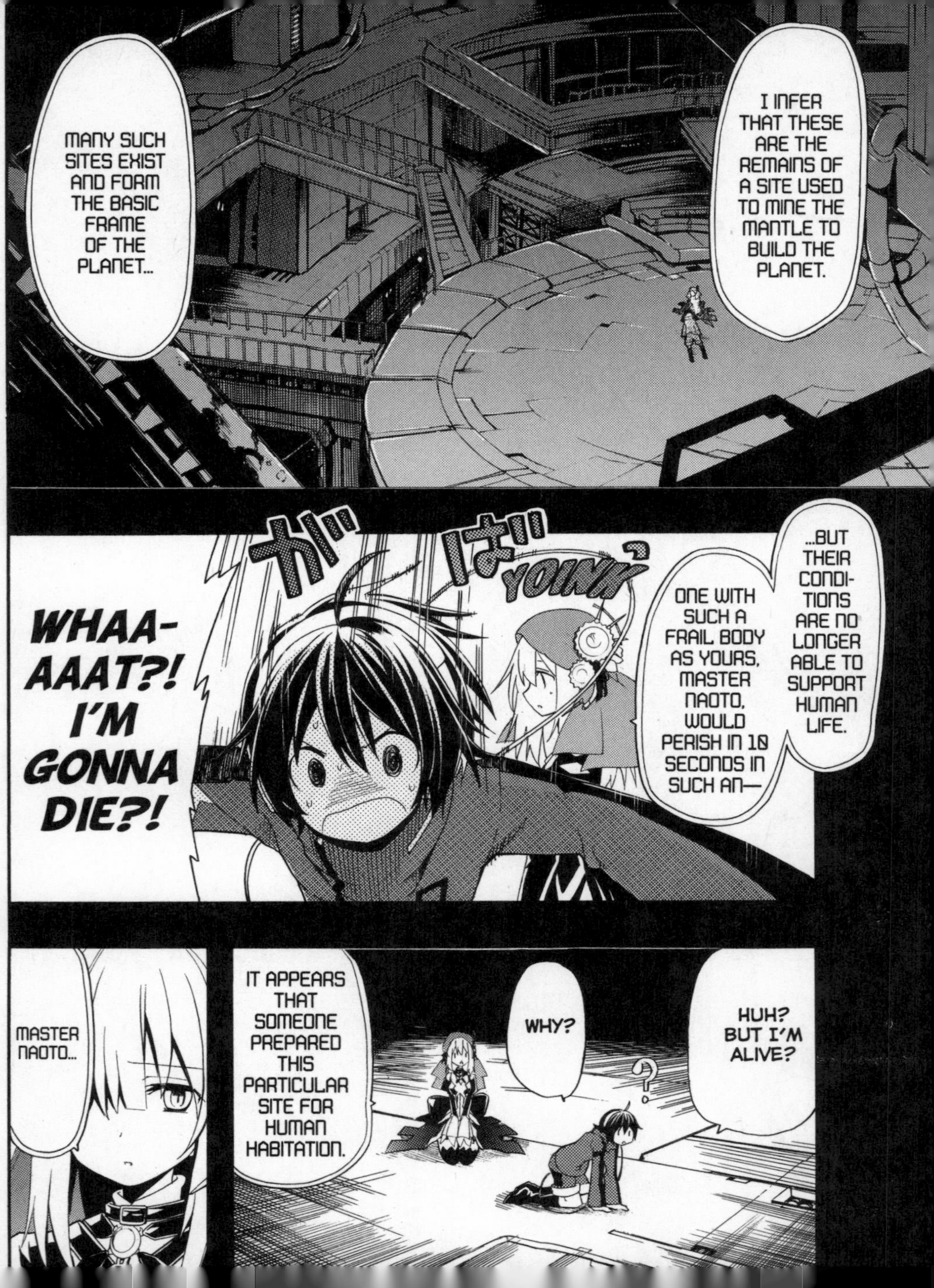
I INFER THAT THESE ARE THE REMAINS OF A SITE USED TO MINE THE MANTLE TO BUILD THE PLANET.
MANY SUCH SITES EXIST AND FORM THE BASIC FRAME OF THE PLANET...
...BUT THEIR CONDITIONS ARE NO LONGER ABLE TO SUPPORT HUMAN LIFE.
ONE WITH SUCH A FRAIL BODY AS YOURS, MASTER NAOTO, WOULD PERISH IN 10 SECONDS IN SUCH AN—
がば
YOINK
WHAA-AAAT?! I'M GONNA DIE?!
HUH? BUT I'M ALIVE?
?
WHY?
IT APPEARS THAT SOMEONE PREPARED THIS PARTICULAR SITE FOR HUMAN HABITATION.
MASTER NAOTO...

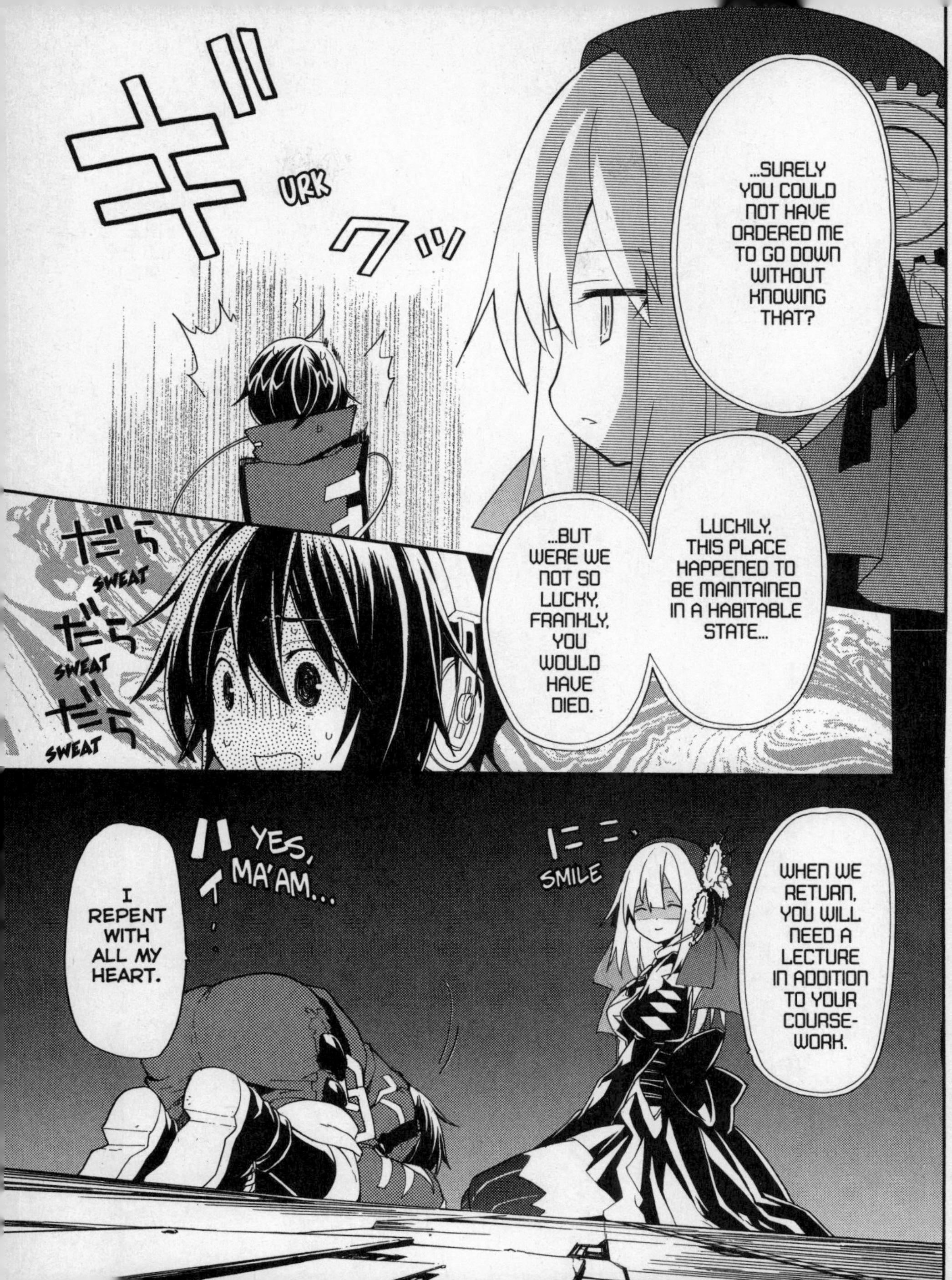
...SURELY YOU COULD NOT HAVE ORDERED ME TO GO DOWN WITHOUT KNOWING THAT?
ギクッ
URK
LUCKILY, THIS PLACE HAPPENED TO BE MAINTAINED IN A HABITABLE STATE...
...BUT WERE WE NOT SO LUCKY, FRANKLY, YOU WOULD HAVE DIED.
だら
SWEAT
だら
SWEAT
だら
SWEAT
にこ
SMILE
WHEN WE RETURN, YOU WILL NEED A LECTURE IN ADDITION TO YOUR COURSE-WORK.
ハイ
YES, MA'AM...
I REPENT WITH ALL MY HEART.

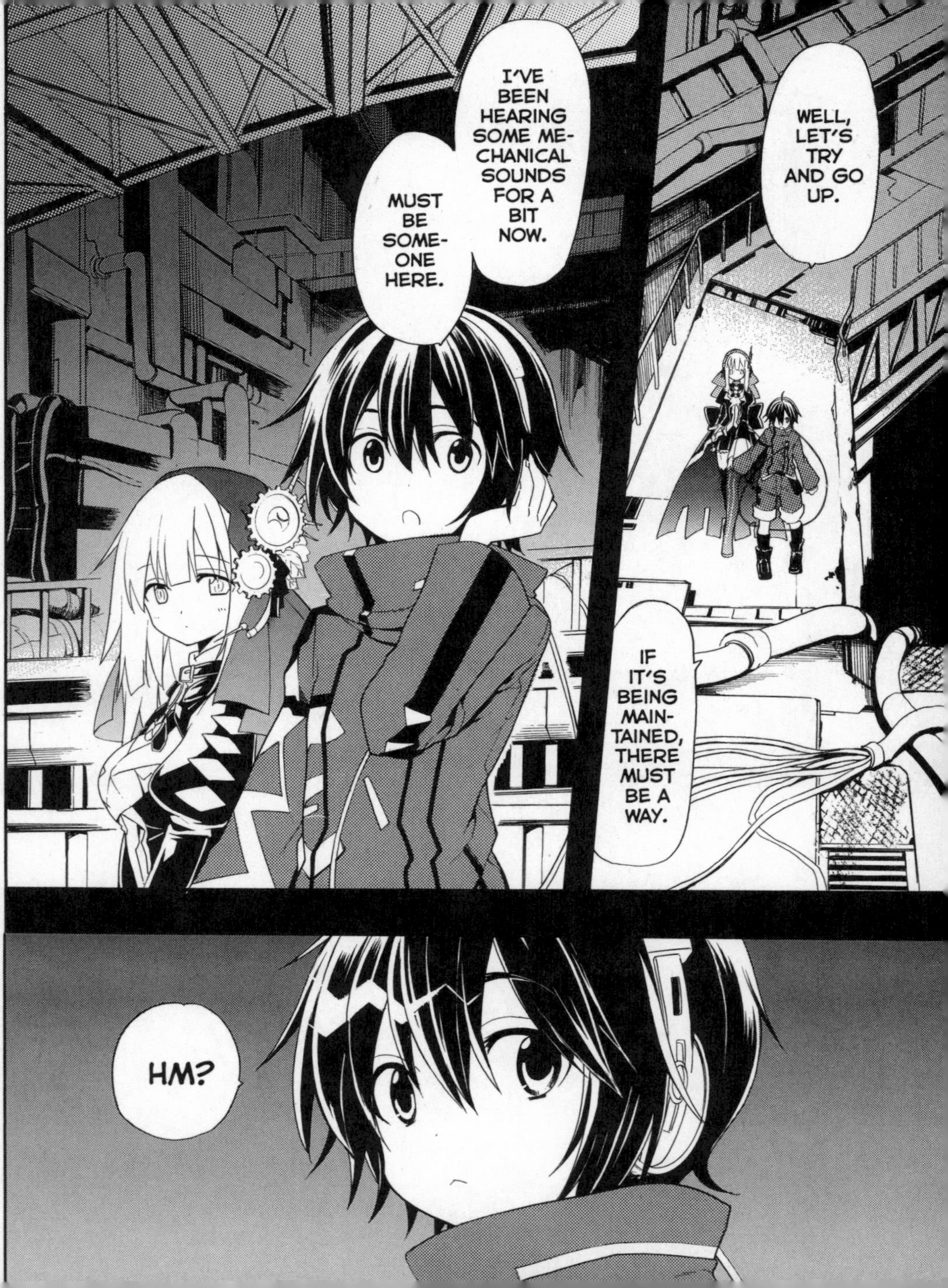
WELL, LET'S TRY AND GO UP.
IF IT'S BEING MAIN-TAINED, THERE MUST BE A WAY.
I'VE BEEN HEARING SOME ME-CHANICAL SOUNDS FOR A BIT NOW.
MUST BE SOME-ONE HERE.
HM?

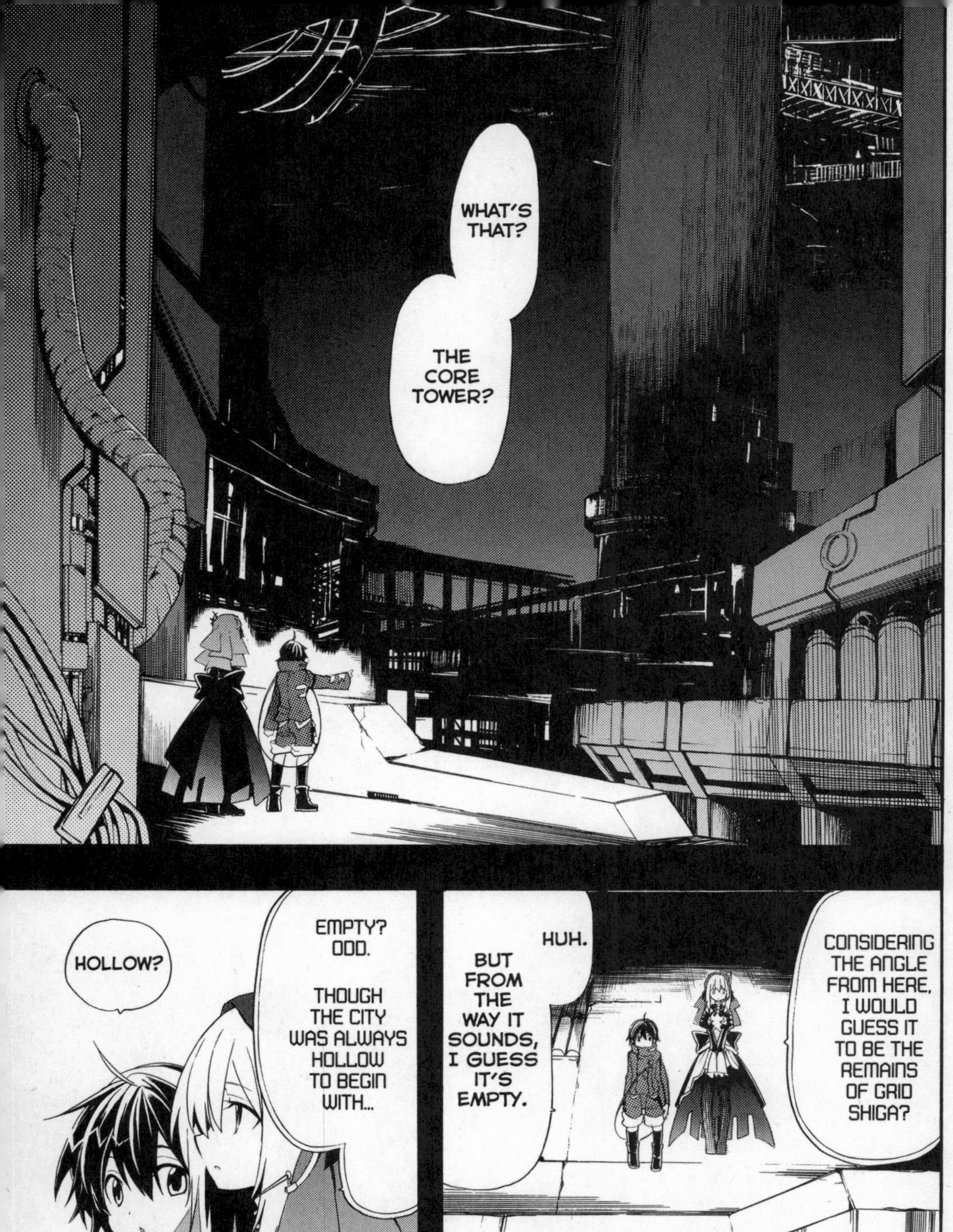
WHAT'S THAT?
THE CORE TOWER?
CONSIDERING THE ANGLE FROM HERE, I WOULD GUESS IT TO BE THE REMAINS OF GRID SHIGA?
HUH.
BUT FROM THE WAY IT SOUNDS, I GUESS IT'S EMPTY.
EMPTY? ODD.
THOUGH THE CITY WAS ALWAYS HOLLOW TO BEGIN WITH...
HOLLOW?

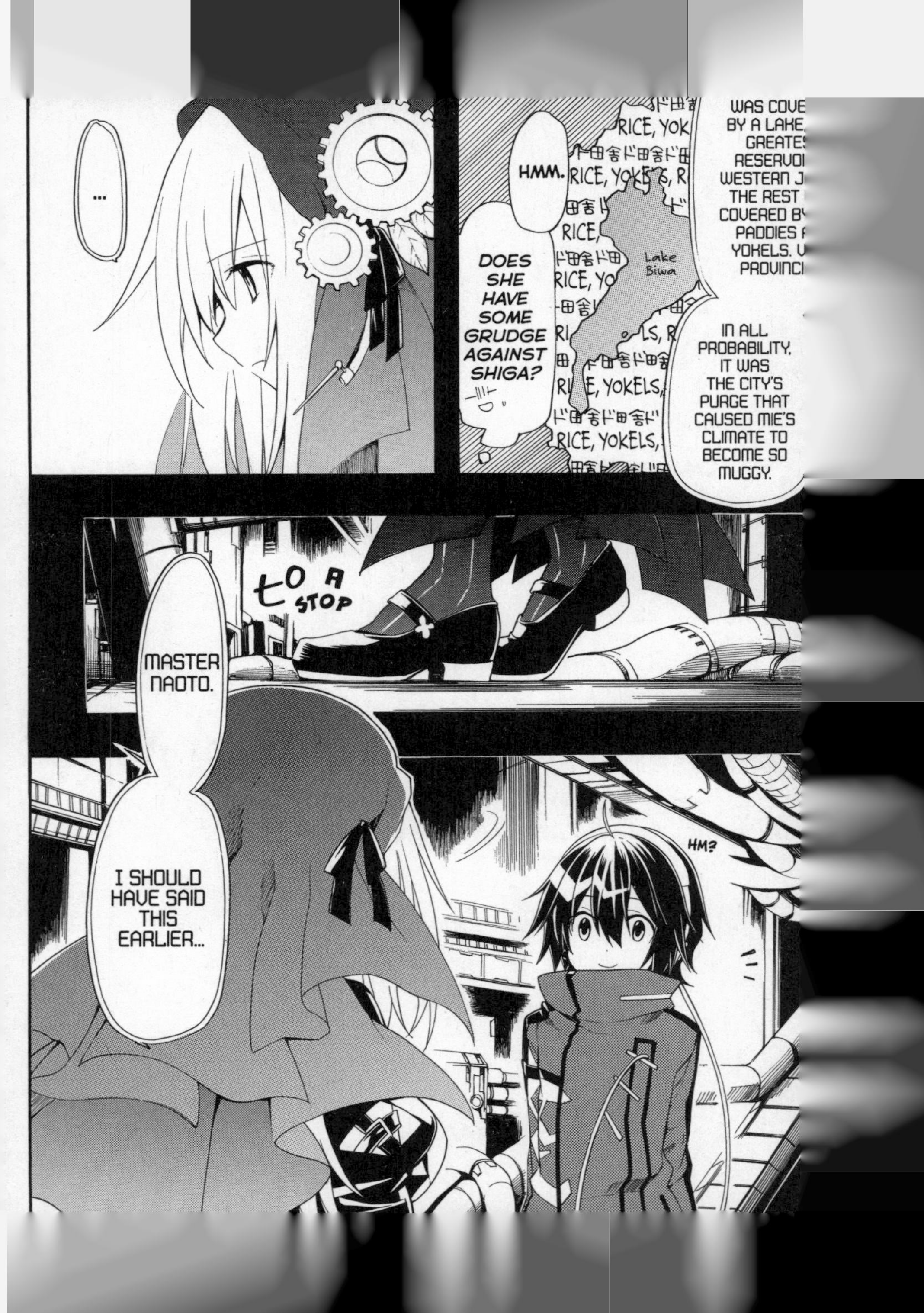

WAS COVE
BY A LAKE,
GREATES
RESERVOI
WESTERN J
THE REST
COVERED BY
PADDIES A
YOKELS. V
PROVINCI
IN ALL PROBABILITY, IT WAS THE CITY'S PURGE THAT CAUSED MIE'S CLIMATE TO BECOME SO MUGGY.
RICE, YOKELS,
ド田舎ド田舎ド
Lake Biwa
HMM.
DOES SHE HAVE SOME GRUDGE AGAINST SHIGA?
...
A STOP
MASTER NAOTO.
HM?
I SHOULD HAVE SAID THIS EARLIER...

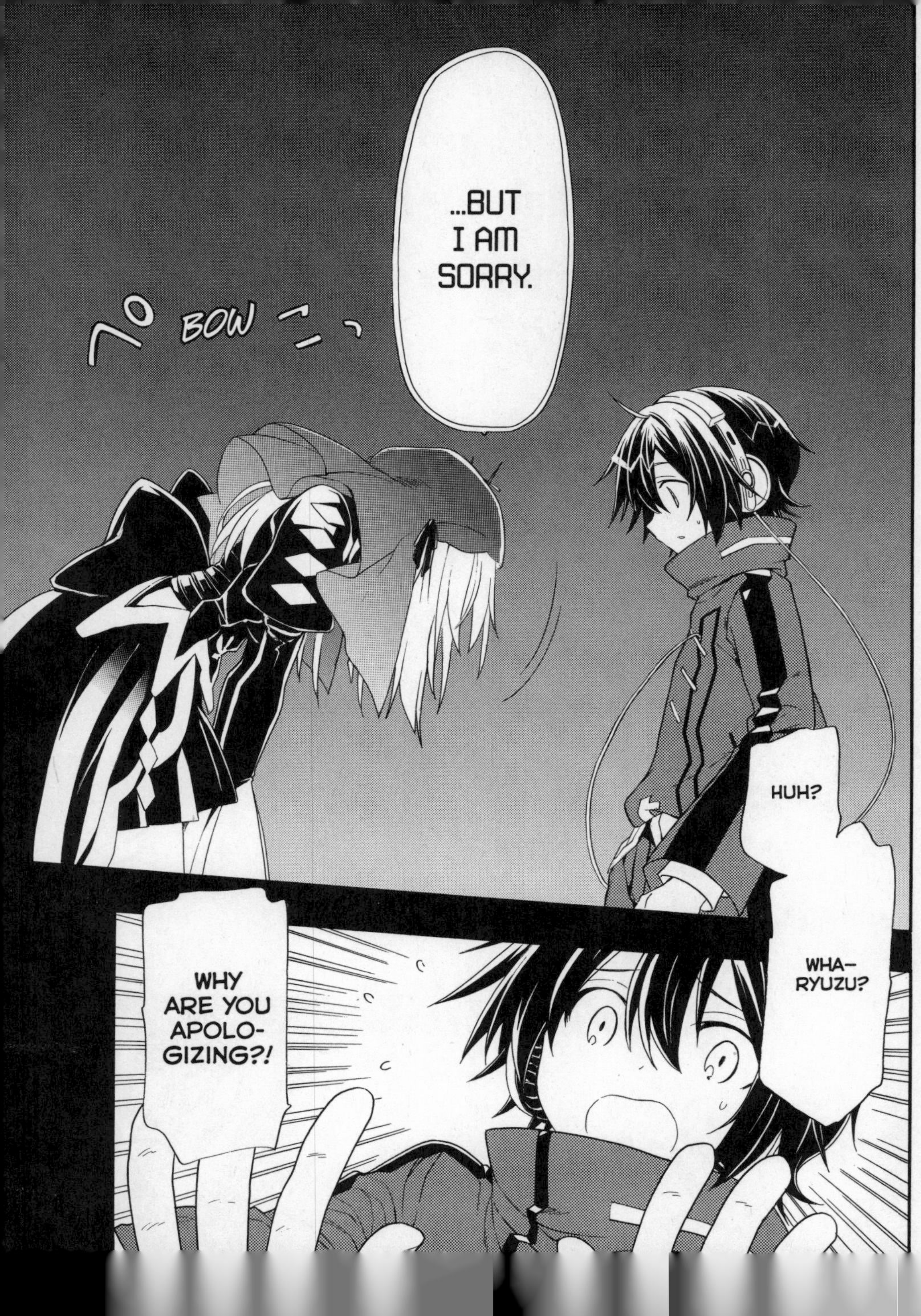
...BUT I AM SORRY.
BOW
HUH?
WHA- RYUZU?
WHY ARE YOU APOLO-GIZING?!

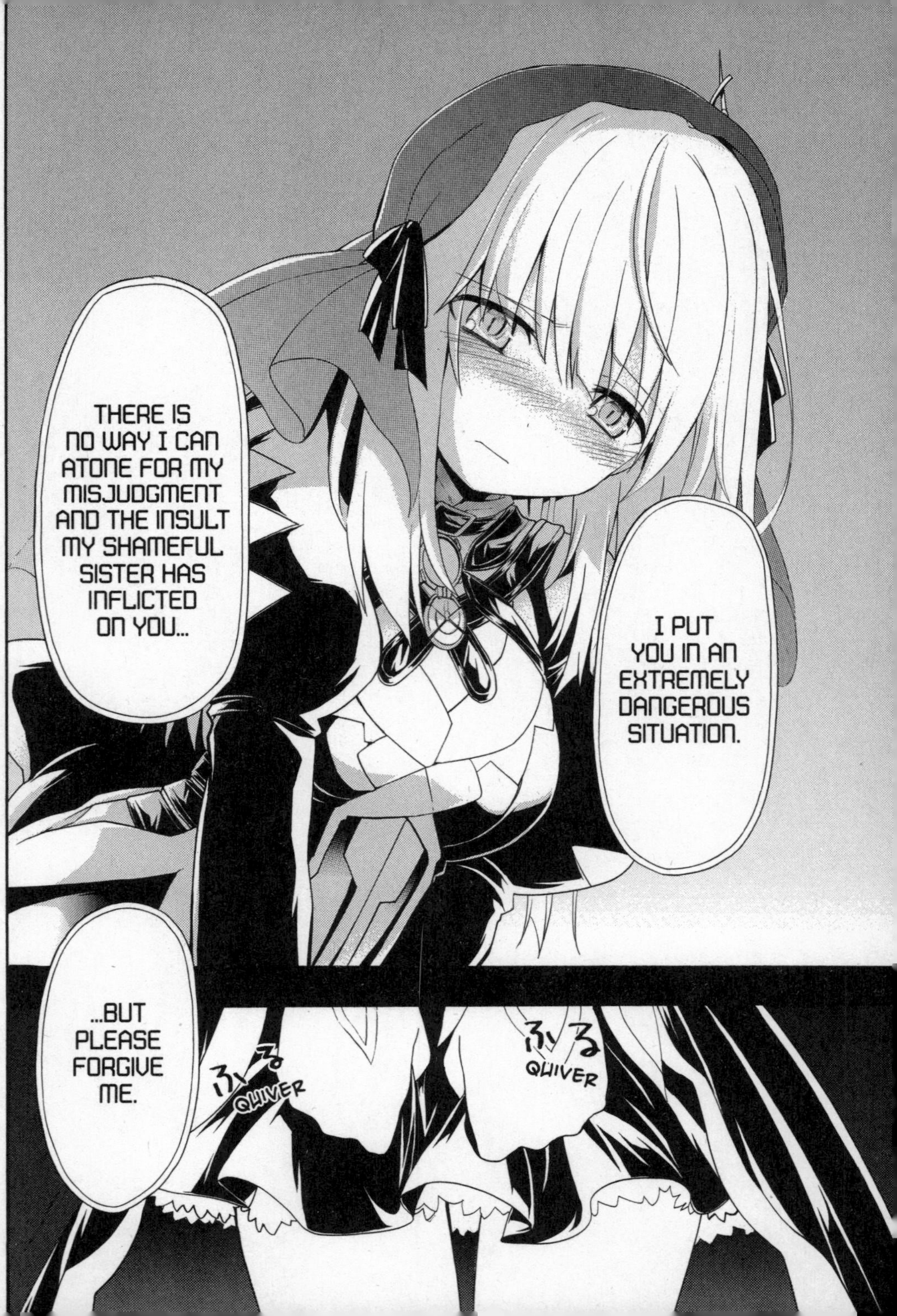
I PUT YOU IN AN EXTREMELY DANGEROUS SITUATION.
THERE IS NO WAY I CAN ATONE FOR MY MISJUDGMENT AND THE INSULT MY SHAMEFUL SISTER HAS INFLICTED ON YOU...
QUIVER
QUIVER
...BUT PLEASE FORGIVE ME.

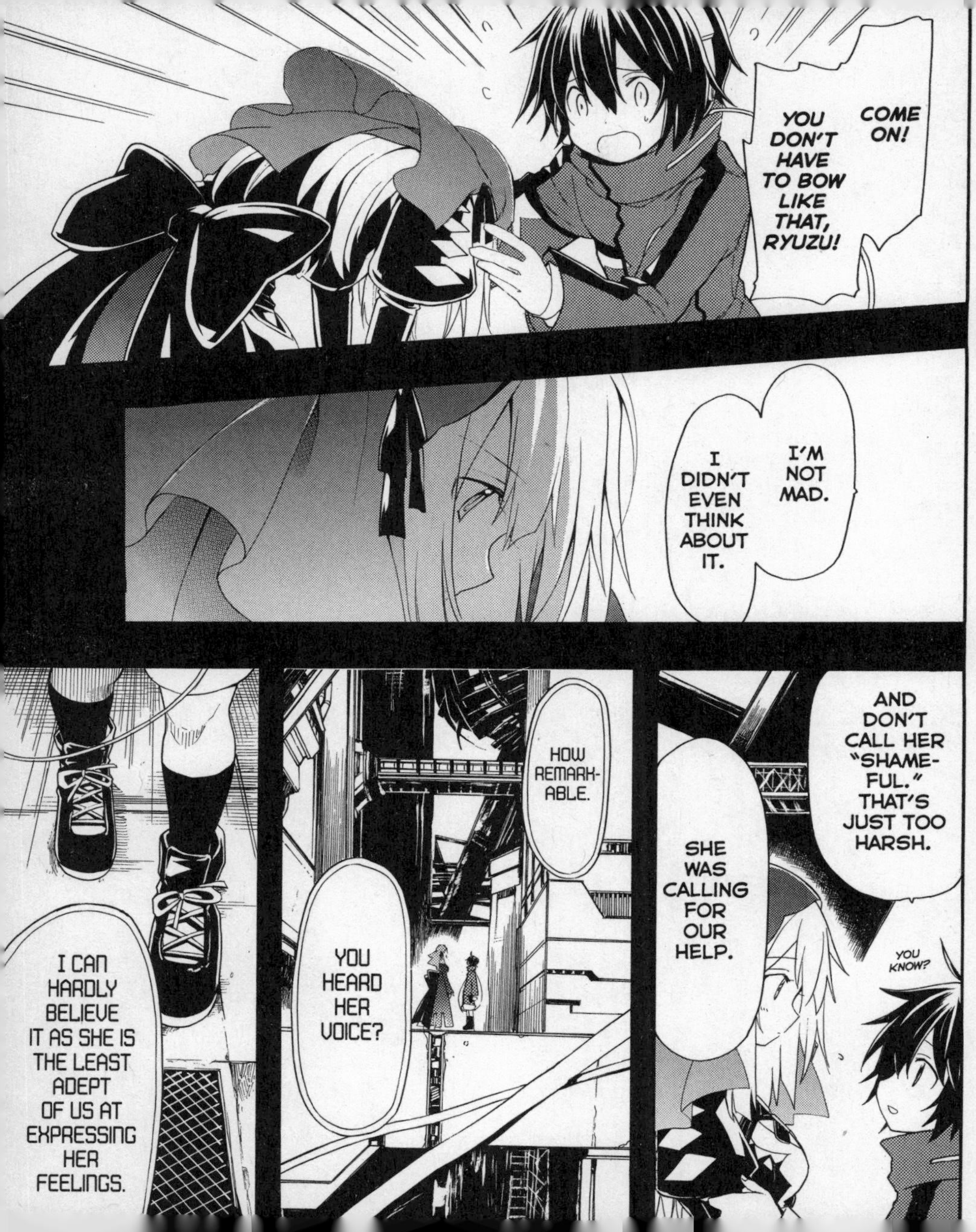
COME ON!
YOU DON'T HAVE TO BOW LIKE THAT, RYUZU!
I'M NOT MAD.
I DIDN'T EVEN THINK ABOUT IT.
AND DON'T CALL HER "SHAME-FUL." THAT'S JUST TOO HARSH.
SHE WAS CALLING FOR OUR HELP.
YOU KNOW?
HOW REMARK-ABLE.
YOU HEARD HER VOICE?
I CAN HARDLY BELIEVE IT AS SHE IS THE LEAST ADEPT OF US AT EXPRESSING HER FEELINGS.

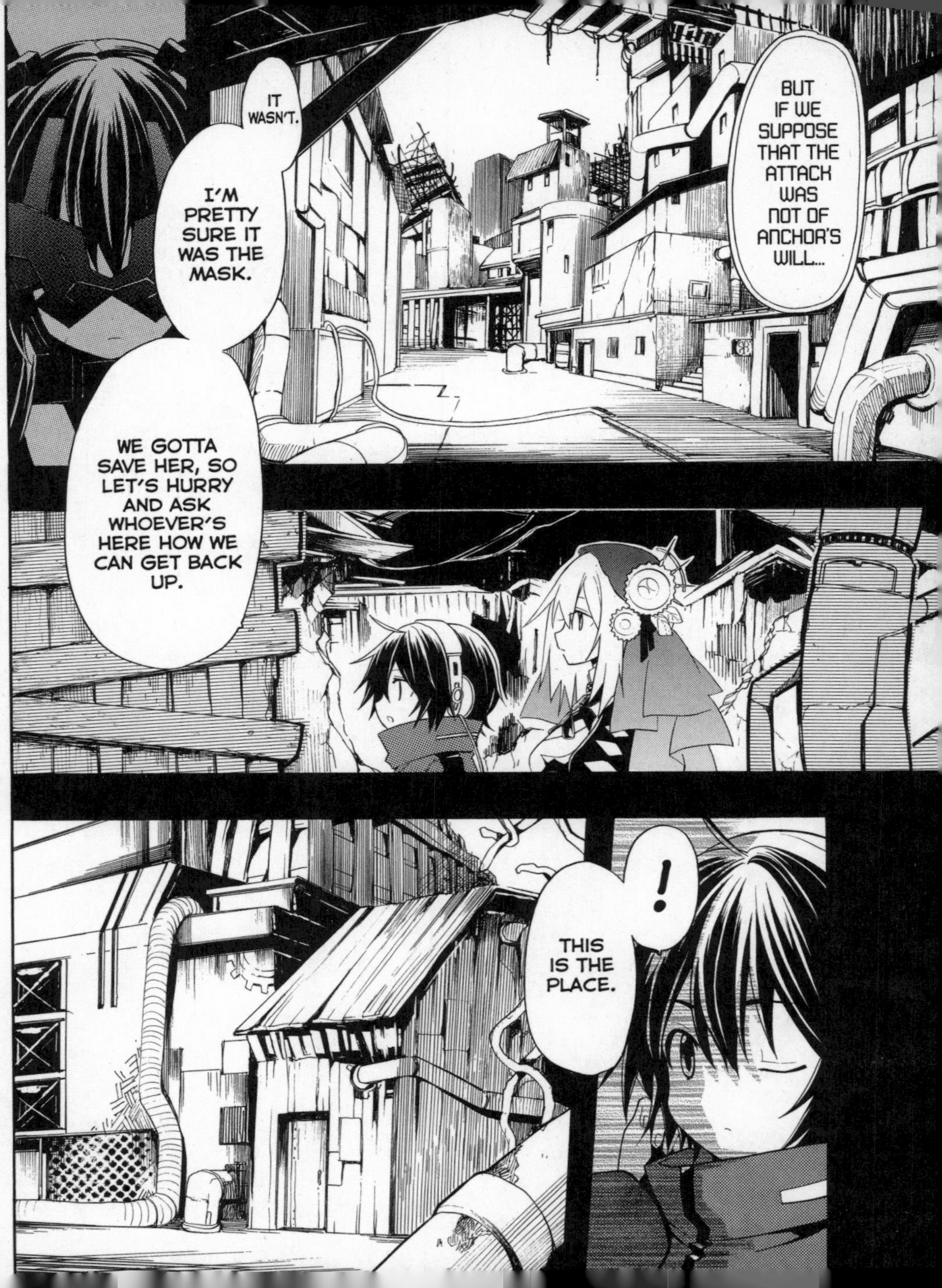
BUT IF WE SUPPOSE THAT THE ATTACK WAS NOT OF ANCHOR'S WILL...
IT WASN'T.
I'M PRETTY SURE IT WAS THE MASK.
WE GOTTA SAVE HER, SO LET'S HURRY AND ASK WHOEVER'S HERE HOW WE CAN GET BACK UP.
!
THIS IS THE PLACE.

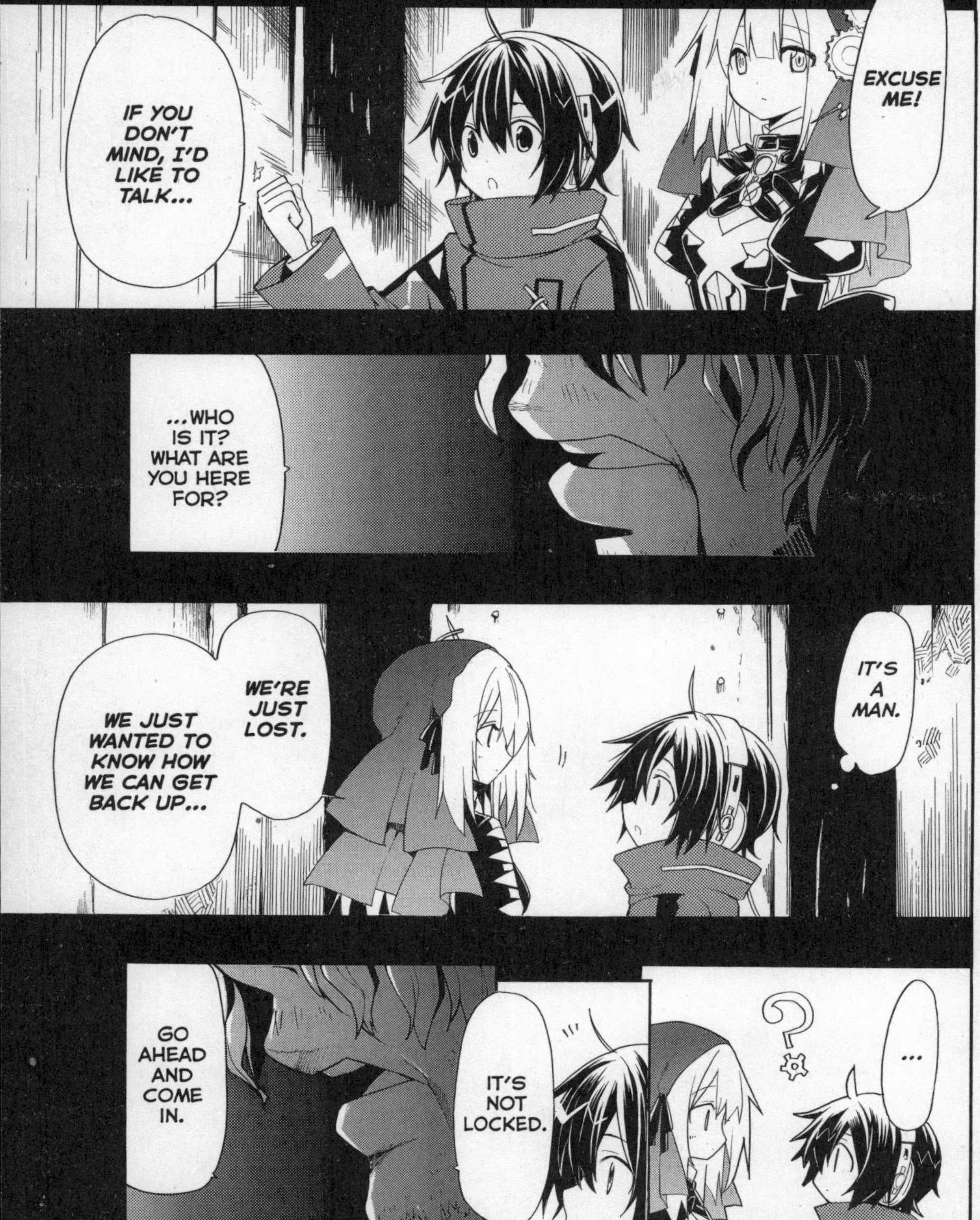
EXCUSE ME!
IF YOU DON'T MIND, I'D LIKE TO TALK...
...WHO IS IT? WHAT ARE YOU HERE FOR?
IT'S A MAN.
WE'RE JUST LOST.
WE JUST WANTED TO KNOW HOW WE CAN GET BACK UP...
...
IT'S NOT LOCKED.
GO AHEAD AND COME IN.

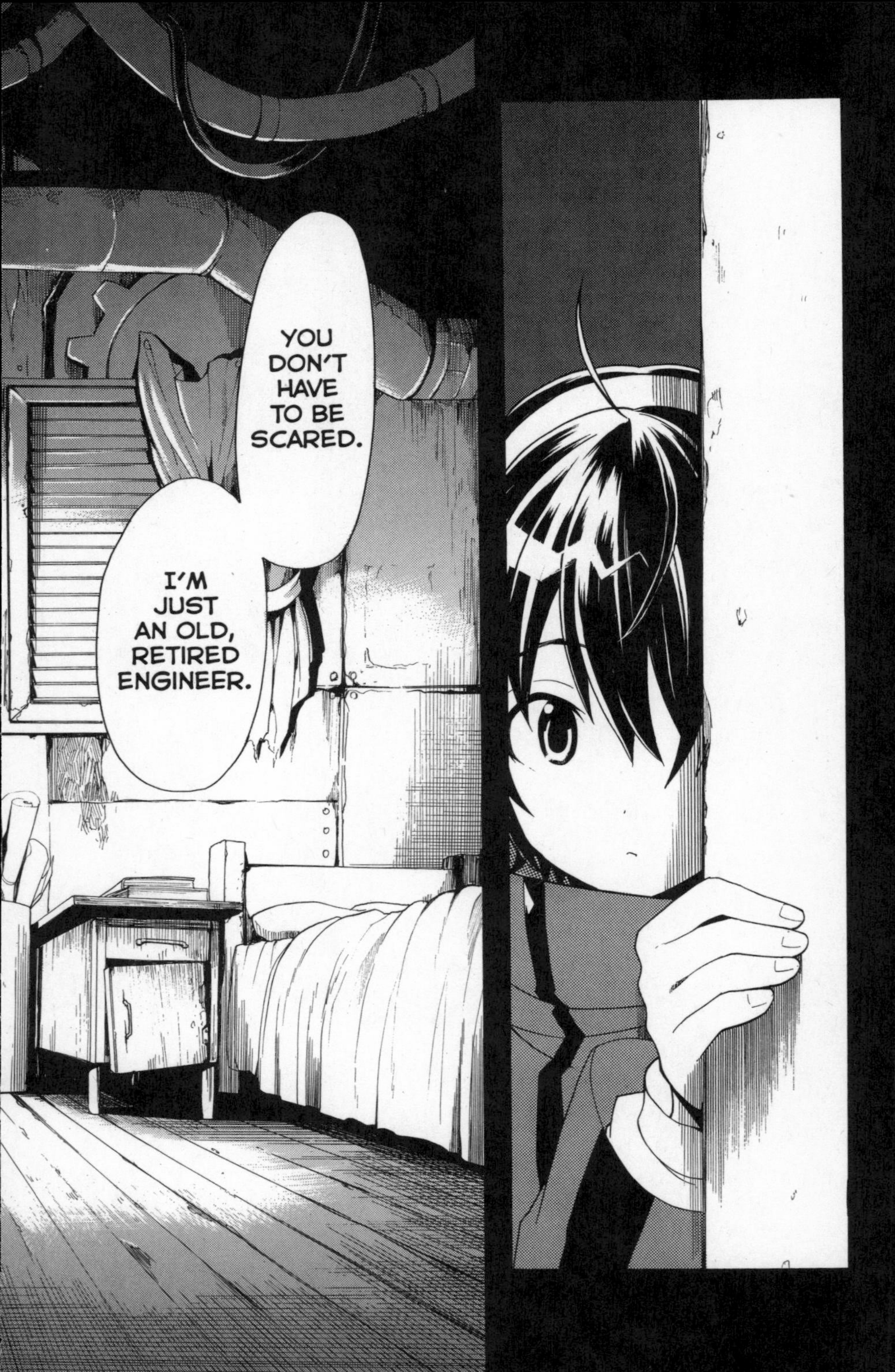
YOU DON'T HAVE TO BE SCARED.
I'M JUST AN OLD, RETIRED ENGINEER.

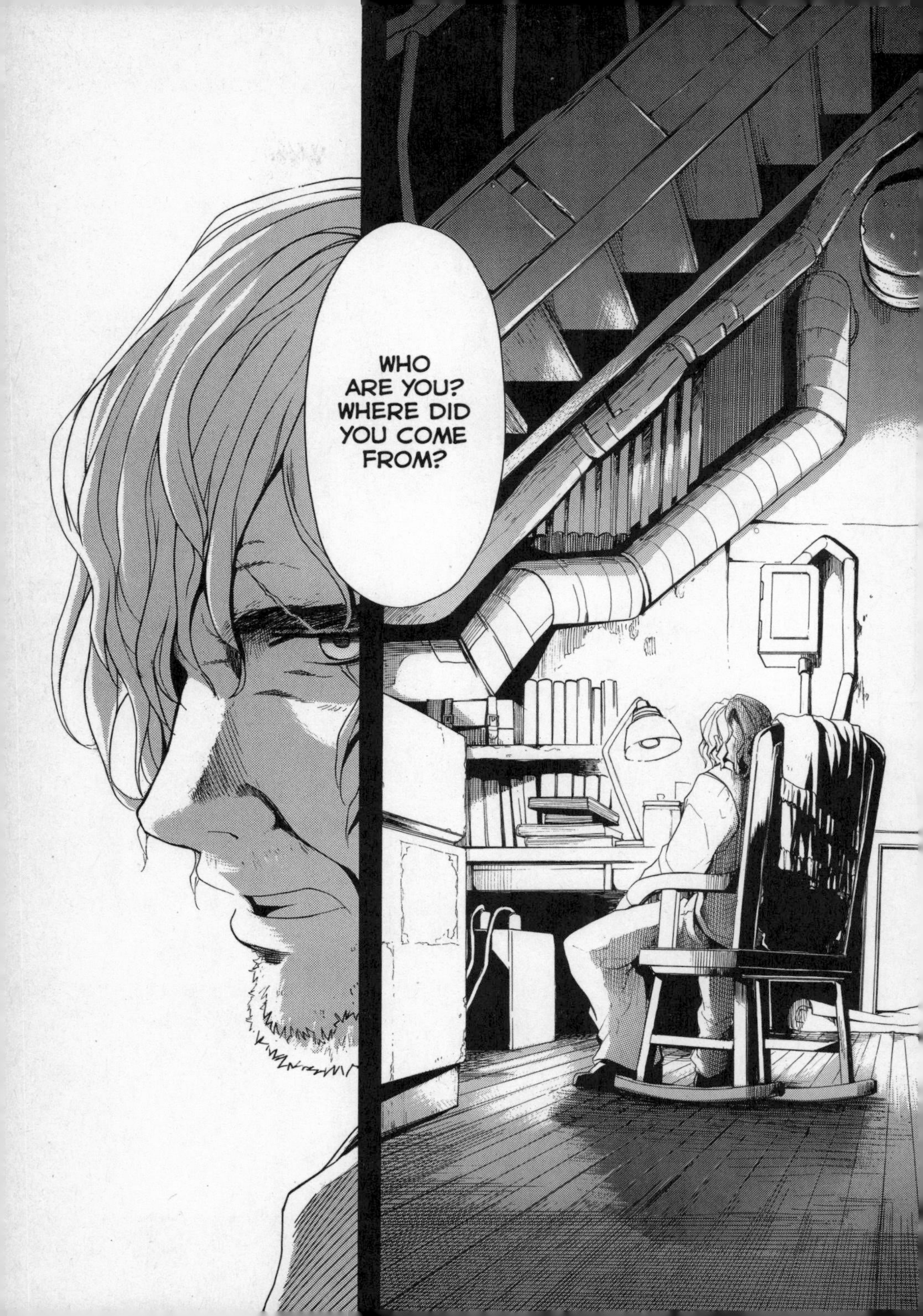
WHO ARE YOU? WHERE DID YOU COME FROM?

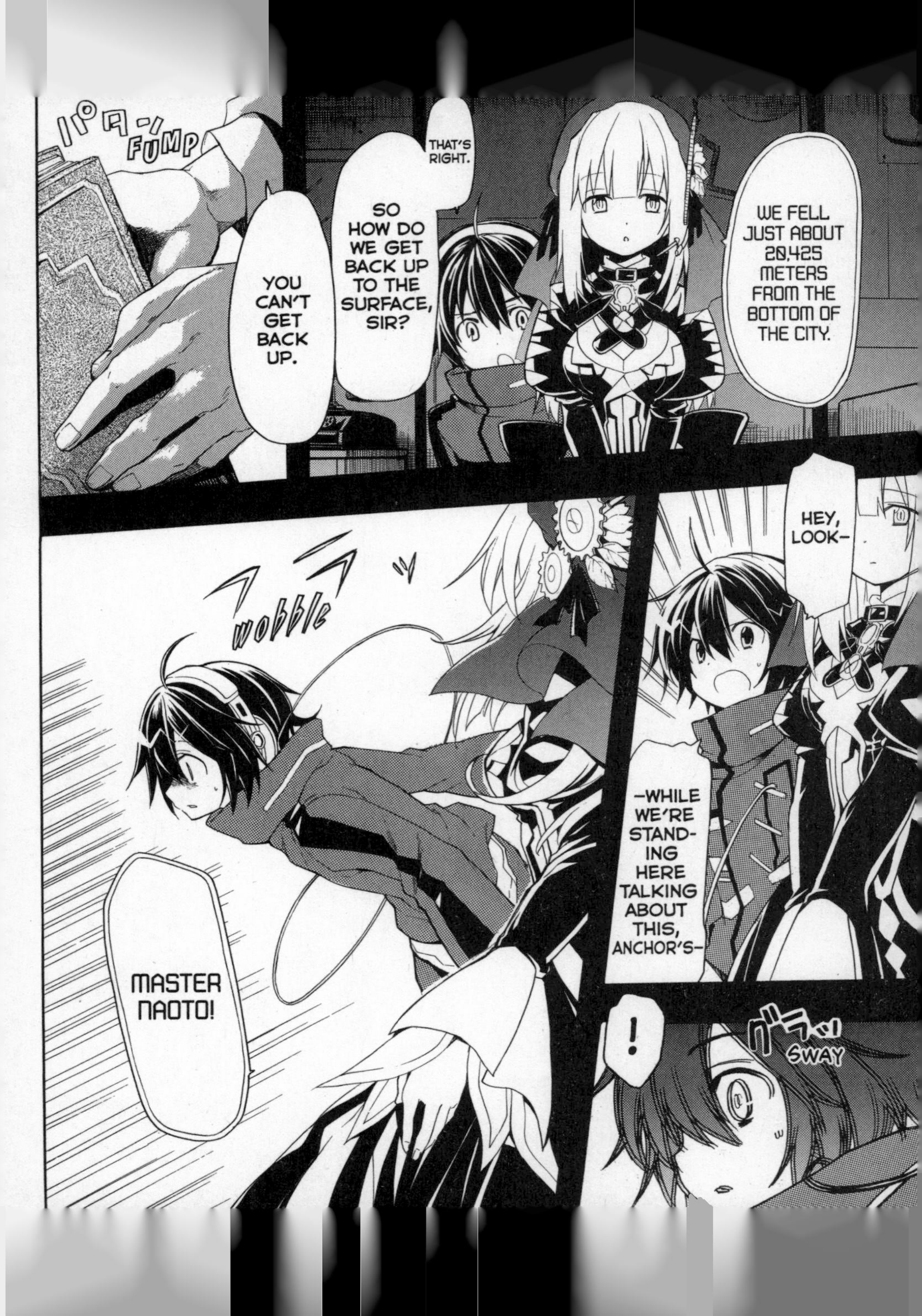
WE FELL JUST ABOUT 20,425 METERS FROM THE BOTTOM OF THE CITY.
THAT'S RIGHT.
SO HOW DO WE GET BACK UP TO THE SURFACE, SIR?
YOU CAN'T GET BACK UP.
FUMP
HEY, LOOK—
—WHILE WE'RE STAND-ING HERE TALKING ABOUT THIS, ANCHOR'S—
!
SWAY
wobble
MASTER NAOTO!

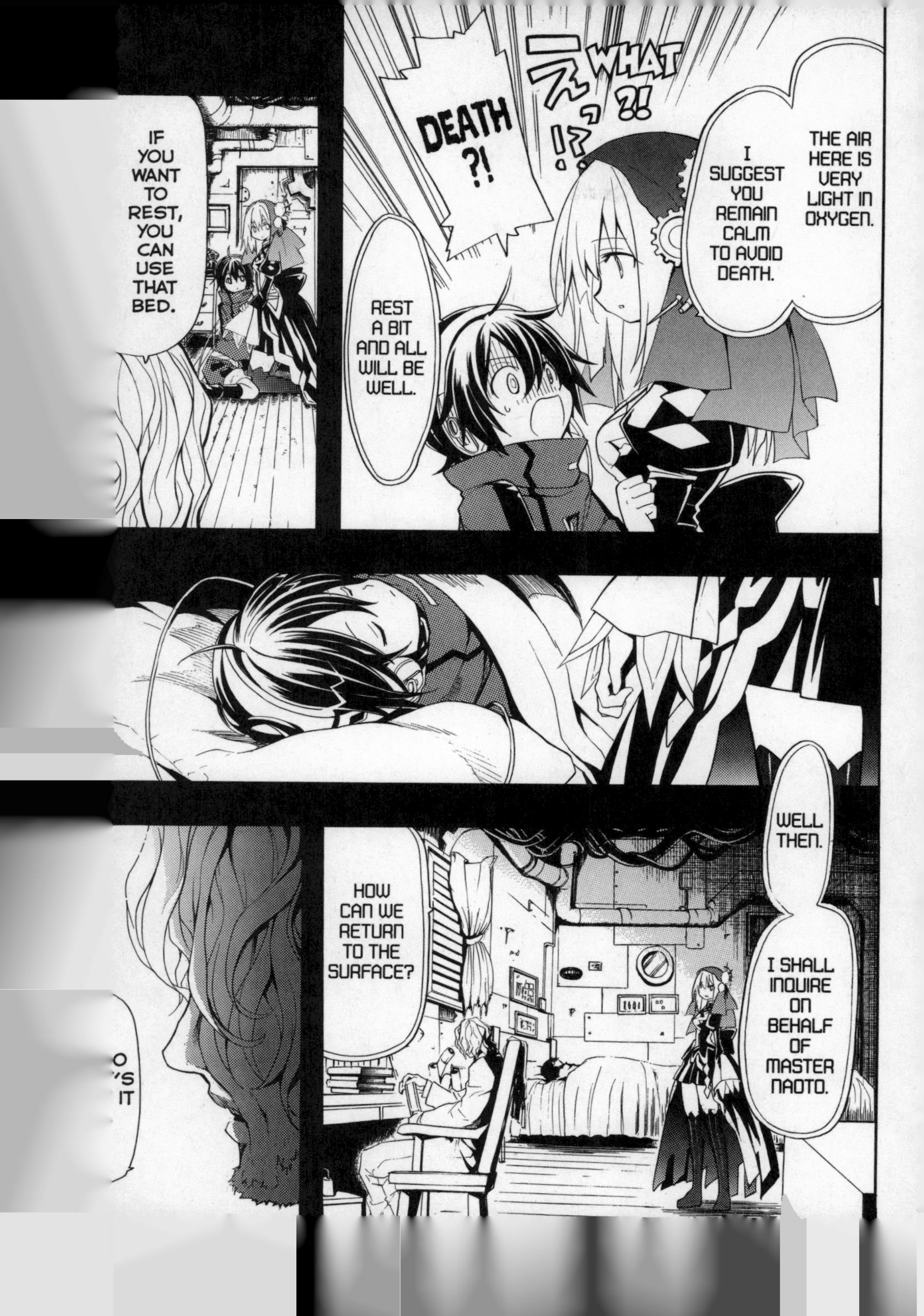
THE AIR HERE IS VERY LIGHT IN OXYGEN.
I SUGGEST YOU REMAIN CALM TO AVOID DEATH.
えっっ!?
WHAT ?!
DEATH ?!
REST A BIT AND ALL WILL BE WELL.
IF YOU WANT TO REST, YOU CAN USE THAT BED.
WELL THEN.
I SHALL INQUIRE ON BEHALF OF MASTER NAOTO.
HOW CAN WE RETURN TO THE SURFACE?

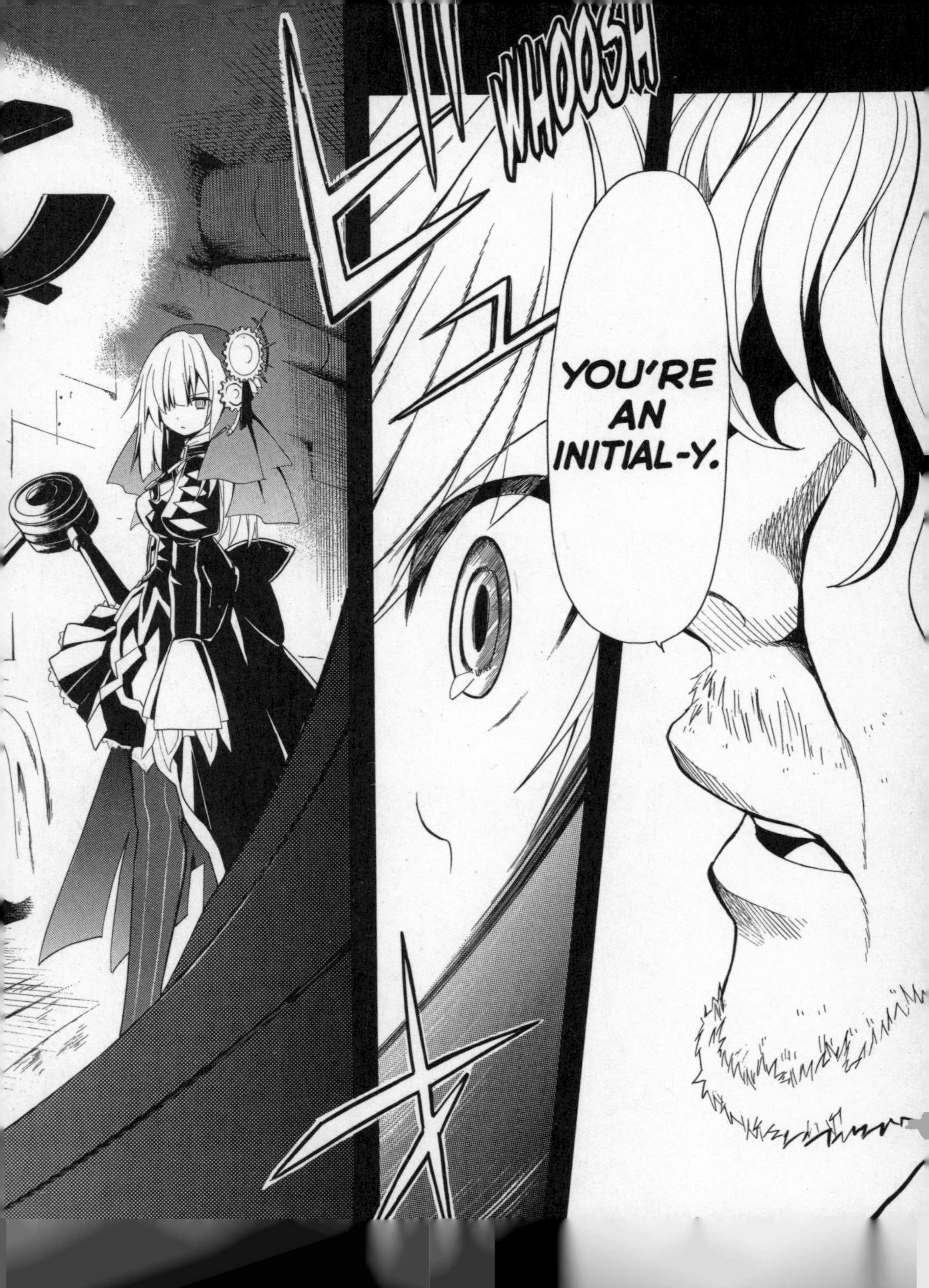
WHOOSH
YOU'RE AN INITIAL-Y.

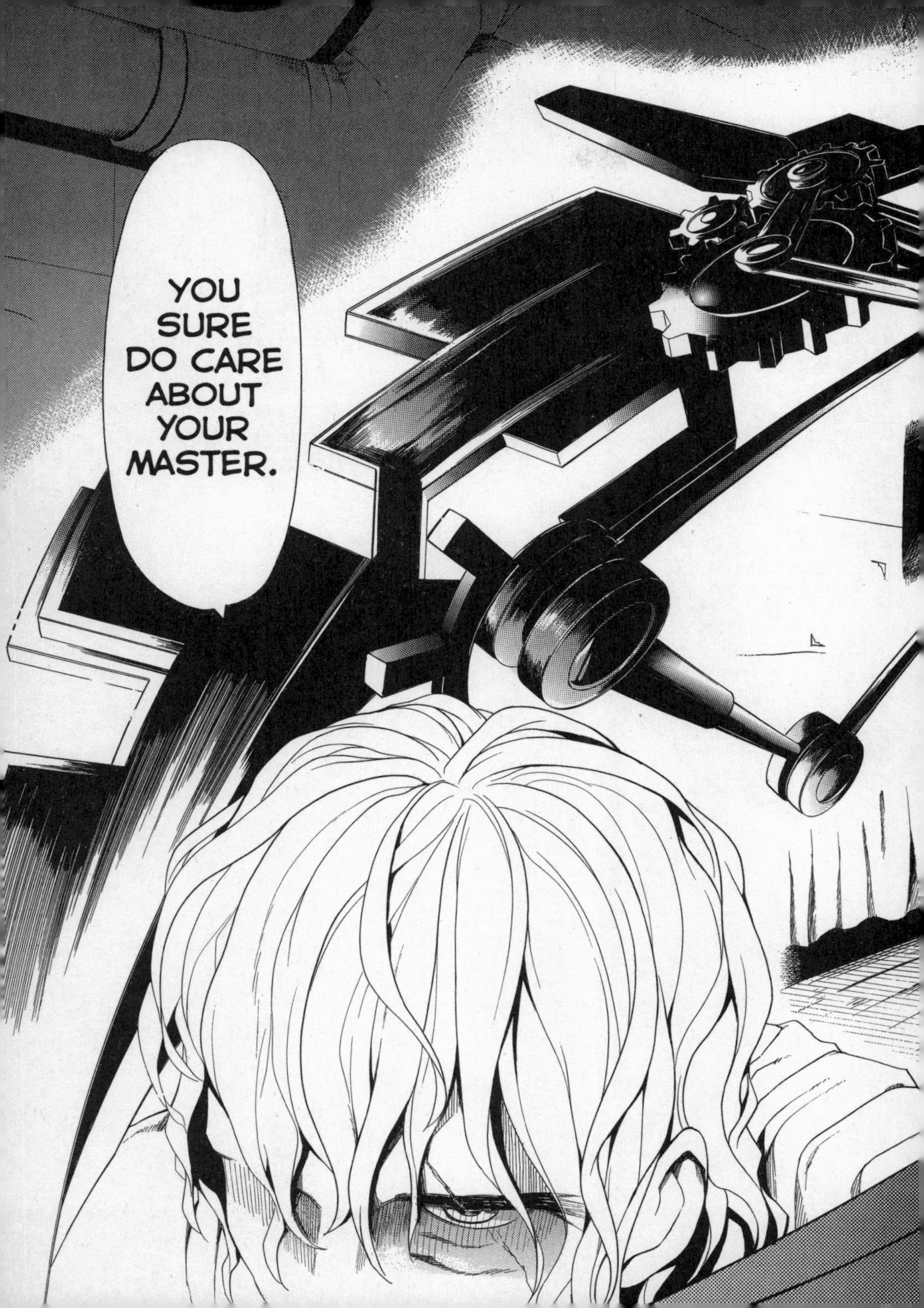
YOU SURE DO CARE ABOUT YOUR MASTER.

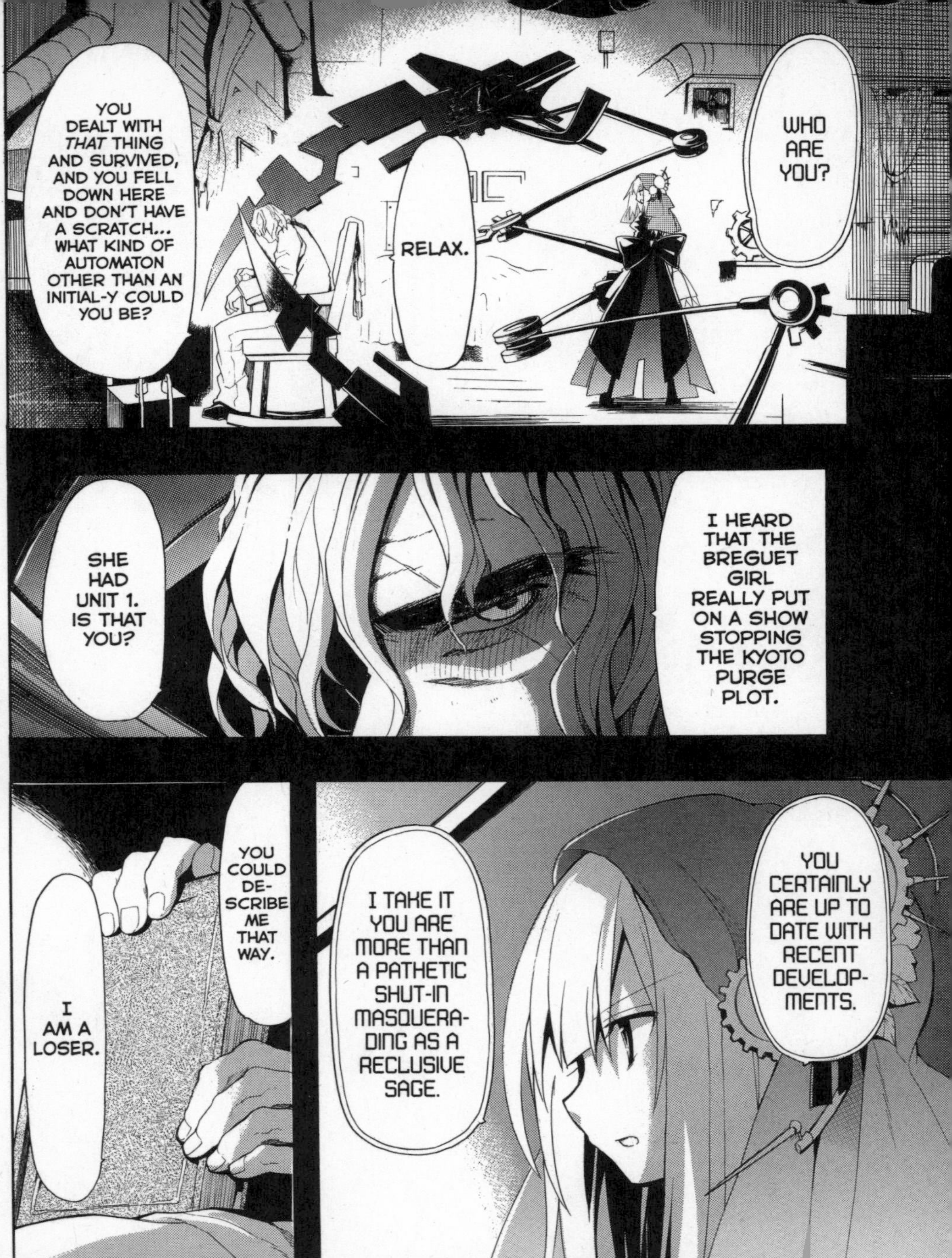
WHO ARE YOU?
RELAX.
YOU DEALT WITH *THAT* THING AND SURVIVED, AND YOU FELL DOWN HERE AND DON'T HAVE A SCRATCH... WHAT KIND OF AUTOMATON OTHER THAN AN INITIAL-Y COULD YOU BE?
I HEARD THAT THE BREGUET GIRL REALLY PUT ON A SHOW STOPPING THE KYOTO PURGE PLOT.
SHE HAD UNIT 1. IS THAT YOU?
YOU CERTAINLY ARE UP TO DATE WITH RECENT DEVELOP-MENTS.
I TAKE IT YOU ARE MORE THAN A PATHETIC SHUT-IN MASQUERA-DING AS A RECLUSIVE SAGE.
YOU COULD DE-SCRIBE ME THAT WAY.
I AM A LOSER.

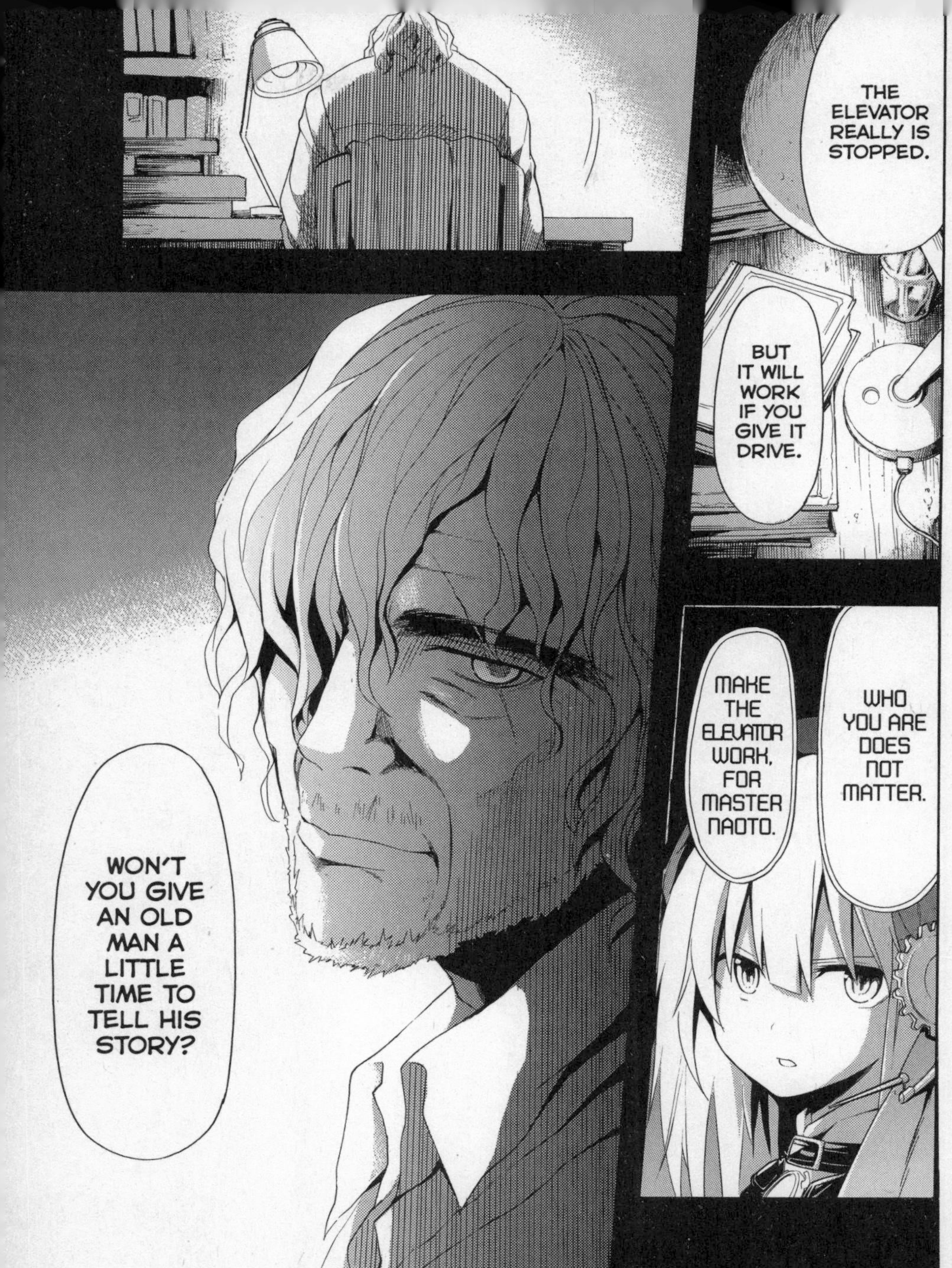
THE ELEVATOR REALLY IS STOPPED.
BUT IT WILL WORK IF YOU GIVE IT DRIVE.
WHO YOU ARE DOES NOT MATTER.
MAKE THE ELEVATOR WORK, FOR MASTER NAOTO.
WON'T YOU GIVE AN OLD MAN A LITTLE TIME TO TELL HIS STORY?

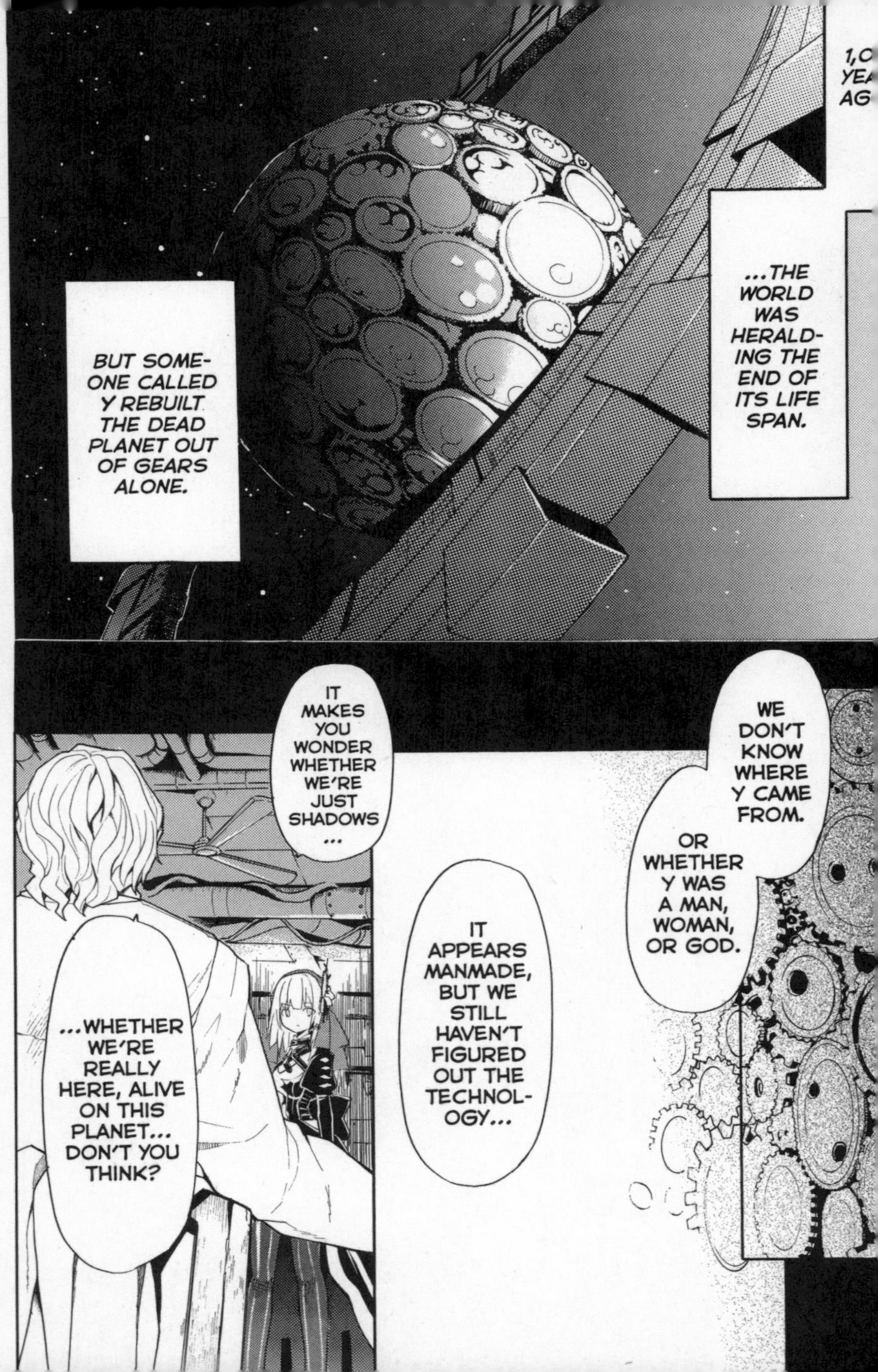
...THE WORLD WAS HERALDING THE END OF ITS LIFE SPAN.
BUT SOMEONE CALLED Y REBUILT THE DEAD PLANET OUT OF GEARS ALONE.
WE DON'T KNOW WHERE Y CAME FROM.
OR WHETHER Y WAS A MAN, WOMAN, OR GOD.
IT APPEARS MANMADE, BUT WE STILL HAVEN'T FIGURED OUT THE TECHNOLOGY...
IT MAKES YOU WONDER WHETHER WE'RE JUST SHADOWS...
...WHETHER WE'RE REALLY HERE, ALIVE ON THIS PLANET... DON'T YOU THINK?

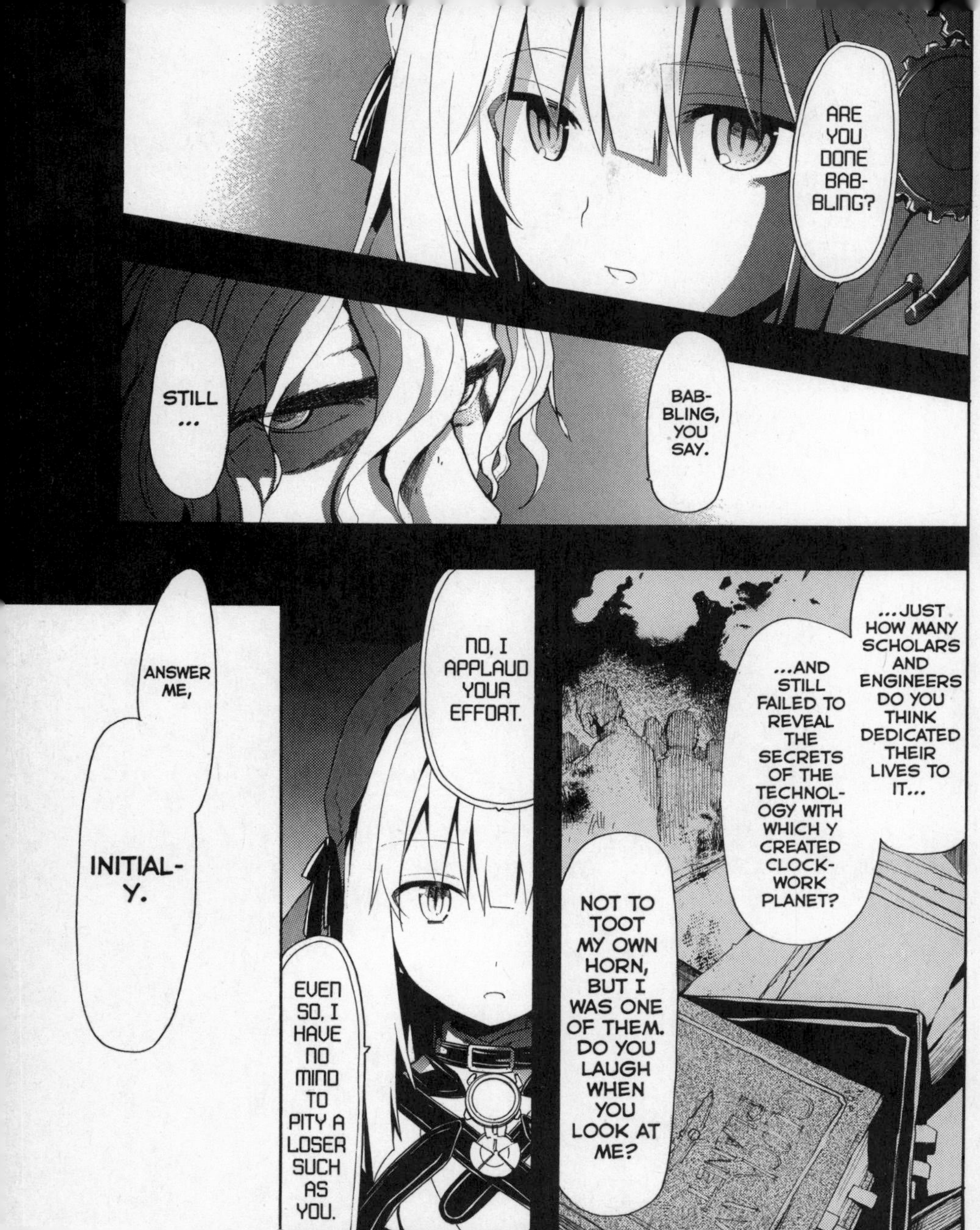
ARE YOU DONE BAB-BLING?
BAB-BLING, YOU SAY.
STILL...
...JUST HOW MANY SCHOLARS AND ENGINEERS DO YOU THINK DEDICATED THEIR LIVES TO IT...
...AND STILL FAILED TO REVEAL THE SECRETS OF THE TECHNOL-OGY WITH WHICH Y CREATED CLOCK-WORK PLANET?
NOT TO TOOT MY OWN HORN, BUT I WAS ONE OF THEM. DO YOU LAUGH WHEN YOU LOOK AT ME?
NO, I APPLAUD YOUR EFFORT.
EVEN SO, I HAVE NO MIND TO PITY A LOSER SUCH AS YOU.
ANSWER ME,
INITIAL-Y.

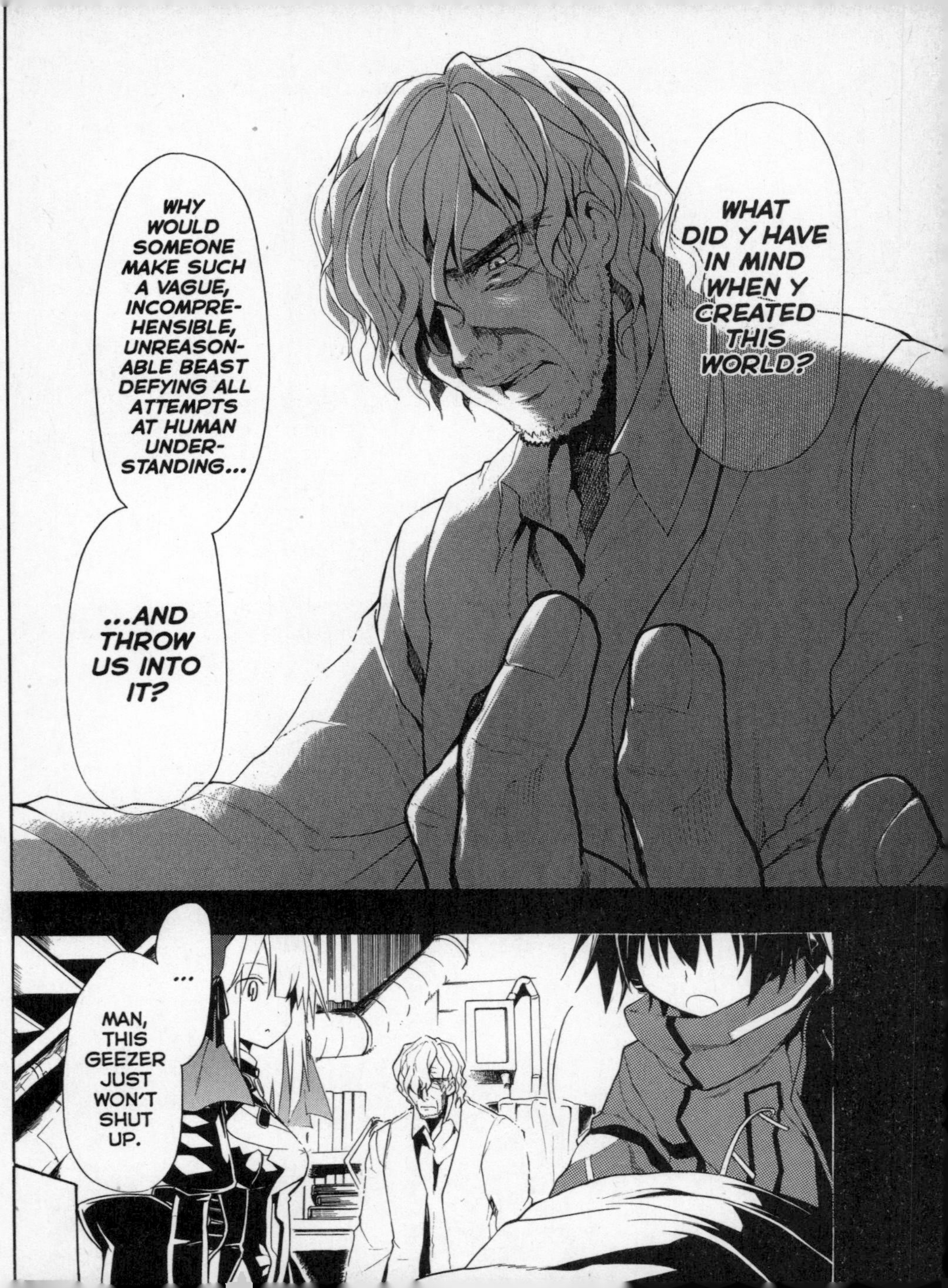
WHAT DID Y HAVE IN MIND WHEN Y CREATED THIS WORLD?
WHY WOULD SOMEONE MAKE SUCH A VAGUE, INCOMPRE-HENSIBLE, UNREASON-ABLE BEAST DEFYING ALL ATTEMPTS AT HUMAN UNDER-STANDING...
...AND THROW US INTO IT?
... MAN, THIS GEEZER JUST WON'T SHUT UP.

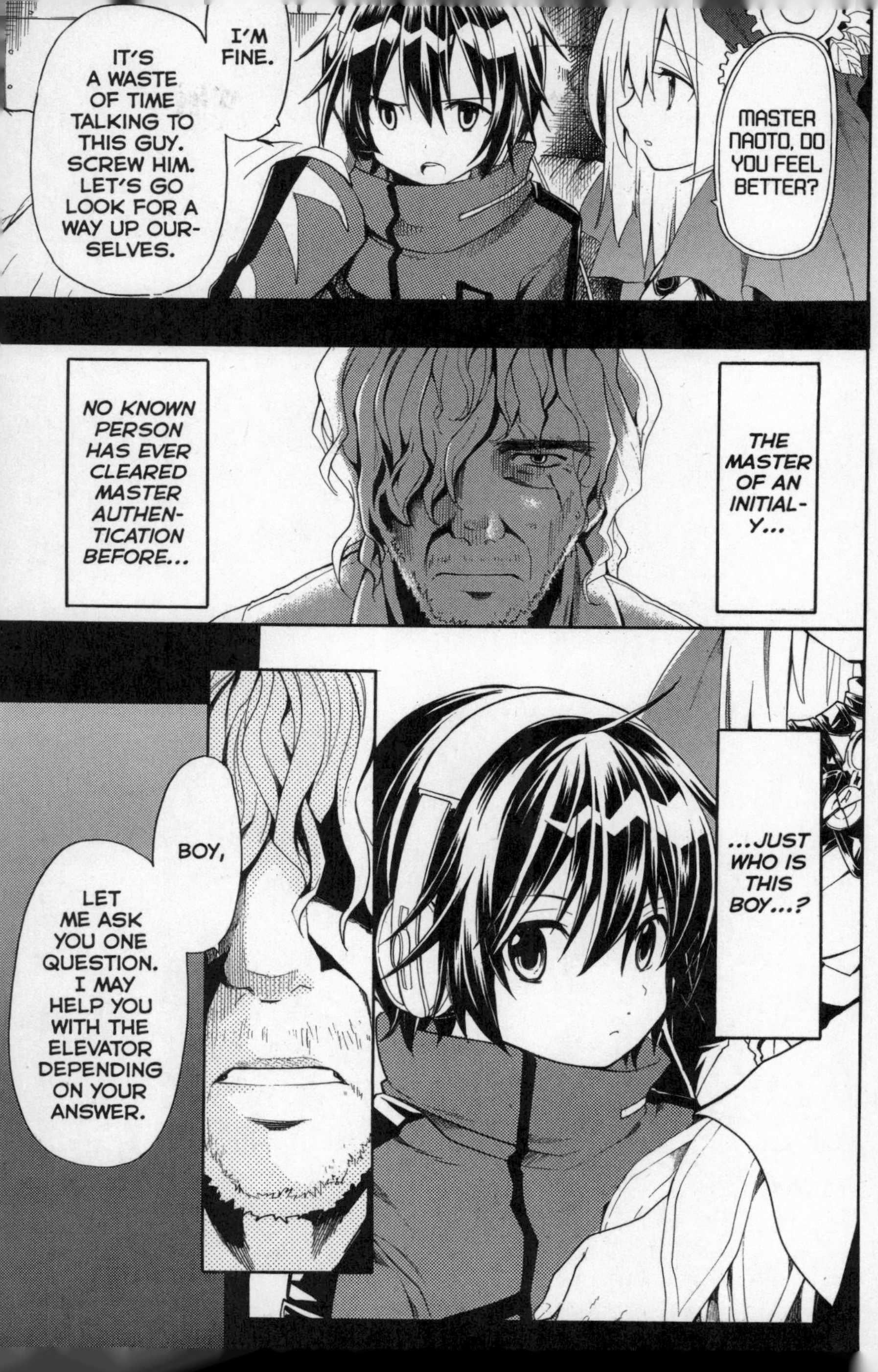
MASTER NAOTO, DO YOU FEEL BETTER?
I'M FINE.
IT'S A WASTE OF TIME TALKING TO THIS GUY. SCREW HIM. LET'S GO LOOK FOR A WAY UP OURSELVES.
THE MASTER OF AN INITIAL-Y...
NO KNOWN PERSON HAS EVER CLEARED MASTER AUTHENTICATION BEFORE...
...JUST WHO IS THIS BOY...?
BOY,
LET ME ASK YOU ONE QUESTION. I MAY HELP YOU WITH THE ELEVATOR DEPENDING ON YOUR ANSWER.

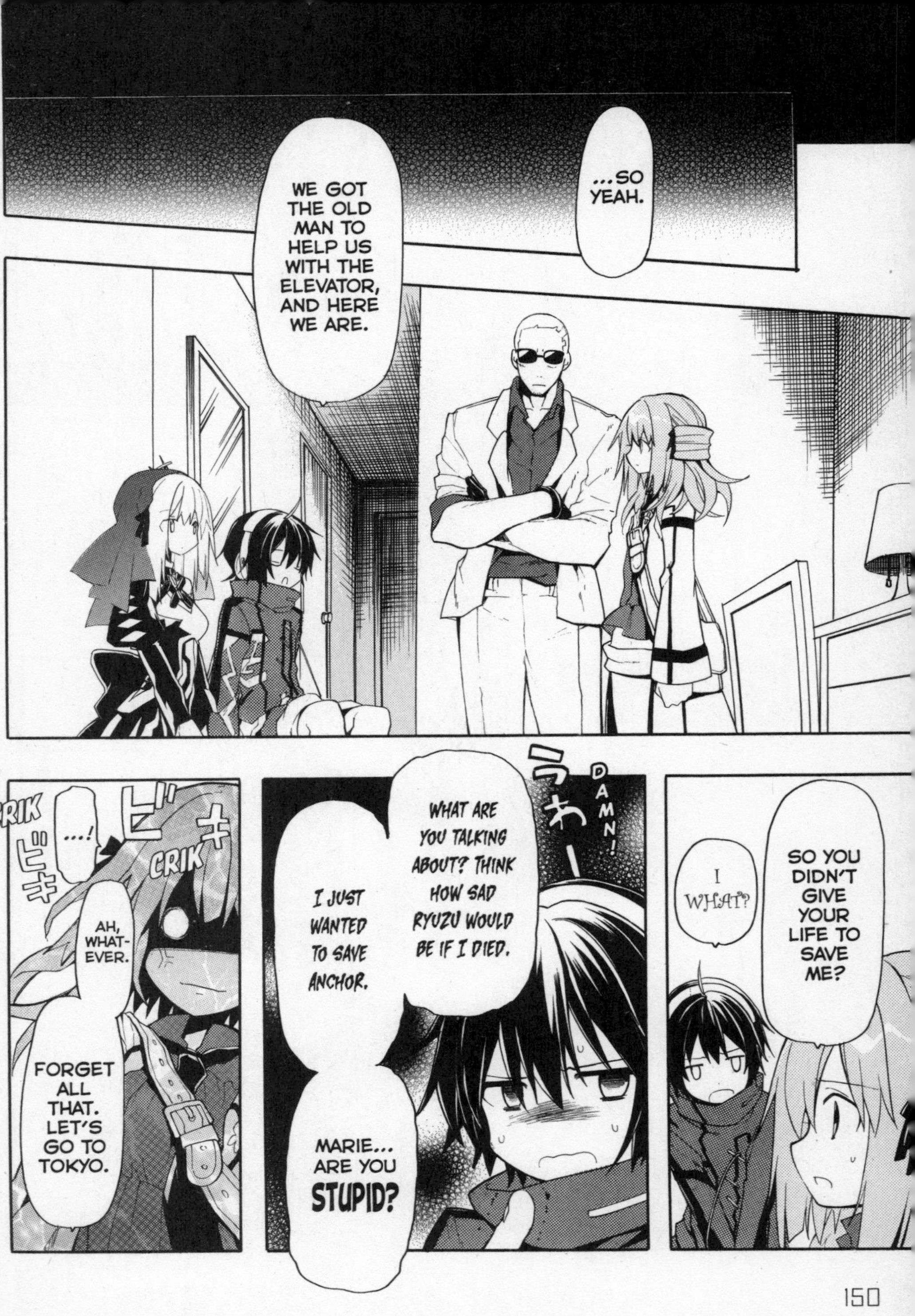
...SO YEAH.
WE GOT THE OLD MAN TO HELP US WITH THE ELEVATOR, AND HERE WE ARE.
SO YOU DIDN'T GIVE YOUR LIFE TO SAVE ME?
I WHAT?
DAMN!
WHAT ARE YOU TALKING ABOUT? THINK HOW SAD RYUZU WOULD BE IF I DIED.
I JUST WANTED TO SAVE ANCHOR.
MARIE... ARE YOU STUPID?
CRIK
CRIK
...!
AH, WHATEVER.
FORGET ALL THAT. LET'S GO TO TOKYO.

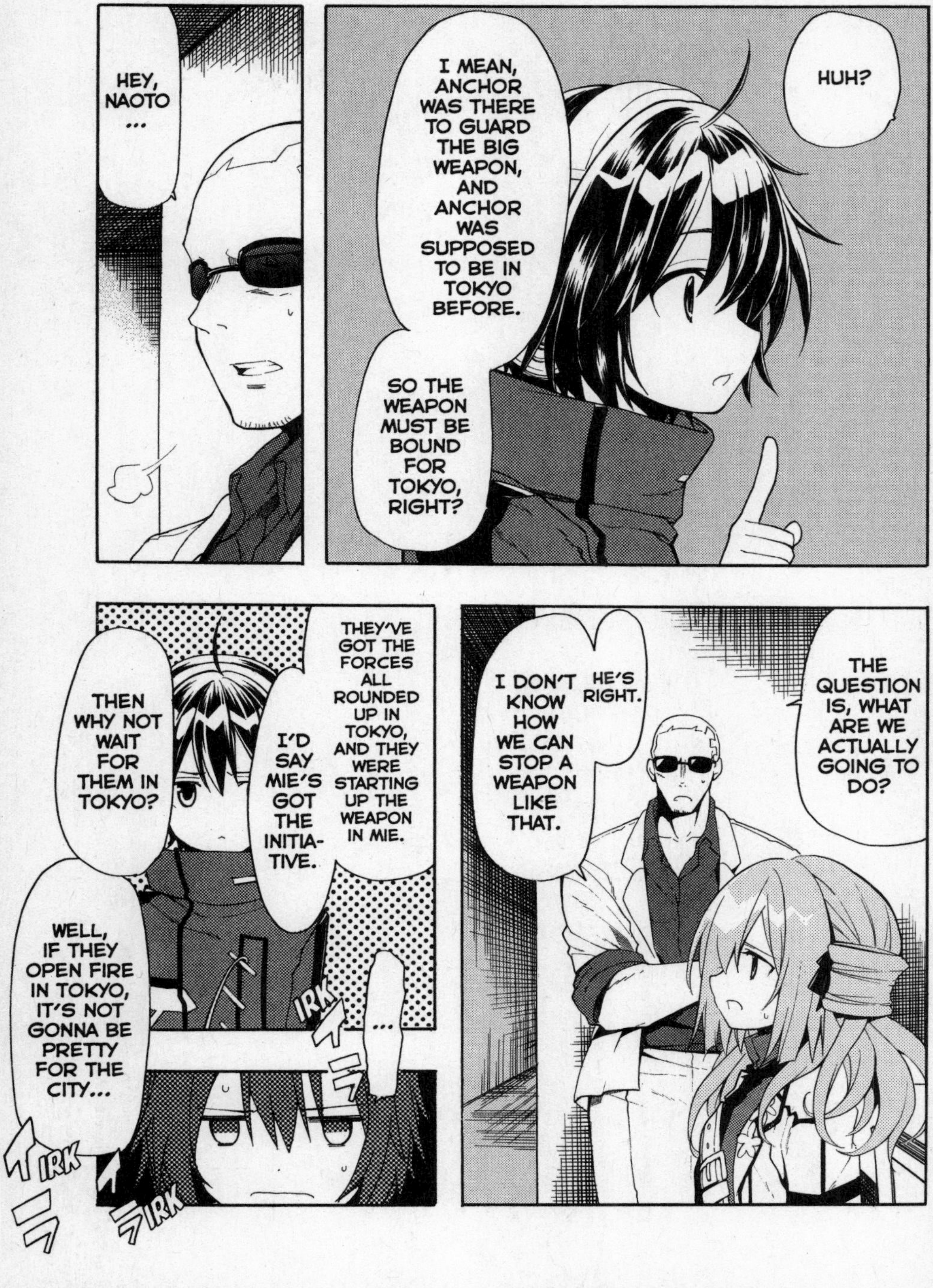
HUH?
I MEAN, ANCHOR WAS THERE TO GUARD THE BIG WEAPON, AND ANCHOR WAS SUPPOSED TO BE IN TOKYO BEFORE.
SO THE WEAPON MUST BE BOUND FOR TOKYO, RIGHT?
HEY, NAOTO ...
THE QUESTION IS, WHAT ARE WE ACTUALLY GOING TO DO?
HE'S RIGHT.
I DON'T KNOW HOW WE CAN STOP A WEAPON LIKE THAT.
THEY'VE GOT THE FORCES ALL ROUNDED UP IN TOKYO, AND THEY WERE STARTING UP THE WEAPON IN MIE.
I'D SAY MIE'S GOT THE INITIA-TIVE.
THEN WHY NOT WAIT FOR THEM IN TOKYO?
...
IRK
WELL, IF THEY OPEN FIRE IN TOKYO, IT'S NOT GONNA BE PRETTY FOR THE CITY...
IRK
IRK

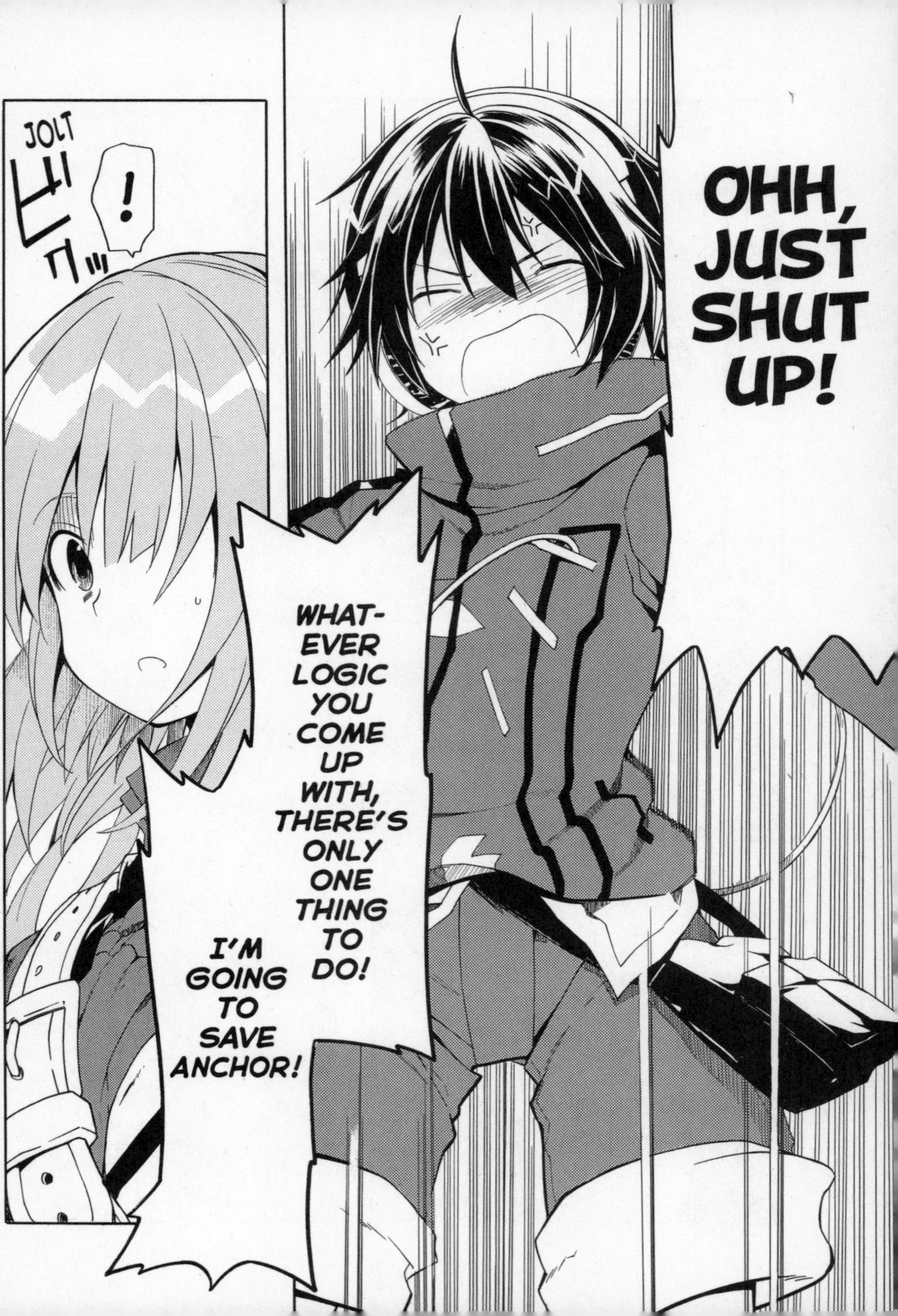
OHH, JUST SHUT UP!
WHAT-EVER LOGIC YOU COME UP WITH, THERE'S ONLY ONE THING TO DO!
I'M GOING TO SAVE ANCHOR!
JOLT
ビクッ
!

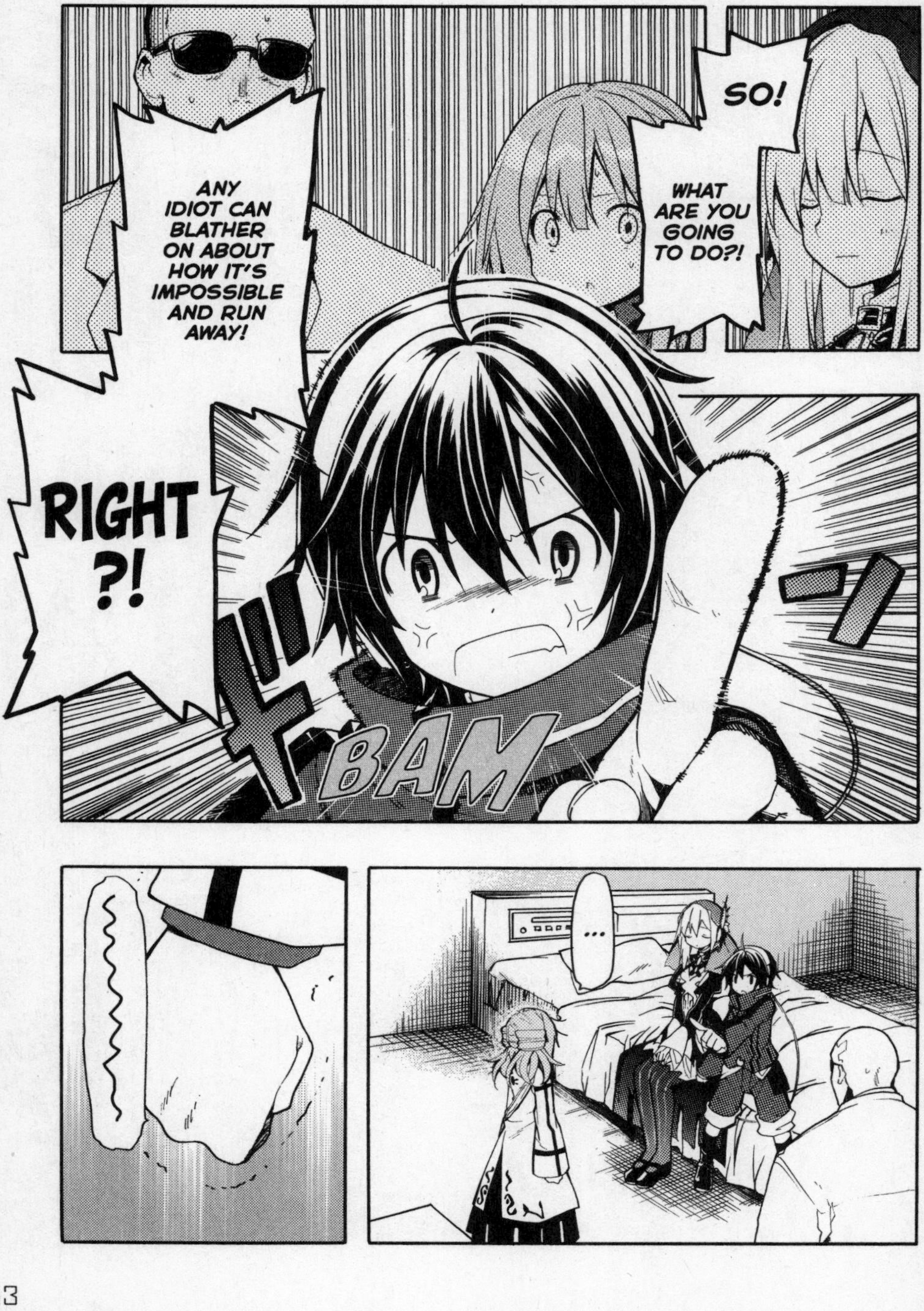
SO!
WHAT ARE YOU GOING TO DO?!
ANY IDIOT CAN BLATHER ON ABOUT HOW IT'S IMPOSSIBLE AND RUN AWAY!
RIGHT ?!
BAM
...

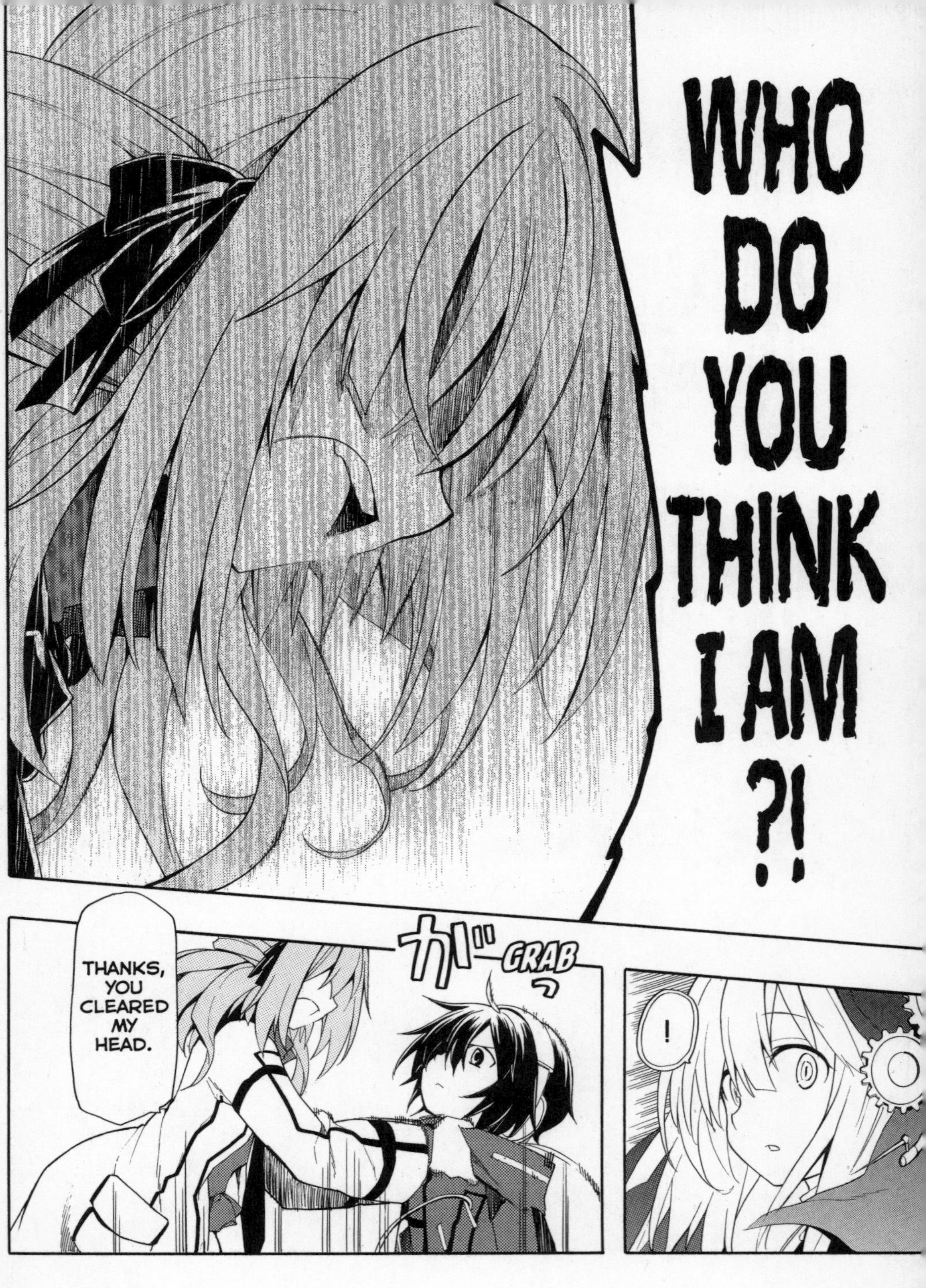
WHO DO YOU THINK I AM ?!
!
GRAB
THANKS, YOU CLEARED MY HEAD.

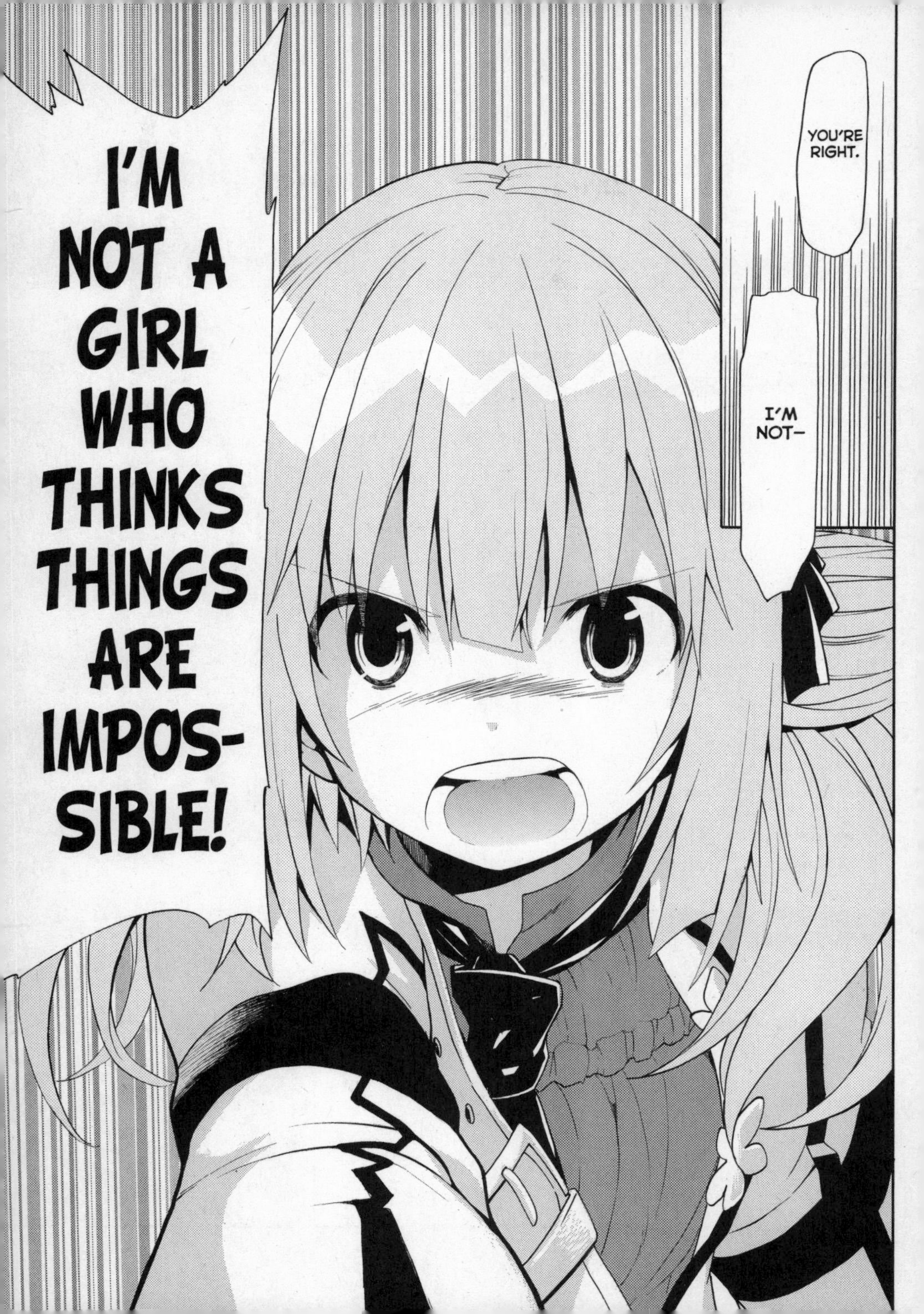
YOU'RE RIGHT.
I'M NOT—
I'M NOT A GIRL WHO THINKS THINGS ARE IMPOSSIBLE!

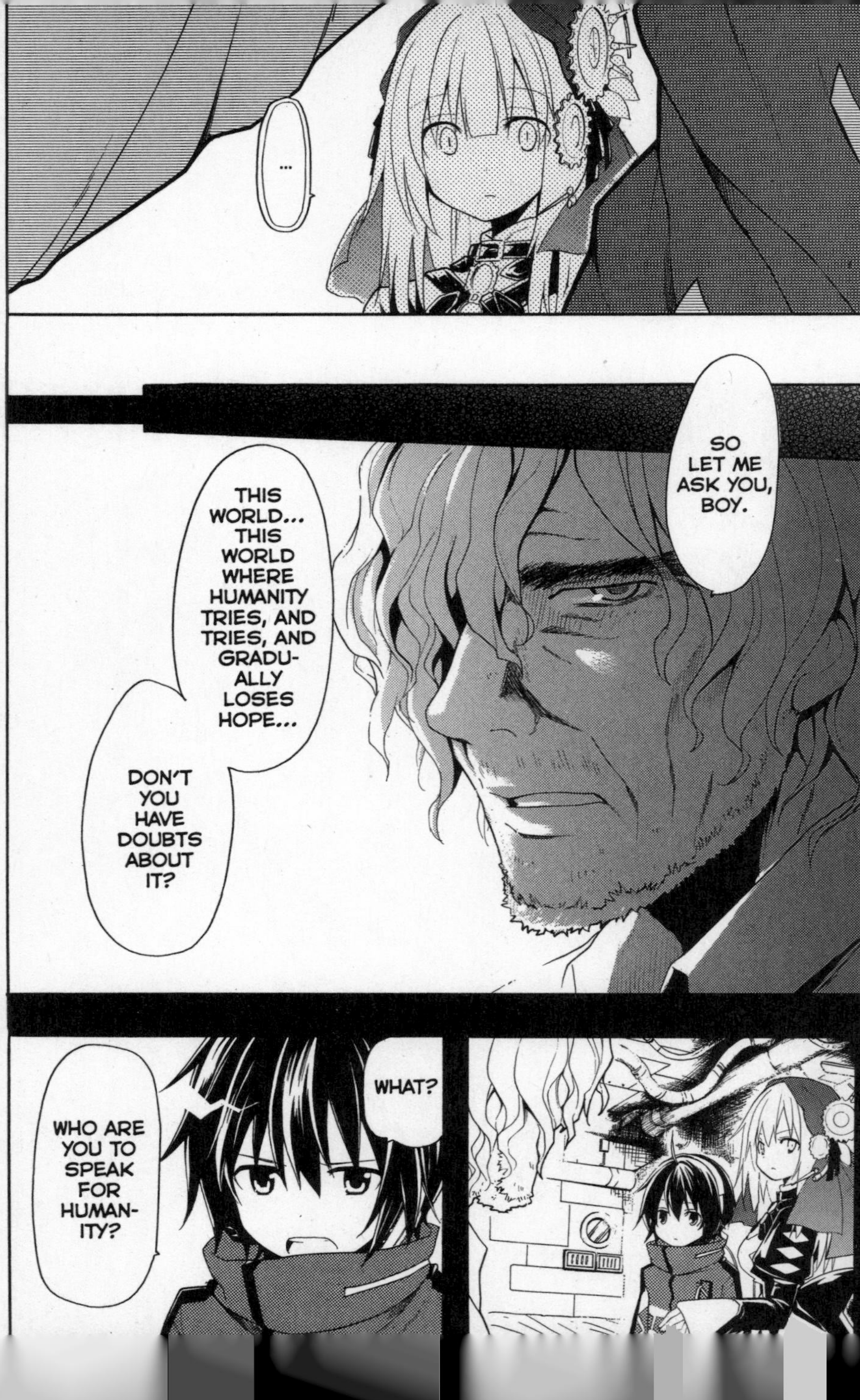
...
SO LET ME ASK YOU, BOY.
THIS WORLD... THIS WORLD WHERE HUMANITY TRIES, AND TRIES, AND GRADUALLY LOSES HOPE...
DON'T YOU HAVE DOUBTS ABOUT IT?
WHAT?
WHO ARE YOU TO SPEAK FOR HUMANITY?

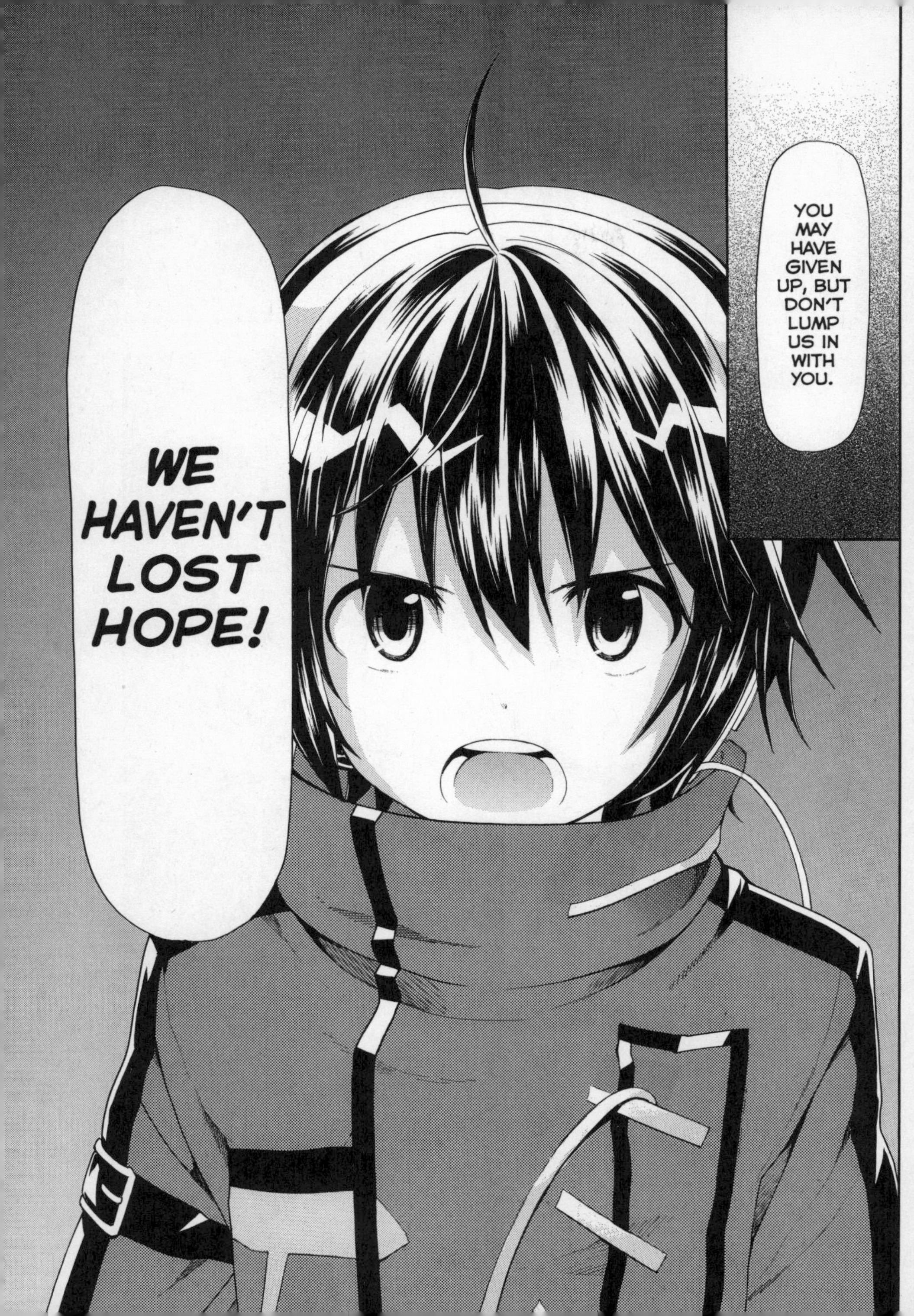
YOU MAY HAVE GIVEN UP, BUT DON'T LUMP US IN WITH YOU.
WE HAVEN'T LOST HOPE!

NO. ABSURD.

COULD THESE TWO...

SO.

YOU SAVE ANCHOR.

I'LL SAVE THE WORLD.

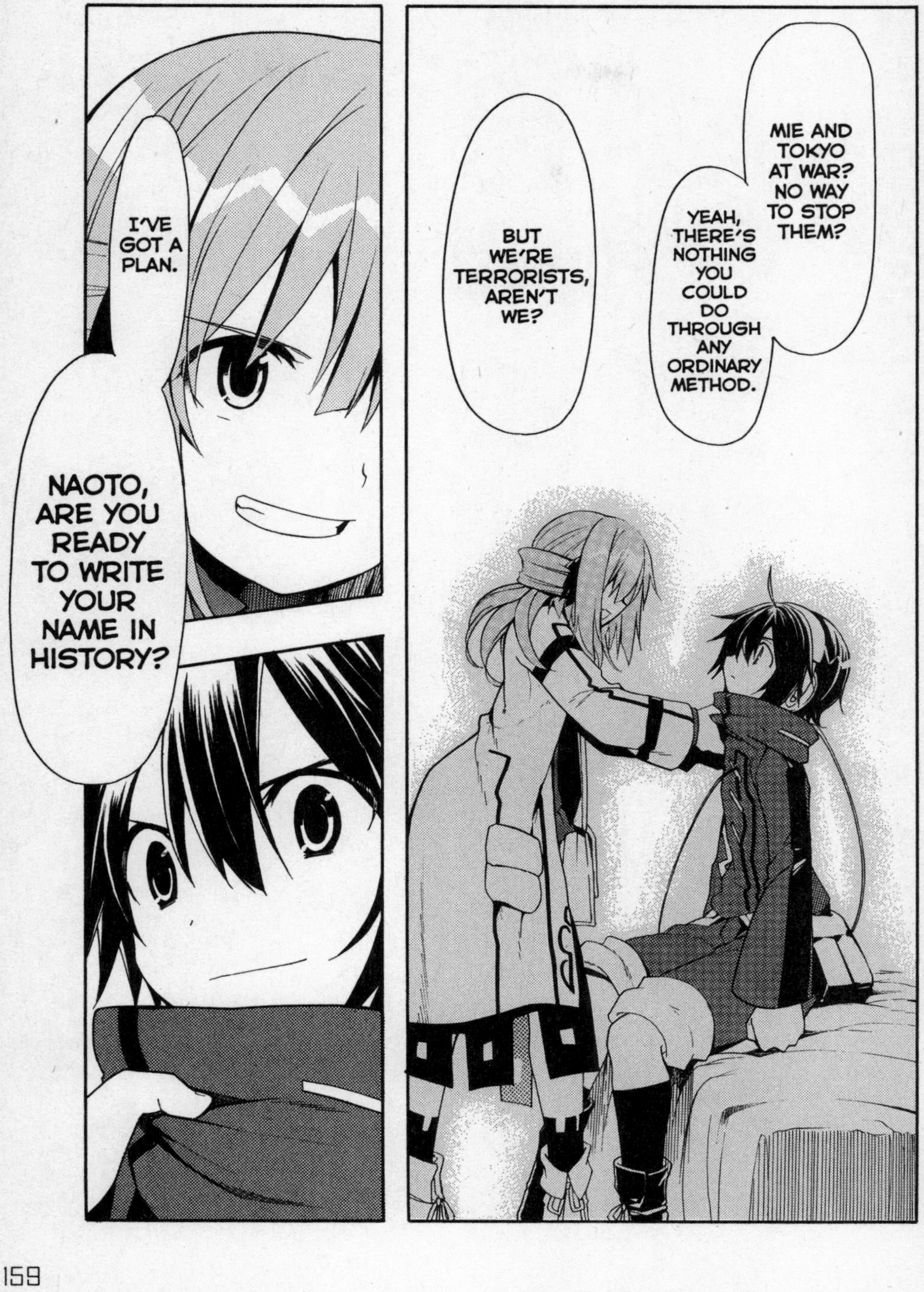
MIE AND TOKYO AT WAR? NO WAY TO STOP THEM?
YEAH, THERE'S NOTHING YOU COULD DO THROUGH ANY ORDINARY METHOD.
BUT WE'RE TERRORISTS, AREN'T WE?
I'VE GOT A PLAN.
NAOTO, ARE YOU READY TO WRITE YOUR NAME IN HISTORY?

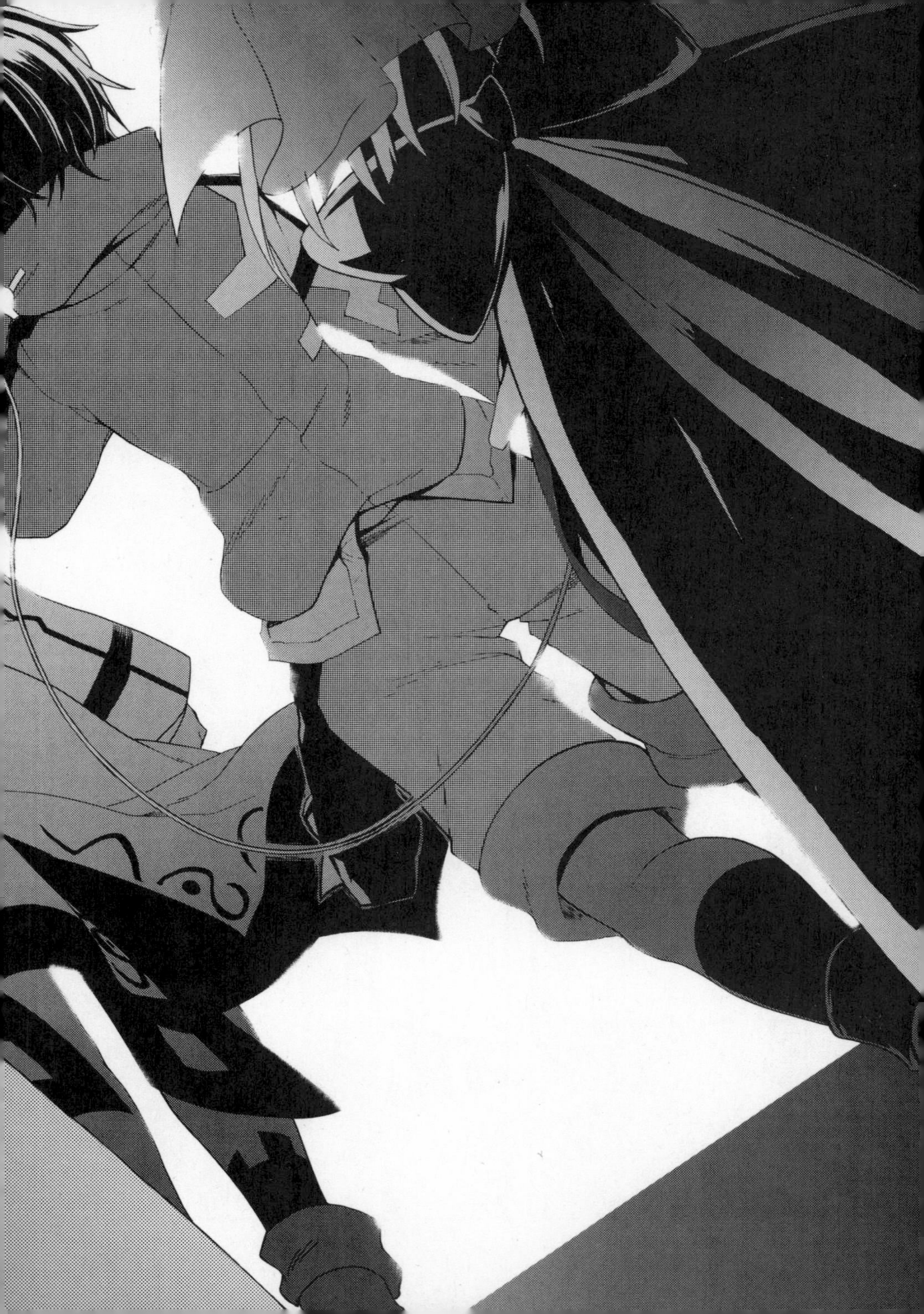

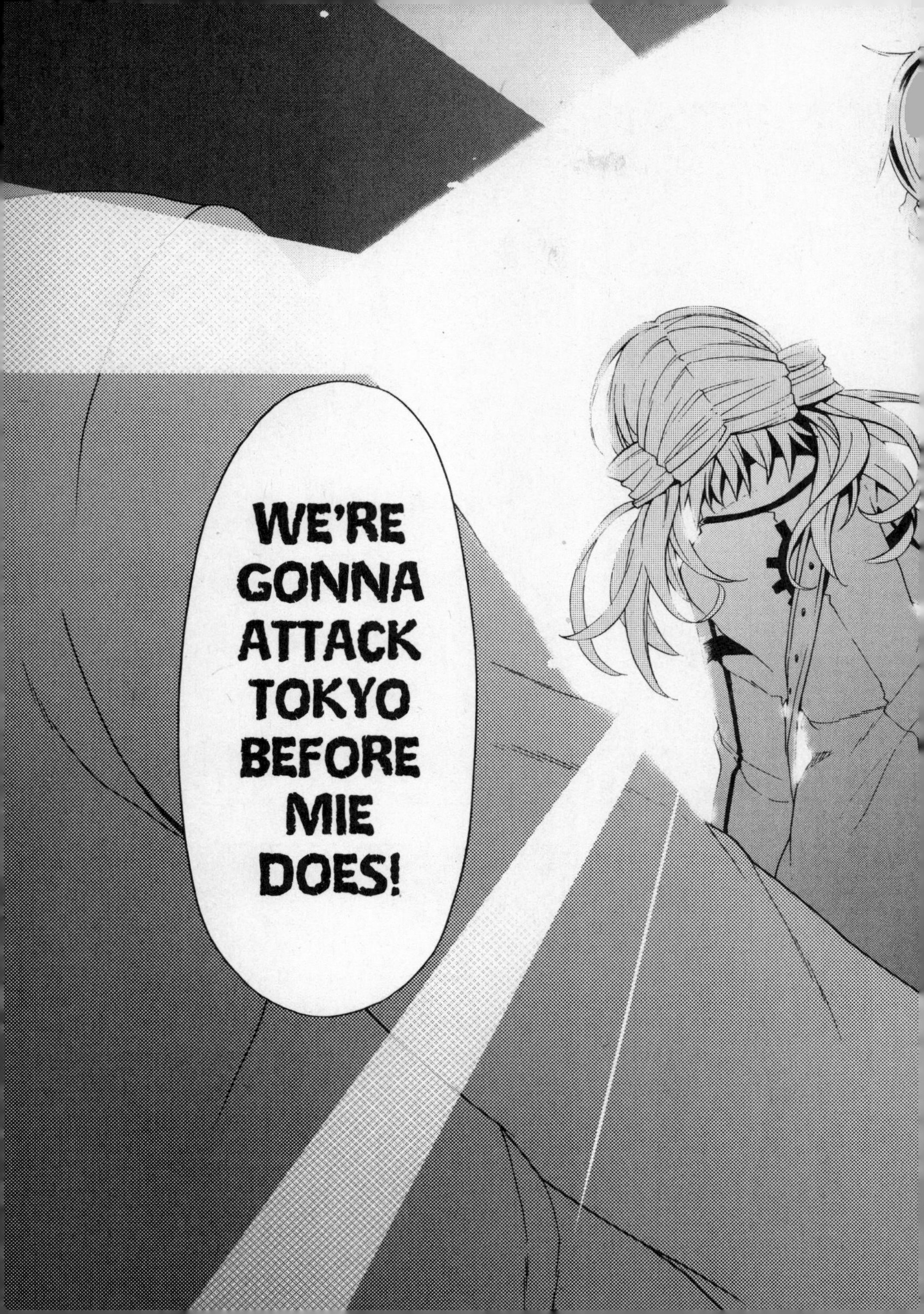
WE'RE GONNA ATTACK TOKYO BEFORE MIE DOES!

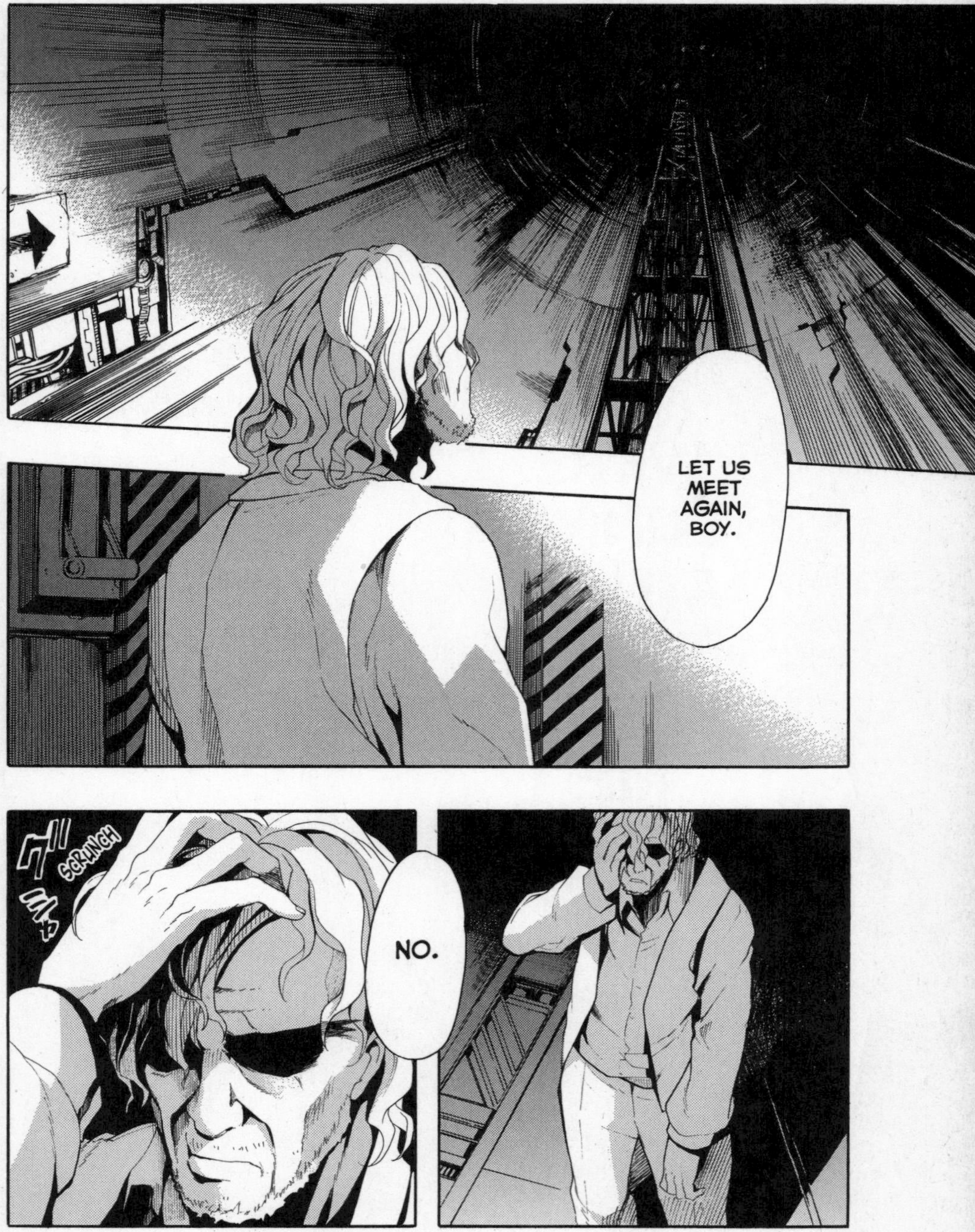
LET US MEET AGAIN, BOY.
NO.
SCRUNCH

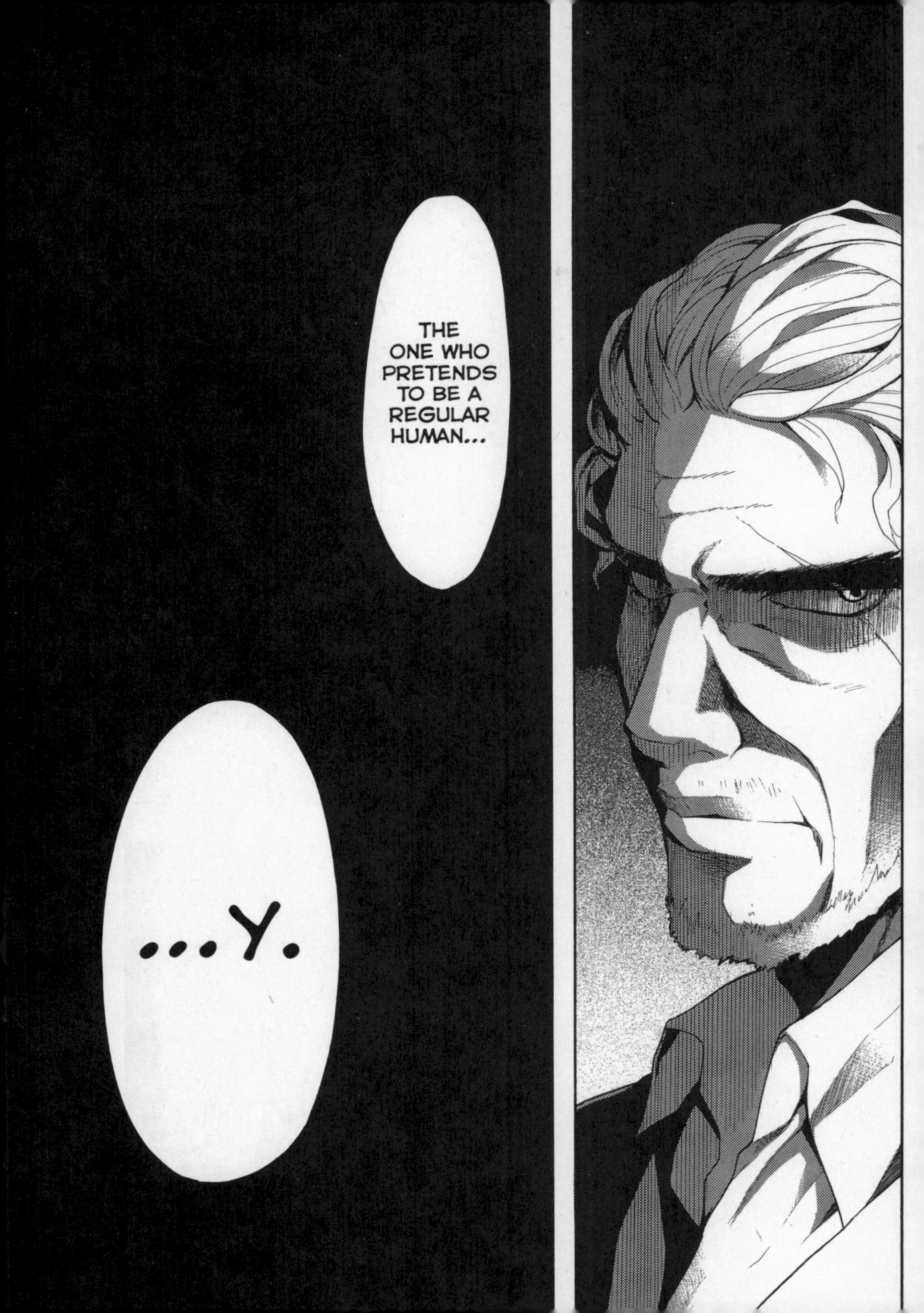
THE ONE WHO PRETENDS TO BE A REGULAR HUMAN...
...Y.

Clockwork Planet

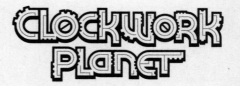

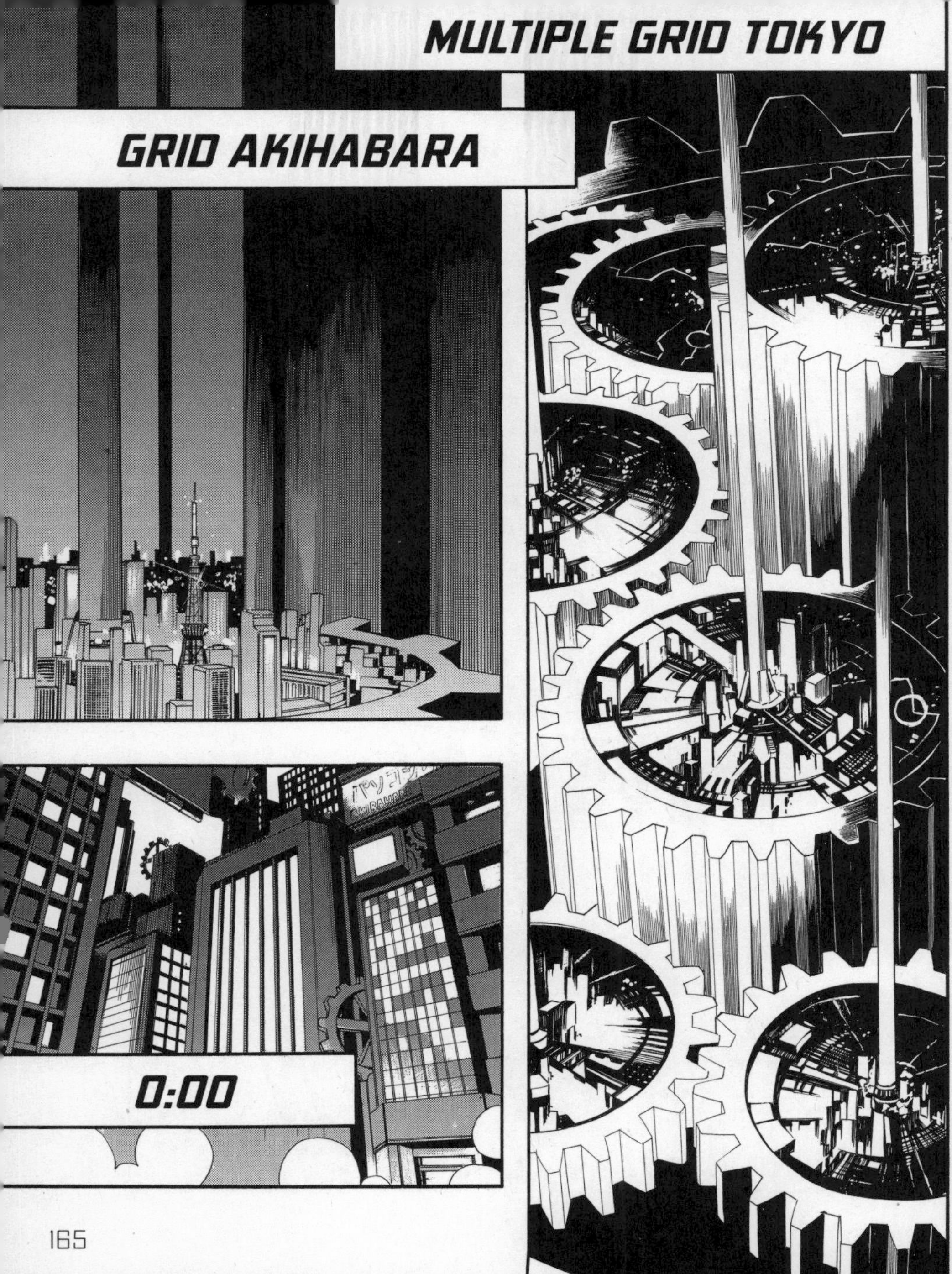
MULTIPLE GRID TOKYO
GRID AKIHABARA
0:00

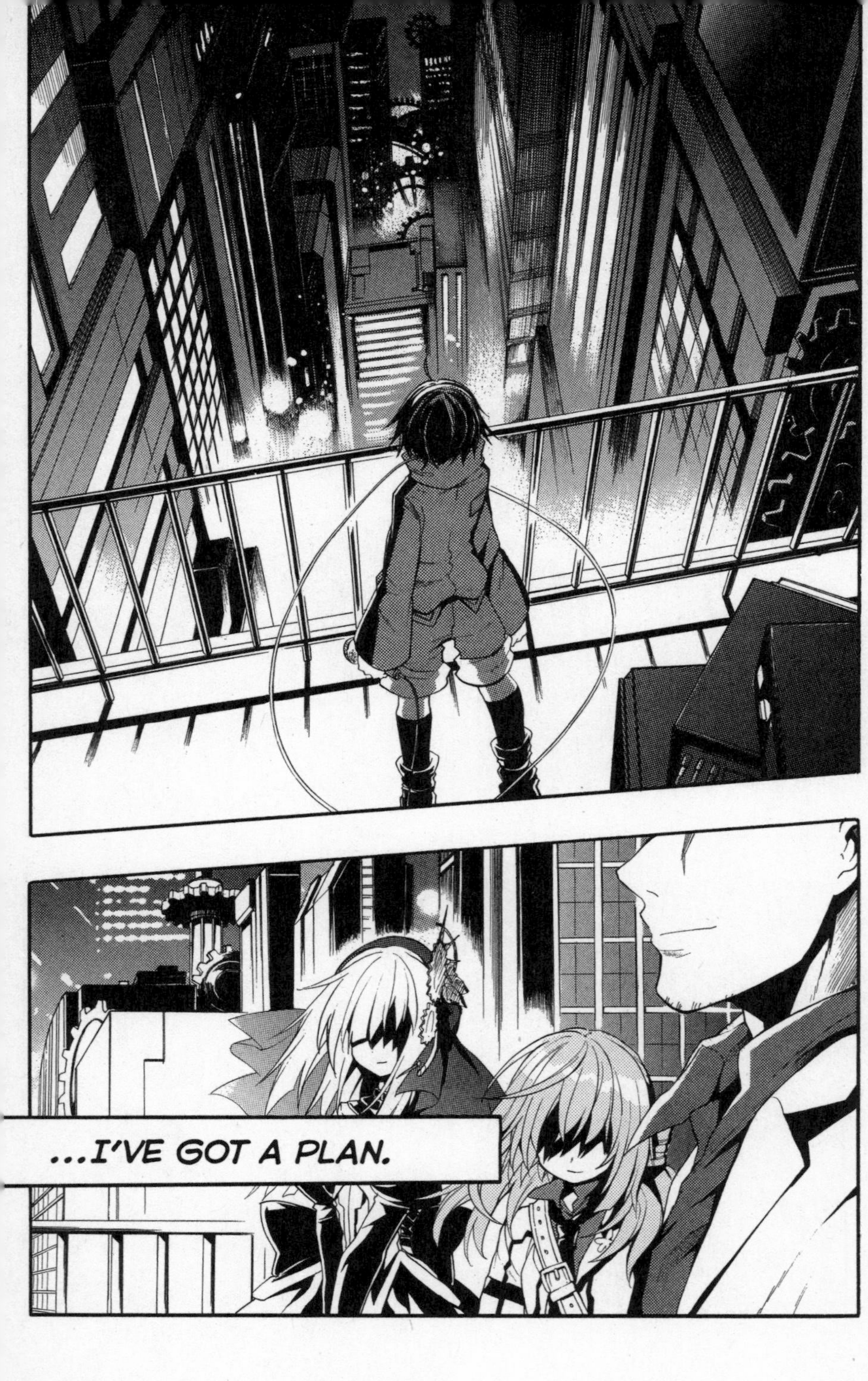
...I'VE GOT A PLAN.

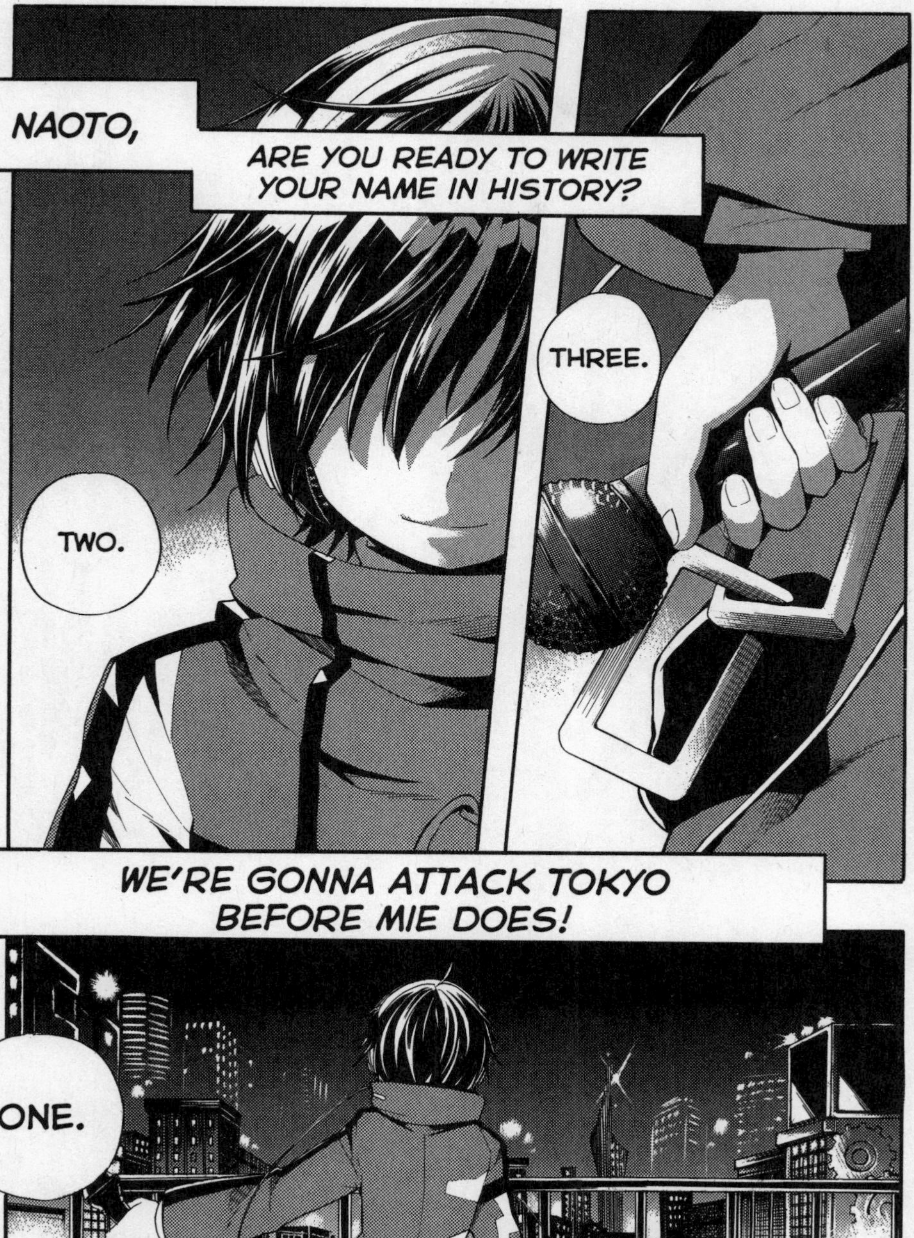
NAOTO,
ARE YOU READY TO WRITE YOUR NAME IN HISTORY?
THREE.
TWO.
WE'RE GONNA ATTACK TOKYO BEFORE MIE DOES!
ONE.

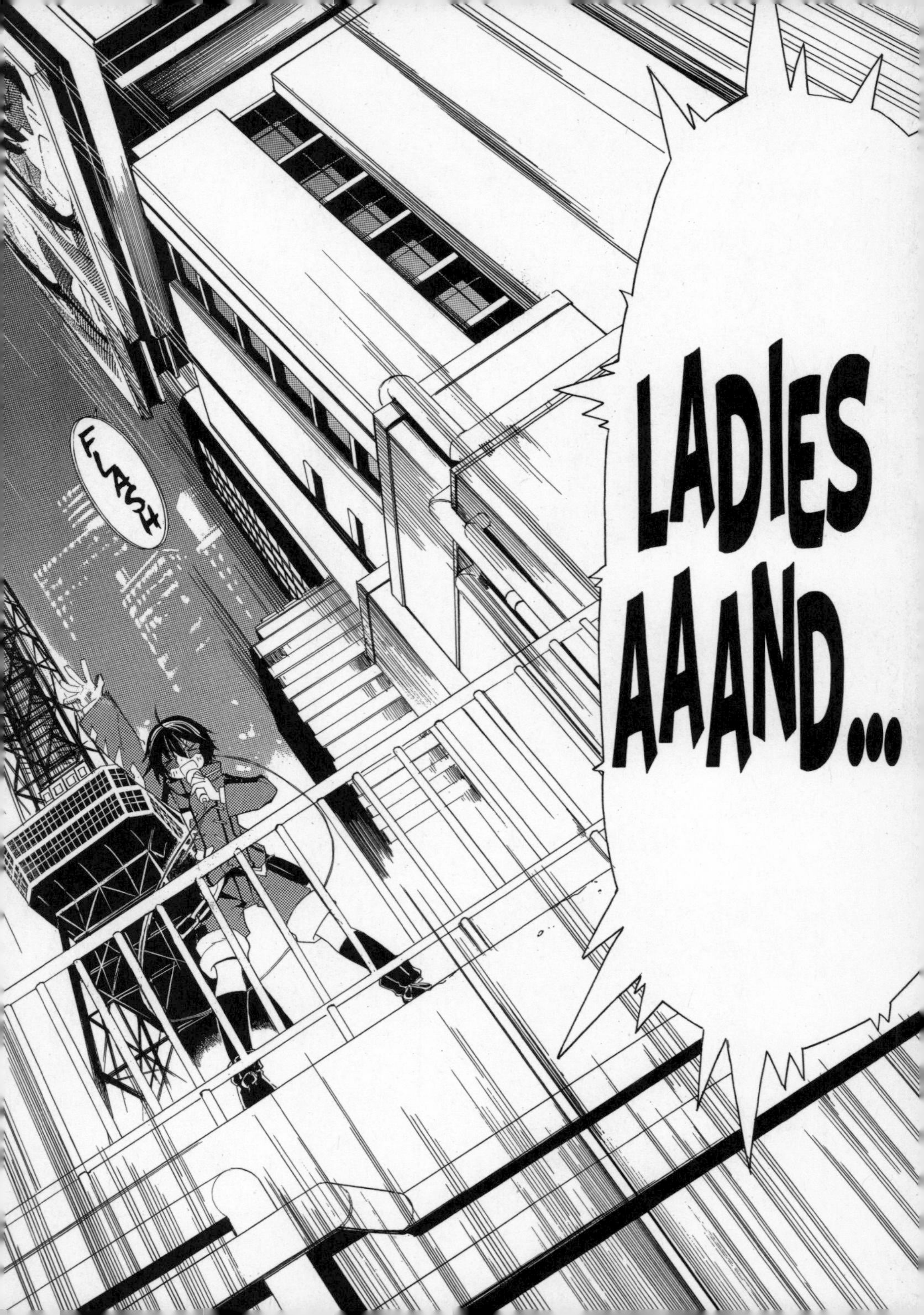
LADIES AAAND...
FLASH

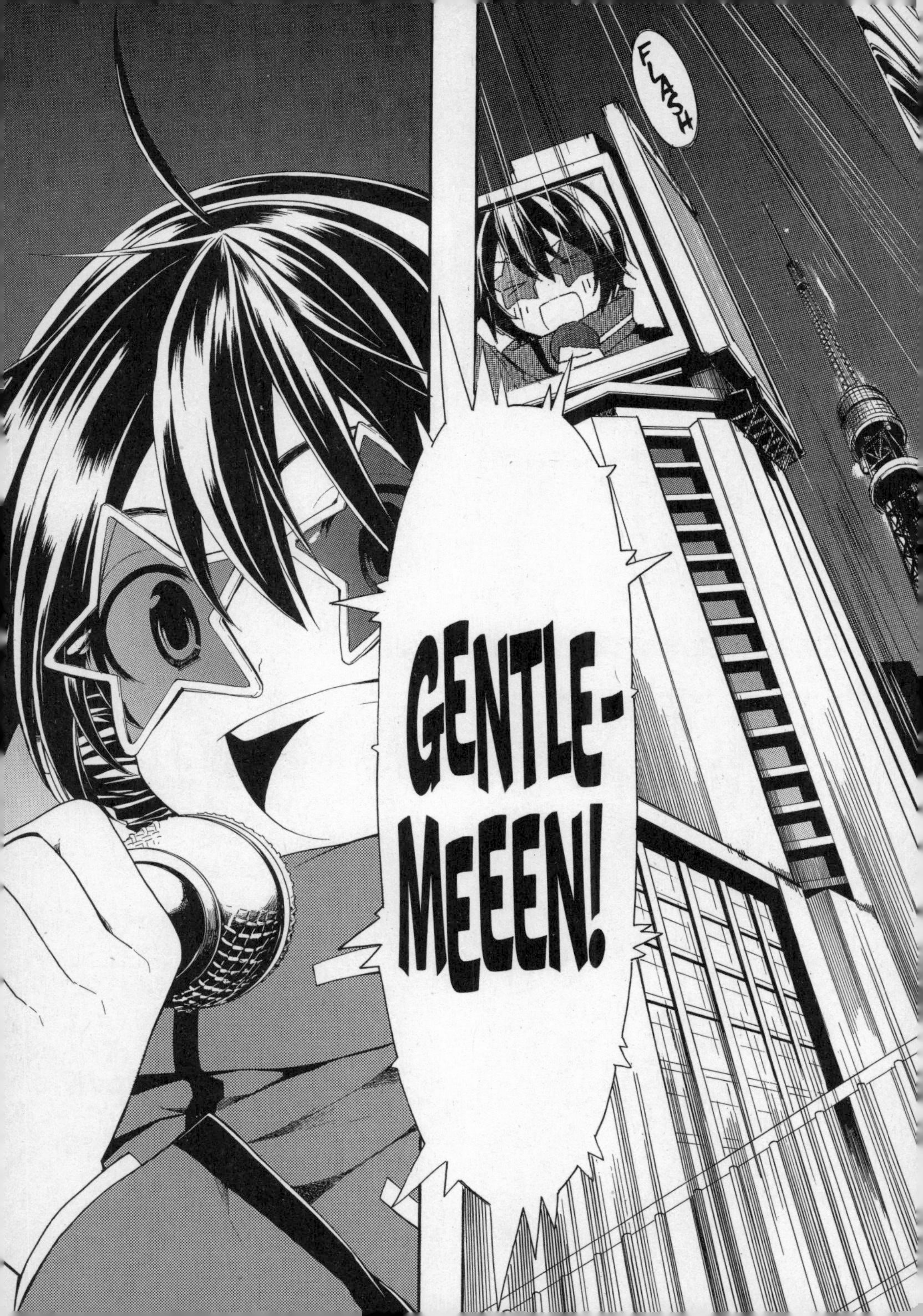
FLASH
GENTLE-
MEEEN!

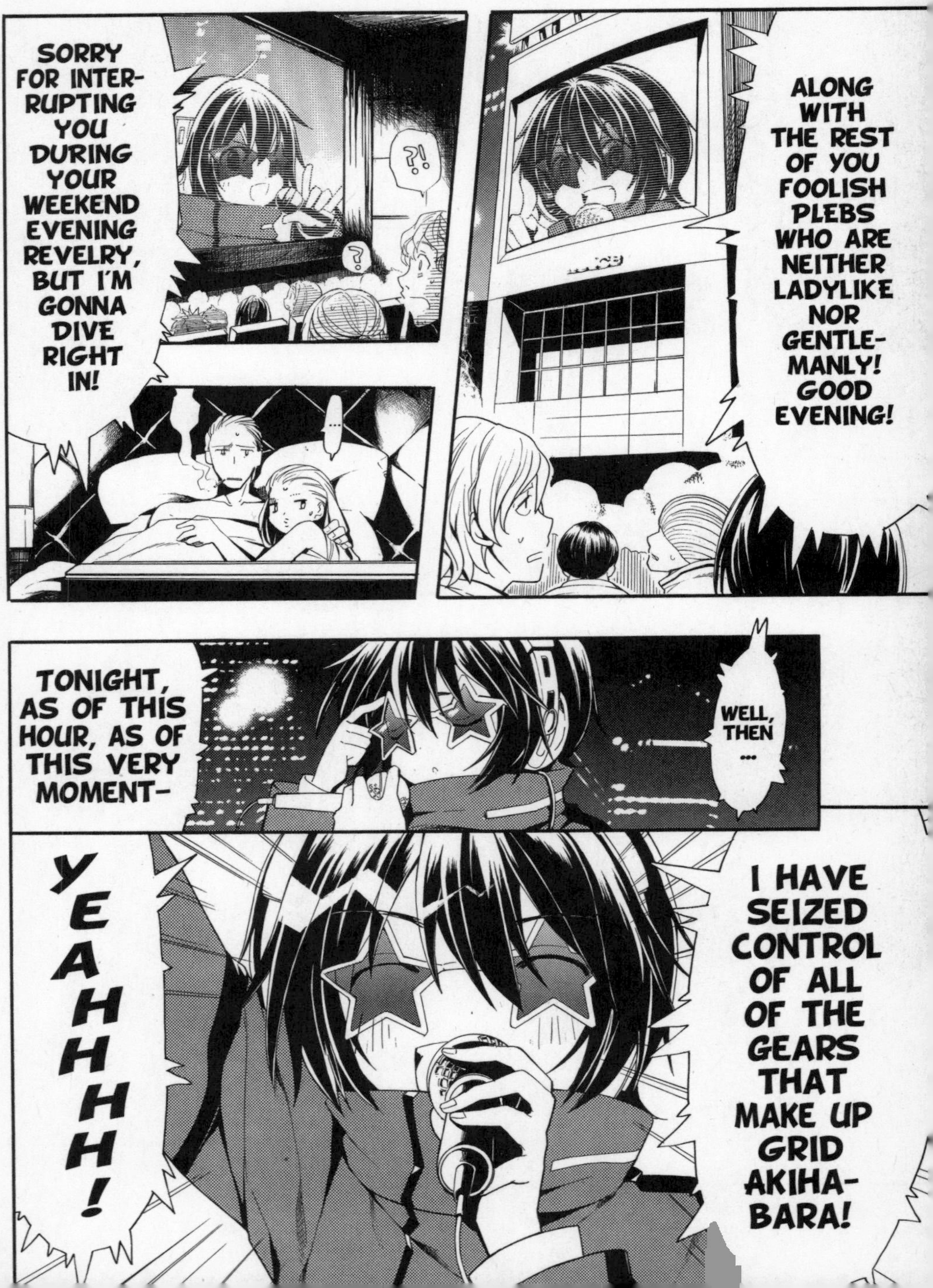
ALONG WITH THE REST OF YOU FOOLISH PLEBS WHO ARE NEITHER LADYLIKE NOR GENTLE-MANLY! GOOD EVENING!
SORRY FOR INTER-RUPTING YOU DURING YOUR WEEKEND EVENING REVELRY, BUT I'M GONNA DIVE RIGHT IN!
?!
?
...
WELL, THEN ...
TONIGHT, AS OF THIS HOUR, AS OF THIS VERY MOMENT-
I HAVE SEIZED CONTROL OF ALL OF THE GEARS THAT MAKE UP GRID AKIHA-BARA!
YEAHHHHH!

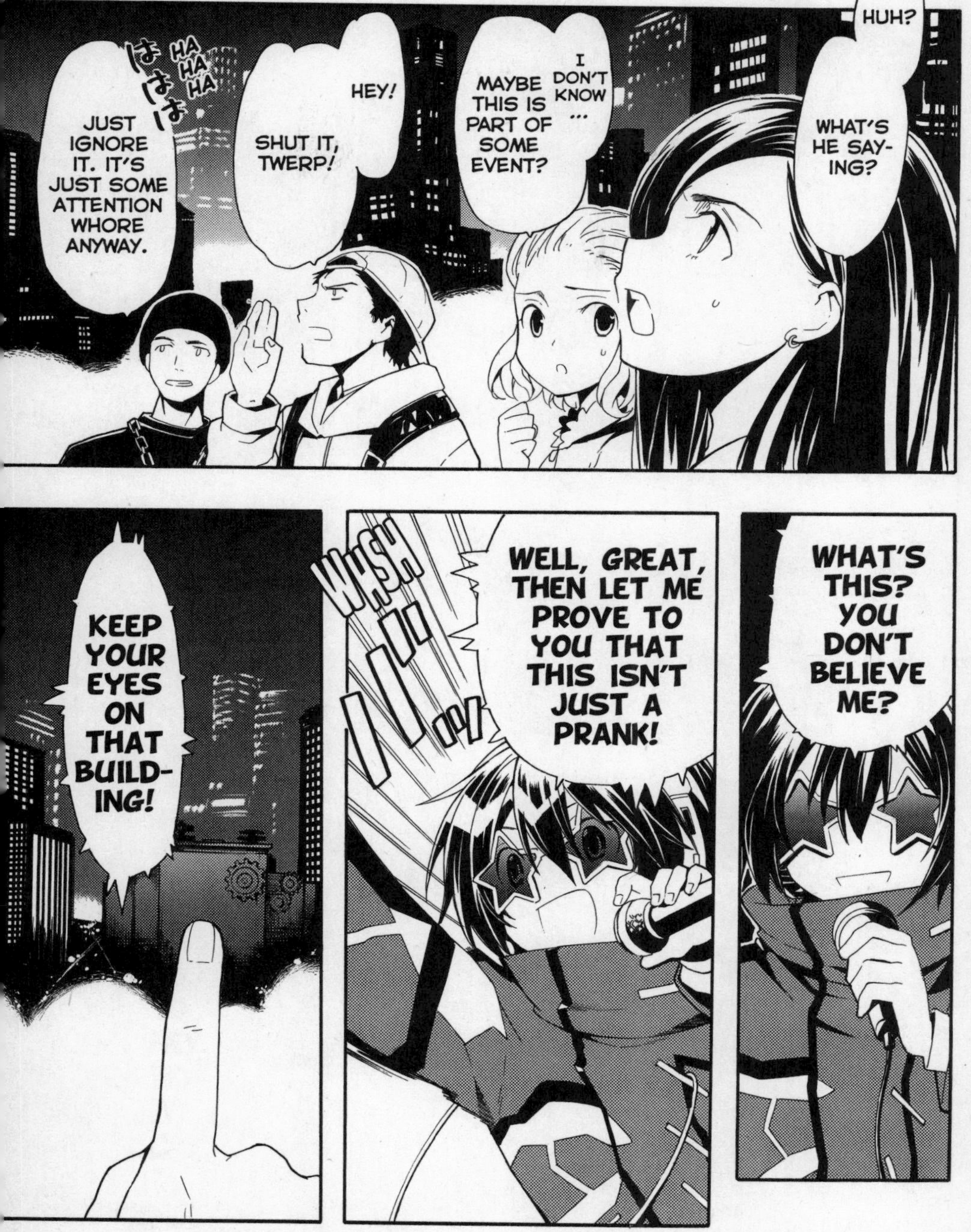
HUH?
WHAT'S HE SAYING?
I DON'T KNOW ...
MAYBE THIS IS PART OF SOME EVENT?
HEY!
SHUT IT, TWERP!
ははは
HA HA HA
JUST IGNORE IT. IT'S JUST SOME ATTENTION WHORE ANYWAY.
WHAT'S THIS? YOU DON'T BELIEVE ME?
WHSH
WELL, GREAT, THEN LET ME PROVE TO YOU THAT THIS ISN'T JUST A PRANK!
KEEP YOUR EYES ON THAT BUILDING!

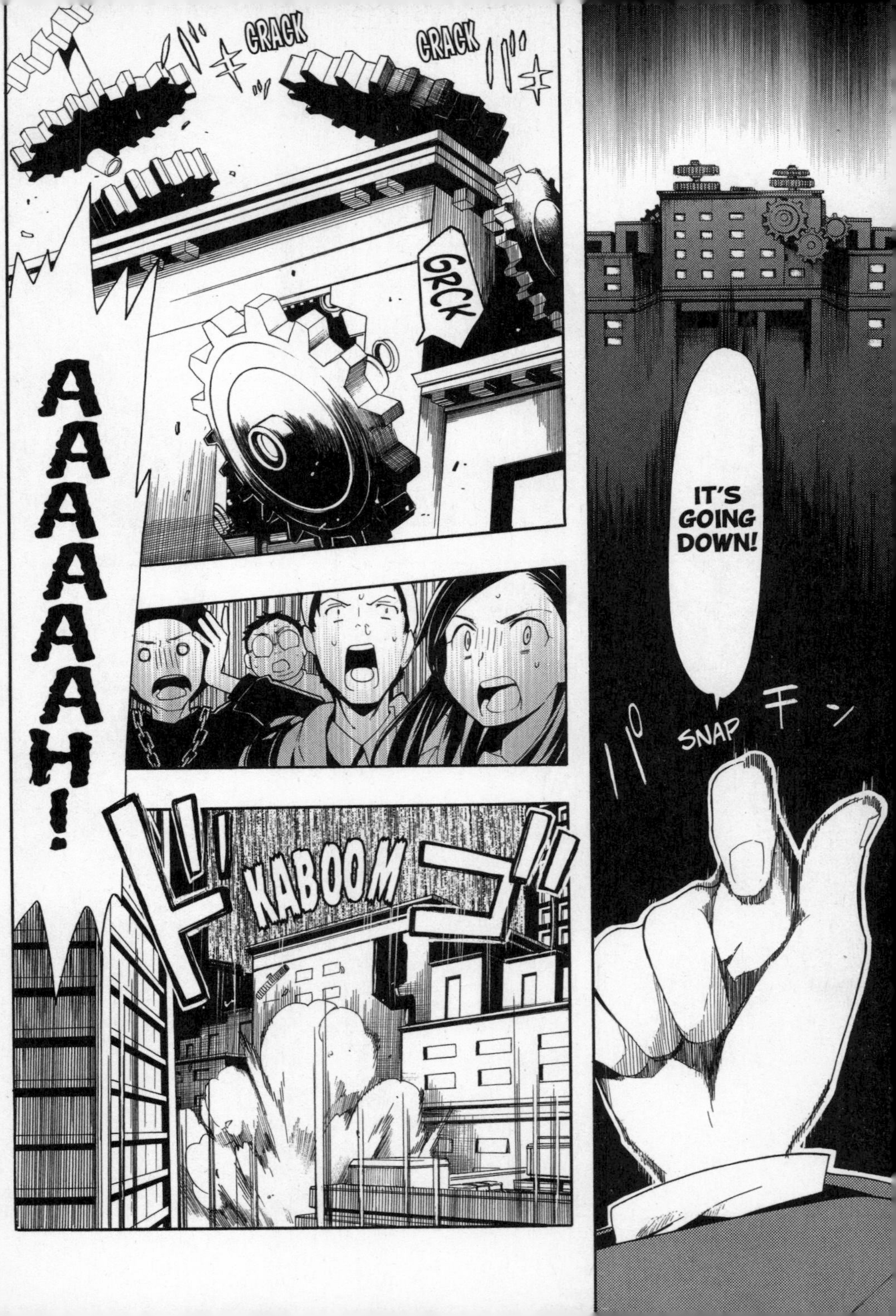
IT'S GOING DOWN!
SNAP
CRACK
CRACK
GRCK
AAAAAAH!
KABOOM

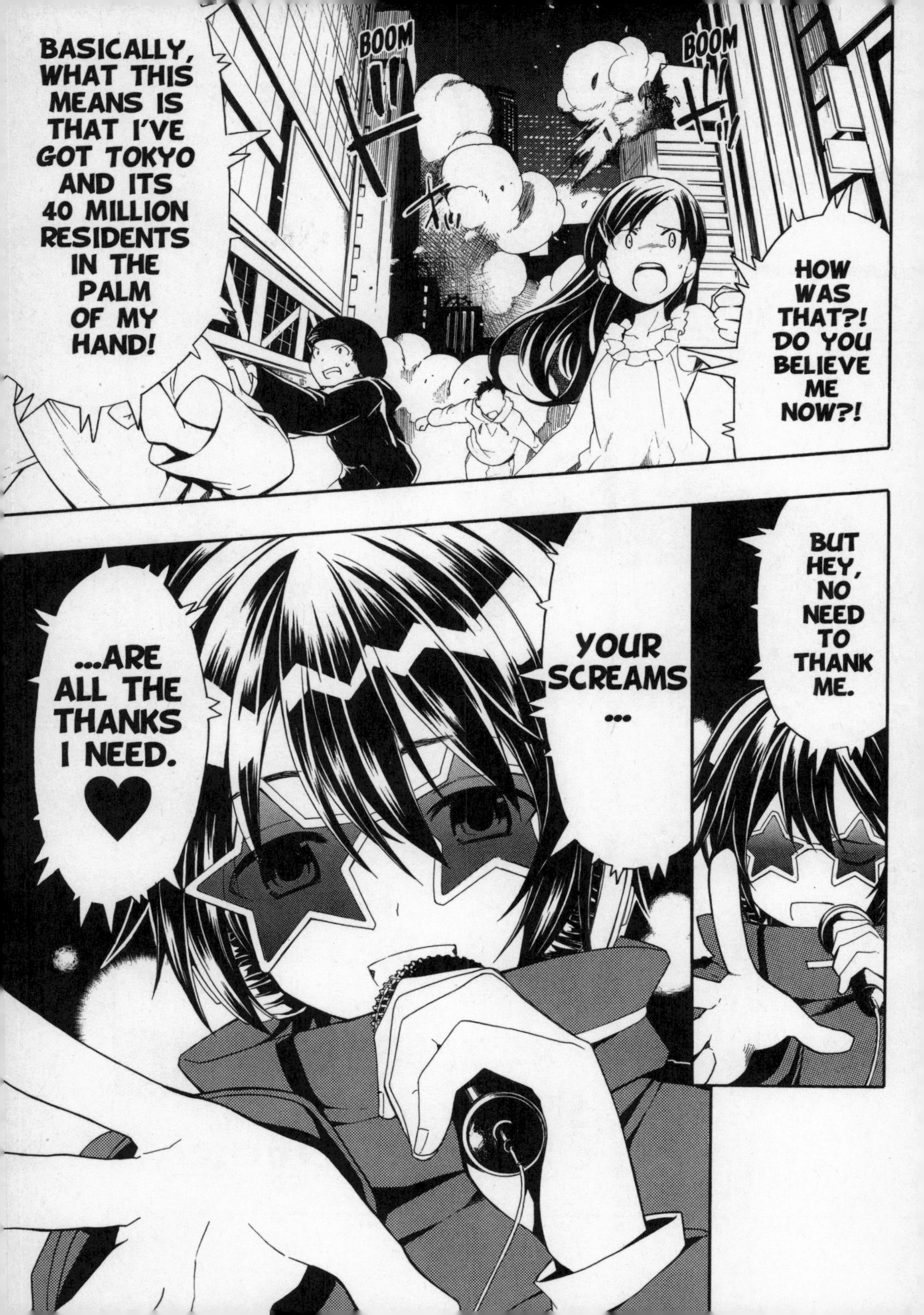
BOOM
BOOM
BASICALLY, WHAT THIS MEANS IS THAT I'VE GOT TOKYO AND ITS 40 MILLION RESIDENTS IN THE PALM OF MY HAND!
HOW WAS THAT?! DO YOU BELIEVE ME NOW?!
BUT HEY, NO NEED TO THANK ME.
YOUR SCREAMS ...
...ARE ALL THE THANKS I NEED. ♥

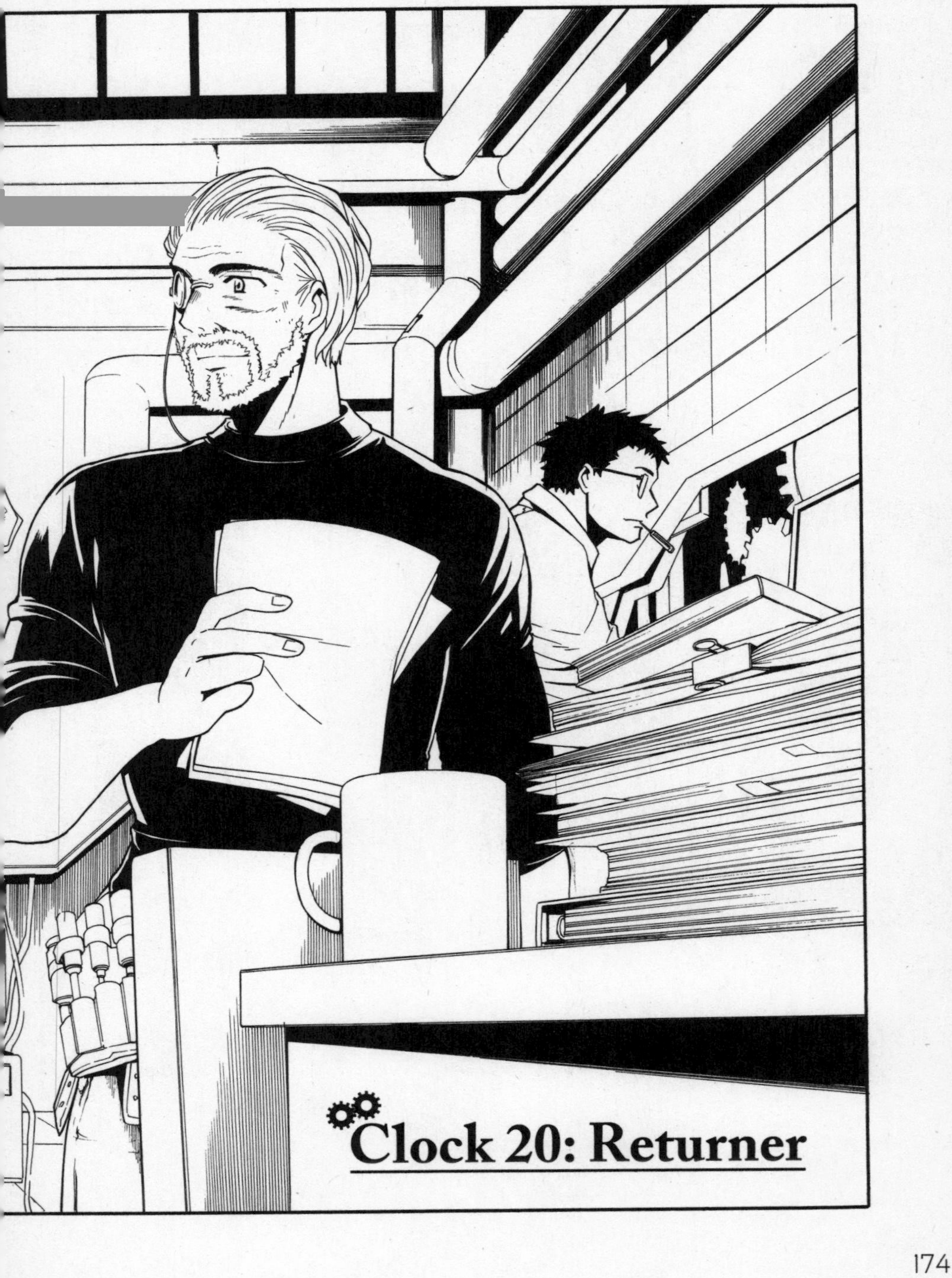
Clock 20: Returner

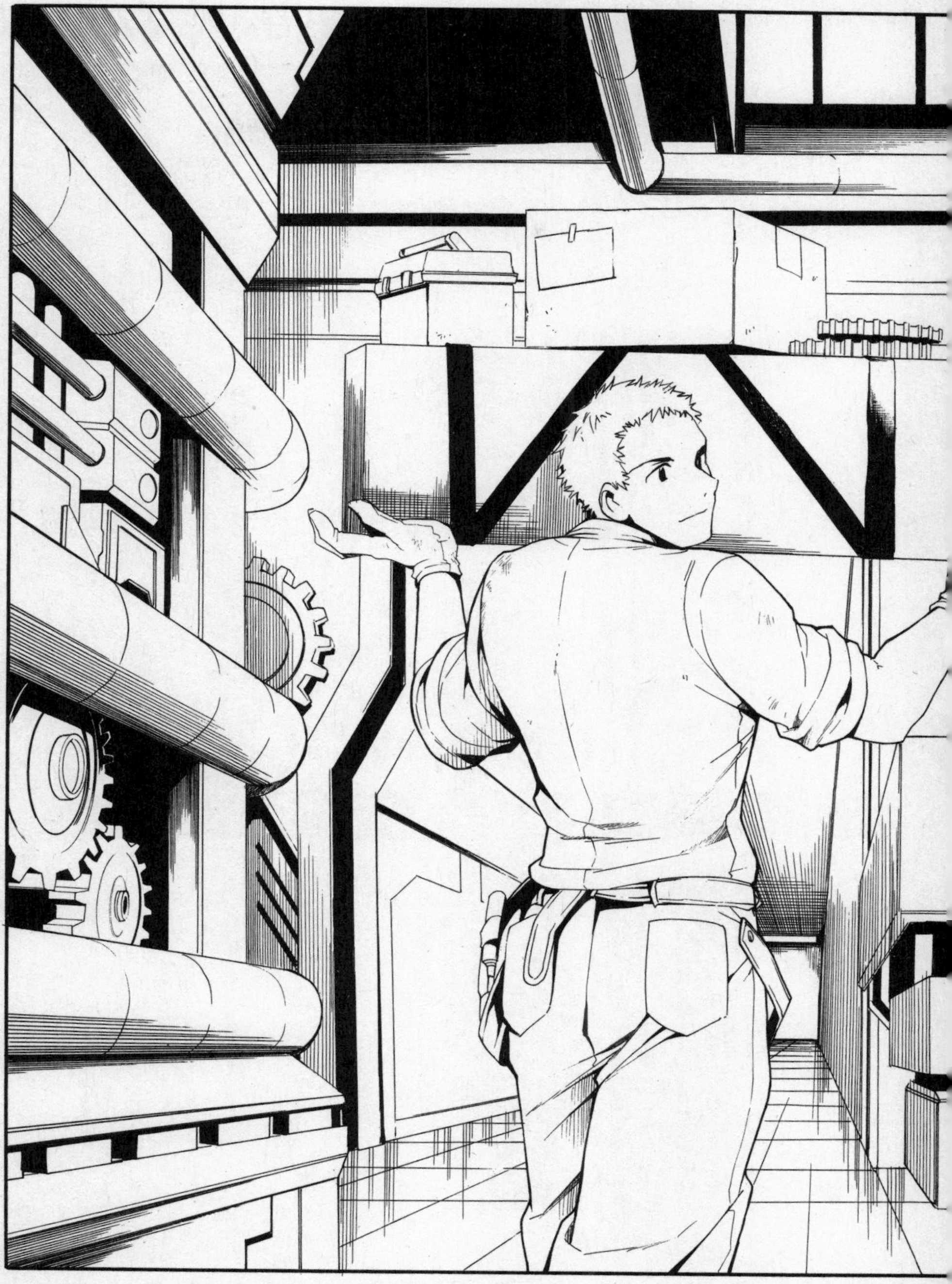

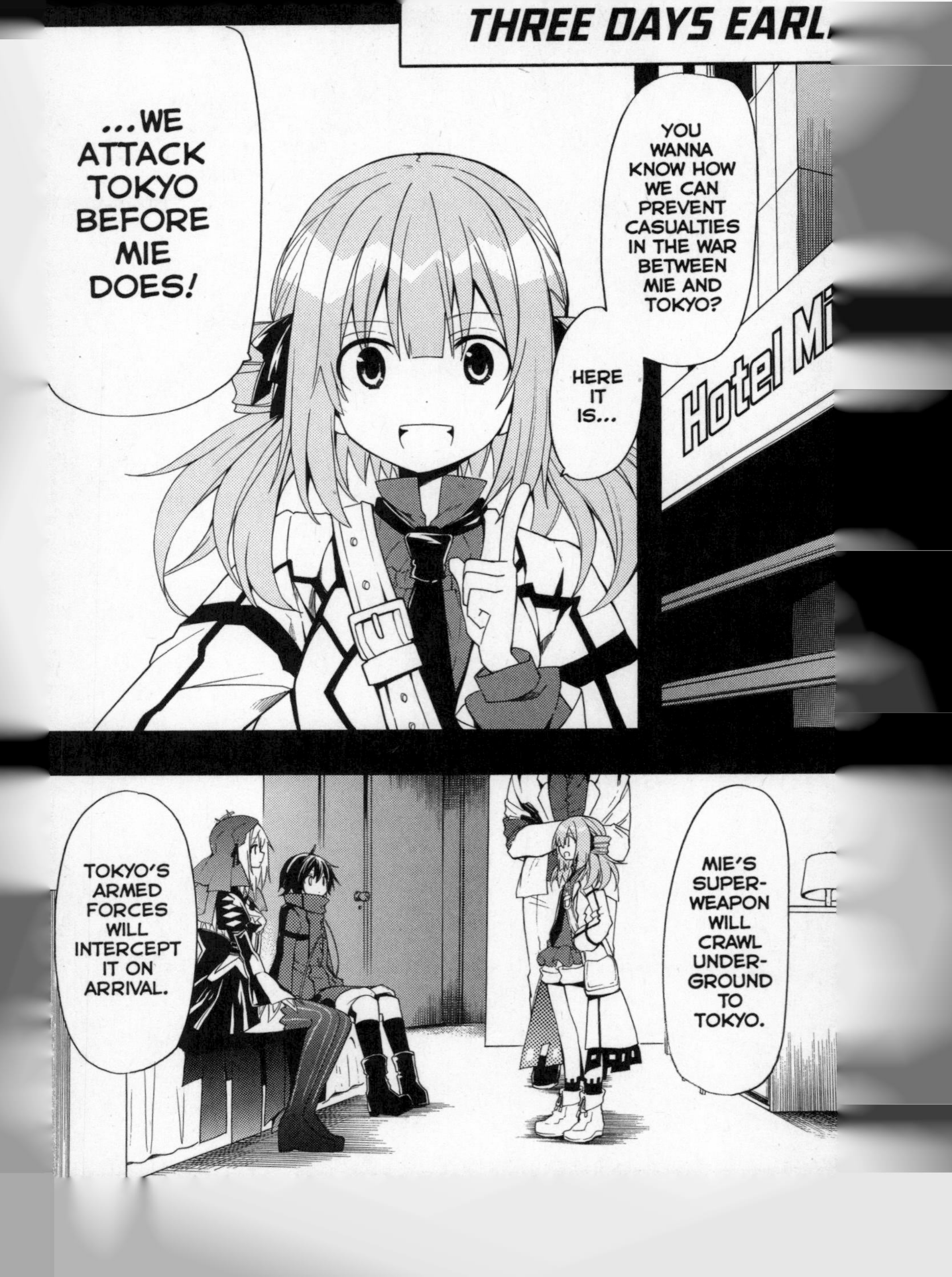
THREE DAYS EARL
YOU WANNA KNOW HOW WE CAN PREVENT CASUALTIES IN THE WAR BETWEEN MIE AND TOKYO?
HERE IT IS...
...WE ATTACK TOKYO BEFORE MIE DOES!
Hotel Mi
MIE'S SUPER-WEAPON WILL CRAWL UNDER-GROUND TO TOKYO.
TOKYO'S ARMED FORCES WILL INTERCEPT IT ON ARRIVAL.

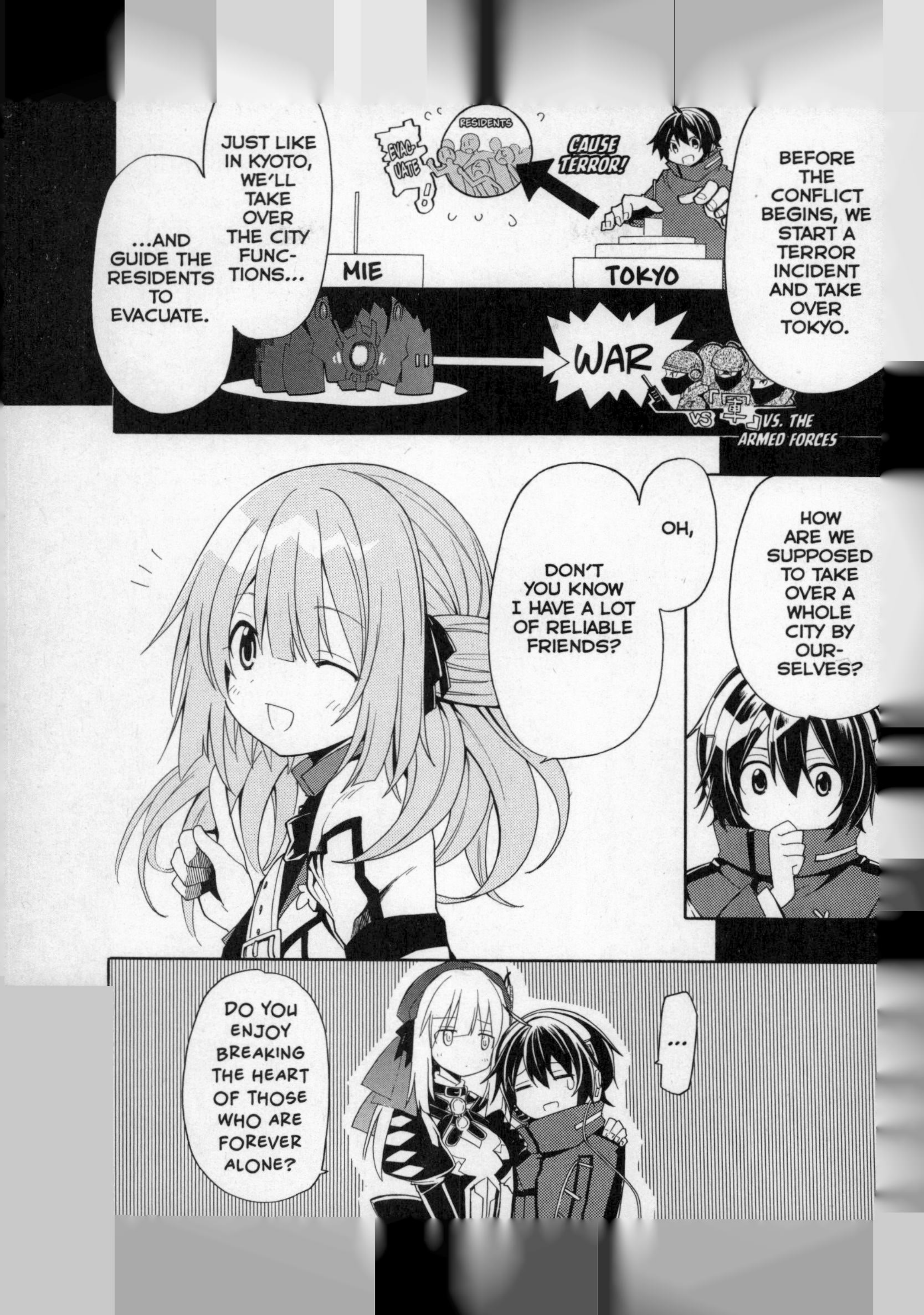
BEFORE THE CONFLICT BEGINS, WE START A TERROR INCIDENT AND TAKE OVER TOKYO.
CAUSE TERROR!
RESIDENTS
EVAC-UATE
TOKYO
WAR
VS. THE ARMED FORCES
MIE
JUST LIKE IN KYOTO, WE'LL TAKE OVER THE CITY FUNC-TIONS...
...AND GUIDE THE RESIDENTS TO EVACUATE.
HOW ARE WE SUPPOSED TO TAKE OVER A WHOLE CITY BY OUR-SELVES?
OH,
DON'T YOU KNOW I HAVE A LOT OF RELIABLE FRIENDS?
...
DO YOU ENJOY BREAKING THE HEART OF THOSE WHO ARE FOREVER ALONE?

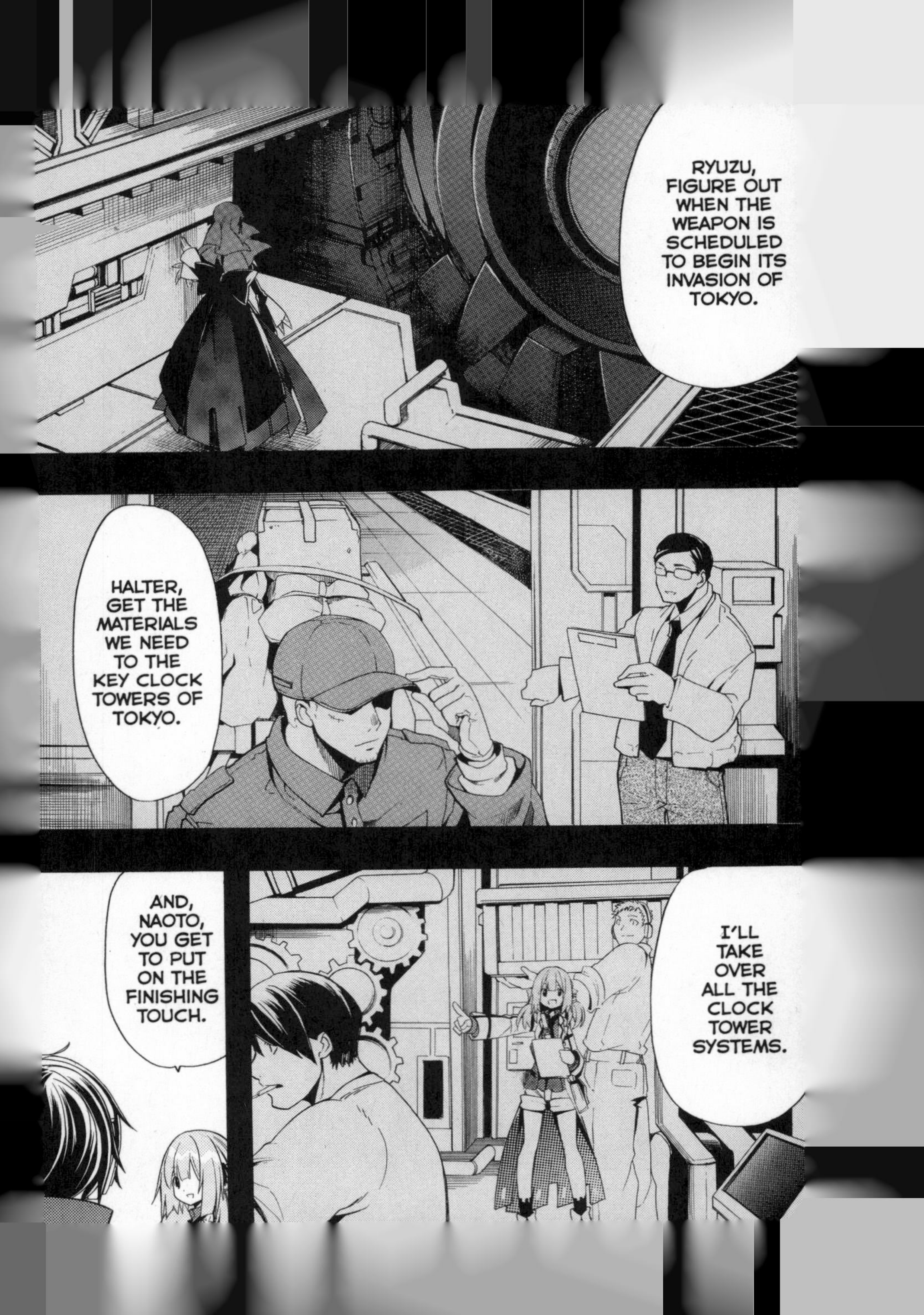
RYUZU, FIGURE OUT WHEN THE WEAPON IS SCHEDULED TO BEGIN ITS INVASION OF TOKYO.
HALTER, GET THE MATERIALS WE NEED TO THE KEY CLOCK TOWERS OF TOKYO.
I'LL TAKE OVER ALL THE CLOCK TOWER SYSTEMS.
AND, NAOTO, YOU GET TO PUT ON THE FINISHING TOUCH.

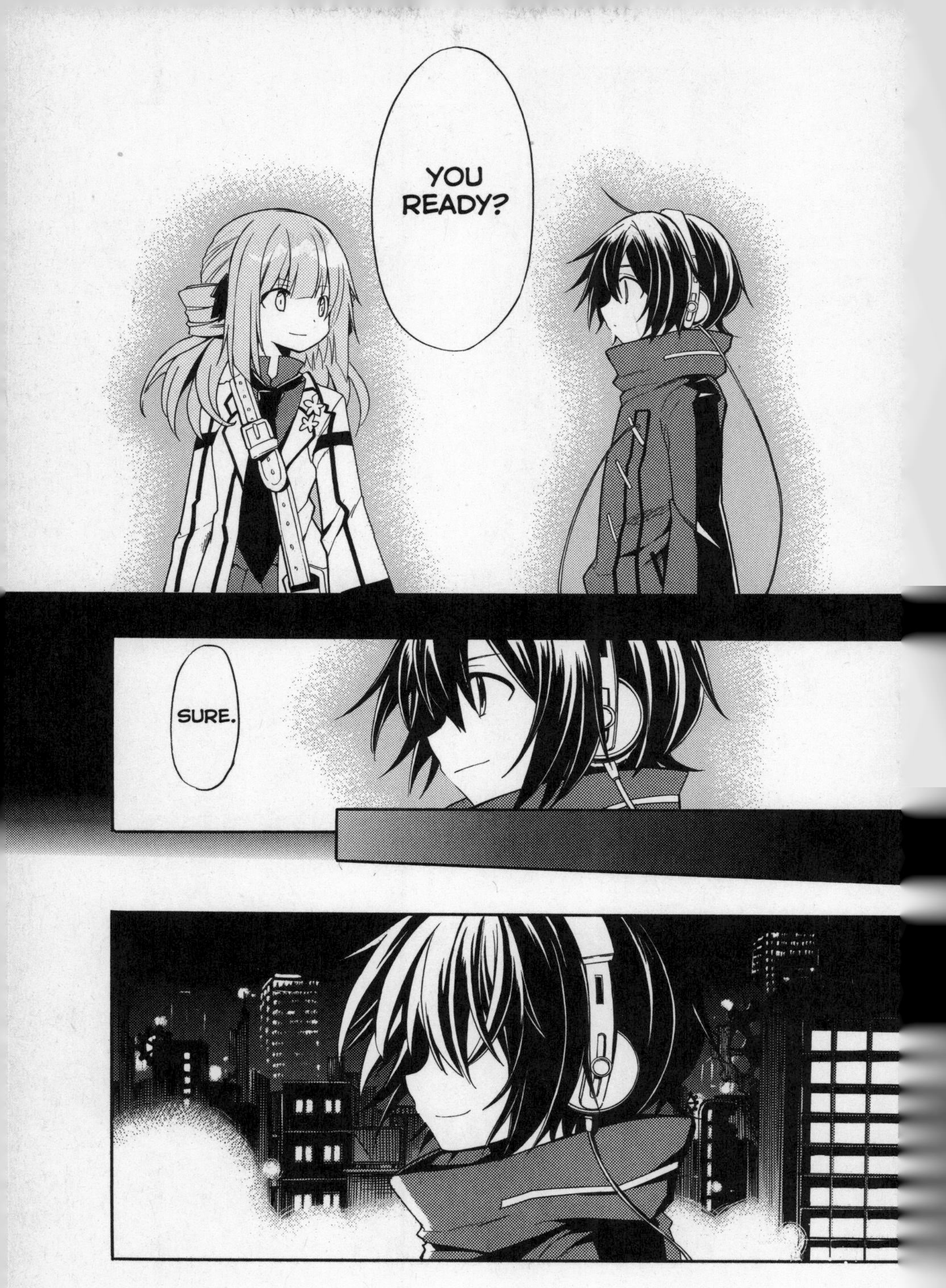
YOU READY?
SURE.

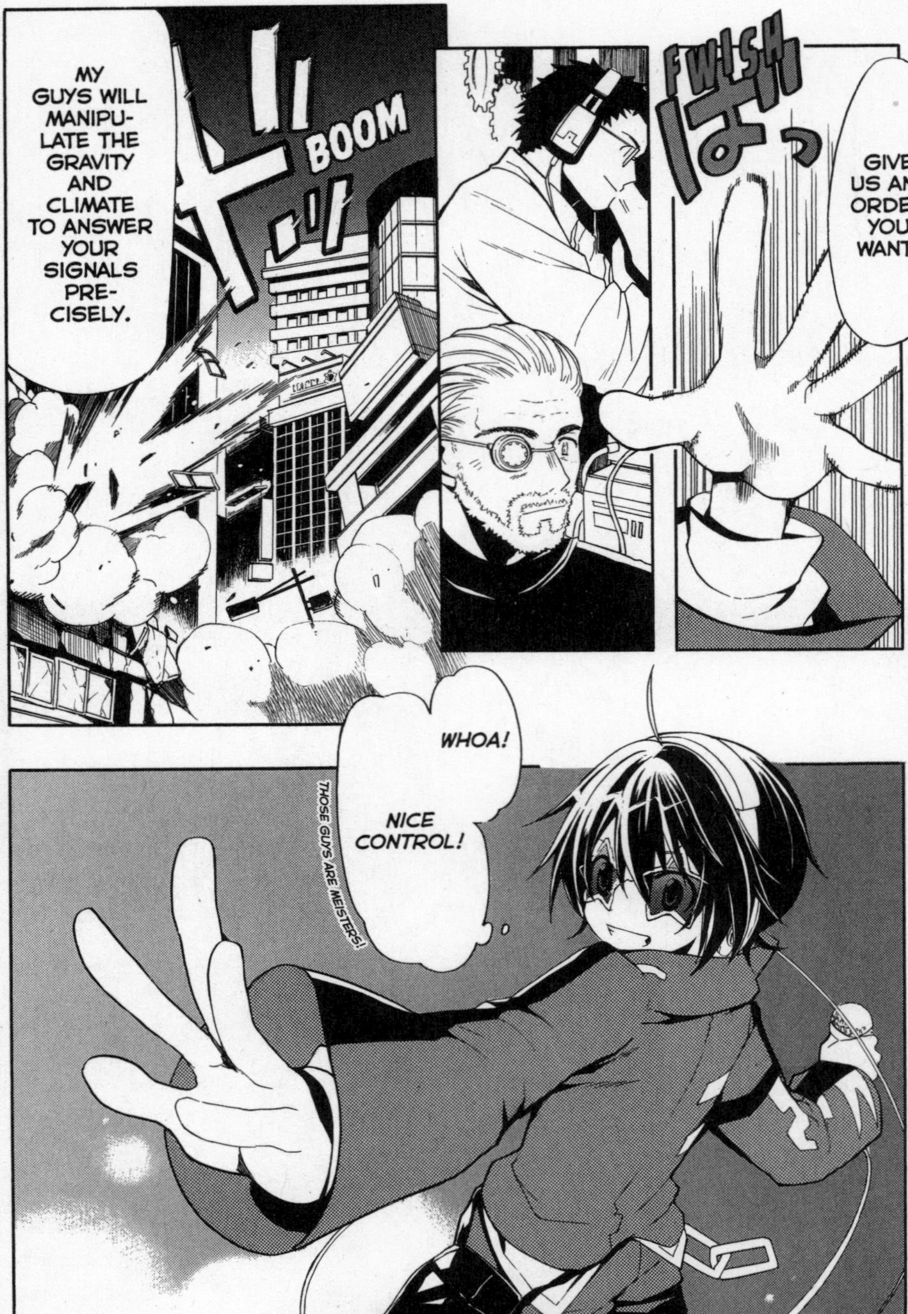
FWISH
ぱっ
GIVE US ANY ORDER YOU WANT.
BOOM
MY GUYS WILL MANIPU-LATE THE GRAVITY AND CLIMATE TO ANSWER YOUR SIGNALS PRE-CISELY.
WHOA!
NICE CONTROL!
THOSE GUYS ARE MEISTERS!

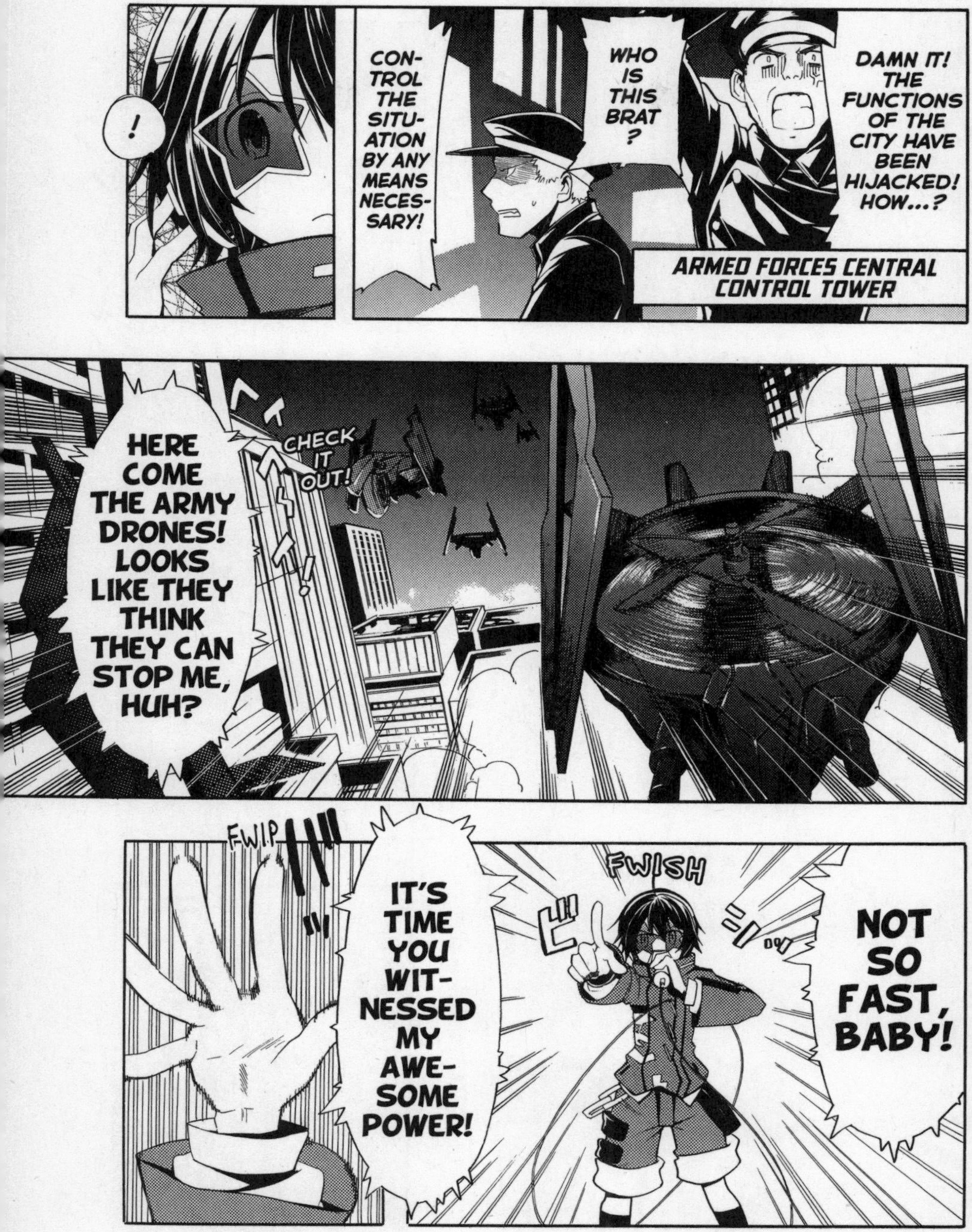
DAMN IT! THE FUNCTIONS OF THE CITY HAVE BEEN HIJACKED! HOW...?
ARMED FORCES CENTRAL CONTROL TOWER
WHO IS THIS BRAT?
CONTROL THE SITUATION BY ANY MEANS NECESSARY!
!
CHECK IT OUT!
HERE COME THE ARMY DRONES! LOOKS LIKE THEY THINK THEY CAN STOP ME, HUH?
NOT SO FAST, BABY!
FWISH
IT'S TIME YOU WITNESSED MY AWESOME POWER!
FWIP

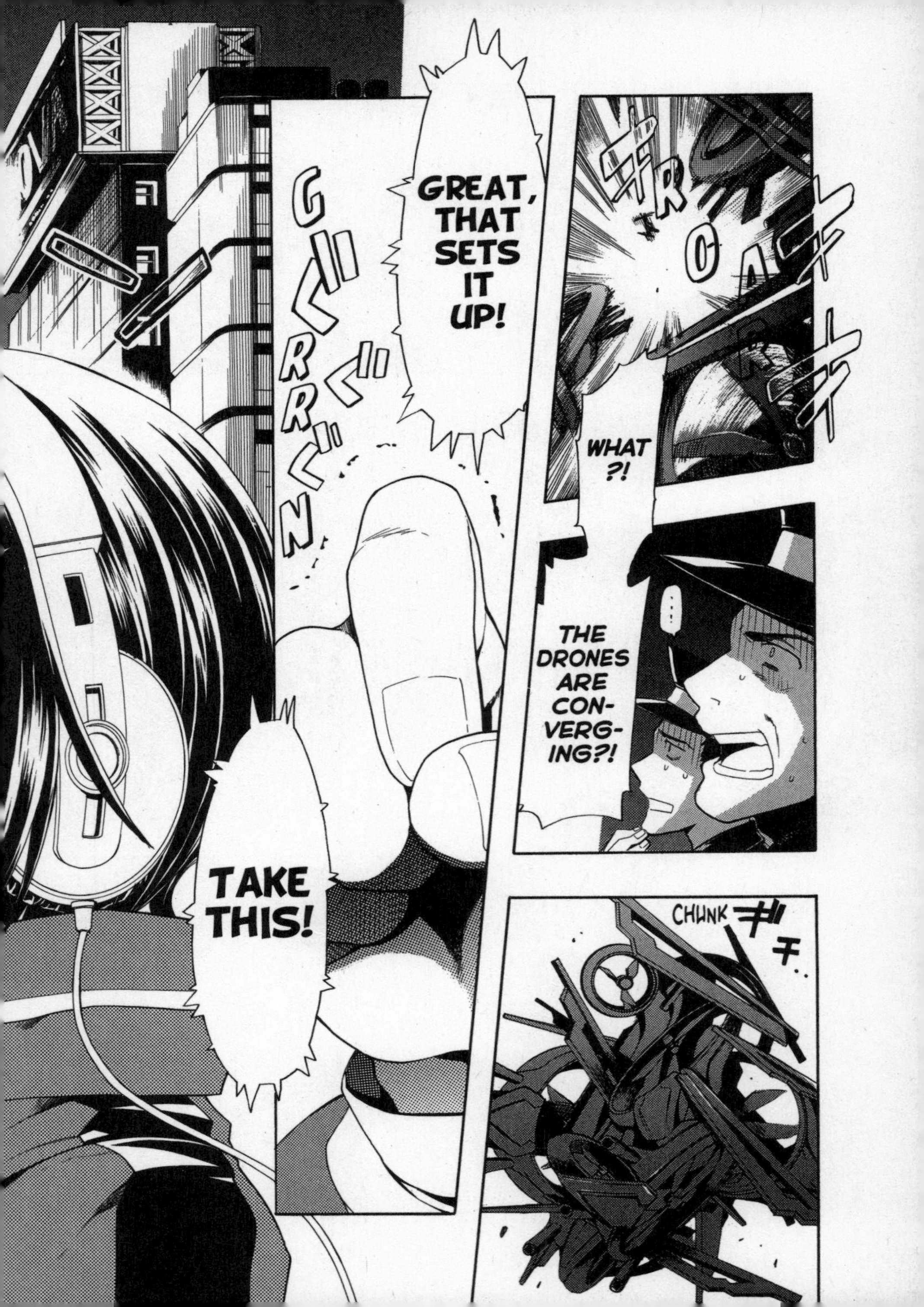
WHAT?!
...
THE DRONES ARE CON-VERG-ING?!
CHUNK
GREAT, THAT SETS IT UP!
GRRRN
TAKE THIS!

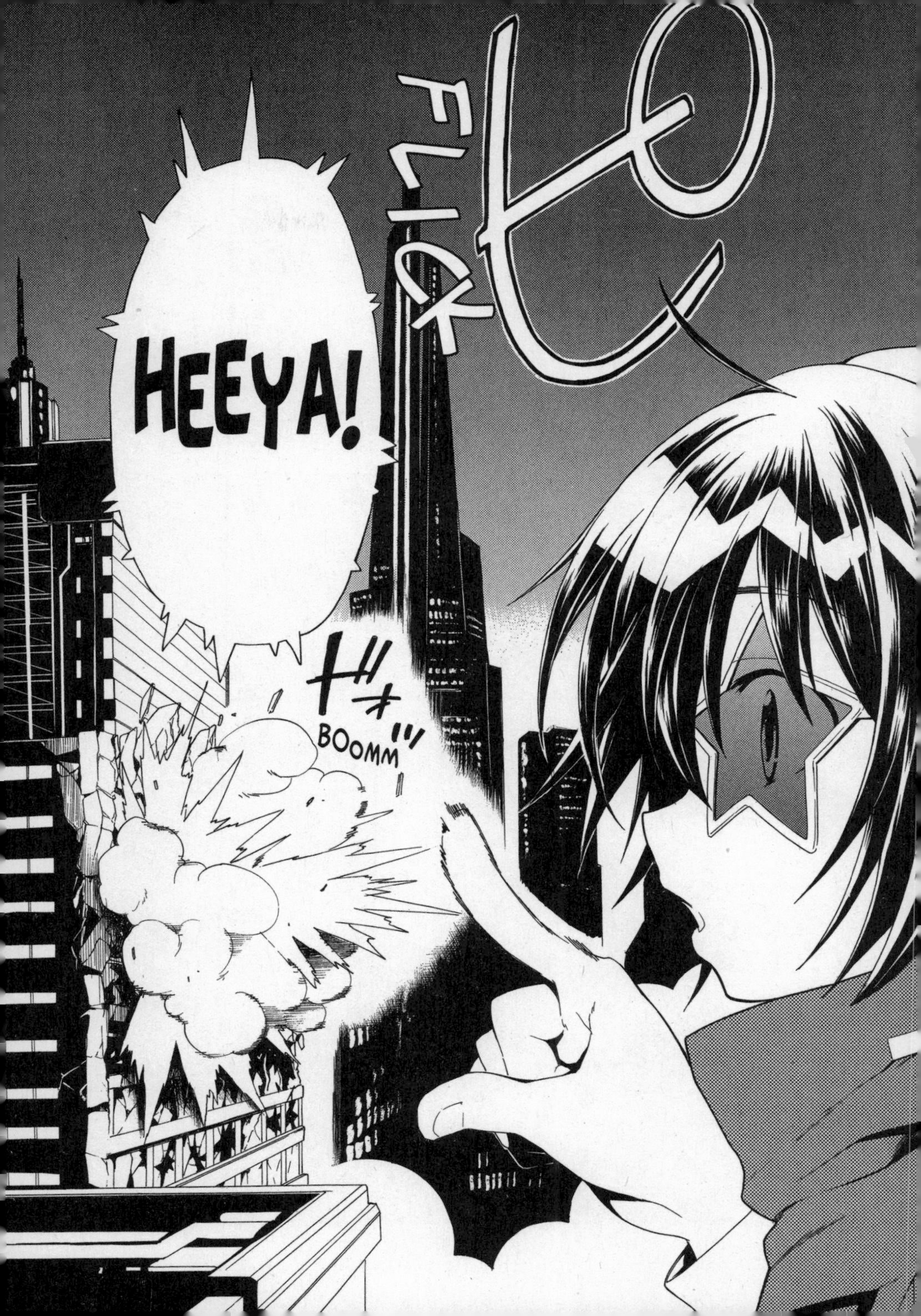
FLICK
HEEYA!
BOOMM

ALL RIIII-GHT!
IT'S TIME FOR THE MOMENT YOU'VE ALL BEEN WAITING FOR!
THE BIG FINALE! NOW, WHAT WOULD MAKE FOR A GRAND, STIRRING CLIMAX?
I KNOW!
THE TOKYO TOWER!

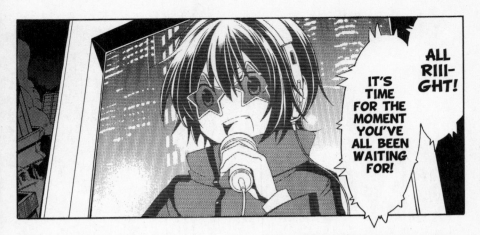

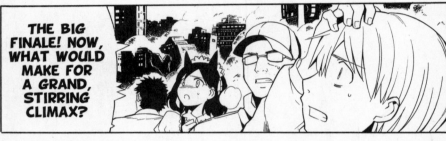

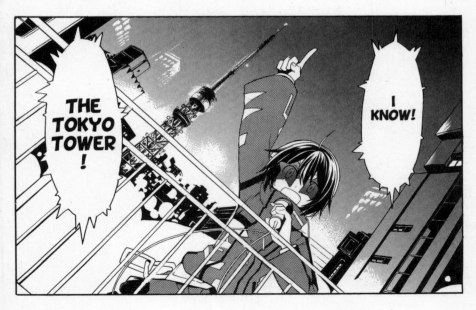

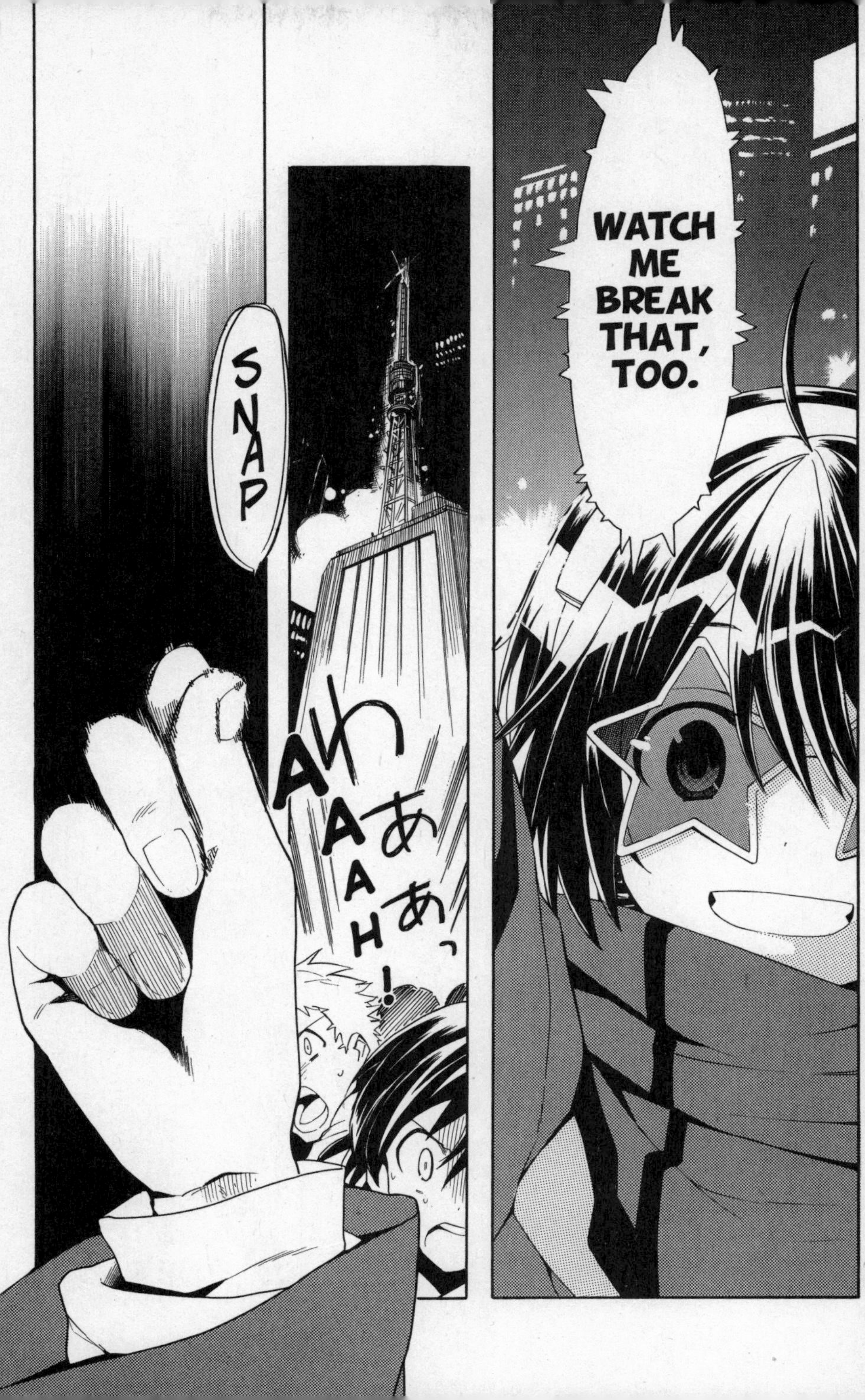
WATCH ME BREAK THAT, TOO.
SNAP
AHHH ああ、
AAAH!

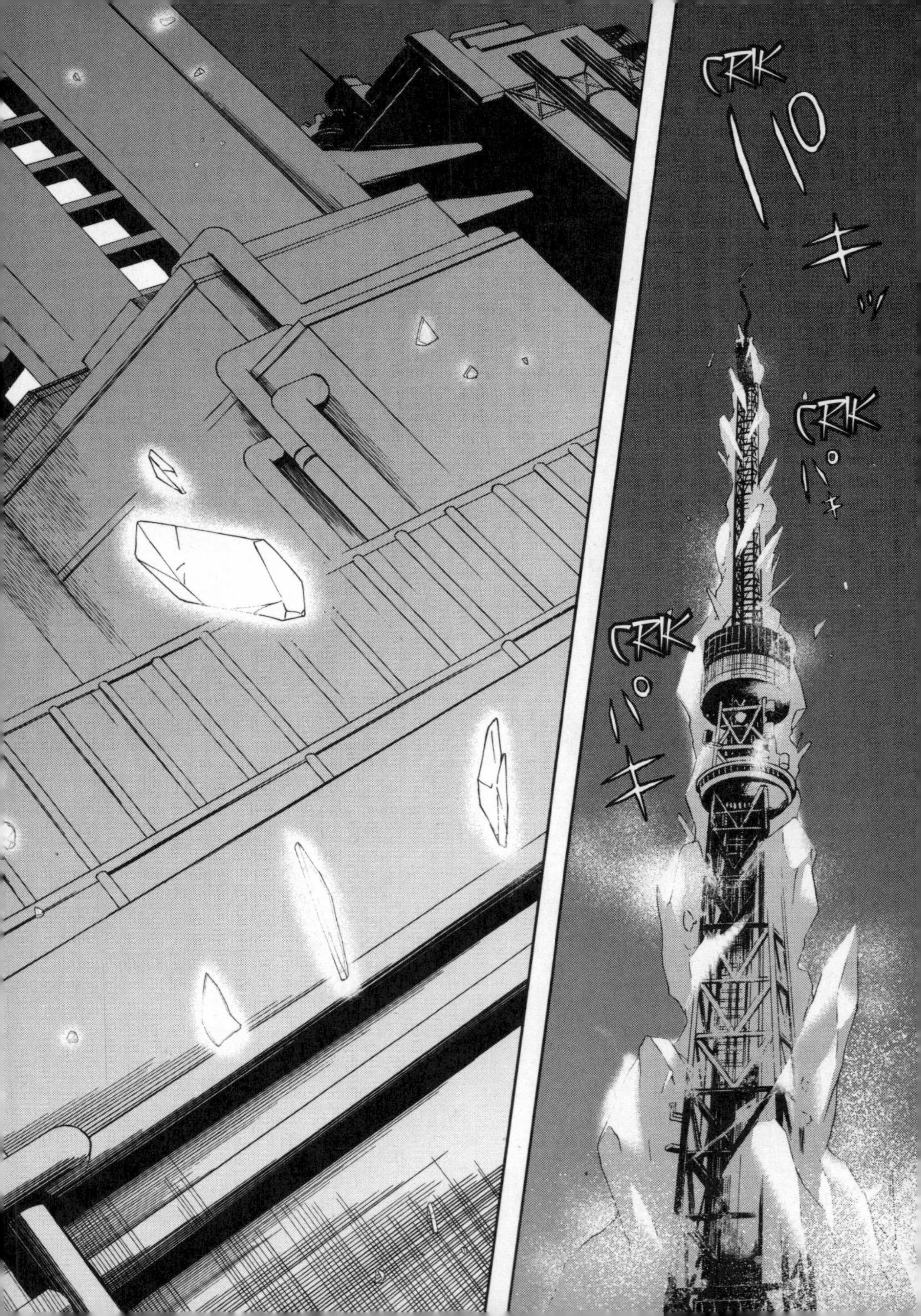
CRIK
パキッ
CRIK
パキ
CRIK
パキ

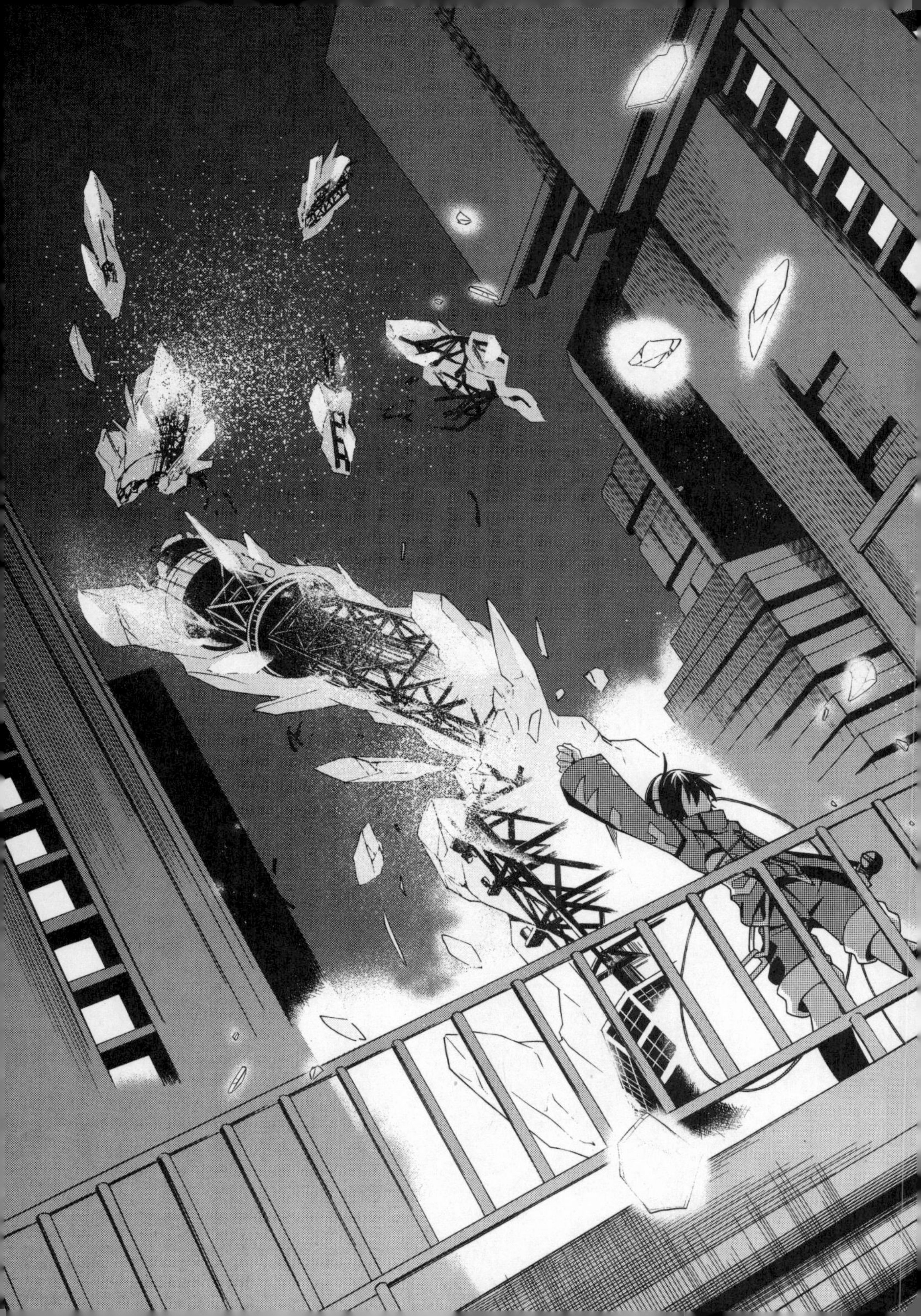

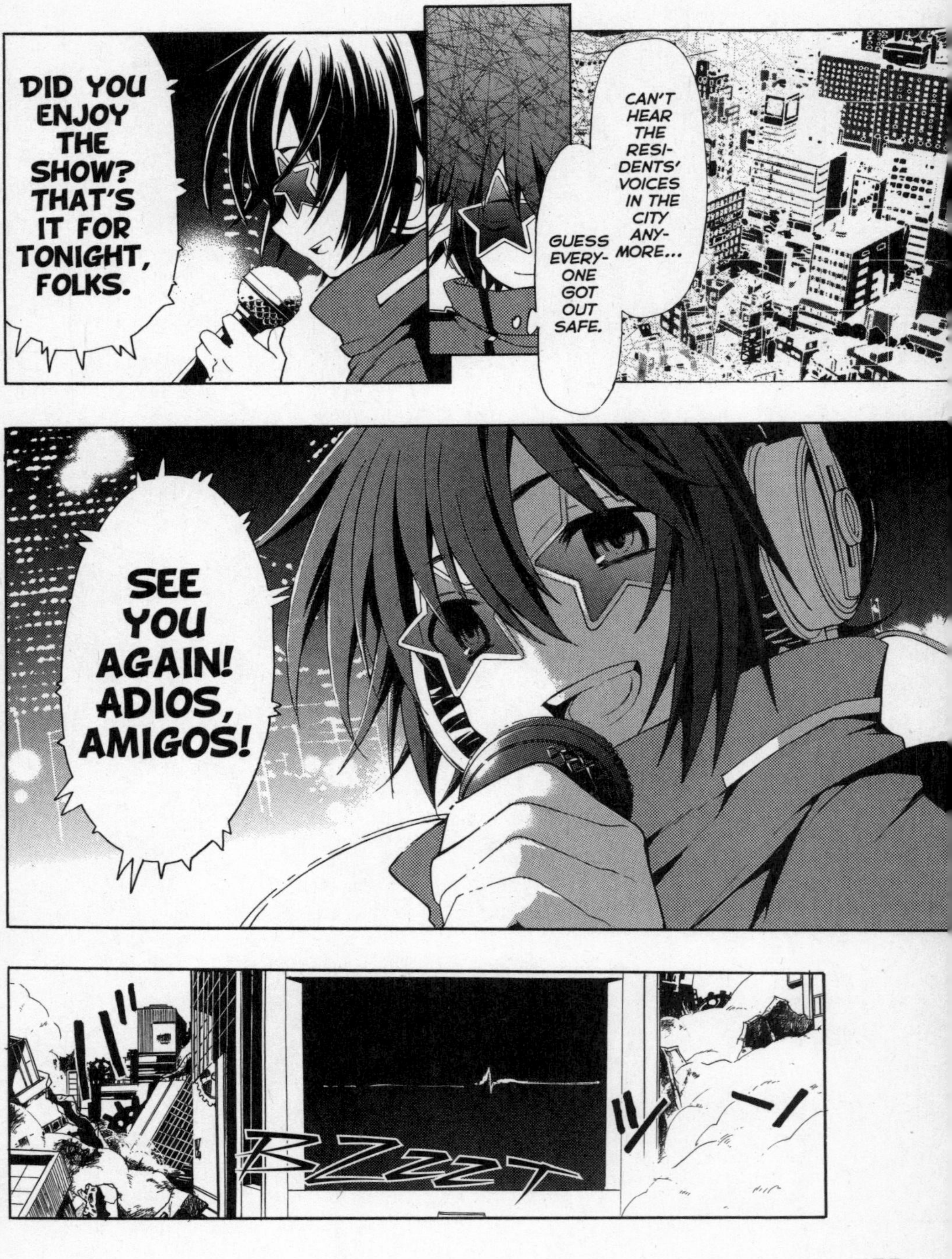
CAN'T HEAR THE RESIDENTS' VOICES IN THE CITY ANYMORE...
GUESS EVERYONE GOT OUT SAFE.
DID YOU ENJOY THE SHOW? THAT'S IT FOR TONIGHT, FOLKS.
SEE YOU AGAIN! ADIOS, AMIGOS!
BZZZT

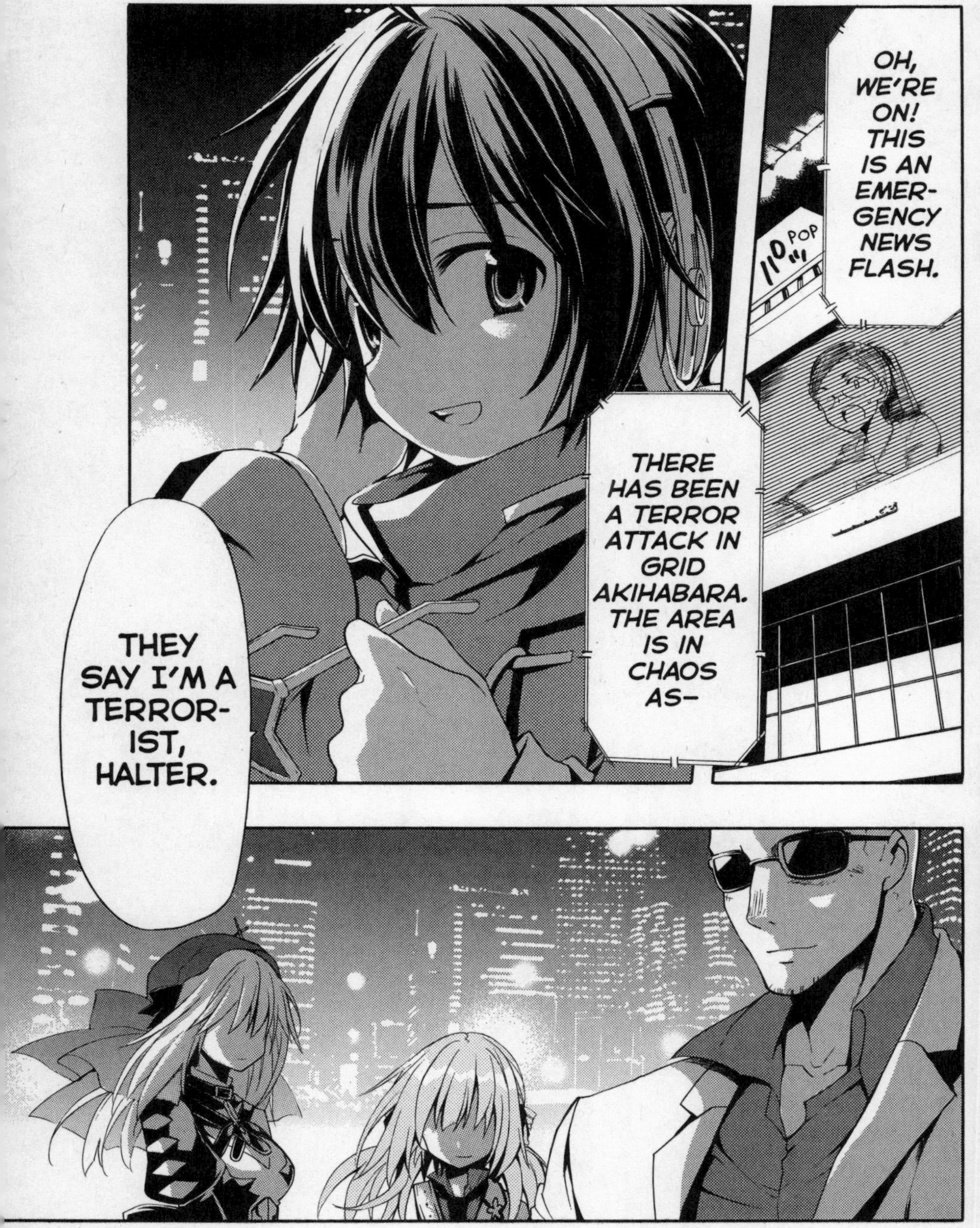
OH, WE'RE ON! THIS IS AN EMERGENCY NEWS FLASH.
POP
THERE HAS BEEN A TERROR ATTACK IN GRID AKIHABARA. THE AREA IS IN CHAOS AS—
THEY SAY I'M A TERRORIST, HALTER.

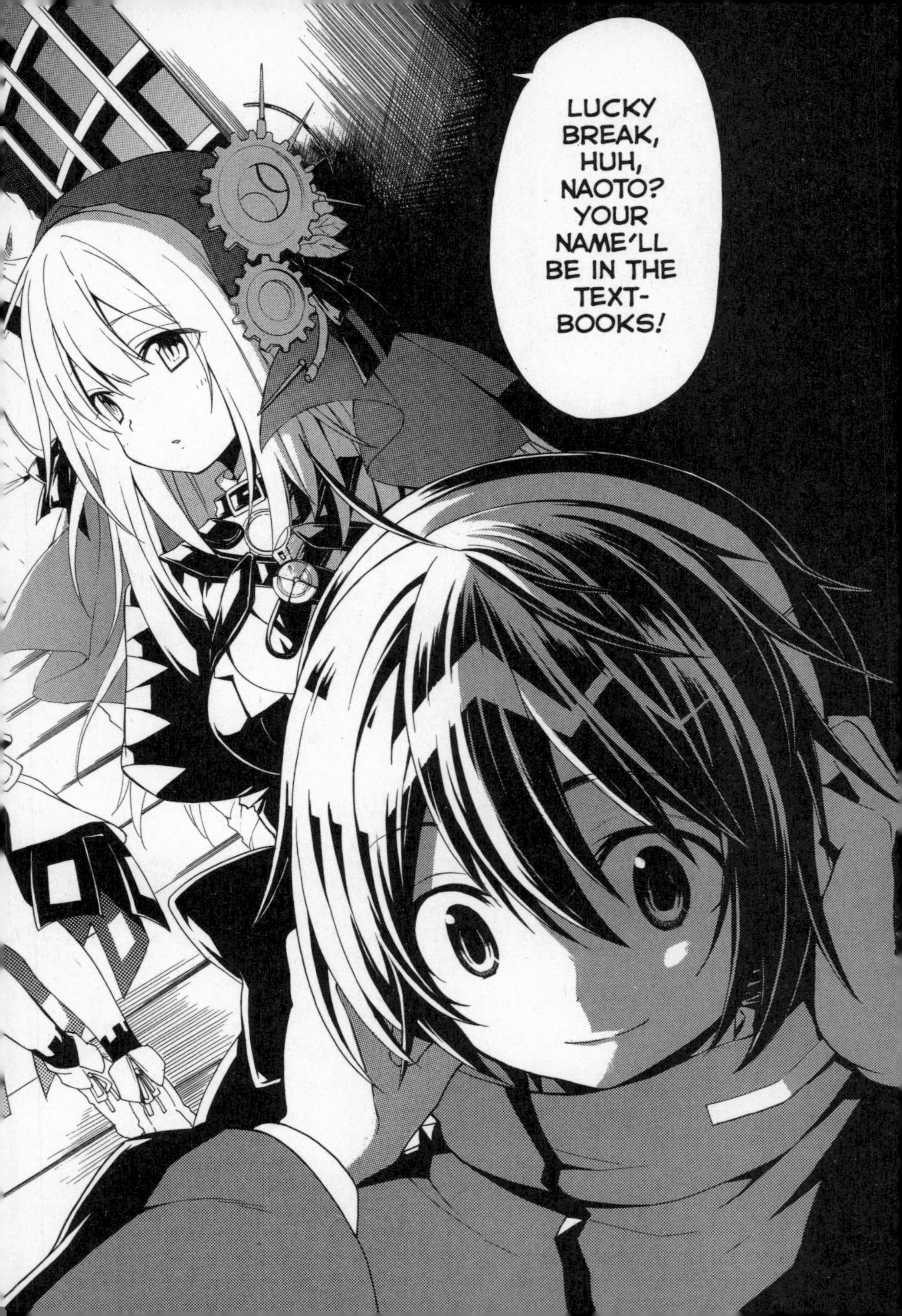
LUCKY BREAK, HUH, NAOTO? YOUR NAME'LL BE IN THE TEXT-BOOKS!

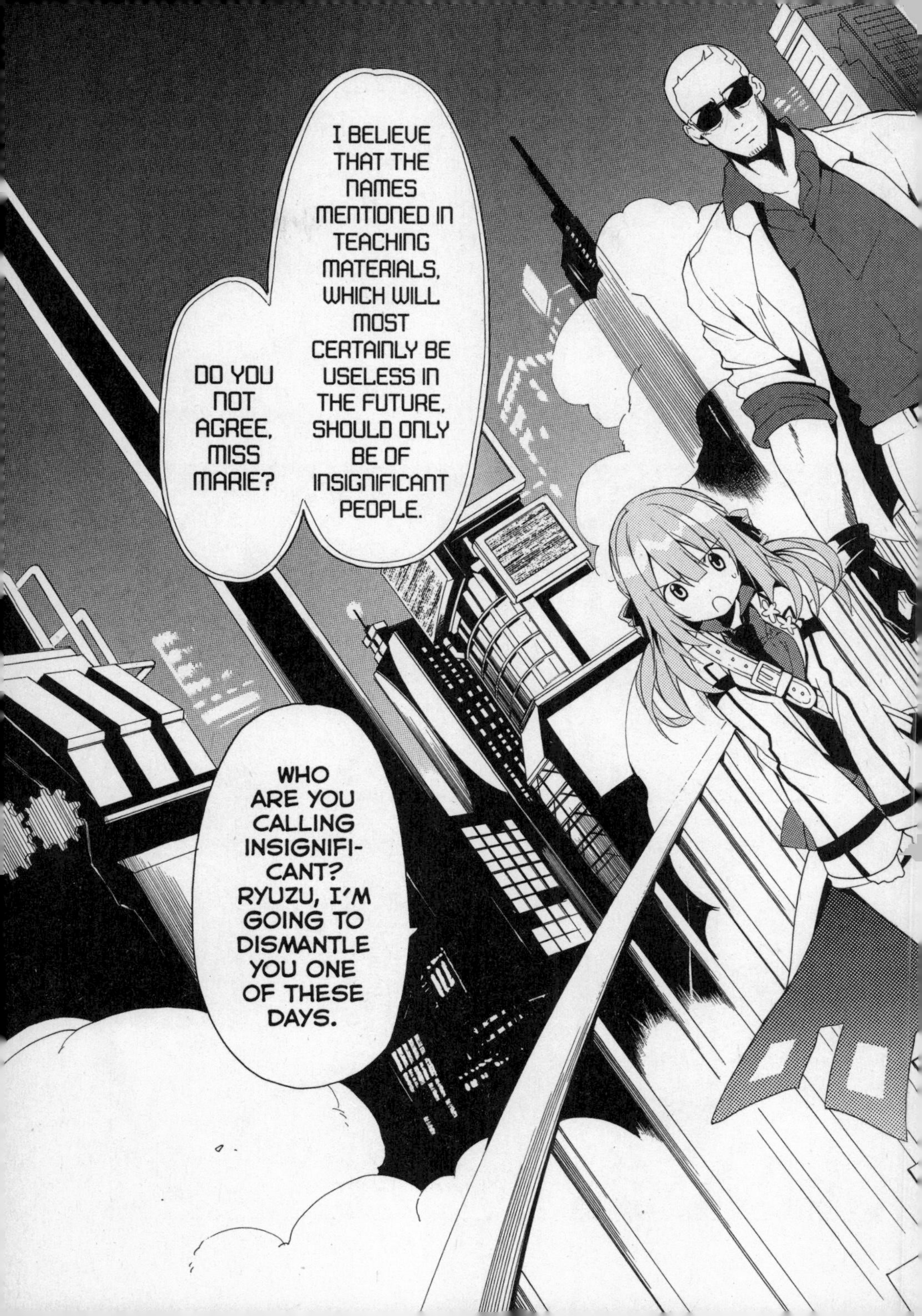
I BELIEVE THAT THE NAMES MENTIONED IN TEACHING MATERIALS, WHICH WILL MOST CERTAINLY BE USELESS IN THE FUTURE, SHOULD ONLY BE OF INSIGNIFICANT PEOPLE.
DO YOU NOT AGREE, MISS MARIE?
WHO ARE YOU CALLING INSIGNIFI-CANT? RYUZU, I'M GOING TO DISMANTLE YOU ONE OF THESE DAYS.

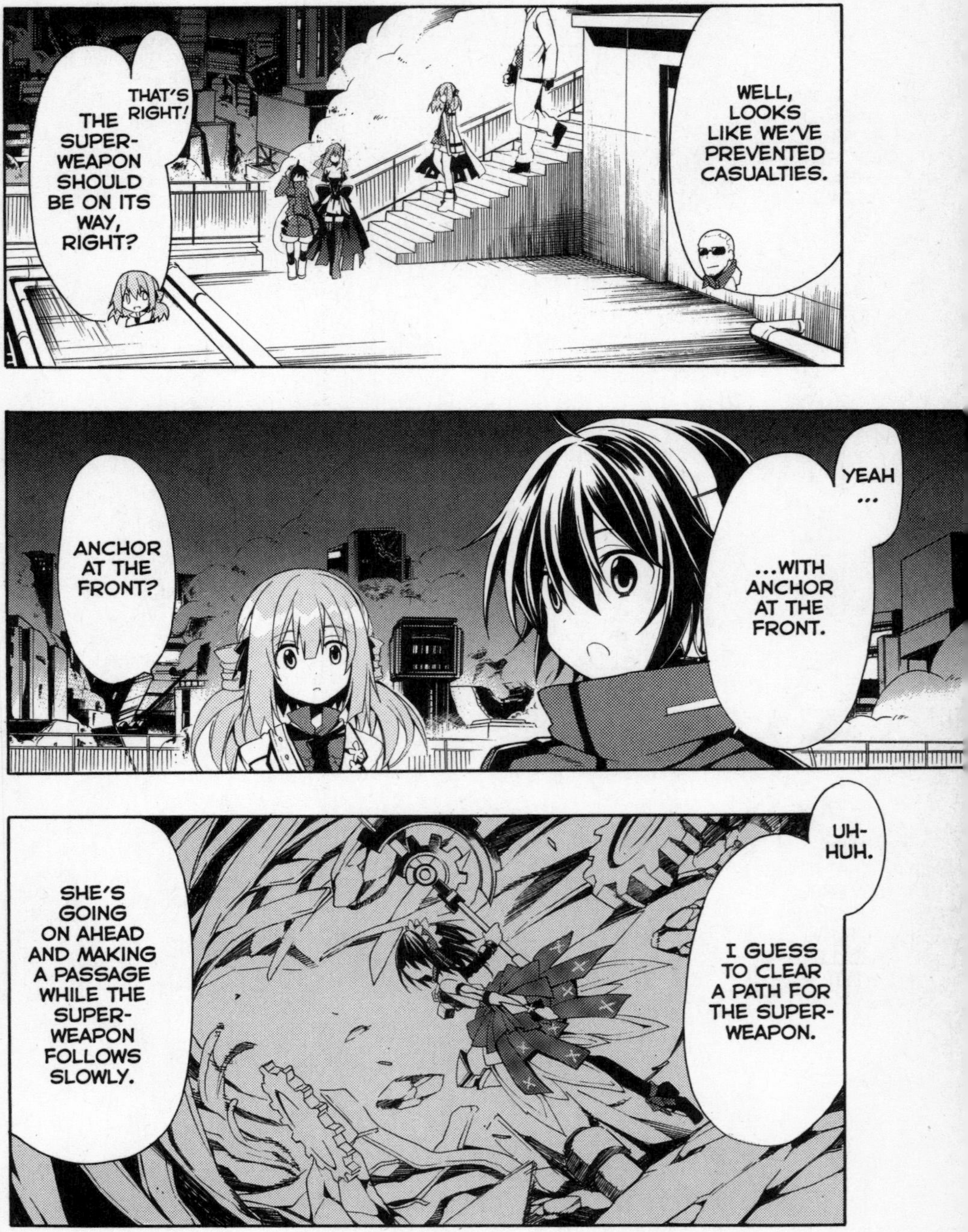
WELL, LOOKS LIKE WE'VE PREVENTED CASUALTIES.
THAT'S RIGHT! THE SUPER-WEAPON SHOULD BE ON ITS WAY, RIGHT?
YEAH ...
...WITH ANCHOR AT THE FRONT.
ANCHOR AT THE FRONT?
UH-HUH.
I GUESS TO CLEAR A PATH FOR THE SUPER-WEAPON.
SHE'S GOING ON AHEAD AND MAKING A PASSAGE WHILE THE SUPER-WEAPON FOLLOWS SLOWLY.

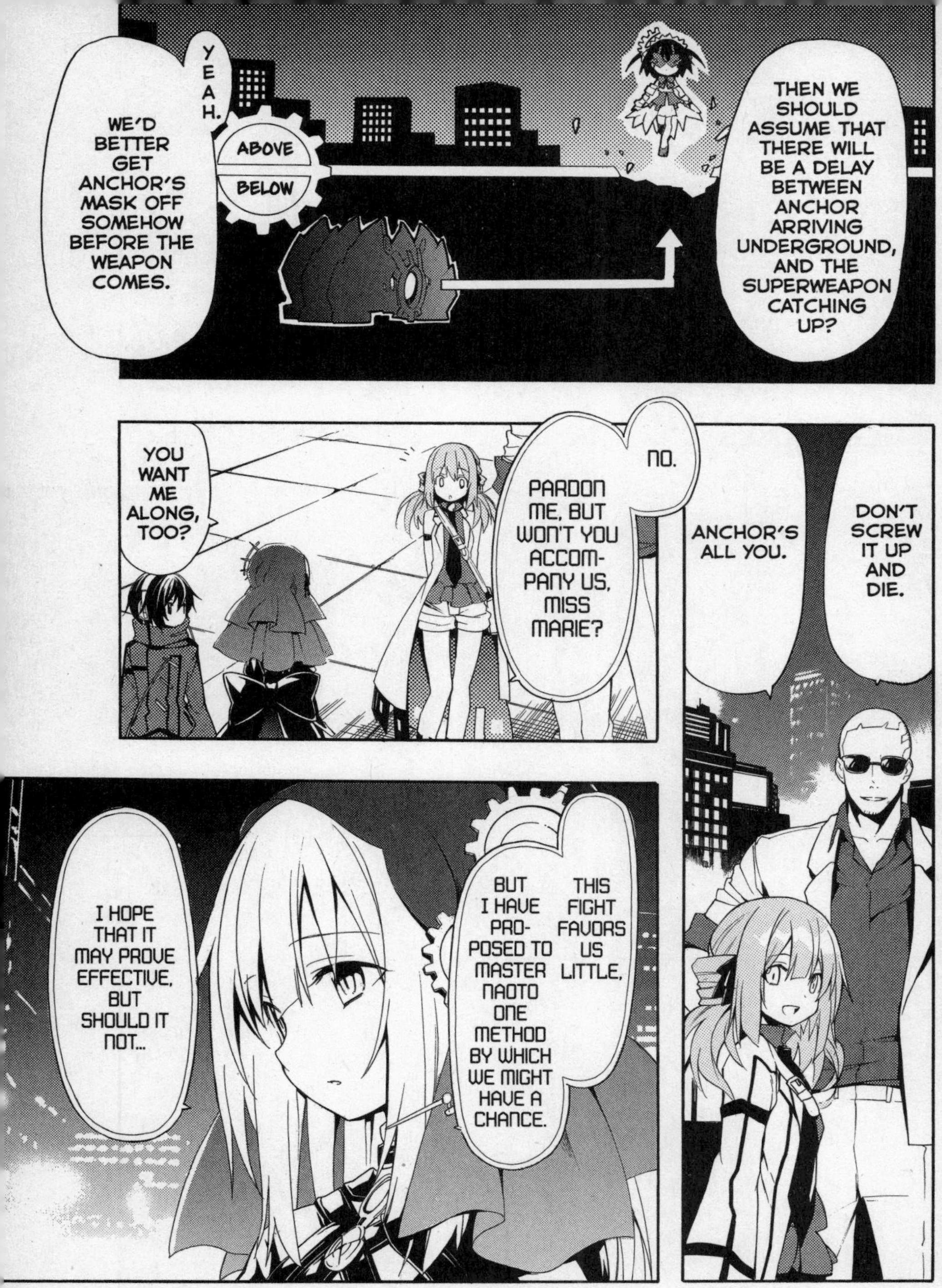
THEN WE SHOULD ASSUME THAT THERE WILL BE A DELAY BETWEEN ANCHOR ARRIVING UNDERGROUND, AND THE SUPERWEAPON CATCHING UP?
ABOVE
BELOW
YEAH.
WE'D BETTER GET ANCHOR'S MASK OFF SOMEHOW BEFORE THE WEAPON COMES.
DON'T SCREW IT UP AND DIE.
ANCHOR'S ALL YOU.
NO.
PARDON ME, BUT WON'T YOU ACCOM-PANY US, MISS MARIE?
YOU WANT ME ALONG, TOO?
THIS FIGHT FAVORS US LITTLE,
BUT I HAVE PRO-POSED TO MASTER NAOTO ONE METHOD BY WHICH WE MIGHT HAVE A CHANCE.
I HOPE THAT IT MAY PROVE EFFECTIVE, BUT SHOULD IT NOT...

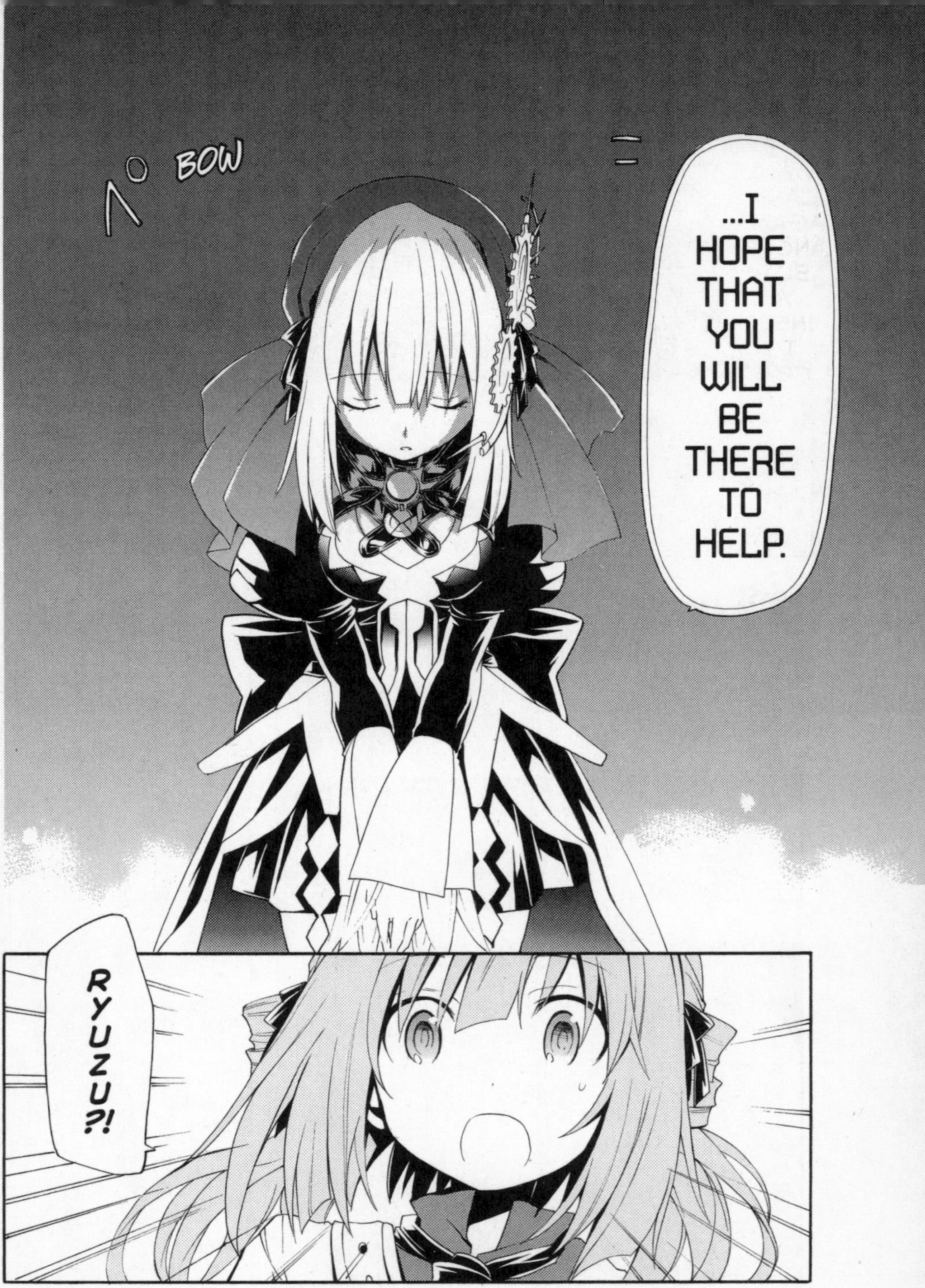
...I HOPE THAT YOU WILL BE THERE TO HELP.
BOW
RYUZU?!

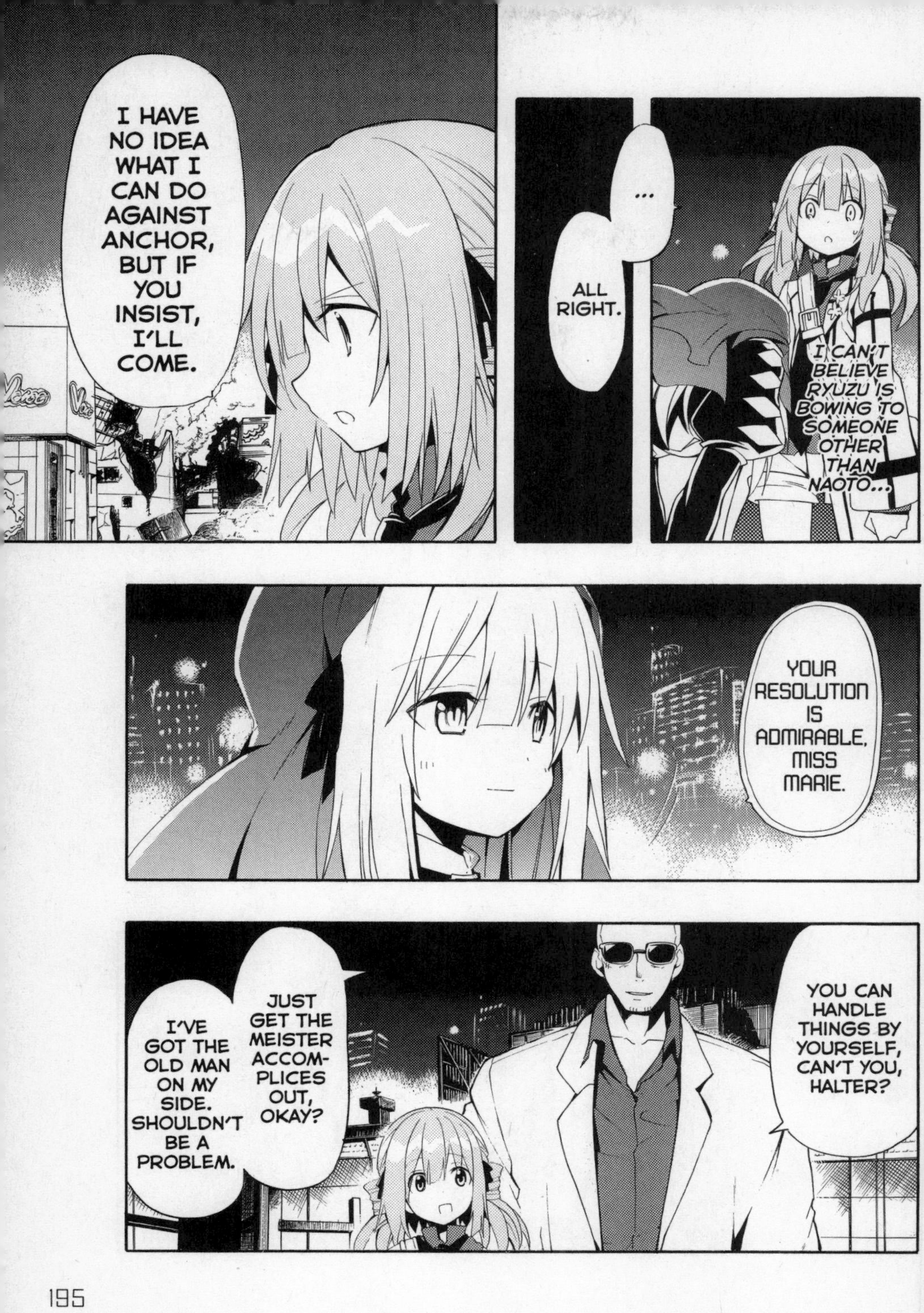
I CAN'T BELIEVE RYUZU IS BOWING TO SOMEONE OTHER THAN NAOTO...
...
ALL RIGHT.
I HAVE NO IDEA WHAT I CAN DO AGAINST ANCHOR, BUT IF YOU INSIST, I'LL COME.
YOUR RESOLUTION IS ADMIRABLE, MISS MARIE.
YOU CAN HANDLE THINGS BY YOURSELF, CAN'T YOU, HALTER?
JUST GET THE MEISTER ACCOM-PLICES OUT, OKAY?
I'VE GOT THE OLD MAN ON MY SIDE. SHOULDN'T BE A PROBLEM.

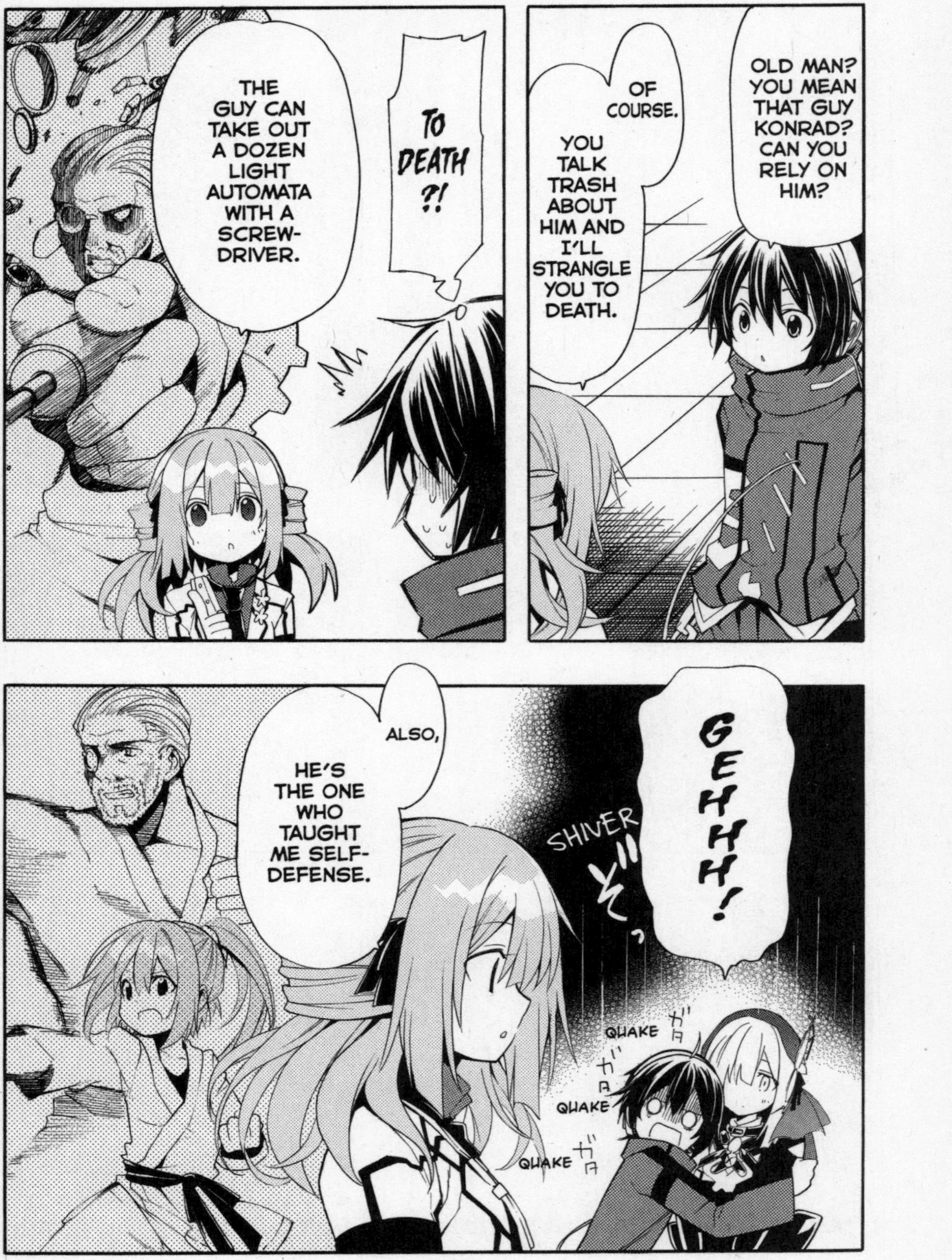
OLD MAN? YOU MEAN THAT GUY KONRAD? CAN YOU RELY ON HIM?
OF COURSE.
YOU TALK TRASH ABOUT HIM AND I'LL STRANGLE YOU TO DEATH.
TO DEATH?!
THE GUY CAN TAKE OUT A DOZEN LIGHT AUTOMATA WITH A SCREW-DRIVER.
GEHHH!
SHIVER
ALSO,
HE'S THE ONE WHO TAUGHT ME SELF-DEFENSE.
QUAKE
QUAKE
QUAKE

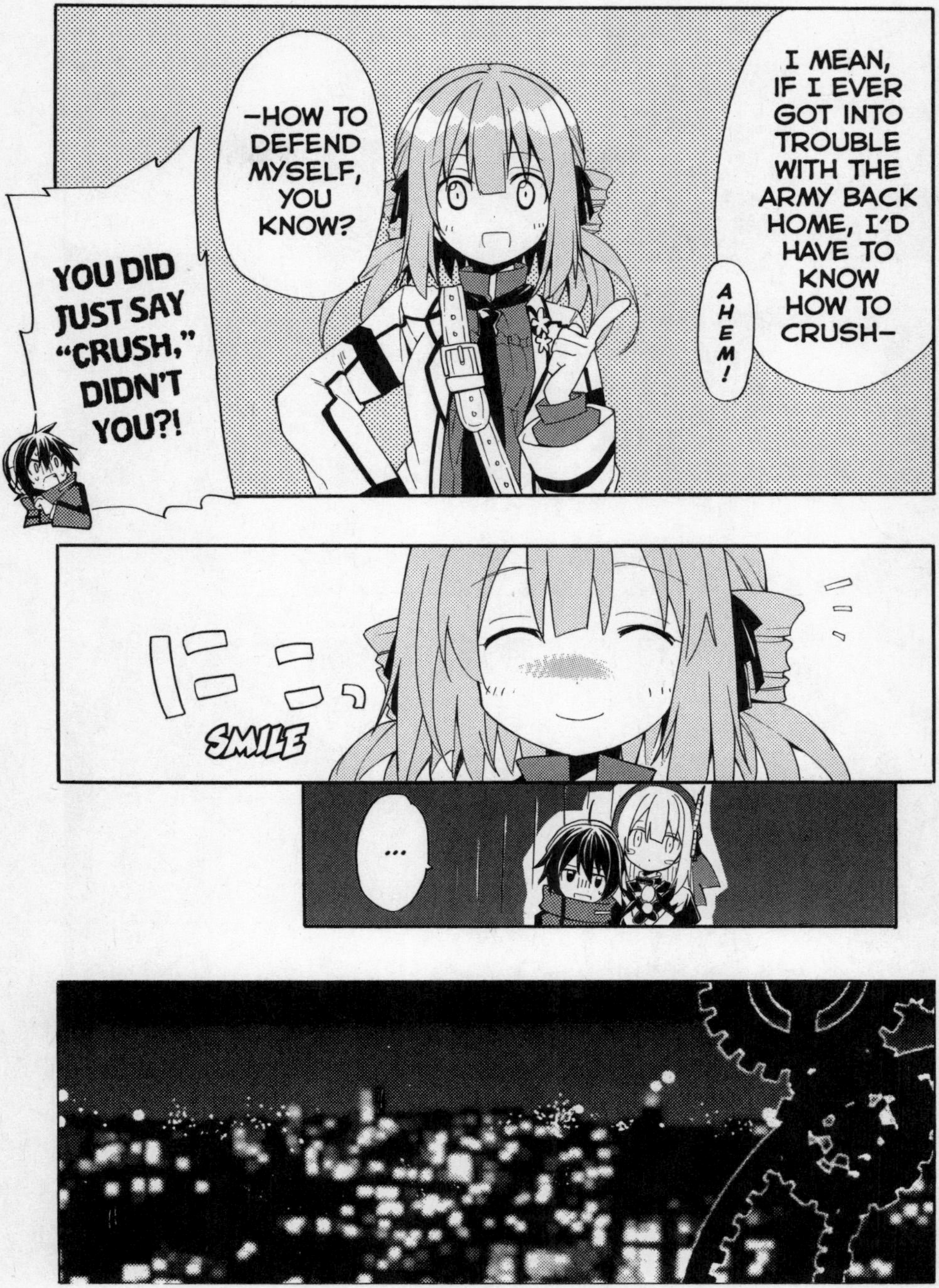
I MEAN, IF I EVER GOT INTO TROUBLE WITH THE ARMY BACK HOME, I'D HAVE TO KNOW HOW TO CRUSH–
AHEM!
–HOW TO DEFEND MYSELF, YOU KNOW?
YOU DID JUST SAY "CRUSH," DIDN'T YOU?!
にこっ
SMILE
...

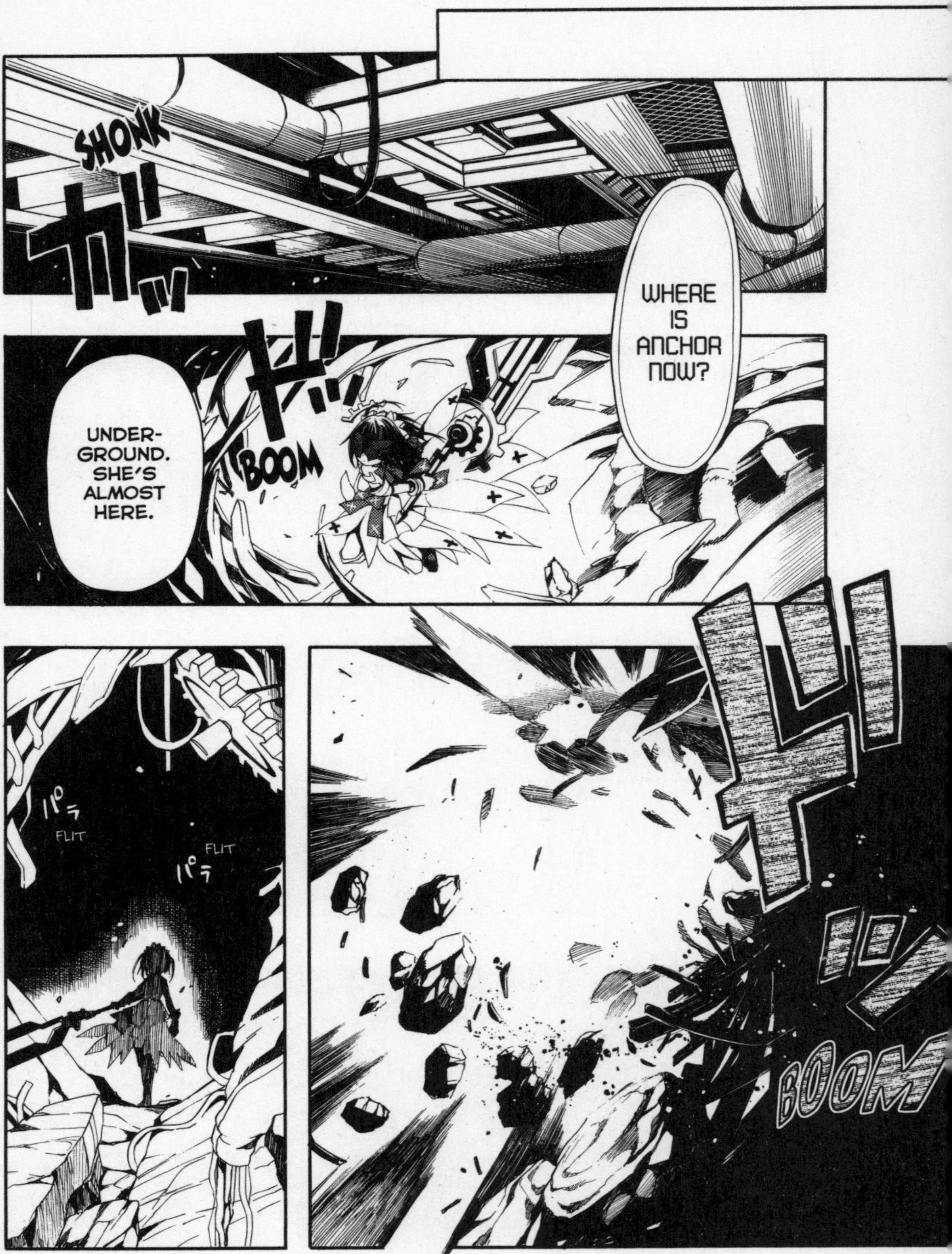
SHONK
WHERE IS ANCHOR NOW?
BOOM
UNDER-GROUND. SHE'S ALMOST HERE.
BOOM
パラ
FLIT
パラ
FLIT

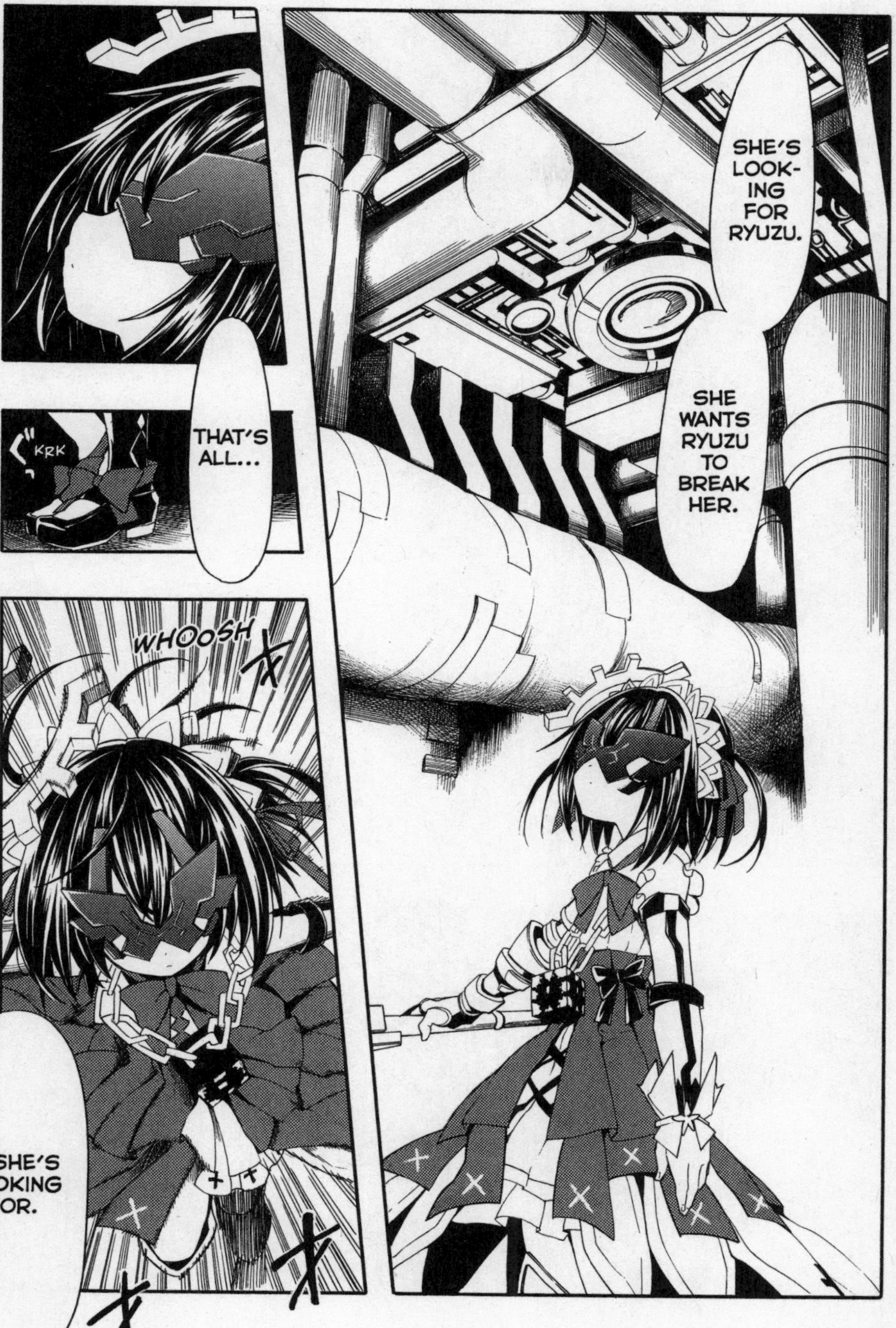
SHE'S LOOKING FOR RYUZU.
SHE WANTS RYUZU TO BREAK HER.
KRK
THAT'S ALL...
WHOOSH
...SHE'S LOOKING FOR.

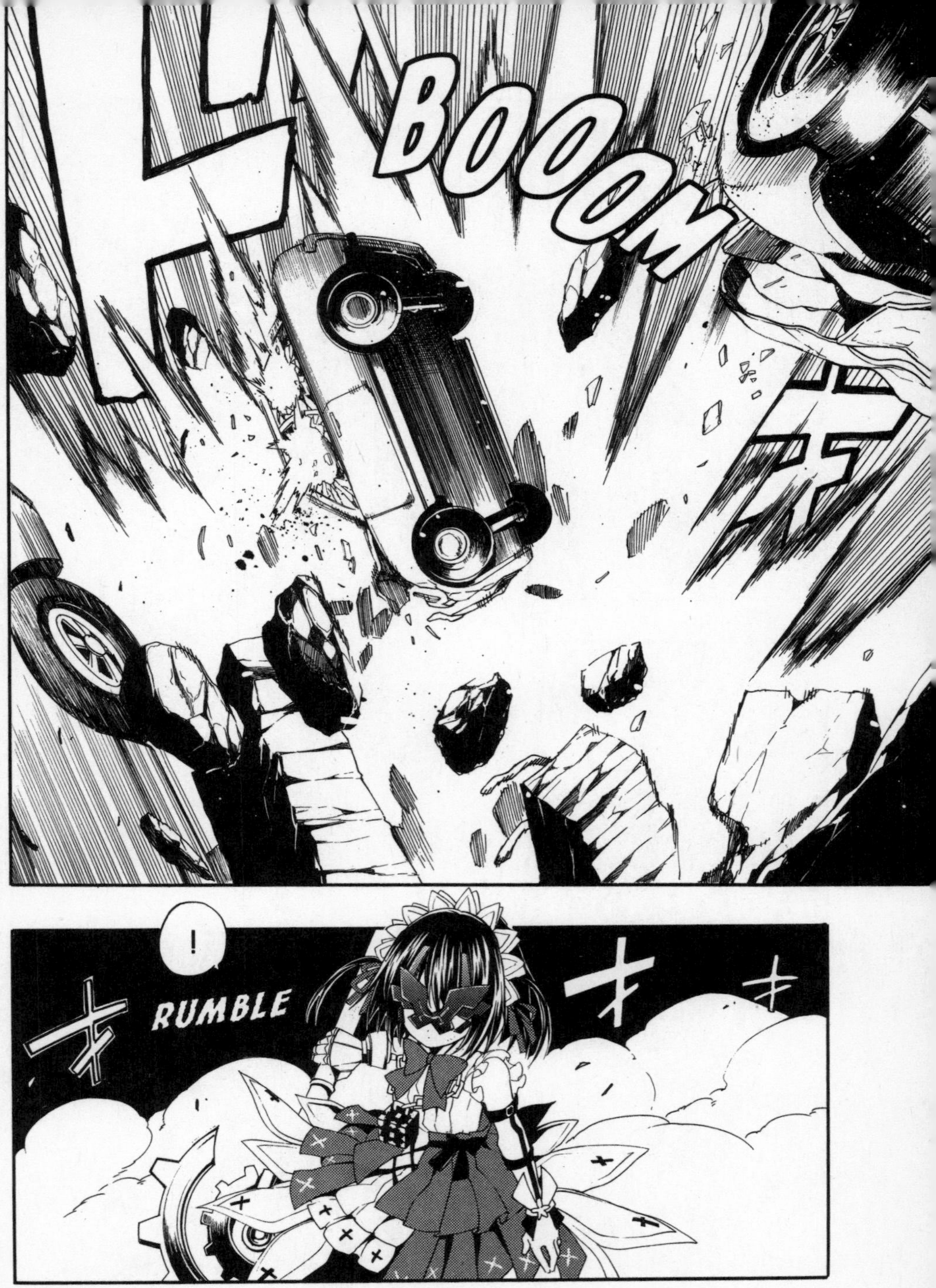
BOOOM
!
RUMBLE

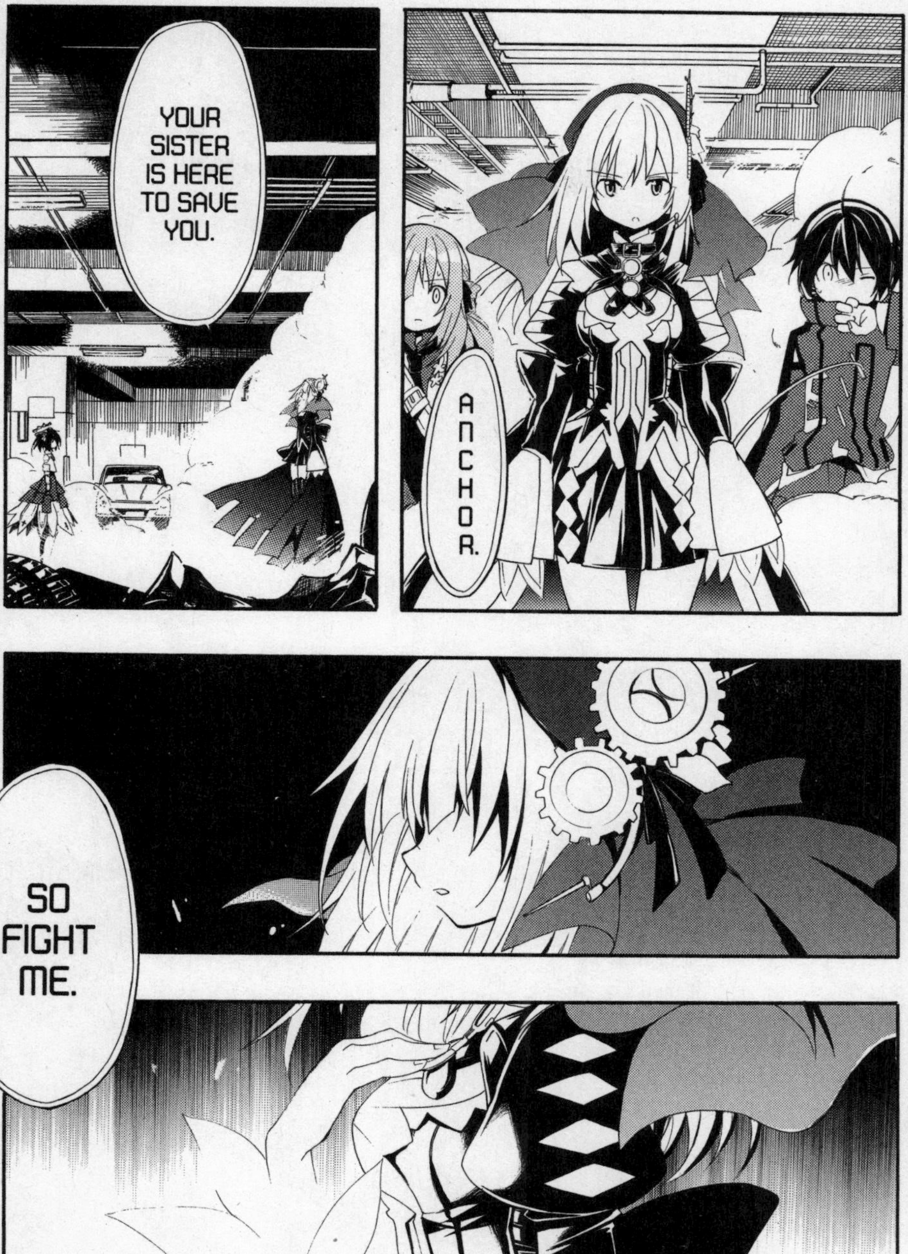
ANCHOR.
YOUR SISTER IS HERE TO SAVE YOU.
SO FIGHT ME.

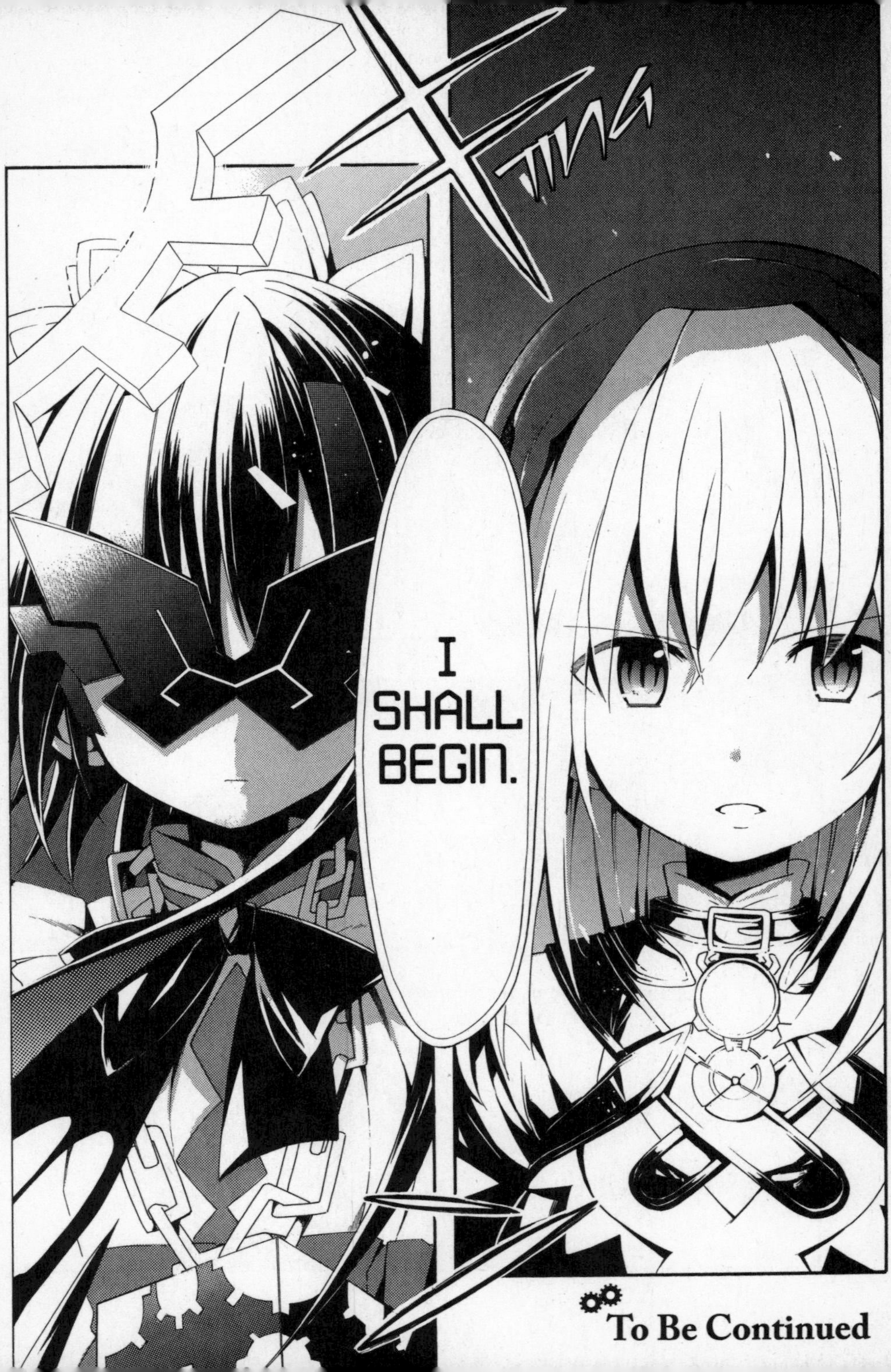
TING
I SHALL BEGIN.

To Be Continued

CLOCKWORK PLANET

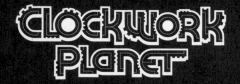

YK: So, here's volume 4 of the manga of *Clockwork Planet*.

TH: Yeahhh! Clap, clap, clap!

YK: And as usual, they told us, "Say something funny."

TH: If we could say something funny on command, we'd be funny guys professionally. I always wonder if there are people who actually read this section... You got something?

YK: Mmm... Yesterday I was eating pizza and I bit my tongue and it bled. Shall we talk about that?

TH: Who cares about your tongue? You have one too many in the first place. Uhhh, okay, how about—gender neutrality sure is making a lot of progress these days, huh? Also, lots of place have legalized gay marriage recently, too.

YK: Sorry political topics aren't allowed. Well, topics unrelated to the story are allowed, actually.

TH: You say that just after talking about your tongue? Okay, you know what? You rejected the idea, but I'm starting to think I was really right when I said Halter should be gay.

...

YK: Tsubaki, my boy, I don't mean to boast, but I am a tolerant man. I have no objection to your resorting to homosexuality because women won't give you the time of day. As long as you are happy, I shall celebrate it. But, that aside, I have two requests. First, that you change your place of residence, and, second, that you refrain from bringing your predilections into—

TH: Come on! You know I'm more purely devoted to little girls than Kazufusa! We've known each other for more than ten years and I still have to say that?!

YK: Oh, that's nice. I'm glad you figured out where you're moving to. (*Dials 110.*)

TH: N—n-n-no, it's not like that! Please, man, just take another look at this.

From line 16 on p. 65 of the first draft of vol. 1 of the original novel series:

> She looked like a smart-ass brat in her early teens. Halter repressed a chuckle as he chided her.
> "Meister Breguet, we may be in a car, but consider how you look and remember to act like a lady."
> "Leave me alone."
> "That's not feasible. Look, your skirt is so far up your undergarments are about to show."
> "So? You want to see it?"
> "Meister Breguet, what are you doing trying to seduce me?"
> "Seduce you? What, you're gay. I could get buck naked and you wouldn't care."
> "I would care."
> "You would? But you're gay!"

YK: So you're saying this guy has this conversation? (*Looks at the cover art.*) You're one sick animal.

TH: No, I mean, at the time, Halter wasn't Marie's bodyguard, but a butler employed by the Breguet company to wait on her, remember? Good-looking butlers are all gay, right? (*Note: B.S.*)

YK: Why don't I give you 5 parsecs (*approximately 155 petameters*) and assume that's valid. Then we figure that Halter should be a bald, beefy butler. And that that's supposed to make for BL.

TH: ...Oh, good point. That's not BL, it's more macho, burly men.

YK: Welp, it may have taken my partner's coming-out to do it, but it looks like we've about filled the page.

TH: Hold on, hold on, Mr. Y; so guys who look like girls and little boys are okay, but BL—

YK: (*shutting him up*) Later! (*We're working to get vol. 4 done before the comic catches up with us, so check out the novels, read the comic, peace!*)

Yuu
Kamiya
&
Tsubaki
Himana

Afterword

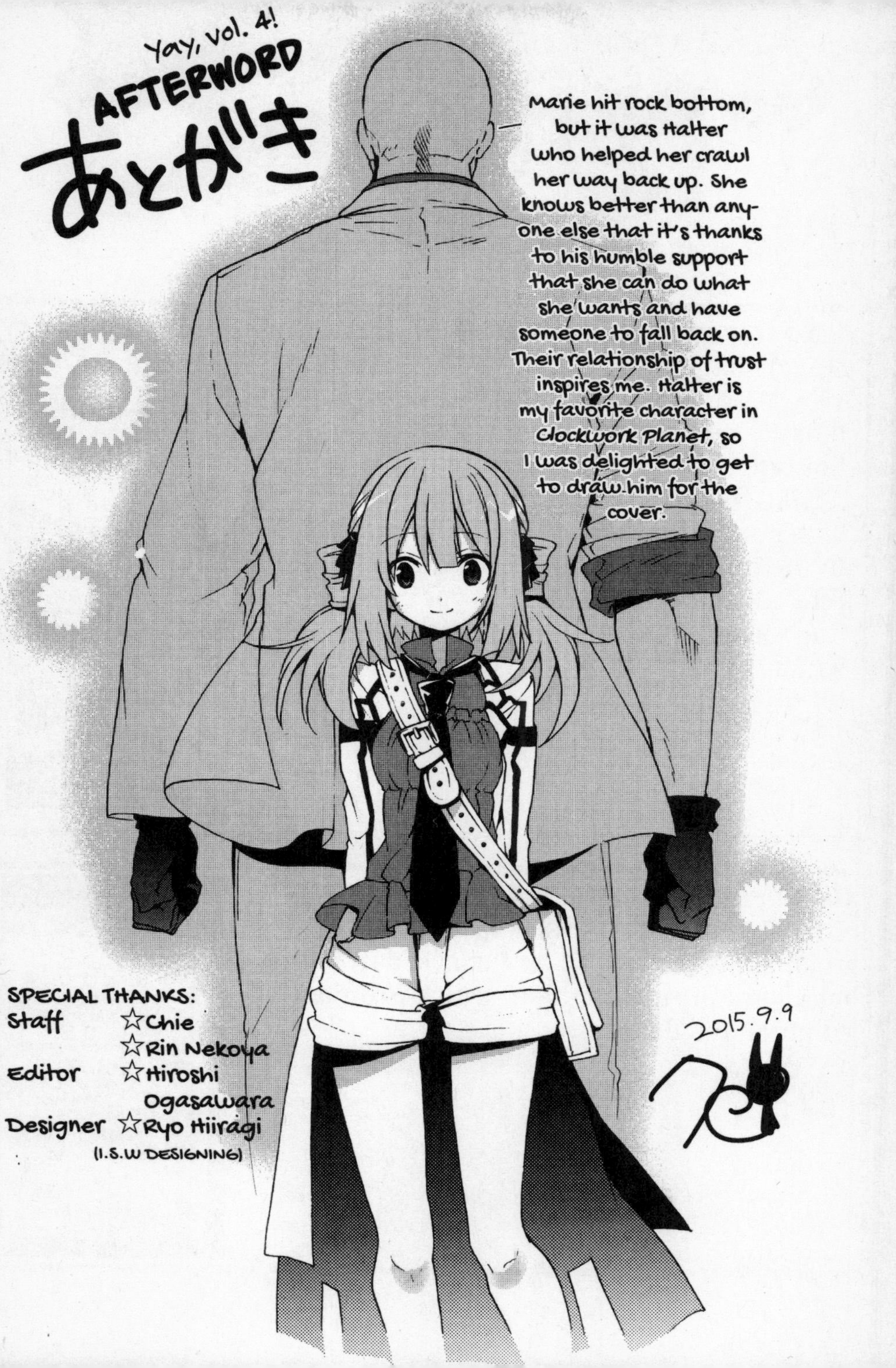
Yay, vol. 4!
AFTERWORD
あとがき
Marie hit rock bottom, but it was Halter who helped her crawl her way back up. She knows better than anyone else that it's thanks to his humble support that she can do what she wants and have someone to fall back on. Their relationship of trust inspires me. Halter is my favorite character in Clockwork Planet, so I was delighted to get to draw him for the cover.
SPECIAL THANKS:
Staff ☆Chie
☆Rin Nekoya
Editor ☆Hiroshi Ogasawara
Designer ☆Ryo Hiiragi
(I.S.W DESIGNING)
2015.9.9

Translation Notes

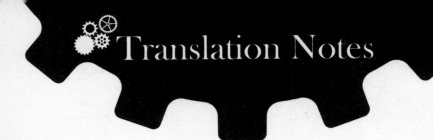

Like it wasn't damp enough in the sewer, page 114

This is originally a pun between *gesui*, literally meaning "bottom water" and figuratively "the sewer," paired with *jōsui*, which literally translates to "top water" and figuratively, to "clean water." In the original Japanese, it would have read along the lines of, "We got out of the bottom water and now it's the top water?"

THIS SUCKS. LIKE IT WASN'T DAMP ENOUGH IN THE SEWER!

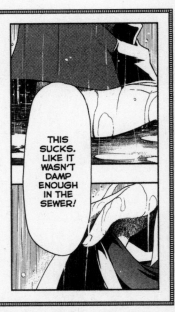

Rice paddies and yokels, page 132

This concept is expressed by a single word in Japanese, *do-inaka*, or "smack-dab in the middle of the countryside" which is quite a common insult.

HMM.
DOES SHE HAVE SOME GRUDGE AGAINST SHIGA?
Lake Biwa
RICE, YOKELS,

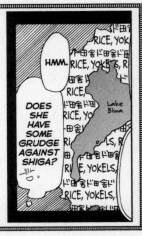

Forever alone, page 177
Botchi, is a slang word derived from *hitoribotchi*, which means all alone. (*Hitoribotchi* in turn comes from *hitoribōshi*, which means lone monk.)

Ladies and gentlemen, pages 168–169
Naoto says this in English for comic effect.

See you again, page 188
Naoto says this in English, too.

Kazufusa, page 204
Kazufusa is the main character from the manga *Love-yan,* who likes young girls. The story is a comedy in which an angel tries to help Kazufusa get his act together.

110, page 204
110 is Japan's emergency police number.

BL, page 204
BL (boys' love) refers to fiction portraying male–male romance and sexuality. Often found in idealized comics most commonly made by and for women.

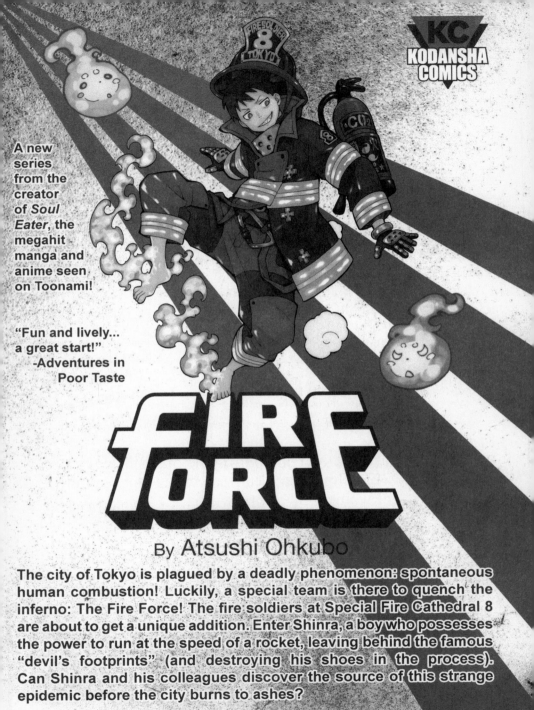

A new series from the creator of *Soul Eater*, the megahit manga and anime seen on Toonami!

"Fun and lively... a great start!"
-Adventures in Poor Taste

FIRE FORCE

By Atsushi Ohkubo

The city of Tokyo is plagued by a deadly phenomenon: spontaneous human combustion! Luckily, a special team is there to quench the inferno: The Fire Force! The fire soldiers at Special Fire Cathedral 8 are about to get a unique addition. Enter Shinra, a boy who possesses the power to run at the speed of a rocket, leaving behind the famous "devil's footprints" (and destroying his shoes in the process). Can Shinra and his colleagues discover the source of this strange epidemic before the city burns to ashes?

The award-winning manga about what happens inside you!

"Far more entertaining than it ought to be... what kid doesn't want to think that every time they sneeze a torpedo shoots out their nose?"
—Anime News Network

Strep throat! Hay fever! Influenza! The world is a dangerous place for a red blood cell just trying to get her deliveries finished. Fortunately, she's not alone…she's got a whole human body's worth of cells ready to help out! The mysterious white blood cells, the buff and brash killer T cells, even the cute little platelets— everyone's got to come together if they want to keep you healthy!

Cells at Work!

はたらく細胞

By Akane Shimizu

Japan's most powerful spirit medium delves into the ghost world's greatest mysteries!

Story by Kyo Shirodaira, famed author of mystery fiction and creator of *Spiral*, *Blast of Tempest*, and *The Record of a Fallen Vampire*.

Both touched by spirits called yôkai, Kotoko and Kurô have gained unique superhuman powers. But to gain her powers Kotoko has given up an eye and a leg, and Kurô's personal life is in shambles. So when Kotoko suggests they team up to deal with renegades from the spirit world, Kurô doesn't have many other choices, but Kotoko might just have a few ulterior motives...

IN/SPECTRE

STORY BY KYO SHIRODAIRA
ART BY CHASHIBA KATASE

Having lost his wife, high school teacher Kōhei Inuzuka is doing his best to raise his young daughter Tsumugi as a single father. He's pretty bad at cooking and doesn't have a huge appetite to begin with, but chance brings his little family together with one of his students, the lonely Kotori. The three of them are anything but comfortable in the kitchen, but the healing power of home cooking might just work on their grieving hearts.

"This season's number-one feel-good anime!" —Anime News Network

"A beautifully-drawn story about comfort food and family and grief. Recommended." —Otaku USA Magazine

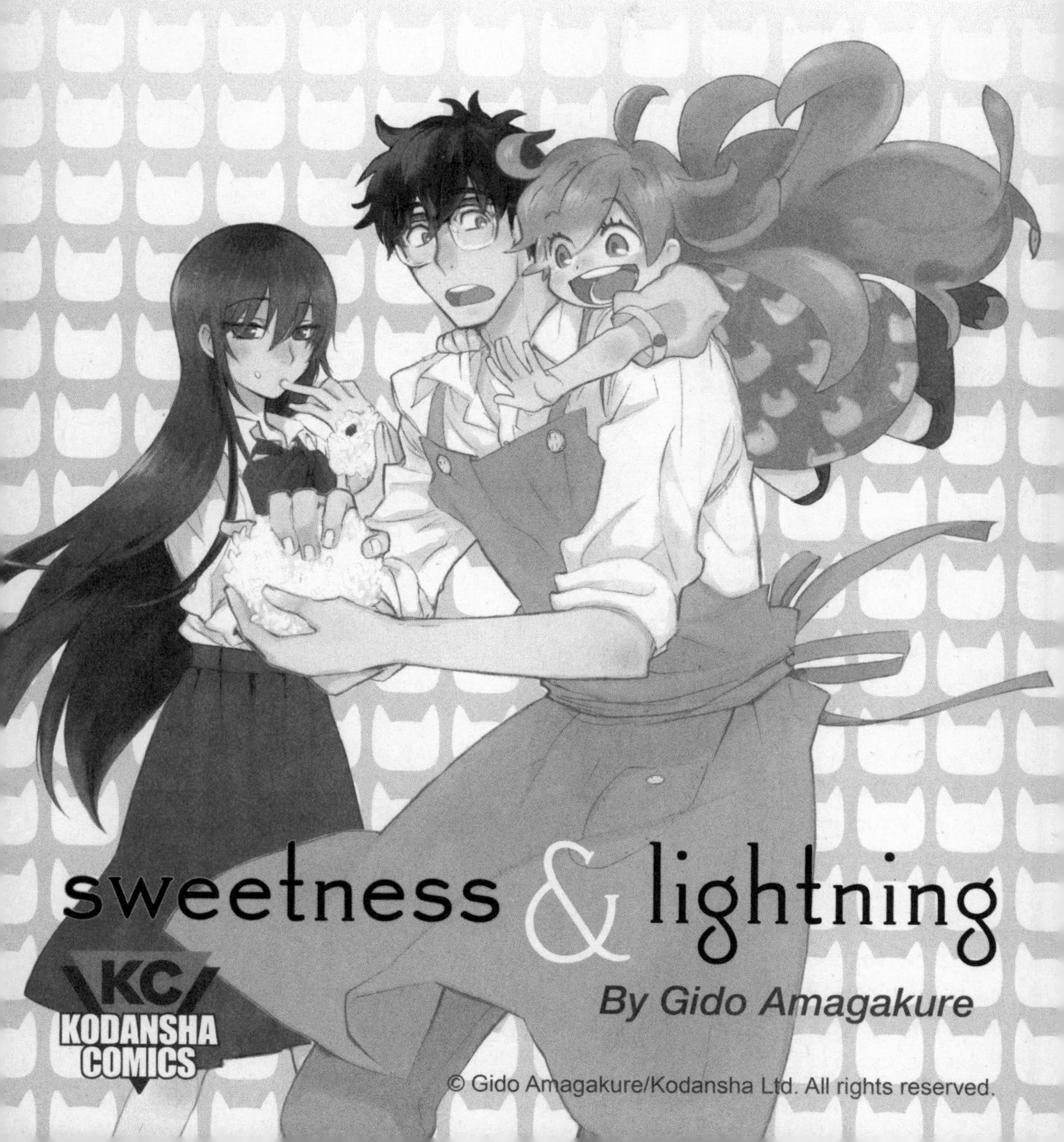

sweetness & lightning

By Gido Amagakure

KODANSHA COMICS

Maria
THE VIRGIN WITCH

"Maria's brand of righteous justice, passion and plain talking make for one of the freshest manga series of 2015. I dare any other book to top it."
—UK Anime Network

PURITY AND POWER

As a war to determine the rightful ruler of medieval France ravages the land, the witch Maria decides she will not stand idly by as men kill each other in the name of God and glory. Using her powerful magic, she summons various beasts and demons —even going as far as using a succubus to seduce soldiers into submission under the veil of night—— all to stop the needless slaughter. However, after the Archangel Michael puts an end to her meddling, he curses her to lose her powers if she ever gives up her virginity. Will she forgo the forbidden fruit of adulthood in order to bring an end to the merciless machine of war?
Available now in print and digitally!

KC
KODANSHA
COMICS

MARDOCK マルドゥック・スクランブル SCRAMBLE

Created by
Tow Ubukata

Manga by
Yoshitoki Oima

"I'd rather be dead."

Rune Balot was a lost girl with nothing to live for. A man named Shell took her in and cared for her...until he tried to murder her. Standing at the precipice of death, Rune is saved by Dr. Easter, a private investigator. He uses an experimental procedure known as "Mardock Scramble 09" on Rune, and it grants her extra-ordinary abilities. Now, Rune must decide whether or not to use her new powers to help Dr. Easter bring Shell to justice. But, does she even have the will to keep living a life that's been broken so badly?

MARDOCK
マルドゥック・スクランブル
SCRAMBLE
1
created by
TOW UBUKATA
manga by
YOSHITOKI OIMA

Ages: 16+

KODANSHA COMICS

VISIT KODANSHACOMICS.COM TO:

- View release date calendars for upcoming volumes
- Find out the latest about upcoming Kodansha Comics series

Clockwork Planet volume 4 is a work of fiction. Names, characters, places, and incidents are the products of the author's imagination or are used fictitiously. Any resemblance to actual events, locales, or persons, living or dead, is entirely coincidental.

A Kodansha Comics Trade Paperback Original
Clockwork Planet volume 4 copyright © 2015 Yuu Kamiya/Tsubaki Himana/Sino/Kuro
English translation copyright © 2017 Yuu Kamiya/Tsubaki Himana/Sino/Kuro
All rights reserved.

Published in the United States by Kodansha Comics, an imprint of Kodansha USA Publishing, LLC, New York.

Publication rights for this English edition arranged through Kodansha Ltd, Tokyo.

First published in Japan in 2015 by Kodansha Ltd., Tokyo

9 8 7 6 5 4 3 2 1
Translation: Daniel Komen
Lettering: Scott O. Brown
Editing: David Yoo, Haruko Hashimoto
Kodansha Comics edition cover design by Phil Balsman